Responses to Oliver Stone's *Alexander*

Publication of this volume has been made possible, in part, through the generous support and enduring vision of WARREN G. MOON.

Responses to
Oliver Stone's *Alexander*

Film, History, and Cultural Studies

Edited by

Paul Cartledge

and

Fiona Rose Greenland

THE UNIVERSITY OF WISCONSIN PRESS

The University of Wisconsin Press
1930 Monroe Street, 3rd Floor
Madison, Wisconsin 53711-2059
uwpress.wisc.edu

3 Henrietta Street
London WCE 8LU, England
eurospanbookstore.com

5   4   3   2   1

Printed in the United States of America

Library of Congress Cataloging-in-Publication Data
   Responses to Oliver Stone's Alexander : film, history, and cultural
studies / edited by Paul Cartledge and Fiona Rose Greenland.
      p.   cm.— (Wisconsin studies in classics)
   Includes bibliographical references and index.
   ISBN 978-0-299-23284-9 (pbk.: alk. paper)
   ISBN 978-0-299-23283-2 (e-book)
   1. Alexander (Motion picture).   2. Alexander, the Great, 356–323 B.C.—
In motion pictures.   3. Historical films—History and criticism.   4. Stone,
Oliver—Criticism and interpretation.   I. Cartledge, Paul.   II. Rose,
Fiona, 1975–   III. Series: Wisconsin studies in classics.
PN1997.2.A425R47   2010
791.43'72—dc22
2009010258

Contents

Acknowledgments

We are most grateful to the contributors to this book, whose patience, hard work, creative efforts, and provocative questions were essential to its successful completion. Warm thanks go, also, to Professor Patricia Rosenmeyer (University of Wisconsin–Madison) and to Raphael Kadushin of the University of Wisconsin Press for their insights and generous support. Finally, we thank Oliver Stone and his historical consultant, Robin Lane Fox, for making this project possible.

Responses to Oliver Stone's *Alexander*

Introduction

PAUL CARTLEDGE and
FIONA ROSE GREENLAND

THE ANCIENT WORLD makes for exceptionally good silver-screen entertainment. More than 600 films about ancient Greece, Rome, and Egypt have been produced since Enrico Guazzoni's silent epic *Quo Vadis* (1912),[1] and among these the historical—or pseudo-historical—epic features prominently. Its enduring popularity is perpetuated by a raft of stereotyped characters and visual backdrops: cunning beauties, waifish slave girls, strapping warriors, and mysterious sages populating a world of thunderous battles, court intrigues, sex, decadence, and cults.

A particularly rich seam was struck in the decade from the mid-1950s to the mid-1960s. The bodybuilder Steve Reeves's Herculean efforts can stand for many. But then disaster struck where it hurts most, at the box office. Joseph L. Mankiewicz's *Cleopatra* (1963) was both the most expensive ancient-world epic movie to date and the biggest box-office flop. There followed, understandably, a gap of over thirty-five years without a major Hollywood film set in antiquity. Yet the period between 2000 and 2004 saw the release of three: *Gladiator* in 2000, directed by Ridley Scott; Wolfgang Petersen's *Troy* in the spring of 2004 (following, and heavily influenced by, a U.S. television mini-series); and Oliver Stone's *Alexander* in the autumn of 2004. These were big-budget, high-tech films with casts of dazzling stars, and with powerful

3

publicity machines behind them. It can fairly be said that the success of the first of the trio—the "*Gladiator* effect"—provided justification and encouragement for the production of the others. The decision to produce these films was in part based on the studios' perceptions about audiences' preferences, but, in the case of *Alexander* at least, it was also driven by a very strong and longstanding personal commitment on the part of the director.

Scott's *Gladiator* was a huge hit, generating more than $32.7 million in ticket sales in its opening weekend in the United States alone. The film went on to earn $457.2 million worldwide.[2] Historians' contempt for the obvious inaccuracies notwithstanding, audiences loved the film (and not least its music), and many critics pointed to its popularity as evidence of the timeless appeal of the swords-and-sandals genre. Petersen's *Troy* met lukewarm reviews, the critics panning the screenplay, the acting (especially the non-acting of the model-turned-actress who played Helen), and the sets, but it still brought in the very respectable sum of $497.3 million internationally.

In contrast, Stone's *Alexander* earned only $167.3 million worldwide in theaters. Even taking into account the increasing numbers of viewers who buy DVDs for home viewing instead of paying for cinema tickets, the film could not be considered a commercial success. Yet *Alexander* had all of the ingredients of a hit: thrilling battle scenes, a well-known, Oscar-garlanded director, recognizable actors, stunning sets, sexy costumes, and, at its heart, the most famous (if not necessarily the best known) of the entire cast of characters from the ancient world: Alexander the Great. One of the questions at the heart of this book, therefore, is why did *Alexander* fail at the box office? Can it really be (just) that audiences lost their appetite for celluloid antiquity so soon after *Troy*'s silver-screen run?[3]

Some of the other issues raised in this book are also specific to Stone's film. What were the consequences of casting a brash young Irishman as Alexander? Why were the women's costumes created in the way they were, and what effect did they have on viewers' judgments about these characters? Other issues relate more broadly to the study of history and film. What happens when we project modern values onto ancient events, or when modern cultural assumptions rub up against ancient quiddities? How does advance publicity affect popular reception? This book engages with these and other questions, as twelve historians, archaeologists, and film scholars respond to the picture's story, characters, costumes, and sets. There is something here, we hope, for filmographers and cultural critics as well as for ancient historians, archaeologists, and those with a general interest in film.

Perhaps uniquely for a study of a historically based film, this book contains framing essays by *Alexander*'s historical consultant (Robin Lane Fox) and its director, with a variety of historical and/or cinematic perspectives in between.[4] All of these contributors, as was our intention, use *Alexander* as a kind of muse—or, one might say, as an intellectual tinderbox that sparks discussion about its actors, costumes, storyline, scenery, sociopolitical setting, and place in cinematic and cinematographic history. There are, in fact, varying degrees of engagement with *Alexander,* from the overt (Jon Solomon, Monica Cyrino) to the subtle (John Cherry), but every chapter addresses an aspect of Stone's project. The result is a volume that is unmistakably devoted to intellectual criticism of Stone's film. A book of twelve film reviews would have been redundant and boring. A book of twelve scholarly discussions of issues raised by the film will, we hope, prove stimulating and contribute to an understanding of the academic and media landscape in the aftermath of the release and reception of *Alexander.*

Before we attempt to summarize very briefly the content and import of these essays, first let us add a few words on the "real," historical Alexander—Alexander III, king of Macedon, posthumously surnamed "the Great" and so far inhabiting that title as to find himself merged with it in the modern Greek portmanteau label "Megalexandros." He was born in 356 B.C.E. to a Macedonian father, King Philip II, and a Greek mother, Olympias, princess of Epirus in northwest Greece, and the most prominent of Philip's seven wives. Their eldest son was deemed worthy to act as regent of Philip's expanding kingdom in 340, when he was barely sixteen years of age. In 338 Philip defeated a coalition of Greek states to the south of Macedon, thereby becoming undisputed leader of the Greek world—a position he sought to exploit by invading the once mighty Persian empire that in its heyday had ruled all of Asia from Pakistan and Afghanistan to the eastern Mediterranean seaboard, and had taken Egypt to boot. But in 336, before Philip could set foot on Asian soil, he was assassinated at his ceremonial capital of Aegae (modern Vergina). His death followed courtly intrigues in which both the estranged Olympias and the estranged Alexander (whose status as heir was uncertain) were suspected to have had a hand.

Alexander thus succeeded to a throne and an empire at the age of twenty, and instantly showed that he was master of his own destiny as well as those of a great many other people. After settling local affairs by personal military interventions as far north as the Danube and as far south as Greek Thebes (which he ordered destroyed in 335), Alexander took charge of the Persian expedition in 334. He would never return to his homeland. He cast the campaign, for propaganda purposes, as a crusade (minus the cross, of course) of revenge for Persian sacrileges committed on Greek soil a century and a half earlier. Actually, from very early on Alexander pursued his own idiosyncratic agenda—precisely what that was, we shall never know, since it is one of the ironies of history that the extant historical sources for reconstructing Alexander's career are rather poor. Not only are they mainly noncontemporary, but they are also partial in both senses—biased and variously incomplete.

In short order, by dint of extraordinary generalship in three major pitched battles—at the River Granicus in 334, Issus in 333, and Gaugamela in 331—Alexander overcame his chief adversary, the Persian emperor Darius III. No sooner was Darius dead (killed by a rival Iranian noble) than Alexander was himself acting as the Persian Great King, king of kings. Riding roughshod over conservative Macedonian recalcitrance, and even outright Greek revolt, Alexander pushed further east and even won a stunning victory over the war-elephants of an Indian rajah in what is today the Punjab. His defeats came at the hands of his own men. In 325 and again in 324 they in effect mutinied, refusing to pursue what they considered Alexander's impossible dream of universal dominion. Very reluctantly, Alexander withdrew westward, to Iran and then to Iraq. Yet his fighting spirit would not be quenched, and to the end he was formulating new plans of conquest: against the Arabs first, then—who knows?—the Carthaginians, maybe even the Romans.

But whatever exactly he intended—or dreamed—the shape and character of his new and vastly enlarged empire ultimately should be, his life ended before he could achieve any sort of political or cultural conclusion. In June of 323, at Babylon, he took ill and died, more likely from malarial fever than from an assassin's poisoned draught, still short of his thirty-third birthday. Small surprise, therefore, that Alexander became a legend in his own lifetime. That his legend has spread so fast and so far—from Iceland to China—is due very largely to the Egypt that he had conquered and to the Greek language of the conquerors. The *Alexander Romance* became the main medium of transmitting his fame through late antiquity and the middle ages, in non-Western (Islamic) as well as Western (Christian) countries.

Thanks to this legend, and for other reasons, too, Alexander became in various countries and at various times a hero, a quasi-holy man, a

Christian saint, a new Achilles, a philosopher, a scientist, a prophet, and a visionary. But in antiquity he was most famous of all as a conqueror. Here is the Greek writer Arrian, our principal surviving narrative historian of Alexander, writing in the early second century C.E. under the influence of the Roman emperor Trajan's recent conquests in Parthia (in modern Iran):

> For my part I cannot determine with certainty what sort of plans Alexander had in mind, but none was small and petty, and he would not have stopped conquering even if he had added Europe to Asia and the Britannic Islands to Europe. (Arr. *Anab.* 7.1.4)

A millennium and a half later, Shakespeare's Hamlet comments rather irreverently in the graveyard scene on the possible earthy fate of Alexander's corpse:

> Alexander died, Alexander was buried, Alexander returneth into dust; the dust is earth; of earth we make loam; and why of that loam, whereto he was converted, might they not stop a beer-barrel?

That is just a local English illustration of the way in which Alexander has featured in the national literatures of some eighty countries, stretching from our own Britannic islands to the Malay peninsula by way of Kazakhstan. That, in its turn, is another way of saying that Alexander is probably the most famous of the few individuals in human history whose bright light has shot across the firmament to mark the end of one era and the beginning of another. To quote Arrian again:

> I am persuaded that there is no nation, city or people then in being where his name did not reach; for which reason, whatever origin he might boast of, or claim to himself, there seems to me to have been some divine hand presiding both over his birth and his actions, inasmuch as no mortal on earth either excelled or equaled him. (*Anab.* 7.30.2)

That last assertion would have especially galled one Julius Caesar, in whose life Arrian's Greek contemporary Plutarch found a parallel to that of Alexander. In some respects, Caesar came quite close to equaling Alexander, though only after many more years of trying, and he did give his name to a type of autocratic ruler (Kaiser, Czar). But he was not, quite, another Alexander—as he himself recognized early on. On a tour of duty in Spain, he is said to have gazed at a statue of Alexander, who had died at thirty-two, king of so many people, and wept because he himself at the same age had not yet achieved any brilliant success.

Many more illustrations of Alexander's fame—negative as well as positive—could be given. St. Augustine was not hugely impressed: in a rather startlingly modern image, he described him as a rogue with a global appetite for plunder. St. John Chrysostom, patriarch of Constantinople, objected to the way in which coins bearing Alexander's image were often bound to people's heads and feet as apotropaic talismans. (The modern equivalent is perhaps to be found on the tennis court, where the Australian athlete Mark Philippoussis, whose father is Greek, wears an Alexander tattoo.) Dante consigned Alexander to the seventh circle of his *Inferno,* along with thieves, murderers, and tyrants. Those, however, were strictly minority viewpoints.[5]

Such in fact is Alexander's continuing fame, even in today's very differently structured, globalized world, that business journalists write management books purporting to derive and convey "lessons from the great empire builder," and American filmmakers and their financial backers are prepared to commit millions of dollars to exploring, re-creating, and perhaps even enhancing the fame of the original.

Our book engages openly with the question of commercial failure, and possible answers to that question are succinctly summarized by Jon Solomon in his chapter, "The Popular Reception of *Alexander,*" which examines contemporary politics and cultural issues in order to contextualize the film more fully. Joanna Paul's contribution, "Oliver Stone's *Alexander* and the Cinematic Epic Tradition," likewise places the film in a broader cultural setting and reminds us that Stone's project ought to be examined in its wider generic framework, that of the celluloid epic. She argues for situating Alexander in a moment in time when receptions of antiquity (across all media) are becoming ever more attractive, and will show that the film plays a key role in this trend, regardless of its aesthetic value. The director faced stiff competition while planning and raising funds for his film, with rival studios trying to beat him to the screen with their own Alexander films. Numerous groups made claims on Alexander, and this struggle had an effect on the type of Alexander that emerges in the film.

The king of Macedon, as noted above, has always had a transcendent charisma and allure, and his life was soon fictionalized. The innately dramatic quality of his life and career also makes him a fitting subject for more or less fictionalized representation in modern films, plays, and novels. Stone has called him "one of the purest dramatic protagonists and paradoxes of ancient times." But when he adds that Alexander "eluded dramatization for 2,300 years," and "not one Greek or Roman,

Elizabethan or Victorian" has portrayed him on stage, he exceeds the strict bounds of truth.[6] Terence Rattigan and Robert Rossen put Alexander on stage and in film, respectively, before Stone embarked on his project. Robin Lane Fox's chapter on Rattigan's *Adventure Story* (1949) and Kim Shahabudin's chapter on Rossen's *Alexander the Great* (1956) offer critical assessments of these works and continue this book's sustained dialogue with Oliver Stone's *Alexander*.

The film operates at two distinct but interpenetrating levels: that of Alexander the world-historical figure, the event-making hero, and that of Alexander the human individual, the intimate Alexander. The latter is the focus of the essays grouped in part 3. Elizabeth Carney ("Olympias and Oliver: Sex, Sexual Stereotyping, and Women in Oliver Stone's *Alexander*") and Monica Cyrino ("Fortune Favors the Blond: Colin Farrell in *Alexander*") interrogate the gender stereotypes inherent in Stone's choice of Angelina Jolie to play Olympias, Alexander's mother, and of Colin Farrell as the hero himself. As the authors point out, there were drawbacks in casting these particular Hollywood stars in these roles (verisimilitude was not served, for example, by Jolie's being in real life just one year older than Farrell, and filmically making no concession whatsoever to the true age—or aging—of Olympias). Resisting the temptation simply to pan the actors' skills, Carney and Cyrino offer sophisticated analyses of the repercussions of Stone's decisions in terms of myth perpetuation and viewer manipulation.

Meanwhile, Marilyn Skinner, in her chapter "*Alexander* and Ancient Greek Sexuality: Some Theoretical Considerations," explains how sexual codes functioned within ancient Greek societies (they differed from society to society, as between Athens and Sparta, for example, not to mention Macedon). She examines what was permitted sexually, and why, and discusses the societal purpose or purposes that homoerotic bonding appears to have served. In this context, it is interesting to find that Alexander's relationship with Hephaestion, and Achilles' with Patroclus (as portrayed—or rather caricatured—in Petersen's *Troy*), both fell outside the parameters of the norm in various ways.

Who was this Hephaestion? Alexander's boyhood friend and adulthood battlefield companion, and (possibly) paramour at both stages of life, is as intriguing off the screen as he is on it. Outside the realm of cinematography, Hephaestion enjoys continued fame thanks to a devoted group of fans who keep him alive on the internet. This is an excellent example of how mythopoiesis is a continuing process in the modern world, not a feature peculiar to ancient Greece, and Jeanne Reames's chapter, "The Cult of Hephaestion," rightly seeks to do justice to it. She brings into prominence the fact that, despite ancient historians' tendency to give Hephaestion short shrift, Alexander's right-hand man is hugely important to his contemporary "fan-girls." In response, Reames asks who Hephaestion might really have been, historically speaking, and suggests why the demographics of his fanbase might explain the neglect by historians that these very fans bemoan.

An even more firmly historical approach to *Alexander* is pursued in the essays grouped in part 4. Among the aspects of Alexander that appealed most to Oliver Stone were the Macedonian's vision of intercultural co-operation and the fact that "he could be extraordinarily gentle and extravagantly savage."[7] A major theme of his film is Alexander's desire to bring together culturally discrete, often mutually hostile, peoples into a peaceful, Hellenistic (post-Classical) kingdom. Stone's view of Alexander in this respect is in keeping with popular perceptions, but it is a view that requires a critical interrogation. Both Tom Harrison and Lloyd Llewellyn-Jones study "the Other"—in this case Persians—as they are represented in the film. Harrison's "Stone's *Alexander* and the Unity of Mankind" (the title is a calque of a well-known scholarly debate between Sir William Tarn and Professor Ernst Badian of Harvard) demonstrates that the civilizing mission undertaken by Alexander in the film, during which he purports to bring freedom to oppressed Persians and to unite them with Greeks, amounts to a historiographical mirage. Llewellyn-Jones, who served as costume consultant on the film's production team, focuses on the Eastern women's dress. In his chapter, "Help me, Aphrodite! Depicting the Royal Women of Persia in *Alexander*," he explores the representation of the royal women of Persia and Bactria and the effect that costume choices had on viewers' conceptualization of the women. He argues that Orientalization and ornamentalization are the key interpretative concepts to bring to bear, inasmuch as certain costume choices unfairly portrayed the women as exotic, erotic, and, often, barbaric.

Verity Platt's "Viewing the Past: Cinematic Exegesis in the Caverns of Macedon" offers a scholarly conversation with visual media connected with Stone's film. In this case the media are incorporated centrally into the plot of the film itself, in a particular scene in which Philip takes the boy Alexander into caves beneath the royal palace at Vergina to look at wall paintings that depict classical myths. Platt studies the (real) ancient prototypes on which the cinematic paintings were based, and analyzes the (*sur*real) use of them in the film to define Alexander's heroic heritage and future authority. Stylistic signifiers, such as linear

Geometric forms, she argues, guide the audience's understanding of the multiple layers of history that make up the Alexander myth itself.

The web-based cult of Hephaestion, as we saw above, presents one way of viewing Stone's *Alexander* from outside the cinema. Museum exhibitions timed to coincide with the film's release present another, and add a significant dimension to its full contextualization. John Cherry's chapter, "Blockbuster! Museum Responses to Alexander the Great," looks at attempts to tell the story of Alexander through displays of relevant ancient art and artifacts. Alexander-themed exhibitions in the twenty-first century are, in a sense, blockbusters themselves, with the "Treasures from an Epic Era of Hellenism" display at the Onassis Cultural Center in New York (December 2004 to April 2005) being a particularly striking example. Cherry argues that such blockbuster museum exhibitions are concerned not so much with stimulating new scholarship or academic debates as with generating profit through ticket or gift shop sales. Museums' responses to Stone's *Alexander,* in other words, might be summed up as a case of hitching their wagon to the Hollywood star vehicle.

Finally, Oliver Stone has his say. His film was heckled for its plodding narrative, stilted acting, and the liberties it took with history. But it also raised important questions. How do we know about (the real) Alexander? How much do we know about him? How do we convey what we know about him? In a powerful afterword to this volume, Stone responds to the criticisms of his film by the contributors to this book and by others,[8] and he offers his own views on Alexander, historical accuracy, gender stereotyping, and storytelling techniques. Acknowledging that he cannot re-shoot the film, Stone concedes, "I am unable to let the film go from my consciousness."[9]

If we may exercise the editorial prerogative to claim the last word, Oliver Stone in our view merits enormous credit for presenting a complex protagonist whose intriguing romantic interludes, episodic savagery, and eventual self-destruction are not whitewashed in the typical Hollywood fashion and diverted into a conventional happy ending. Indeed, Stone's *Alexander* is alluring for scholars precisely because it acknowledges the problems of the evidence and the complexity of procuring historical knowledge, and makes us think about what historical narratives can mean and how they convey meaning. Stone's artistically bold—and perhaps financially risky—decision to present an Alexander freely transgressing cultural, sexual, and racial boundaries sparked outrage among critics and certain segments of the public (especially in America), and prompted a wider discussion about the sort of man

we ought to be thinking about when we conjure Alexander of Macedon.[10] But that, we believe, is just how it should be: may the discussion
continue.

Notes

1. Jon Solomon, *The Ancient World in the Cinema*, 2nd ed. (New Haven, CT:
Yale University Press, 2000).

2. All figures are drawn from The Numbers website (http://www.the
-numbers.com/). When adjusted for inflation, *Gladiator*'s $457.2 million trans-
lates into $494.4 million in 2004, the year *Troy* and *Alexander* were released.

3. See the volume edited by Martin Winkler, *Troy: From Homer's Iliad to Hollywood Epic* (Oxford: Blackwell, 2006).

4. We should like to draw special attention to Robin Lane Fox's remarkable
The Making of Alexander (Oxford: R & L, 2005). Lane Fox also shares with Oliver
Stone the commentary on the DVD of the theatrical release.

5. See further Paul Cartledge, *Alexander the Great: The Hunt for a New Past*
(Woodstock, NY: Overlook Press, 2004; rev. ed., New York: Vintage, 2005).

6. Stone, "Foreword," in Lane Fox, *The Making of Alexander*, n.p.

7. Ibid.

8. Stone, writing in the foreword to the prerelease pressbook of the film
(Paris, July 2004). However, he has been able to do the next best—or worst—
thing, which is to re-cut and re-re-cut the footage he shot, issuing first a (slightly
shorter) DVD version that lacked some material that was in the theatrically released film and reintroduced material not originally included, and then a second, longer DVD version—truly a final cut in the sense that, as he himself announced, there was nothing left in the can! Throughout the book, we refer to the
three versions of the film as follows: *Alexander* (2004 theatrical release, 2005
DVD, 175 minutes), *Alexander: Director's Cut* (2005 DVD, 167 minutes), and *Alexander Revisited: The Final Cut* (2007 DVD, 214 minutes).

9. For similar thoughts see Stone's foreword to the pressbook. Stone's 2007
DVD release—the version he calls the Final Cut (*Alexander Revisited*)—is a significant restructuring of the original film, with scenes rearranged and previously
cut material included. This version has received critical acclaim (see, e.g., the
following reviews: www.dvdtalk.com/reviews/26729/alexander-revisited-the
-final-cut/; www.filmsinreview.com/2007/02/27/alexander-revisited-%E2%80
%93final-cut/) and is, Stone asserts, more in keeping with the project he initially envisaged.

10. We should note the appearance of another edited volume on film and an-
tiquity, which was published too late for a thorough consideration here: Irene
Berti and Marta García Morcillo, eds., *Hellas on Screen: Cinematic Receptions of
Ancient History, Literature and Myth* (Stuttgart: Franz Steiner Verlag, 2008).

Part 1

Stone's *Alexander*

Oliver Stone's *Alexander* and the Cinematic Epic Tradition

JOANNA PAUL

THE RELEASE OF *Alexander* in late 2004 (early 2005 in the United Kingdom) was a cinematic event generating excitement and anticipation in audiences eager to see what Oliver Stone would do with this "incomparably famous" ancient ruler.[1] The excitement was countered by the controversy and condemnation that surrounded the project at every stage of its development, and lingered long after the film's release.[2] My intention here is not to defend Stone's film against unfavorable judgments but, instead, to analyze it as the most recent in a long chain of receptions of Alexander the Great, a character whose capacity for reshaping and rereading was evident even in antiquity. *Quot auctores, tot Alexandri,*[3] and the Stone-authored Alexander is as worthy of consideration as any of them. Furthermore, assessing *Alexander* as a particular kind of film—an "epic"—and trying to understand its place within the wider cinematic epic tradition will help shed light on its implications, not only for receptions of Alexander, but for the continued place of classics in popular culture more generally.

The definition of an epic film is, rightfully, shifting and elusive, but for my purposes some parameters are necessary. Here, "epic" refers to a mainstream film, large-scale in both production values and budget, set in antiquity, with a historical or mythological narrative (or both).[4]

On this definition, the renewal of such filmmaking in the twenty-first century (beginning with *Gladiator* in 2000)—and *Alexander*'s role in this renewal—should not only tell us *how much* Alexander and other ancient figures still matter, but also lead us to ask *why*.

Competing for Alexander: Preproduction Controversies

Stiff competition beset Stone's film from the start as numerous "Alexanders" attempted to battle their way into cinematic production. This story has been helpfully untangled by Stone's academic consultant, Robin Lane Fox, in his invaluable account of the making of the film and more recently by Gideon Nisbet.[5] But it is worth stopping to consider how these cinematic struggles both shaped and reflected the reception of Alexander, and how they are aligned with other conflicts over the territories of Alexander's sexuality and ethnicity that manifested themselves during production and that reveal his potent currency as a contested figure even into the twenty-first century.

The varying fortunes of the rival projects attracted a good deal of media attention—not only because they were grist for the Hollywood rumor mill, but also because they provoked concern about the precise portrayal of Alexander that each would produce. A headline from London's *Sunday Times* in November 1998—"Alexander the Great Wimp Gets Lost in a Hollywood Conspiracy"—suggested unease over Alexander's heroism, or lack of it. The article discussed a Christopher McQuarrie script that allegedly made Alexander "a peace-loving wimp," while Stone's emerging project would apparently present an Alexander who was subject to court conspiracies, thus aligning the ruler with the director's presidential biopics of John F. Kennedy and Richard Nixon. With so many possible readings of the character, life, and legacy of the Macedonian king, it was clear even at this relatively early stage that any film that attempted to recount his biography was going to attract a great deal of attention.

Also apparent in this frenzy of preproduction debate was a particular slant to the rhetoric. Consciously or unconsciously, the struggle to film the story of Alexander's life is often described in ways that precisely reflect that narrative, using the language of battle, conflict, expansion, and conquest. There are faint echoes of this even in academic discourse, as when Diana Spencer's account of receptions of Alexander described the "tortured progress" of the Scorsese/Scott/Stone struggle, at its peak when she was writing in 2001-2,[6] but this rhetoric is especially prevalent in the media. The *New York Times* described the Hollywood heavyweights involved in the projects as "an army of screen conquerors," and after box-office disappointment in the United States, *Variety* declared, "Stone redraws battle plans."[7] In an interview with *Cineaste*, Stone himself observes that "a lot of people begin rooting for one side or the other to 'win'";[8] and *Variety* wrote of "the battle between sellers of the two films [Stone's and Luhrmann's] to divide and conquer foreign territories."[9] Clearly, *Alexander* and its competitors were rooted in the conventions of the cinematic epic tradition from an early stage. As Vivian Sobchack has observed, the epic genre in film "*formally repeats* the surge, splendor and extravagance, the human labor and capital cost entailed by its narrative's *historical content* in both its *production process* and its *modes of representation*."[10] Thus, particularly in accounts of the making of a film, this particular kind of cinema is likely to trope that process in terms that reflect the internal narrative, in an extratextual "*mimetic interpretation* of the historical events it is dramatizing."[11] Though Sobchack's observations are based primarily on mid-century epics, the practice has continued with *Gladiator* and *Alexander*, thereby signaling a certain continuity within the epic tradition that is explored in greater depth below.

Describing these cinematic conflicts in terms of battles and conquest may seem to be simply Hollywood and media hyperbole, but the arenas (itself a loaded term) in which these struggles actually began to make their presence felt suggest otherwise. Film fans and academics might have their own reasons for arguing for a particular Alexander, but for other interest groups the issues involved can be profound. From an early stage, Alexander's sexuality was a hotly debated issue. He had been "adopted" as a historical hero for the gay rights movement, thanks in part to Mary Renault's trilogy of Alexander novels (1977–88) and, before that, Klaus Mann's *Alexander: Roman der Utopie* (1929).[12] Newspaper reports on homosexuality in the armed forces place Alexander at the head of any list of famous gay warriors,[13] and there is a wealth of Internet discussion on the topic. Though many observers— not least Stone himself—were quick to point out that labeling Alexander "gay" was anachronistic, there was an understandable eagerness to see how his sexuality would be treated, especially once rumors spread that his relationship with Hephaestion would be central to the film.[14] Such speculation prompted "Alexander the Gay" headlines and a strong conservative backlash (especially in large areas of the U.S.

South), which the director believed were largely responsible for the film's failure.[15] So far, so predictable. But the conflict was more complex. The Director's Cut of *Alexander* came under fire from the Gay and Lesbian Alliance Against Defamation in the United States, which claimed that Stone had "compromised his own artistic integrity" by editing out a scene between Alexander and Hephaestion.[16] For many, sexuality was the main area of contestation for ownership of Alexander, a struggle that took on even greater significance when it became intertwined with other emotive issues.

Another twist in the production controversies came in 2003, when the Greek culture minister, Evangelos Venizelos, formally withdrew support for Stone's project, calling the anticipated portrayal of Alexander as bisexual "a disgrace" and "a slur on Greece."[17] Again, this basically conservative response to the film (or to early reports on it) is predictable, but it derives complexity from the ethnic and nationalist debates that surround Alexander and that led the Greeks to stake a claim to "their" Alexander at an early stage in the production. Regarding the competing claims of Greeks and Macedonians,[18] suffice it to say that the symbolic potential of Alexander the Great's cultural capital is immense, generating far greater passion and acrimony than his sexuality. In the dispute over who has the right to call themselves Macedonians—Greeks or the inhabitants of what is currently named the Former Yugoslav Republic of Macedonia—Alexander has been enlisted as a figurehead for both sides. It was inevitable that this prominent new reception of Alexander fanned the flames of the conflict and attracted media attention.[19] Presumably, each side hoped that the film might present an Alexander who was recognizably "theirs"—but this was ultimately an issue that Stone would find easier to duck than that of Alexander's sexuality. Although Fiachra Gibbons in the *Guardian* observed that the contribution of Robin Lane Fox was seen as a victory for the Greeks (since both Greeks and Macedonians regard him as a Hellenist), Stone himself wisely avoided commenting on the issue.

The only production detail that seems to shed light on the issue of competing nationalisms is the use of Irish or Celtic accents for Alexander and his Macedonians, in contrast to the English "Received Pronunciation" usually associated with cinematic epic diction, and here reserved for the Greeks. Though Gibbons speculated that "Macedonians of all complexions are content with this, each convinced it favours their cause," the neutral observer is surely more likely to interpret the Macedonian-Irish/Greek-English distinction as a way of figuring the

Macedonians as "Other," marginal even—and therefore not Greek. However, as Daniel Mendelsohn observed, the force of the distinction is undermined by the fact that Aristotle is actually the only "Greek" who offers a contrast for the Macedonian accent.[20] Given that media reports on the ethnicity issue were less numerous and colorful than reports on sexuality, audiences could remain unaware of the symbolic power a new Alexander might hold in some parts of the world. Still, for the academic observer, it is clear evidence of the potency still held by ancient figures, and of the potential for "popular" receptions of antiquity to have an impact far beyond the sphere of simple entertainment.

Alexander: A Film for Our Time?

Apart from contestations over Alexander and his legacy, a prominent theme in media coverage of the film was its identification as belonging to a particular tradition of filmmaking, the (Hollywood) epic. Fluctuations in this tradition have long fascinated audiences and film scholars alike.[21] After the apparent death of the Hollywood epic of the ancient world in the 1960s—after dominating the industry for much of cinema's early history, and especially the 1950s—the genre was unexpectedly (and successfully) reborn with the release of *Gladiator*. With only Wolfgang Petersen's *Troy* intervening between Ridley Scott's film and Oliver Stone's *Alexander*, many people were as interested in the latter's resurrection of the cinematic epic tradition as in its revivified protagonist.[22] Many media reports suggested that *Gladiator* was "paving the way" for *Alexander*, even though we now know that Stone had conceived of his film long before *Gladiator* came along. Certainly the earlier film's success legitimized the new projects and their potential for box-office success.

In this section I examine the extent to which *Alexander*'s continuation of a film genre and its self-conscious "newness" reveal themselves in the production and shape responses to the film. This involves considering *Alexander* not simply alongside *Gladiator* (and, to a lesser extent, *Troy*), but also in the wider context of the cinematic epic throughout the twentieth century. It has long been recognized that literary works— especially high-status ones, such as epic poetry—can be understood differently when regarded as part of a tradition. Each new work entering a tradition may consciously or unconsciously appeal to that tradition, situating itself in the context of its predecessors, or it may assert its distance from them, signaling its newness and difference; often, it does

both simultaneously.[23] The notion of tradition—not often fully explored in film criticism—can usefully be employed when interpreting
cinematic epic, not least because of the complex and provocative generic resonances between epic in literature and in cinema.

First, is there evidence that Stone and his production team consciously sought to move on from the epic film tradition that flourished
in the past? Cinematic technology is one potential marker of a film's innovation and was certainly seen as such after *Gladiator*'s celebrated use
of computer-generated imagery (CGI). Martin Winkler described that
film as "a new epic, displaying in its computer-generated images a kind
of cyber-Rome."[24] Yet Stone's DVD commentary on the theatrical release, particularly remarks relating to the battle of Gaugamela, shows
that he resisted the overuse of CGI. Though certain sets, such as the exterior view of Babylon, were computer-generated, *Alexander*'s aesthetic
is less reliant on this technology than *Gladiator*'s.[25] In one sense, though,
the use of new technology is not necessarily a marker of innovation in
the cinematic epic tradition, since the film epic has always been driven
by new developments: the advent of sound, color, widescreen, computer technologies, and so on have all encouraged filmmakers to turn
to the big-budget spectaculars that the ancient world provides as a
means of showing off these new developments to the full.[26] Stone's relatively *limited* use of new technology may in fact signal a departure
from his predecessors' eagerness to exploit every available process—
though we should not overstate the case here. Although Stone does not
rely heavily on CGI, he shows a willingness to experiment with other
visual techniques. The most notable example is the filming of the final
battle scene in India. As a way of indicating Alexander's frenzied state
of mind, director of photography Rodrigo Prieto used infrared film
stock, which bathes the scene in vivid hues, and also manipulated the
focus. Just as *Gladiator*'s frantic, rapidly cut battle scenes[27] represented a
departure from the relatively static treatment of such scenes in earlier
films, like *Spartacus* (1960), the hallucinogenic quality of Alexander's
Indian combat, coupled with the disorientation of the dust-filled plain
at Gaugamela, demonstrates a relatively novel approach to the conventional epic battle.

More than its use of visual technologies, a film's relationship to current affairs may be particularly powerful in marking it out as "a film for
our time." Evidence for the topicality of Scott's film ranges from its reflection of the modern fascination with entertainment violence to its allusions to contemporary American politics.[28] We have already noted

two areas, sexuality and ethnicity, that underline *Alexander*'s contemporary relevance. Though reticent on the latter issue, Stone, as we have seen, was committed to confronting Alexander's sexuality, and regardless of its impact on the film's success, he was well aware that this was one of its most original aspects. Recognizing that Hephaestion's visit to Alexander on his wedding night might trouble some people, he remarked, "What can I say? This isn't *Braveheart!*"[29]

More complex than Alexander's love life—and far more topical—was his co-option as a symbol of contemporary politics and militarism. This aspect of Alexander's reception is nothing new. The nature of his campaigns, and the extent of his army's territorial reach, means that he has long been a personification of imperialism, whether as the archetypal questing conqueror, aiming to unite mankind under a peaceful, beneficent ruler, or as a prototype of bloodthirsty, brutal colonial exploitation.[30] Stone adheres to the first view. For him, Alexander was "not a typical Western imperialist."[31] He presents him as treating his conquered territories well, not exploiting them, and spreading civilization under the banner of an idealized multiculturalism, a perspective clearly informed by contemporary notions of imperialism and its evils.

But Stone's quite traditional reading of Alexander's imperialism was open to rereading by audiences who were inclined to see Alexander's exploits as commenting on the Iraq War. This kind of ancient/modern analogy was already being tested in *Troy*. From Herodotus onward, it has been commonplace to describe the Trojan War as the archetypal conflict between East and West; for Alexander, whose conquests took him through the Middle East, including modern-day Iraq, the comparisons were even more readily available. It was all too easy to equate him with George W. Bush as a power-hungry Western ruler interfering with the East to satisfy a demand for material and political rewards. Since Stone clearly envisioned Alexander as a beneficent ruler (and evidently did not take such a view of Bush), such suggestions were unwelcome; but, perhaps bowing to the insistence with which the analogy was pushed, he eventually confronted the Iraqi conflict. As the critic Gary Crowdus observed, the film itself "does not push such parallels," but it still proved a fruitful topic for Stone:

> I don't think Alexander would have made the fatal mistake Bush did of disbanding the Iraqi army, or of alienating the locals with a lack of central authority and presence. He never wavered in going after a band of robbers or a rebel tribe. He would track down such people for weeks if necessary, even months. . . . I don't think that President Bush ever figured

that out. How could we as a nation turn away from the promised chase
for Osama Bin Laden, and divert our resources into Iraq? This was fundamentally flawed military policy, which Alexander would have avoided
at all costs.[32]

Stone turned to contemporary parallels mostly to illuminate his own
reception of Alexander, but their currency had an impact on the film.
The director addresses the question of Iraq several times in his DVD
commentary—demonstrating his awareness that this message was
available to be read into his cinematic narrative, whatever his original
intentions were.[33] Even as Stone tries to deflect such interpretations, we
are reminded of their pervasiveness. The comparison with Bush, he
says, "is revisionist, because you're putting a twenty-first-century view
on Alexander, and you have to talk about what glory and freedom
mean to Alexander. He was the first, he was the prototype of the West-
erner who went East."[34] But how else, we might ask, can one read Alexander except through twenty-first-century eyes? As much as Stone,
after years of careful study and consultation with advisors, might wish
us to use his film to approach the real Alexander—and understand
what glory and freedom meant to him!—surely Stone's reading of Alexander is as constructed and contingent as one that compares him to
President Bush.

Alexander's engagement with current affairs, while inevitably figuring it as "a film for our time," does not necessarily differentiate it
much from its peers in the cinematic epic tradition, which could also
be marked by contemporary political engagement. To find what is
unique about the film, we must consider the basic content of *Alexander*'s narrative—that is, ancient Greek history. Throughout the twentieth century, the clear majority of cinematic epics set in the ancient
world were concerned with Roman history.[35] Although a few movies
looked to Greek history (*The 300 Spartans* [1962], for example), Rome
was of far greater interest, and seemingly more suitable as cinematic
material, partly because of the stereotypes of the "bloody gladiatorial
spectacles and seductive Oriental queens," which were instantly appealing spectacular subjects for filmgoers,[36] but also because we have
constructed certain "grand narratives" for Rome—the rise of Christian-
ity, the decline and fall of a great empire—that work particularly well as
epic narratives.

Oliver Stone's choice to film Greek history, then, signals a certain distance from epic convention. *Troy* was concerned with Greek material,
too. But though it declared its narrative to be predominantly historical,

not mythical—a distinction explored further below—its use of Homeric and other mythological texts had precedents in the fifties and sixties, such as *Ulysses* (1955), *Helen of Troy* (1956), and *Jason and the Argonauts* (1963). Greek history—and specifically the life of Alexander the Great—may have appealed precisely because of the relative lack of attention so far. Robert Rossen's 1956 *Alexander the Great* was the only previous Hollywood attempt on this narrative;[37] it is therefore ironic that so many other filmmakers conceived of the same idea at the same time. Negative responses to Stone's *Alexander* may have been partially shaped by that very choice of Greek history: where Stone saw nothing but the drama of Alexander's life, audiences reared on Roman films failed, perhaps, to appreciate fully the story being played out in relatively unfamiliar times and locations.

Still, this ought not to have mattered; audiences' failure to engage with Alexander's life surely had more to do with the structuring of the narrative (discussed in the next section) than the fact that he was Greek. Whatever pitfalls the choice to "go Greek" may have presented, Stone's treatment of his historical material is interesting and sometimes quite original for epic film. Perhaps as a result of the sheer number of years spent on the project, the *amount* of historical detail he incorporated is considerable. Some critics highlighted this as one of the film's failings: Crowdus, for example, suggested that Stone's extensive reading and personal investment in the subject led to a film "rich in historical detail . . . but much of it will be invisible to the average moviegoer or, even when apparent, will lack sufficient dramatic or historical context to be anything other than bewildering for most viewers."[38] This may well be a fair reflection of popular consensus. For our purposes, though, it is interesting to observe Stone engaging with the historical record in a way that sheds light on the shifting boundary between popular and academic notions of history, and on the question of historical authenticity.

Many accounts of films set in the ancient world are concerned with how "accurate" they are, and there is often disagreement over what kind of accuracy a filmmaker can, or indeed should, strive for in a fictional film.[39] *Alexander* provides an invaluable addition to this discourse, largely thanks to Robin Lane Fox's detailed accounts—in his book, DVD commentary, and other media reports—of working as Stone's advisor. Though an observer might expect the academic historian to push historical authenticity at the expense of everything else, Lane Fox's reflections instead clarify with sensitivity just what role and responsibility the historian has when working on such a project. When the facts are known, they can be followed, but Stone's project also forces us to confront those aspects of ancient history that are not certain. Lane Fox's description of the battle scenes, for example, re- counts his conversations with Dale Dye, the ex-Marine who had often worked on the military aspects of Stone's films, and whose detailed— but nonacademic—knowledge of ancient warfare led him to some very different conclusions about, say, phalanx formation.[40] Lane Fox ac- knowledges that *Alexander* made him reconsider some of his own the- ories about the Macedonian king—for example, reassessing the signifi- cance of Alexander's marriage to Roxane.[41] It is also surely right that a cinematic reception of the ancient world should make us—particularly academics—question our ownership of antiquity, or at the very least recognize how different, and how powerful, competing visions of the ancient world might be. The filmmaker must strike a balance between the "authentic" account offered by the scholar—fragile as it may be— and what audiences feel things *ought* to be like.[42]

Another aspect of *Alexander*'s engagement with history is its interro- gation of the boundaries between myth or fiction and history. As sug- gested above, *Troy* also negotiated this distinction by recasting the Tro- jan War as a historical event, expunging supernatural elements of the Homeric myth and using cinematic devices such as maps and dating intertitles ("3200 years ago") to give the narrative a definite spatio- temporal location. *Alexander* proceeds in a different way. Alexander's existence is of course historically attested, but the film develops as a theme the process of self-mythologization engendered in Alexander's own lifetime, and the even more concerted mythologizing process from the moment of his death. The prevalence of the heroes of Greek mythol- ogy in the film (such as Alexander's identification with Achilles) under- lines this process, and is discussed in more detail in the next section, but the figure of the older Ptolemy, who punctuates the narrative, is partic- ularly emphatic. As he dictates his own history in the Library at Alex- andria, he shows how even the first historical accounts, those written by Alexander's contemporaries, may not be understood as objective truth. "Did such a man as Alexander exist?" he asks at the beginning. "Of course not. We idolize him, make him better than he was." Pinning down just who Alexander "was" is impossible. Stone dramatizes, in- stead of denying, one of the key features of the modern world's rela- tionship with antiquity—the difficulty of uncovering verifiable truth under the layers of receptions piled up over the centuries. And, of course, even as the film adumbrates the complexities of Alexander receptions, and their mythologization of history, it cannot escape being part of that collection of mythologizing responses itself.

Alexander and Its Epic Predecessors

It now remains to discuss the ways in which Stone's film responds to or is affected by its position in the wider cinematic epic tradition. Unsurprisingly, many of the conventions of cinematic epic are central to *Alexander* as well. For example, spectacle—which is often regarded as the central constitutive feature of epic, such that the two terms can be synonymous—is clearly an important aspect of the film. Though certain aspects of *Alexander*'s spectacular display may seem innovative, it is, for the most part, entirely in keeping with what we have come to expect from ancient world epics. Sets and costumes receive lavish attention, and the usual set-pieces provide moments of climactic spectacle, such as the battle scenes and the triumphal entry into Babylon. Stone himself is aware of, and sometimes a little defensive about, the conventionality of such details: commenting on Alexander's speech to his troops at Gaugamela, for example, he acknowledges that "people will say they've seen this before"—the pre-battle speech is a memorable feature of films such as *Spartacus* and *Gladiator*—but he justifies it as the most effective way of communicating Alexander's message.

The film's marketing strongly recalled earlier epics, from small details such as the use of a Roman-style font for the film's title to its embodiment of the scale of production through a kind of "rhetoric of numbers." An article in the *Sunday Times*, for example, listed the use of 2,000 Moroccan military extras and 120 horses, 20,000 costumes, 3,000 swords and shields, 4,000 bows, 9,000 arrows, 200 lances, 350 clubs and axes, and 20 elephants and riders—all highly reminiscent of the way in which 1950s epics were also advertised in terms of their consumption.[43] The film's score is what we might expect from a Hollywood epic; Stone himself said that he "wanted big, I wanted operatic; Sergio Leone or something epic, and I knew that Vangelis was on the right track."[44] Casting choices may also have been informed, to an extent, by similar practices in other epics, especially *Gladiator*. Neither film employed an especially well known (at the time) actor in the leading role, but both filled supporting roles with renowned "veterans." *Gladiator* cast Richard Harris, Derek Jacobi, and Oliver Reed; *Alexander* uses Brian Blessed, Anthony Hopkins, and Christopher Plummer. The use of Plummer in particular

casts a light on *Alexander*'s membership of a tradition. Besides the abstract notion of epic "gravitas" that such actors impart, their association
with previous productions set in the ancient world provides a more distinct line of continuity between the tradition's past and present. Plummer had played Commodus in *The Fall of the Roman Empire*, and though
his role in *Alexander* is small, it is not too far-fetched to see his presence
as an appeal to that tradition.[45]

For the most part, though, this discussion must focus on a theme
raised earlier—the characterization of Alexander himself, and the ways
in which this aligns itself with the cinematic epic tradition. Stone's
choice of a simple, one-word title—instead of the *Alexander the Great*
used in 1956—may signal a resistance to emphasizing Alexander's heroic status. As the film's Ptolemy speaks of the difficulty of getting past
the myths about Alexander, Stone—in the title at least—attempts to do
this, refraining from passing judgment by using the established nomen-
clature. But elsewhere, Stone's comments on Alexander show his high
regard for the man and his idealized imperial vision, and the emphasis
on Alexander's identification with Greek mythical heroes shapes and
challenges his heroicization in important ways. Throughout his DVD
commentary, Stone is at pains to point out this recurring theme, which
makes its presence strongly felt in Alexander's childhood—through Aristotle's teachings and the cave paintings that his father, Philip, shows
him—and continues to inform Alexander's sense of self, and his perception by both his contemporaries and modern audiences. Achilles,
Heracles, Oedipus, Prometheus, Jason—each story and each painting
fills the young Alexander with awe, and he claims that "one day I'll be
on walls like these."[46] Stone constructs his narrative so that each mythical template can be seen to play out in Alexander's life, from his prow-
ess in battle to his relationship with his parents to his untimely death.

Alexander does indeed end up immortalized "on the wall" (the
equation of the cave paintings to the cinematic product itself is rather
neat, especially if we choose to read the image of Plato's cave as a kind
of proto-cinema). Although he is understood as hoping to be remembered for his achievements, appealing to these mythical exempla also
allows the possibility that he will be remembered for his flaws and his
struggles—just as Achilles is remembered as much for his anger, and
Oedipus for his self-deluded crimes, as for their typically "heroic"
deeds. The tragic hero is an important model, but for our purposes we
should particularly note how Alexander is portrayed in accordance
with the ancient epic hero. He pursues the archetypal epic "quest" or

journey, accompanied by faithful companions (especially Hephaestion), overcoming many obstacles on the way. He is a powerful individual who also has the capacity to work for the good of his community; on Stone's reading, Alexander strove to benefit mankind as a whole. He inspires great reverence—and his *kleos* will be communicated by those who come after him, from Ptolemy onward—but his flaws may also lead to his downfall. These are all aspects of epic heroism that have had a demonstrable impact on the characterization of the hero in epic cinema. Even though some of the complexities may be ironed out, it is shortsighted to see cinematic heroism as concerned only with positive models of behavior; instead, heroes such as Spartacus, Ben-Hur, and Maximus are equipped with both positive qualities and failings, facing challenges as well as achieving great success. Therefore, not only is Stone's characterization of his Alexander firmly situated within the cinematic tradition, but it also contributes to making that cinematic epic tradition continuous with the wider epic tradition in literature.

Although we might welcome Stone's appeal to the conventions of the mythical hero—epic, tragic, or otherwise—as a way of adding interest to the characterization of Alexander, it leaves the film open to criticism. Tom Shone suggested that this theme resulted in an excessive amplification and aggrandizement of Alexander that was ultimately detrimental to the film. Referring to the Homeric combat in *Platoon*, Shone praises Stone's previous success at "mythologizing men. . . . [But] now that he has an actual myth on his hands, Stone has doubled up and cancelled himself out: we get myth pumped up into über-myth, from which Olympian vantage point Stone shows no signs of descending."[47] This criticism has, I think, only limited validity, since it is precisely the layering of different mythologizing processes—Alexander's own reverence for the epic hero, his own posthumous mythologization, and so on— that creates interest and forces us to examine the means by which historical figures become prominent, and their stories distorted. By sweepingly characterizing Stone's material as "a myth" in the first instance, Shone removes the underlying complexities of this theme.

A more relevant criticism of the film's characterization of Alexander concerns the narrative emplotment of the epic hero's exploits. Though Alexander's life was relatively short, it is still impossible to include every significant event in a single film, and some viewers were inevitably disappointed by what was left out—such as the visit to the oracle at Siwa oasis, where Alexander was proclaimed son of Zeus (a potentially fascinating contribution to the theme of self-mythologization).[48] If the writer feels bound to narrate *a life*, then how should he or she address the fact that Alexander's biography—however short and exciting—does not necessarily have a satisfying dramatic shape? Many critics—and Stone himself, in his commentary—were quick to observe that a conventional narrative arc would have seen the film end after the climactic battle in India. But since this was to be a film of a whole life, it had to carry on until Alexander himself died.

Structure seems to have been a constant headache for Stone. Having observed that Rossen's film faltered after spending too long on Alexander's early years in Macedon he was keen to avoid a similar fate. He also seems to have turned to classical plot structures for guidance, speaking in the commentary of his vision of the story as a three-act narrative (necessarily shortened from an original five-act concept, and thus implicitly appealing to models of Shakespearean tragedy).[49] But the filmmakers might have done well to heed the advice of one of the film's own characters: the suggestion in Aristotle's *Poetics* that the ideal narrative of an epic or tragedy should be constructed around a single *action*, not a single hero (1451a, 1459a). Narratives need not follow Aristotelian precepts in order to be successful, but cinema in particular lends them a good deal of credence, and the *Poetics* may be seen as a kind of proto-screenwriting manual.[50] Given that the criticisms of *Alexander*'s dramatic structure seem to stem mainly from Stone's attempt to cram too much in, we might wonder what would have been done differently had the director listened to Aristotle as carefully as his Alexander did. Indeed, this is where paying more attention to the successes of previous epic films might have helped. It would not have necessitated any less emphasis on the central epic hero—the titles of many of the most famous epic films (*Gladiator, Ben-Hur, Spartacus*) demonstrate how important that central figure is—but the plots of these dramatically satisfying films coalesce around the single action that Aristotle advocates: an act of revenge, or a bid for freedom. Maybe this is inconceivable for a film about Alexander, whose whole life presents such irresistible material: Stone himself criticizes the simplicity of Rossen's "revenge drama" structure. Clearly the compulsion to make a "biopic" about Alexander presents narrative problems that cannot easily be solved.[51]

*A*lexander's struggles with narrative structure mean that it is easy to judge it as inferior to the epic predecessors just mentioned. More generally, the success of *Gladiator* and the heavyweights of the earlier twentieth century presents an intimidating precedent. *Gladiator* was, in a sense, less bound by such fears, given its temporal distance from its predecessors, but it still had to negotiate its position in the tradition—and, indeed, to justify a return to that tradition in the first place. *Alexander* avoided that problem—*Gladiator*'s success not only justified *Alexander*'s existence but also *enabled* it, by giving financiers the confidence to back Stone's project. One might argue that Stone would have carried on regardless, but a more sober view has to take commercial considerations into account. The flipside was, of course, that Stone was measured against his predecessor and found wanting by the many reviewers (and audiences) who dismissed this new film with the comment, "It's not *Gladiator.*" *Troy*'s release only a few months earlier and its lukewarm reception might have been expected to work in *Alexander*'s favor: here was the chance to better Wolfgang Petersen's celluloid (or CGI) Greeks and Trojans. But the fact that *Alexander* was criticized as worse than *Gladiator*, rather than praised as (slightly) better than *Troy*, demonstrates how such traditions work. It is the successful works that loom largest in one's mind.

So much for the critical response. But given the amount of time Stone spent on the project, one would not expect *Gladiator* or *Troy* to have been uppermost in his mind. Rather, we could argue that it was the cinematic epic tradition in its first incarnation—that is, earlier in the twentieth century—that occupied him. The fact that this kind of filmmaking was so different from his earlier work meant that Stone seemed to see himself entering an already illustrious tradition, and relishing that fact. Aligning this film with precedents such as D. W. Griffiths, Cecil B. DeMille, William Wyler, and David Lean, he pronounced it "wonderful" to work in that style, particularly enjoying the license for heightened dialogue and grand gestures.[52] He also seemed to revel in a comment made by "a French critic [who] told me that the film is like Cecil B. DeMille, which I think is great. It *is* a bit of a throwback. He said, 'C'est vieux, mais c'est moderne,' which is a nice compliment."[53] This remark neatly sums up *Alexander*'s relationship to the cinematic epic tradition. Although it does not tell the whole story, the film's dual identification as "ancient, but modern" indicates not only its strategy of retelling an ancient story for the modern world, but also its negotiation between following in the footsteps of a great filmmaking tradition and, at the same time, asserting itself as new and relevant for the twenty-first century.[54]

What, then, of the future? In 2006 we might have asked whether the relative failure of *Alexander* killed off the Hollywood epic even as it seemed to prolong it, but a year is a long time in cinema, as they say, and when *300* returned audiences to Greek history yet again in 2007, it met with remarkable success. All that can be said with any certainty is that the future of the genre remains uncertain, a state of affairs as consistent with Alexander's life as the rival productions' battles for territory and conquest were. One of the most effective ways of confronting the notion of tradition in literary epic has been to trope it as a matter of succession, so that the anxieties over one poet's relation to another are wrapped up in metapoetical relationships between father and heir.[55] The end of *Alexander* encapsulates the theme neatly: dying off before he has achieved all that might be expected of him, with his successors and the future of his empire unknown, Alexander the Great might seem to be an apt symbol of the state of the cinematic epic tradition today.

Notes

1. Cartledge 2004, 6.
2. See Monica Cyrino's chapter in this volume for discussion of these controversies, particularly in relation to Alexander's sexuality.
3. Paul Cartledge, foreword to Mossé 2004, vii.
4. The historical setting of epic film is subject to most debate, with some suggesting that the genre is not limited to ancient history and should encompass films with fantasy or futuristic settings, such as the *Star Wars* series (1977–2005) or *The Lord of the Rings* trilogy (2001–3), alongside modern narratives like *The Godfather* trilogy (1972–90). For the most recent scholarly discussions of the "genre" (itself a slippery term in this debate), see Burgoyne 2008 (who equates "epic" with "ancient"). Previously, Elley 1984 insisted that epic film is limited to pre-eleventh-century settings.
5. Lane Fox 2004; Nisbet 2006, 112–35.
6. Spencer 2002, 211–12.
7. Fleming 2004.
8. Crowdus 2005, 23, 14. This interview also quotes Stone's earlier remark that "if I pull off *Alexander,* it'll be the greatest coup of my life."
9. Fleming 2003.
10. Sobchack 1995, 287 (italics in original).
11. Ibid., 293.
12. Spencer 2002, 212–16; Mossé 2004, 202–5.
13. Ezard 1995.
14. Crowdus 2005, 22–23. Salacious media reporting no doubt increased expectations that there would be a significant amount of homosexual sex in the film. Stone has called these reports exaggerated and said that he had never intended to show much more of Alexander's relationships with Hephaestion or Bagoas than what appeared in the theatrical release—only a few scenes were "trimmed" (ibid., 23).

15. Dalton 2005. The *Independent* reported that American conservatives were warning potential moviegoers to "speak to your pastors immediately because Satan is attempting to enter your mind" (Hiscock and Burleigh 2004).

16. Dalton 2005.

17. Gibbons 2002.

18. See John Cherry's chapter in this volume (specifically his discussion of "Alexander in the Antipodes"). Loring Danforth (1995, 163–74; 2003, 347–64) provides comprehensive accounts of "the Macedonian Question," also reporting that Greek objections to the Stone project were raised as far back as 1998, when the *Hellas Letter,* the monthly bulletin of the Consulate General of Greece in Boston, stated that Stone's "version of the life of Alexander the Great will differ significantly from the historical version" (quoted in Danforth 2003, 359).

19. Gibbons 2004.

20. Mendelsohn 2005, 46.

21. Wyke 1997, Elley 1984, and Winkler 2001 all contain descriptions of the decline and fall (and second rise) of the cinematic epic, including the political and economic factors that came into play. The financial disasters that were *Cleopatra* (1963) and *The Fall of the Roman Empire* (1964) are often held responsible here.

22. See for example the *Sunday Times* (Covington 2004), and a lengthy preview in the *Hollywood Reporter* (Galloway 2004).

23. This is necessarily an extremely simplified description of literary theories dealing with tradition. Recommended discussions of this topic in ancient literature include Hardie 1993, Hinds 1998, and Conte 1986.

24. At the same time he identified it as a film "heavily indebted to cultural and filmic traditions of spectacle" (Winkler 2004b, 89).

25. Stone seems to be of the opinion that excessive use of CGI risks damaging an audience's engagement with the film: some would agree that digital technology "destroys our faith in the honesty of the images . . . we see" (Monaco 2000, 27).

26. See, for example, Belton 1992.

27. Rushton 2001.

28. See in particular Cyrino 2004; Cyrino 2005, 238–56; Rose 2004.

29. DVD commentary (all references are to the commentary on the DVD of the theatrical release). This is not to suggest that homosexuality had previously been absent from the Hollywood epic, though it was certainly suppressed: witness the cutting of the famous "snails and oysters" scene in *Spartacus,* or the reticence over discussing the potentially erotic element of the relationship between Judah and Messala in *Ben-Hur.* Stone's relatively light touch on this matter (Moritz Borman described the Alexander-Hephaestion relationship in terms of *Will and Grace* [Fleming 2003]), and the disproportionately large outcry it prompted, might suggest that things had no changed much since the sixties. Yet the fact that this issue was now open to discussion, instead of being concealed or coyly alluded to, demonstrates the currency of this aspect

of Alexander. It also represents a considerable advance over *Troy*, which completely effaced any sexual aspect of the relationship between Achilles and Patroclus.

30. Spencer 2002, 208–11; Mossé 2004, 197–201.

31. DVD commentary.

32. Crowdus 2005, 22.

33. A particularly insightful commentary is provided by Hywel Williams (2004), who sees through the positive assessments of Alexander that Stone presents in interviews. He suggests that "the deepest reason for the outrage it has excited is that the film is just too explicit about expansionist war. . . . This is a film about imperial over-stretch. At its end Stone, for all his enthused worship, shows us a ruler who is half-psychotic—deranged by dreams of destiny that out-strip his capacity. In the age of Rumsfeld and Bush that is a brave and accurate call."

34. DVD commentary. See also the *Cineaste* interview for Stone's unrealistic wish that audiences watch the film without "twenty-first century glasses. Leave your baggage and prejudices at the door" (Crowdus 2005, 22).

35. Solomon 2001 sets aside eight pages for his survey of films based on Greek history, compared with fifty-two for Roman history.

36. Solomon 2001, 38.

37. See Kim Shahabudin's chapter in this volume.

38. Crowdus 2005, 14.

39. See the articles by A. M. Ward, Kathleen Coleman, and Martin Winkler in Winkler 2004a for an excellent overview of the different approaches that may be taken.

40. Lane Fox 2004, 99–107.

41. DVD commentary. Lloyd Llewellyn-Jones, advisor for the film's costumes, makes a similar point; see his chapter in this volume, as well as Llewellyn-Jones 2004.

42. "A Production Designer must work out a vision of his own because what he needs is a coherent 'look' which will also feel right to the audience. . . . No film wants to show the same old sets, but if a film goes way out into new (often disputed) territory, the audience will lose their 'feel' of the historic scene. The true 'look' of the past can shock, whereas an action-film cannot afford to look too 'wrong' and bemuse its viewers" (Lane Fox 2004, 80).

43. Covington 2004.

44. Koppl 2005, 42.

45. In comments on *Gladiator* (Landau 2000, 50), Ridley Scott explicitly acknowledged the benefits of being able to "revisit the genre" with actors such as Derek Jacobi (Claudius in the BBC's *I, Claudius*) and Richard Harris (apparently originally signed to play Commodus in *Fall*).

46. See Verity Platt's chapter in this volume on the film's cave paintings.

47. Shone 2004.

48. See the critique by Daniel Mendelsohn, who laments the film's missed opportunities "to dramatize its subject" and comments that "what does get packed into the film . . . is often treated so perfunctorily as to be meaningless. . . . A better title for this film would have been *Lots of Things That Happened to Alexander*" (2005, 46).

49. Crowdus 2005, 18. Stone acknowledges that he has still "not really settled the issue [of structure] in my own mind."

50. Hiltunen 2002; Tierno 2002.

51. See Mendelsohn's comment on "the problem inherent in all biography, which is that a life, however crammed with dazzling incident, does not necessarily have the shape of a good drama" (2005, 47). Stone himself has admitted that he never solved the problem of the story's structure, even with the release of the Director's Cut DVD (Crowdus 2005, 18).

52. DVD commentary.

53. Crowdus 2005, 19.

54. See Iampolski 1998, 9: "Novelty and tradition enter into a dynamic fusion that is to a large extent responsible for the production of new meanings."

55. Hardie 1993; Ricks 2002.

Bibliography

Belton, John. 1992. *Widescreen Cinema*. Cambridge, MA: Harvard University Press.

Borza, Eugene N. 2008. "Movie Commentary: *Alexander*." Archaeological Institute of America Online, December 2004. http://www.archaeological.org/pdfs/papers/AIA_Alexander_Review.pdf.

Burgoyne, Robert. 2008. *The Hollywood Historical Film*. Oxford: Blackwell.

Cartledge, Paul. 2004. *Alexander the Great: The Hunt for a New Past*. London: Pan Macmillan.

Coleman, Kathleen. 2004. "The Pedant Goes to Hollywood: The Role of the Academic Consultant." In Winkler 2004a, 45–52.

Conte, Gian Biagio. 1986. *The Rhetoric of Imitation: Genre and Poetic Memory in Virgil and Other Latin Poets*. Ithaca, NY: Cornell University Press.

Covington, Richard. 2004. "Inside the Mind of an Ancient Warrior." *Sunday Times*, December 5.

Crowdus, Gary. 2005. "Dramatizing Issues That Historians Don't Address: An Interview with Oliver Stone." *Cineaste* 30 (Spring): 12–23.

Cyrino, Monica. 2004. "*Gladiator* and Contemporary American Society." In Winkler 2004a, 124–49.

———. 2005. *Big Screen Rome*. Oxford: Blackwell.

Dalton, Stephen. 2005. "Cut to the Quick." *Sunday Times*, July 28.

Danforth, Loring M. 1995. *The Macedonian Conflict: Ethnic Nationalism in a Transnational World*. Princeton, NJ: Princeton University Press.

———. 2003. "Alexander the Great and the Macedonian Conflict." In *Brill's Companion to Alexander the Great*, ed. Joseph Roisman, 347–64. Leiden: Brill.

Elley, Derek. 1984. *The Epic Film: Myth and History.* London: Routledge.

Ezard, John. 1995. "Talk of Alexander and of Others Too." *Guardian*, June 8.

Feeney, Denis. 1996. "Epic Hero and Epic Fable." *Comparative Literature* 38: 137–58.

Fleming, Michael. 2003. "Stone Leaves No Throne Unturned." *Variety*, September 22.

———. 2004. "Stone Redraws Battle Plans." *Variety*, December 27, 6.

Galloway, Stephen. 2004. "Great Expectations." *Hollywood Reporter*, August 3.

Gibbons, Fiachra. 2002. "Kings of Hollywood in Epic Battle to Film Alexander, the First Bisexual Action Hero." *Guardian*, December 30.

———. 2004. "Patriot Games." *Guardian*, November 19.

Hardie, Philip. 1993. *The Epic Successors of Virgil: A Study in the Dynamics of a Tradition.* Cambridge: Cambridge University Press.

Hiltunen, Ari. 2002. *Aristotle in Hollywood: The Anatomy of Successful Storytelling.* Bristol: Intellect Books.

Hinds, Stephen. 1998. *Allusion and Intertext: Dynamics of Appropriation in Roman Poetry.* Cambridge: Cambridge University Press.

Hiscock, John, and James Burleigh. 2004. "*Alexander* Proves to Be Not So Great at Conquering Homophobic America." *Independent*, November 29, 3.

Iampolski, Mikhail. 1998. *The Memory of Tiresias: Intertextuality and Film.* Berkeley: University of California Press.

Koppl, Rudy. 2005. "Vangelis and Oliver Stone—*Alexander*: As the Eagle Soars." *Music from the Movies* 44:36–43.

Landau, Diana, ed. 2000. *Gladiator: The Making of the Ridley Scott Epic.* London: Boxtree.

Lane Fox, Robin. 2004. *The Making of Alexander.* Oxford: R & L.

Llewellyn-Jones, Lloyd. 2004. "The King and I: Costumes and the Making of *Alexander*." *CA News* 31 (December): 1–3.

Mendelsohn, Daniel. 2005. "Alexander, the Movie!" *New York Review of Books*, January 13, 43–47.

Monaco, James. 2000. *How to Read a Film: Movies, Media and Multimedia.* 3rd ed. New York: Harbor Electronic Books.

Mossé, Claude. 2004. *Alexander: Destiny and Myth.* Trans. Janet Lloyd. Edinburgh: Edinburgh University Press.

Nisbet, Gideon. 2006. *Ancient Greece in Film and Popular Culture.* Exeter: Bristol Phoenix.

Ricks, Christopher. 2002. *Allusion to the Poets.* Oxford: Oxford University Press.

Rose, P. W. 2004. "The Politics of *Gladiator*." In Winkler 2004a, 150–72.

Rushton, Richard. 2001. "Narrative and Spectacle in *Gladiator*." *Cinéaction* 56: 34–43.

Santas, Constantine. 2008. *The Epic in Film: From Myth to Blockbuster.* Lanham, MD: Rowman and Littlefield.

Shone, Tom. 2004. "Alexander the Grating." *Daily Telegraph,* November 26.

Sobchack, Vivian. 1995. "Surge and Splendor: A Phenomenology of the Holly-wood Historical Epic." In *Film Genre Reader II,* ed. Barry Keith Grant, 280–307. Austin: University of Texas Press.

Solomon, Jon. 2001. *The Ancient World in the Cinema.* New Haven, CT: Yale University Press.

Spencer, Diana. 2002. *The Roman Alexander: Reading a Cultural Myth.* Exeter: University of Exeter Press.

Tierno, Michael. 2002. *Aristotle's Poetics for Screenwriters: Storytelling Secrets from the Greatest Mind in Western Civilization.* New York: Hyperion.

Ward, A. M. 2004. "*Gladiator* in Historical Perspective." In Winkler 2004a, 31–52.

Williams, Hywel. 2004. "Alexander Was, After All, Defeated." *Guardian,* December 10.

Winkler, Martin. 2001. "The Roman Empire in American Cinema after 1945." In *Imperial Projections: Ancient Rome in Modern Popular Culture,* ed. Sandra Joshel, Margaret Malamud, and Donald McGuire, 50–76. Baltimore: Johns Hopkins University Press.

———, ed. 2004a. *Gladiator: Film and History.* Oxford: Blackwell.

———. 2004b. "*Gladiator* and the Coliseum: Ambiguities of Spectacle." In Winkler 2004a, 87–110.

Wyke, Maria. 1997. *Projecting the Past: Ancient Rome, Cinema and History.* London: Routledge.

The Popular Reception of *Alexander*

JON SOLOMON

*A*LEXANDER GROSSED $13,687,000 during its opening weekend in the United States in late November 2004, a disappointing sum for a film budgeted at approximately $160 million. Over a run of sixty-eight days until it was withdrawn from theatrical release at the end of January 2005, *Alexander* earned just over $34 million from movie-going audiences in the United States.

With foresight, Oliver Stone, Intermedia Films, and Warner Bros. pre-sold the film in many markets through a host of international distributors, guaranteeing that it would at least break even.[1] Opening from November to February, the film brought in over $132 million[2] for a worldwide total of approximately $167 million. None of these totals includes VHS or DVD rentals or sales, cable agreements, or other merchandising. As anyone can see, the film was not a financial failure, despite its disappointing theatrical sales in the United States.

Film Critics and Historians

The failure to attract movie-goers to the box office in the United States cannot be attributed solely to the wide array of negative reviews by both popular and erudite critics. The year 2004 also saw the release of

Troy, which received equally negative reviews but earned $133 million in domestic box-office receipts. In contrast, Fox Searchlight's *Sideways* received glowing reviews and five nominations for Academy Awards, but it earned only $71 million, ranking fortieth in box-office receipts for 2004 and trailing behind *Christmas with the Kranks.* Nor can the disappointing box-office performance of *Alexander* be attributed to the general claim made in the United States that the film is "not Great," as Peter Travers punned in *Rolling Stone,* or "emotionally and intellectually incoherent," as *Newsweek*'s David Ansen claimed.[3] Indeed, a number of American reviewers would have us believe that their greatest objections were to Colin Farrell's blond wig and Angelina Jolie's accent, or to the fact that Jolie at age twenty-nine played the mother of Farrell, age twenty-eight.[4] This kind of flippant criticism did spill over into at least one subsequent review by an Alexander historian. Ian Worthington, amid an otherwise academic review of the film's historical accuracy, felt compelled to add that "Farrell, with dreadful blond hair (although accurate), is simply not credible as Alexander. . . . Angelina Jolie, eyes flashing and snakes coiling around her body, plays Alexander's mother Olympias. More could be made of her scheming nature, and a real distraction was that she is made to speak in an accent that makes her sound like Count Dracula."[5] But these complaints do not add up to a compelling reason for avoiding the film at the theater. A Google search for the words "bad," "wig," and "movie" produces scores of reviews for films ranging from *Blow* and *V for Vendetta* to *Beyond the Sea* and *A Sound of Thunder.* A search for "poor," "accent," and "movie" produces millions of hits.

In fact, when teaching film to students, I never allow them to employ the "Canon of Film Non-Criticisms." This includes attacks on such things as accents and wigs, but it begins with superficial complaints like "It was too long," "It was boring," and "It wasn't like the book." All of these complaints were launched at *Alexander.* Travers called the film a "buttnumbathon." Even such an experienced critic as Stanley Kauffmann in the *New Republic* dwelled on the film's length: "*Alexander* is very long and very torpid . . . and three hours of non-originality is a bit hard on one's behind. . . . After the three hours—though it seemed longer—I was still bewildered."[6] I have yet to discover a creditable essay maintaining that the linchpin problem with *Gone with the Wind, The Godfather,* or *Lawrence of Arabia*—three of the top five films on the American Film Institute's Top 100 Films list—was that they were too long. A theatrical experience can, of course, become tedious, but not

simply because it runs long: it happens because the spectator is not
fully engaged in the experience, a phenomenon to which we will return
later. As for the second no-no, historian/columnist Victor Davis Hanson complained, "In reality, the movie proved not so much scandalous
as boring."[7]

The third rule of the canon, "It wasn't like the book," applies to
Alexander as well. Asked to assess its historical authenticity, Ian Worthington and Victor Davis Hanson fell prey to the same temptation,
faulting the film because it is a film and not a book, and because it does
not portray historical events accurately. Neither graphic novelists nor
arachnologists were asked to guarantee the accuracy of *Spider-Man 2*,
which earned $373 million in 2004, nor were security experts asked to
probe weaknesses in the mechanics of *National Treasure*, which earned
$173 million.

Very few Americans know much about Alexander the Great except
that he was a conqueror who was "Greek," so the film's poor box-office
showing can hardly be blamed on lack of authenticity, particularly
when the alleged errors are either part of a well-established tradition
or the proprietary belief of an authority who spent years formulating
a unique hypothesis of which only a small community of scholars is
aware and with which few agree, irrespective of its academic validity.[8]
It is hard to fault Stone, as Worthington does, for giving some credence
to W. W. Tarn's suggestion that Alexander dreamed of "bringing together all his people in a brotherhood of mankind. This is nonsense,
for he intended no such thing, and I seriously doubt the extent of his
mother's influence."[9] It may well be that Tarn's evaluation was excessively generous, but Stone hardly adopts it wholesale, and it was a
significant part of the Alexander tradition: it took Ernst Badian and
Brian Bosworth decades to challenge it successfully. It can hardly be
described as "nonsense," any more than Shakespeare's non-Plutarchian
"Et tu, Brute" is historical nonsense that deserves to be excised from future productions of *Julius Caesar*.[10] Similarly, while Worthington has
every right as an ancient historian to "seriously doubt" some aspect of
the characterization of Olympias, Stone has every right as a screenwriter to make conjectures and draw conclusions.

Daniel Mendelsohn's high-profile review in the *New York Review of
Books* provides an equally instructive example of what happens when a
critic versed in history attempts to criticize the historicity of a historical
film.[11] Mendelsohn writes: "There is no denying that a lot of the film is
richly detailed, despite some inexplicable gaffes—why a mosaic wall

map in the Greek-speaking Ptolemy's Egyptian palace should be written in Latin is anybody's guess—and absurd pretensions. (The credits are bilingual, with awkward transliterations of the actors' names into Greek characters: To whom, exactly, is it necessary to know that Philip II was played by 'OUAL KILMER'?)." The mosaic map in question has some four dozen place names written on it, all correctly transliterated Greek names (e.g., Pergamon, Athenai, Kupros), written in the Roman alphabet, with the lone exceptions of "Mare Mediterraneum" and "Mare Aegeum." Few in the audience would have understood "Mesogaia." As for the transliteration of Kilmer's first name, "OU" is indeed the correct Greek transliteration for the Roman letter "V."

Mendelsohn goes on, after twice in the first paragraph telling us that the film was "long," to suggest that Stone's "structurally incoherent" film suffers from more than one "serious historical omission." The first "serious" omission involved Alexander's difficulties in relating to the Greeks in Athens; then there was the absence of any development of the relationship with Bagoas. ("The beautiful Persian eunuch Bagoas . . . suddenly appears, in this version, as little more than an extra in the harem at Babylon, and the next thing you know he's giving Alexander baths.") He laments also the omission of the prostration controversy. Dramatizing any of these missing features would have added to the already considerable budget and would have added extra minutes to a film that Mendelsohn complained was too long, while adding little to Stone's (coherently) complex characterization of Alexander. Inexplicably, Mendelsohn seems to be pushing toward a four-hour film when he complains that the conspiracies against Alexander's life and the mutiny in India "are so hurriedly depicted as to leave you wondering what they were about." On the contrary, they consume most of the second half of the film, and I submit that Stone's portrayal of Hephaestion's and Alexander's poisoning at the end of the film—not to mention Ptolemy's admission that he was privy to the poisoning—pretty much confirms that mutiny and conspiracy were afoot.

Historians who criticize films for not being historical enough tend to ignore the fact that an intelligent film director and screenwriter like Stone has read some of the same material they have; he has already made profound and considered decisions about what historical elements and events to include; he incorporates these decisions in formulating a compelling drama; and he consults with his financial backers to consider the projected demographic targets. Historians, who define their discipline in part by developing sophisticated approaches to various kinds of historical evidence, often fail to realize that an experienced film director and screenwriter has spent a career developing many of the same skills, albeit with a look toward dramatization (which necessitates rewriting, conflating, and condensing), not a comprehensive examination of every historically important episode.

Stone has repeatedly answered such criticisms in the past in regard to such controversial, contemporary events as the Kennedy assassination and the Vietnam War. In Robert Brent Toplin's *Oliver Stone's USA*, Stone categorically denied that he considered himself or had ever called himself a historian and rejected even the term "cinematic historian." Instead, he refers to himself consistently as "a dramatist, mixing fact and fiction—the fiction . . . based on a combination of research, intuition, and my private conscience—in the tradition of historical dramatists before me, admitting that no one can get behind the closed doors of history and hear the actual dialogue of its participants . . . something akin to what Shakespeare and the Greek dramatists had done."[12] But if historical inaccuracies and analyses did not keep movie-goers away from *Alexander*, neither did antihistorical comments. Both Mendelsohn and Alonso Duralde, for example, ridiculed Ptolemy's statement that "Alexander was conquered only by Hephaestion's thighs" as if it were a high-camp line scripted by Stone, even though this quip—from the Cynic philosopher Diogenes of Sinope—has been part of the Alexander tradition for over two millennia. Duralde began his review:

> Alas, *Alexander* is anything but great. Were it to contain a few more dance numbers (the film already has two) or a few more unintentional laughs (the film already has several), Stone's portrait of the 25-year-old who conquered the known world might at least rank as a camp classic. As it is, gay audiences will probably remember the film most for a line of Anthony Hopkins's narration following a boyhood wrestling match where Hephaestion bested Alexander: "It was said later that Alexander was never beaten, except by Hephaestion's thighs." Yow![13]

Similarly, for all the amusing jokes about Angelina Jolie's inappropriate "Transylvanian"/"Count Dracula" accent, have any of these critics looked at a map of southeastern Europe, or do they have a Molossian Epirote voice coach they could recommend to the next actress who portrays Olympias?

Stone was roundly criticized for including several scenes and voice-overs narrated by Ptolemy (Anthony Hopkins). Duralde lamented amusingly: "Pity poor Hopkins, who as Ptolemy is given pages and pages and pages of exposition to fill in the many dead spaces of the film. . . . If you've ever thought to yourself, Anthony Hopkins is such a great actor, I'd listen to him read the phone book, here's your chance." Anthony Lane complained that "the exploits of Alexander, of all people, should be relied upon to sell themselves."[14] Here again, however, Stone has made a conscious choice to tell Alexander's story through a variety of narrative techniques: scenes with dialogue, scenes without dialogue, flashbacks, Philip's mythological lecture, and the cinematographic transformation at the end of the road in India, as well as Ptolemy's periodic expository dictations and voiceovers. But we also acquire knowledge about Alexander during the various scenes in which he confides in his mother, Hephaestion, Bagoas, and the younger Ptolemy—the latter atop the snowy Caucasus. Any biography of Alexander has much to say about Alexander; after all, it is the conflicting ancient accounts—some of the earliest extant historical biographies in the Western tradition—that helped earn him his near-legendary status. The historical Ptolemy not only knew Alexander's campaigns as well as any of his generals or successors; he also wrote one of the most important ancient histories of Alexander. The critics who found Hopkins's introductory exposition and evaluation tedious and cinematically ineffective failed to appreciate the importance of Ptolemy's account as an essential source for what we know of the life of Alexander. Indeed, Stone could hardly have included a more "historical" narrative style. The scribe seated before Ptolemy and the Greek letter-forms in the opening credits convey the same textual idea: this is a filmic rendition of the creation of the most important ancient text describing the life of Alexander—set less than one generation after the events that are about to be narrated. Critics of Ptolemy's raison d'être as a narrator also failed apparently to notice, let alone appreciate, the azure set that silently provides the Alexandrian background. This location is visual proof of the immediate and lasting legacy of Alexander's conquests, the capital of Ptolemy's own powerful and enduring empire, and the setting for the great Library that housed the famed and comprehensive collection of Greek writings. If Western historiography could be said to have had an ancient capital, we see it vividly recreated in the opening scene of *Alexander*.[15]

All of these critics and historians spent a few hours experiencing an artistic product that took an established director several years and sixteen tens of millions of dollars to create. I am not attacking them in order to champion Stone's film; I am pointing out instead that their criticisms are irrelevant and counterproductive. They fail to probe either their own real reasons for reacting negatively to the film—which of course they are entitled to do—or audiences' reasons for doing the same thing, or, for that matter, the difficulties Stone himself admits he had in wrestling with a biographical film about the scion of an alcoholic, womanizing father and a manipulative mother, a man who claimed divinity and was forever after known as "the Great." I did not "love" *Alexander* when I first saw it during its brief theatrical release. But as a classicist who has spent thirty years studying films set in antiquity, I am dissatisfied reading the essays of film critics who review these films without understanding the genre of ancient historical films (except as overly lengthy epics, shallow spectacles, and inaccurate biopics), and I am equally dissatisfied with classicists and classical historians who approach these films without respecting the differences between cinematic and historical narratives or the particular demands of filmmaking. The goal for all of us, as many of the chapters in this book suggest, is to understand the film and put it in its proper perspective.[16]

Preconceptions

An imposing work of modern art evokes an emotional response. This is particularly likely when the work is a three-hour film by Oliver Stone on a subject about which most audience members have some preconceptions. In this instance, we can identify at least four preconceptions (and this is not a comprehensive list):

1. This is going to be a film accurately portraying the conquests of Alexander the Great.
2. This is going to be a film with stark representations of homosexuality.
3. This is not going to be a typical Oliver Stone film.
4. This is going to be a film like *Braveheart* or *Gladiator,* with a brawny physical hero who overcomes evil, restores the world to equilibrium, and lives (or dies) happily ever after (or heroically).

The first of these I have addressed above. To point out the obvious: there is no such thing as an accurate representation of history, cinematic or otherwise. By definition, cinematized history cannot pretend to be any more than a product engendered by mimesis in which actors portraying other people are composited through camera lenses onto a chemical surface and projected through artificial light onto a two-dimensional image from one-twentieth to twenty times larger than life. Pontius Pilate's search for truth does not end on the silver screen. The year 2004 also witnessed the release of Michael Moore's documentary

Fahrenheit 9/11, which millions of Americans would hardly identify as an accurate representation of history, while millions of others would argue that neither have the press and the government accurately portrayed their versions of the same events. We will have reason to refer to this film again as a parallel to *Alexander*.

The second preconception engendered a well-publicized lawsuit, brought by Greek American attorneys who had never seen the film.[17] The suit seems to have been groundless and was therefore dropped the week the film premiered, and those who saw the film in those first few days observed only male hugs, longing glances, and Aristotle's approval of men who "lie together in knowledge and virtue." They also observed the rough and starkly naked sexual foreplay of Alexander and Roxane, which was also designed to recall Philip's rape of Olympias earlier in the film. *Brokeback Mountain* this was not. But that did not matter. Rumor with its thousand tongues announced that this was a film involving blatant homosexuality, and so, in his December piece in the *National Review*, Victor Davis Hanson used nearly one-third of his allotted space to detail the ancient evidence for a social history of Homeric, Spartan, Athenian, and Roman homosexuality, none of which pertains to Macedonian soldiers of the mid- to late fourth century or accounts for a reference to "this gay extravaganza" or the conclusion that "Alexander the Great was more likely a bore in the bedroom."

All these pre- and misconceptions probably hurt the film significantly at the box office. It was released during a period of homophobic frenzy in the United States. The *San Francisco Examiner* and *Queer Day Magazine* reported on October 1 that Warner Bros. had delayed the opening from November 5 to November 24 in order to give Stone time to cut some of the gay scenes out of the theatrical release, thereby making the studio's involvement in the controversy public. On November 2 the electorate in eleven states voted to ban same-sex marriages—and by large margins (three to one in Kentucky, six to one in Mississippi).[18] Two weeks later, when *Alexander* premiered in Hollywood, the antigay demographic refused to see it, and the gay demographic was disappointed that the homoeroticism was so understated. Making matters worse, *Alexander* was released into a pre-Christmas market populated by films that featured academically sanctioned (*Kinsey*) or less threatening heterosexuality (*Bridget Jones: The Edge of Reason*) or avoided sexuality completely in family fare (*The Incredibles, The Polar Express, Finding Neverland, The SpongeBob SquarePants Movie,* and *Christmas with the Kranks*). All of these were released within two weeks of *Alexander*.

Attending European premiers a few weeks later, Stone asked: "Who could have imagined that the election would turn on the issue of homo-sexuality? But it also became the headline of this movie. . . . They called him Alexander the Gay. That's horribly discriminatory, but the film simply did not open in the South, in the Bible belt. There was clear re-sistance to the homosexuality. . . . On *JFK*, I gambled on the audience's intelligence and won. Here, I lost."[19]

This was the sociopolitical climate faced by *Fahrenheit 9/11*. Within days of its June 26 release, it had earned a higher per-screen take than *The Passion of the Christ*, and it went on to gross $119 million domes-tically and $221 million worldwide. Subsequently it won numerous awards (including the Palme d'Or at the Cannes Film Festival). And yet later that fall it garnered not a single nomination from Hollywood's supposedly left-leaning Academy of Motion Picture Arts and Sciences. The country's sociopolitical mood had changed that much in just a few months. This was the climate in which Stone, already the director of three anti–Vietnam war films, an anti-Nixon film, and an anti–Warren Commission film, and a prominent voice against the Iraq War, released *Alexander*.

This brings us to the third and fourth preconceptions: audiences' (and most critics') expectation of a more linear and heroic film. David Ansen in *Newsweek* asked, "We're supposed to root for this guy?" In his *New Yorker* review, Anthony Lane asked if it would not have been "smarter and more gratifying to follow the path of *Gladiator*, in which a fictional hero, his progress molded to have shape and momentum, can be carefully locked into a landscape of verifiable history?"

Were they unaware of Oliver Stone's sizable portfolio of contro-versial films that deconstruct American icons and reshape them in anti-iconic formulations? Or perhaps the American movie-goers who shied away from the new film remembered that he was the anti-establishment auteur who had made them squirm as they watched *Pla-toon* and *Born on the Fourth of July*, who portrayed the idolized Jim Mor-rison as a self-proclaimed divinity living in a shocking world of drugs, alcohol, sex, and blood ritual, whose *Wall Street* rendered the American icon of the smart, wealthy businessman into a corrupt and corrupting symbol of American greed, and whose *Natural Born Killers* created a shocking portrait of the media and its marriage to American violence. To some he was a cinematic antihero, a representative of the generation that had protested against the establishment in the 1960s and 1970s as well as a filmmaker who vividly realized that era on the screen. *Platoon* cost some $6 million to produce in 1986, and it earned sixteen times that amount at domestic box offices. *Wall Street* (1987) turned a $15 million investment into $43 million, and *Born on the Fourth of July* (1989) turned $14 million into $70 million. But since the mid-1990s *Nixon* (1995) had lost $35 million, and *U Turn* (1997) lost $12 million. Although *Any Given Sunday* (1999) recouped the previous loss, it nonetheless trailed the profits of the more popular 1996 football movie *Jerry Maguire*. Stone himself, his films widely criticized and their profitability inconsistent, began to develop doubts about his future in filmmaking.[20] Soon, however, the opportunity to create an epic on Alexander the Great presented itself, even if competition forced him to seek funding overseas. When asked by *Time*, "How difficult is it today for a liberal filmmaker to find backing?" Stone responded: "It's impossible. There's a decision, a consensus, that a certain kind of movie 'will not work.'"[21] His next film, *World Trade Center*, he did not write.

Stone is widely recognized as "controversial." This controversy stems both from his political position as a left-leaning filmmaker in an increasingly right-leaning sociopolitical climate and from his innovative and iconoclastic filmmaking techniques, which are in many respects very well suited to rendering his dramatized historical films. In addition, he has, particularly since *Nixon*, repeatedly challenged basic notions of spectatorship theory, the basic processes of how a story is told, how characters are presented and developed, how audiences respond emotionally to these fictional characters, and how a film delivers messages. Whether one adheres to Roland Barthes's literary model, which allows for an interplay of thematic (hermeneutic), character (semic), and action (proairetic) codes, or David Bordwell's fourfold hierarchy of filmic meaning (diegetic, explicit, implicit, symptomatic), or Murray Smith's "structure of sympathy" in the film-viewing experience (with its three progressive steps: recognition, alignment, and allegiance), the typical reaction to Stone's visually and politically aggressive style seems to challenge these theories or form an exception at almost every step.[22]

Roger Odin emphasizes the positive connection between film and spectator in identifying "mutual comprehension between the actants, which gives the impression that communication resides in the transmission of a message from a Sender to a Receiver."[23] But he also discusses the distinction between "*mise en phase*," a phrase describing a genuine resonance between the diegesis (narrative), cinematic delivery method, and spectator comprehension, and "*déphasage*," a term describing, in the vernacular, "a movie that the audience doesn't get."[24] Audiences tend to become shocked, confused, or disappointed in the latter case, particularly American audiences, who (to generalize) prefer a process in which the narrative, characters, and themes are more familiar, digestible, and, in many instances, stereotypical. Very often the desired emotion is meta-Aristotelian in producing a catharsis by ending the terror (and violence) threatened (and administered) by the evil protagonist and reestablishing the sociocultural equilibrium, or by delighting the spectators throughout with charm, wit, dazzling computer-enhanced imagery, and, of course (heterosexual) sex. The dozen top money-making films of 2004 all fit these parameters: *Shrek 2, Spider-Man 2, The Passion of the Christ, Meet the Fockers, The Incredibles, Harry Potter and the Prisoner of Azkaban, The Day After Tomorrow, The Bourne Supremacy, Polar Express, National Treasure, Shark Tale,* and *I, Robot.* In fact, five of the first six are sequels or remakes.

Most of the films of Oliver Stone upset the equilibrium of both the protagonist and the viewer by rendering the former as an untraditional tragic figure and forcing the latter down the tragic slope with him. This was certainly true of Jim Morrison in *The Doors,* Richard Nixon in *Nixon,* John Kennedy as well as Jim Garrison in *JFK,* and Alexander in *Alexander.*

The Ancient World

Stone introduces ancient characters or characterizations into his films in a variety of guises. His writings, interviews, and DVD commentaries repeatedly refer to ancient Greek tragedy not just as a dramatic genre but as a general perspective on the human condition. In *The Doors* he thrice referred to Jim Morrison as a new Dionysus—as did the Doors' drummer John Densmore in his account of his years with the group[25]—to suggest that Morrison transcended human existence and sacrificed himself. In the waning minutes of *Nixon,* the outgoing president confides in General Alexander Haig and Henry Kissinger that he has become the sacrificial victim: "It came over from Vietnam, you know. . . . That smell. I mean, everyone suffered so much, their sons killed. They need to sacrifice something, y'know, appease the gods of war—Mars, Jupiter. I am that blood general. I am that sacrifice, in the highest place of all."

Similarly, in *U Turn* he created a unique character billed simply as the "Blind Man," played by Jon Voight, whose attributes recall those of the ancient Theban prophet Teiresias. He is blind, he worships a

primordial earth divinity, he is cantankerous toward the doomed protagonist Bobby Cooper (Sean Penn), he speaks in aphorisms, and he
forecasts the future. Cooper visits with him three times, and each time
more is revealed. Another example, from Roman history, occurs in *Any
Given Sunday,* when the African American star quarterback Willie Bea-
men (Jamie Foxx) visits the Italian American head coach, Tony D'Amato
(Al Pacino). Front and center in the coach's apartment is a large, state-
of-the-art plasma television on which we see the chariot race from the
1959 MGM version of *Ben-Hur.* The quarterback walks into the apartment and immediately observes, "Ah, the gladiators of their times,"
intentionally conflating charioteers, gladiators, and modern athletes,
particularly football players. In fact, he is walking toward the screen
just as one of the charioteers is run over by an oncoming chariot, suggesting that he, too, will serve as a symbolic sacrifice for a civilized
world that delights in violent forms of entertainment.[26]

Although Roger Ebert, Stanley Kauffmann, Anthony Lane, and
other well-known critics complained that Stone's epic film did not provide a user-friendly, traditional narrative leading the viewer through
the course of Alexander's life and anabasis, near the outset of the film
Stone generously provided a road map identifying its thematic elements. This is the purpose of Ptolemy's much maligned introductory
exposition and the scene illustrating Alexander's Aristotelian education. The diegetic mode here at the outset of the film is entirely unnec-
essary in that Alexander's conquests demand no introduction even to
the most casual of observers. Instead, Stone carefully has Aristotle help
instill in the young Alexander a yearning or *pothos* (*contra* Mendelsohn) to reach the shores of the Outer Ocean, and then he has Philip
take the young Alexander into an underground passage (suggestive of
recent archaeological finds in Vergina), where he articulates in detail—
Woody Allen might have "AUTHOR'S MESSAGE" blinking at the
bottom of the screen—the mythological and thematic structure of the
screenplay.

Philip and the Ages of Gods and Humans

This unique sequence summarizes in minutes some of the most significant lessons we can glean from reading deeply into ancient Greek
poetry.[27] Stone has Philip begin by conflating the Hesiodic myths of
Ouranos and Kronos to illustrate generational struggles. Stone specifically dates this myth to the epoch of Titans to foreshadow and elevate

the struggle between the historical Macedonian king and prince. This is not an archetypically human but a cosmically eternal Titanic struggle. Later Stone will distinguish between the epochs and the status of men, of gods, and of Titans, the latter representing a stratum of existence and achievement toward which Alexander yearns because of its association with greatness.

In the next painting he moves chronologically to the age of mankind's original manufacturer, Prometheus. As the film unfolds, Prometheus will become a symbol for human triumph over the ancient realm of the gods. To be a Titan or god would seem to be a sign of greatness, but Alexander learns that his greatness will lie in remaining a triumphant, albeit overachieving, human.

Stepping down from Titans and their progeny, he comes next to the Homeric Achilles, Alexander's favorite, "for loving his friend and choosing a glorious short life." But Philip adds a different lesson, adapted from or at least worthy of Aeschylus: there is no glory without suffering. And as the film will reveal, Alexander will suffer the assassination of Philip, he will suffer the murder of Cleitus, he will suffer the mutiny of his army, he will suffer mutiny in India, he will suffer the death of Hephaestion, and he will suffer his own wounding, poisoning, and death. His glory will come only after much suffering—hence Colin Farrell's much criticized but warranted tears.

Fourth is Oedipus. The purpose of this mythical lesson is not the usual and inaccurate Freudian reading that Oedipus hated his father and loved his mother excessively; the lesson is that we suffer and commit our sins because we gain knowledge too late. A number of films in the past twenty years have offered reinterpretations of the Oedipus myth (e.g., *The Unbearable Lightness of Being, The Empire Strikes Back*), but this bold reinterpretation strips the myth of its sexuality and generational conflict—which had just been offered in the more timeless Kronos myth—and renders it as an admonition about the inevitable deficiency of the human intellect. We continue down the levels of existence from Titan to Olympian to Medea, who provides the most mundane lesson thus far: beware of women, a fitting warning from someone like Philip.

And last is Heracles, for here we have a half-mortal hero who murders what he loves because the gods and Fate make him mad, destroying everything he has created. Like the lament of an ancient Greek dramatic chorus for the tragic trajectory of human life, this four-minute sequence of mythological exemplars brings Alexander's education to a close. We are ready for and move immediately to Gaugamela.

This sequence succinctly and clearly establishes many of the thematic elements of the film as well as its inherent dramatic relationships and conflicts between Alexander and his father, his mother, Roxane, and his Macedonian generals, as well as the limits he will discover to the extent of the world, Aristotelian knowledge, and his own destiny.

The story arc of *Alexander* resembles that of *Lawrence of Arabia*: its young hero is well schooled and ambitious, achieves legendary victories in exotic lands, and then fails through the disorganization of his empire. Stone fills out this path with quasi-Homeric animal similes—particularly the snake (Olympias), eagle (Zeus), panther (Roxane), and lion (Heracles). He frames it with two frequently praised and contrasting battle scenes, one triumphant, one tragic, and leads his hero to the top of the Caucasus to discuss with Ptolemy (the same Ptolemy who throughout the film recalls many such encounters with Alexander) his disappointment at discovering finally that reaching the Outer Ocean or the heights of Prometheus are just illusions, and that what he must suffer is characteristically human, albeit nearly superhuman. At this important juncture in his life, "his failures," as Stone's Ptolemy points out to the disappointment of Anthony Lane, did indeed "tower over other men's successes." Blind to this coherent structure, most critics seem to have relegated themselves to some place between the Caucasus and the cinematic land of *déphasage*.

Notes

1. Michael Fleming, "Stone Redraws Battle Plans," *Variety*, December 27, 2004, 6.

2. This sum includes receipts from Spain ($14 million), Japan ($11 million), Germany ($10.1 million), Italy ($10 million), France ($7.7 million), Russia ($7.5 million), South Korea ($5.6 million), Mexico ($5.5 million), Greece ($3.7 million), and Turkey ($2 million)—the latter two, ironically, being ancient subjects of the protagonist. For specific amounts, which are unofficial, see such online compilations as Lee's Movie Info (http://www.leesmovieinfo.net/wbotitle.php?t=2648) and the Internet Movie Database (http://us.imdb.com/title/tt0346491/business).

3. Peter Travers, "Alexander," *Rolling Stone*, November 16, 2004 (http://www.rollingstone.com/reviews/movie/6156186/review/6630406/alexanderreview); and David Ansen, "Not So Great," *Newsweek*, November 29, 2004, 60.

4. E.g., *U.S. Playstation Magazine* 96 (September 2005): 95: "Colin Farrell . . . sporting a blond shag stripped off a shih tzu"; and Alonso Duralde,

"Alexan-dreck," *Advocate,* December 21, 2004, 54: "She vamps around handling snakes and speaking in a Russian accent that's pure Natasha of Rocky and Bullwinkle. Maybe she thought this was a movie about Catherine the Great."

5. Ian Worthington, "Alexander," *American Historical Review* 110 (2005): 533–34.

6. Stanley Kauffmann, "Conquests," *New Republic,* December 27, 2004, 28–29. Cf. the introductory quip by Mike Clark, *USA Today,* December 10, 2004: "Short life, long movie."

7. Victor Davis Hanson, "Gay Old Times," *National Review,* December 27, 2004, 40–41.

8. Of course, even historical consultants for films have limited influence on the final product; cf. Kathleen M. Coleman, "The Pedant Goes to Hollywood: The Role of the Academic Consultant," in *Gladiator: Film and History,* ed. Martin M. Winkler (Oxford: Blackwell, 2004), 45–52. For authenticity in historical films, see also Martin M. Winkler, "*Gladiator* and the Traditions of Historical Cinema," ibid., 21–23.

9. Worthington, "Alexander," 533–34.

10. In fact, Stone deliberately labeled the film *Alexander* to suggest that he was probing the very question of greatness: "The movie is called *Alexander,* not Alexander the Great, so the judgment is left up to the viewer," he told Gary Crowdus ("Dramatizing Issues That Historians Don't Address: An Interview with Oliver Stone," *Cineaste* 30 [Spring 2005]: 12–23). I cannot cite properly the criticism I heard on National Public Radio in the spring of 2004 in regard to the proliferation of CGI effects in Hollywood, which lamented that the computer-enhanced shot of Greek ships sailing for Troy "made it seem like there were one thousand of them."

11. Daniel Mendelsohn, "Alexander, the Movie!" *New York Review of Books,* January 13, 2005, 43–47 (http://www.nybooks.com/articles/17685). In addition to telling us twice in the first paragraph that the film was "long," Mendelsohn's second sentence accuses it of providing "obvious boredom" to theatrical audiences.

12. Robert Brent Toplin, *Oliver Stone's USA: Film, History, and Controversy* (Lawrence: University Press of Kansas, 2000), 5–6, 40–41.

13. Duralde, "Alexan-dreck," 54.

14. Anthony Lane, "War-Torn: Oliver Stone's 'Alexander,'" *New Yorker,* December 6, 2004, 125–27; cf. Roger Ebert (*Chicago Sun-Times,* November 24, 2004), as he describes a break from "the endless narration of Ptolemy the historian, who functions here like the Bill Kurtis of antiquity."

15. As of spring 2009, three versions of the film are in circulation on DVD. I refer to the DVD of the original theatrical release unless otherwise noted.

16. I tried to do this in a previous publication: Jon Solomon, "Model of a Lesser God," *Arion* 13, no. 1 (2005): 149–60.

17. For a summary of the reactions to the bisexuality in the film, see http://www.isidore-of-seville.com/alexander/14.html.

18. Arkansas, Georgia, Kentucky, Michigan, Mississippi, Montana, North Dakota, Oklahoma, Ohio, Utah, and Oregon.

19. Fleming, "Stone Redraws Battle Plans."

20. Jeffrey Ressner, "10 Questions for Oliver Stone," *Time*, April 19, 2004, 8: "I had reached the place where I did what I had set out to do—and more. So I just stopped. My movies were much criticized, and at a certain point you say things like, 'What's the point?' and you begin to wonder." Stone's subsequent films suggest that he has indeed done some profound soul searching.

21. Ibid.

22. See Judith Mayne, *Cinema and Spectatorship* (London: Routledge, 1993), 14-16; Murray Smith, "Altered States: Character and Emotional Response in the Cinema," *Cinema Journal* 33 (1994): 34-56.

23. Warren Buckland, *The Cognitive Semiotics of Film* (Cambridge: Cambridge University Press, 2000), 82-86, quote on 83.

24. Ibid., 94-95.

25. E.g., John Densmore, *Riders on the Storm: My Life with Jim Morrison and the Doors* (New York: Delacorte Press, 1990), 2-3.

26. Again, quibbling about the differences between gladiators and charioteers misses the point. Audiences understand the parallel.

27. See also Verity Platt's chapter in this volume.

Part 2

Precursors of *Alexander*

Alexander on Stage

A Critical Appraisal
of Rattigan's Adventure Story

ROBIN LANE FOX

URING FILMING Oliver Stone described his film to me as a wheel with five spokes, moving in three different times. The "spokes" are the five main settings: Alexandria in Egypt, Macedon, Babylon, Bactria, and India. Each of them is distinguished by distinctive coloring and light exposure: a crisp contrast of gray and white for Ptolemy's Alexandrian palace as the new future after Alexander's death; sunny sky blue with clean white clothes to evoke the distant past world of Macedon as remembered from childhood and youth; blue, above all, for the Babylon palace and an enhanced splendor, including much more gold (with a chillier exception for Hephaestion's final bedroom); muted reds, blacks, and a sandy brown interior for Roxane's Bactrian castle; pinks and greens for the Indian warriors, enhanced by the silvering effect of the bold use of special film that was risked for the elephant battle and by the orange-yellow canopy for the drinking party in the Indian palace. The color coding marks off each "spoke" from the others. The "three times," meanwhile, are the period when the old Ptolemy is dictating his memoirs (283/82 B.C.E.), the main events of Alexander's adult life (336–323 B.C.E.) as remembered (and mis-remembered) by Ptolemy, and Alexander's childhood and youth (ca. 352–336 B.C.E.), partly evoked by Ptolemy but mainly evoked mentally by Alexander himself within his later career. As the film goes on, the scenes from these earlier years are not simple flash-backs. They are "parallel stories" that return to Alexander's conscious-ness at particular moments. They are placed (particularly in the Direc-tor's Cut and Final Cut DVDs) at what Stone interprets as parallel moments in Alexander's adult life.

Film can exploit color, light, and texture in a way that a text, even a drama, cannot. These elements direct or orientate viewers, but they should not be so obtrusive that they overwhelm them: Stone's elements worked excellently, almost too well for many film critics to notice them. The changing times in which the "wheel" moves, their intercutting (less pronounced in the first cinema version), and the implicit indication of "parallel stories" make *Alexander*'s structure quite unlike that of any previous epic narrative based on ancient history. The first cinema audi-ences were not expecting this structure after *Gladiator* or *Troy*, nor were film critics, who fastened on Ptolemy as if he were simply a narrator, violating rules of film that Stone knows as well as (or far better than) any of them and expressing views that they took rather crudely to be Stone's own. When the final turnabout comes and Ptolemy says that he "never believed in Alexander's dream," a simplistic reception of the film is cut down, leaving viewers to rethink (Stone hoped) the point of view that had previously been leading them on. Ptolemy then tells his scribe to replace the words with something else. Implicitly a point is made here about the written evidence that survives, often to mislead future historians.

The five-part structure, the color coding, the interrelating times were all devised to give form and drama to a long life that in reality was more an epic of deeds and failures than a plot with its own self-evident shape. During and after filming Stone observed to me how striking it was that Alexander had never been a subject for dramatists. The search for a dra-matic structure had occupied Stone and previous scriptwriters for more than seven years of intermittent attempts at the project. The disastrous march through the Gedrosian desert was tried in the foreground for the opening scenes in 2002; the first big battle scene, in one version, was supposed to be Chaeronea in 338 B.C.E. Meanwhile the struggle to write a concentrated but comprehensive script remained an unsolved prob-lem for the rival Baz Luhrmann and De Laurentiis project: they even fa-vored versions in which Alexander died, preposterously, in India.

There are, in fact, two significant dramas about Alexander in English, neither of which was known to Stone and his scriptwriters. One is Nathaniel Lee's *Rival Queens* of the 1670s, which was still being staged and rewritten a hundred years later. An echo of it did find its way into Stone's script—"let me rot in Macedonian rags," as spoken by Cleitus at his final drinking party—but this echo came only from my quotation of Lee's lines as an epigraph to one part of my 1973 book about Alexander. The original play is still worth reading. The "rival queens" are Roxane and Stateira, the daughters of Darius whom Alexander eventually married in 324 B.C.E. In the light of Stone's film, the most striking themes are Lee's stress on Roxane's jealousy ("there's not a glance of thine / But like a basilisk comes winged with death") and the final speeches of Alexander, "with disordered wildness in his looks," after he is poisoned by Cassander (whom Roxane had actually been urged to marry, with the advice to kill Alexander and thus assure the succession for her unborn son). In Lee's play Roxane's jealousy is not provoked by Hephaestion (as in Stone's film) but by the new wife, Stateira (whom Plutarch alleges that Roxane poisoned: Lee had read Plutarch and also Curtius). Lee's Alexander regards Hephaestion as "my second self, my friend," whereas the object of his mad love is Princess Stateira. It is for her (not Hephaestion) that Alexander threatens to pave the "bower of Semiramis" (the Hanging Gardens of Babylon) with gold and "draw dry the Ganges" for her tomb. As the poison starts to work, his mind runs wild ("Bear me Bucephalas, among the billows . . ."), and finally he cries out, "Through Ammon's voice, I know it. . . . Father, I come . . ." He knows he has been less than a good ruler: "The god shall send you in my stead a *nobler* prince / One that shall lead you forth with matchless conduct." In Lee's drama, Philip's ghost haunts Cassander in Babylon, telling him to "forbear" among all the turmoil and grievances of Alexander's final years. In Stone's film, Philip flashes into Alexander's mind and is seen spitting blood, significantly, after Cleitus's murder, but he appears again, indicating approval, as Alexander announces under pressure the decision to return from India. Of his mother, Olympias, Lee says not a word. His Alexander is passionately heterosexual.

Near the end of Stone's film, important scenes of "parallel violence" (Philip's to Olympias) recur to Alexander as he assaults Roxane after Hephaestion's death. The brilliantly distorted colors of the last fatal drinking party then lead on to episodes, back-lit or flaming, from the previous years while Alexander (poisoned?) lies dying. These scenes are the free brushstrokes of a master of "parallel story" and "disordered wildness" in film. The female jealousies of polygamy, the Orientalism, and the plots and grievances of a disgruntled court assured Lee's script its very long appeal to eighteenth-century tastes. But its focus was on Alexander's final months, into which significant "wildness" was mostly transposed (the murder of Cleitus, a mention of the murky "murder" of Philotas). The problems of dramatizing a life and giving it a structure were evaded. Instead, feminine jealousy and courtly discontents elaborated a fictitious melodrama around a flawed but passionate king.

The other modern drama in English is my main focus here. On March 17, 1949, Terence Rattigan's *Adventure Story* opened in London's West End with a burst of publicity. The first night saw a standing ovation (like the first night of Stone's *Alexander* in Los Angeles and again in New York's Lincoln Center, before reviews appeared). The stalls, observed the diarist Chips Channon, were applauding Rattigan, while the circle cheered for the leading actor, the twenty-six-year-old Paul Scofield. ("Though it is magnificently produced," Channon had remarked from the stalls on the first night of the play's trial run in Brighton, "Paul Scofield as Alexander did not particularly impress any of us.") When press reviews appeared, they began by being complimentary but soon deteriorated into gleeful hostility. The respected Harold Hobson in the *Sunday Times* considered it "the most adult political comment in the modern theatre," which "breathes a message as poetically beautiful as it is politically sad." The majority thought it symptomatic of a "Rattigan Tragedy," the attempt by a dramatist with one particular gift to do something that he could do "only moderately well," if that. It was a "plod" through thirteen years of a man's life. It was a boring failure.

The play had gone into production with the highest hopes: Alec Guinness had read the script and greatly liked it, but had finally refused the title role because he could not guarantee the twelve-month run on which the producers were already insisting in their contract. In fact, the play would close after only four months. A big budget of £8,000, three times larger than usual, was put up for the production, to be designed by George Wakhevitch: Rattigan put in his own money, including £1,400 for Benjamin Frankel to compose the music. The cast of actors was also big, a star-studded twenty-six. Paul Scofield stepped in when Alec Guinness pulled out; Jack Hawkins was initially cast as King Darius until he realized that the play would have a six-week trial outside London and that his role was not as big as Alexander's. Filming drew him away. Gwen Ffrangcon-Davies agreed to play the important role of the Persian queen mother, her first role in England after seven years abroad. The young Richard Burton was cast as Hephaestion but was discarded in rehearsals for reasons that were variously understood. Burton later said that Rattigan had told him that he was afraid that the audiences (and the censors of the Lord Chamberlain's office) might assume that there was a homosexual relationship between Hephaestion and Alexander because of the actors' good looks. Scofield recalled no such issue, but Rattigan did indeed write to Burton assuring him that there was no problem with his "excellent performance," but that the writer and the producer felt that they needed someone with "a physique and personality different from yours." Burton also claimed that he had received and resented a drunken pass from Rattigan during rehearsals. Looks, certainly, were part of the problem: Burton was replaced by Julian Dallas, and sexual issues were not raised again.

Audiences were eager to see such a new departure from a top dramatist hitherto known for light-hearted plays or oblique dramas about honesty and humiliation in modern settings. The production had a welcome postwar splendor, and when the first-night curtain went up on "a courtyard at night in Babylon," the audience broke into applause before a word was even spoken. The enthusiasm was not to last, nor did it quickly die down. *Adventure Story* remained Rattigan's only venture into ancient history, but it lived on as a target for a new generation of critics, led by the young Kenneth Tynan: "Rather than risk the embarrassment of rhetoric," he declared, "Rattigan has developed a talent of drawing undramatic people." *Adventure Story*'s reception caused Rattigan to write article after article in self-defense and then admit that he had not succeeded in pulling his themes together. Nonetheless, the play's run left two notable legacies. Just before it began in London, a young lover of Rattigan's, the actor Kenneth Morgan, was discovered to have gassed himself after leaving a pained suicide note. The playwright had to confront his play's reception at an acutely distressing time, but the disaster led to the germ of his subsequent success, *The Deep Blue Sea*. Three years later this play would begin with an attempted suicide by use of a gas fire, albeit by a female involved in a heterosexual love affair. *Adventure Story*'s lead actor, Paul Scofield, was the only one to have a wholly happy reward: he met and married Joy Parker, who was playing Roxane to his Alexander. They were married for sixty-five years, until his death in 2008.

Social class, homosexuality, an expressive lifestyle (a Rolls Royce for "Play-as-you-earn Rattigan" in postwar Labour Britain): all of these prejudices were used in the invective against Rattigan by a new wave of theater talent that was staking out the Royal Court Theatre as the modern rallying point against a "middlebrow" London West End. Their critical rhetoric and their preference for kitchen-sink drama and "looking back in anger" (as in the play of 1956) did little justice to Rattigan's understated talents or all that he and a group of like-minded authors continued to put on for the London stage. His play about Alexander had been based on his personal interest in the subject since boyhood. It was seen as a turning point, the test of whether Rattigan's talent was truly great or not. The answer was a firm "no," although the critic for the left-wing *Daily Worker* did at least declare it "a gallant failure worth a dozen so-called successes."

Unwittingly, these words were to be echoed in 2004 by Stone's Ptolemy: "If Alexander failed, why, his failures were greater than other men's successes." So many elements in the story of *Adventure Story* prefigure elements in the story of Stone's *Alexander*: the high expectations, the big budget, the stunning sets, the star casting, the rapid shift in the critical reception, the castigation for "failure," the admission by the director that changes needed to be made. Rattigan could not reissue a "Director's Cut" or "Final Cut," and he failed repeatedly to interest New York even in a revised version, but he did condense a shorter version for television (it appeared in 1959, starring Sean Connery, no less). Like Rattigan, Stone attracted criticism that went beyond the drama in question. His press critics' undeclared baggage included continuing resentment on account of his *JFK* (reopening the question of Kennedy's murder) or his *Nixon* (showing a Republican President as drunk) or the recent television documentaries on such un-American subjects as Fidel Castro and Yasser Arafat. The homoerotic element was either too feebly shown (for the undeclared interest of critics who themselves were gay) or too explicit (for strident minority voices in Christian groups or in Greece itself). In 2004 Stone was a target waiting to be assaulted for various undeclared reasons. Others simply disliked the film or found it confusing and too long.

Throughout Rattigan's life *Adventure Story* remained the play that he was most pleased to hear appreciated. I want to look beyond its obvious weaknesses, some of which are even clearer with the passing of time. The most pervasive are the style and language. As Tynan observed, "His pagan legionaries move like gods and talk like [school] prefects." "Been cheeking Alexander again, I expect," Parmenion says about his son Philotas, who is under arrest. The very title has the tone of a school or an English officers' mess. It turns out to be a poignant story, a misadventure, but it equates Alexander's life with a "Boy's Own" escapade. Middle-class politeness is written into it. At the end of the prologue, the dying Alexander exclaims, twice, "Where did it first go wrong?" The critics pounced on these prophetic words with glee and helped their readers never to forget them. Much of the answer is implicit in the intervening script. "Goodbye, my friend," Alexander actually says to a soldier who pays his respects at the bedside. "Thank you for caring."

As the play is rarely, if ever, reread nowadays, I will pick out details, first from the five scenes of act 1, then, after the interval, from the five scenes of act 2. Rattigan had been a scholar at Harrow School and then a History scholar at Trinity College, Oxford. As a schoolboy his range of reading was famously wide, and only six months before his attempt at Alexander, he had put on his admired *The Browning Version*, which included lines 951–52 of Aeschylus's *Agamemnon* in Greek at a crucial point (in 1948, it was still plausible for Rattigan to imply that this work had been read by a sixteen-year-old English public schoolboy in class). Quite independently the years of *Adventure Story*'s scripting (1947–49) were a cardinal moment for scholarly publications on Alexander in English. Can we work out what he read?

Unlike Stone, Rattigan did not turn to a historical consultant, but he did turn to identifiable sources, ancient and modern. He did far more than simply dramatize bits of Plutarch's *Life of Alexander*, the prevailing view among his critics and biographers. His Alexander both is and is not a creation at a particular point in Alexander studies. I wish to emphasize the details in his play that arose from particular books and also the details, no less telling, that went deliberately against modern authorities. In the film, too, there are sentences that Stone included because an ancient source contained them (sometimes they are the ones that critics and audiences found "absurd"). Like Rattigan, he also alluded to, and departed from, modern sources.

Rattigan's dramatic manner was always at its best when implicit, showing more than it said: if we look beneath the chirpy style, there is plenty in the play. It is both remarkably like and unlike Stone's film. Neither Stone, we must remember, nor his previous scriptwriters had read *Adventure Story*. If the two scripts survived from antiquity, scholars would certainly assume Stone's to be partly based on Rattigan's. But it is not.

Both Rattigan and Stone engaged with their subject as authors outside the official genealogy of Alexander studies. Rattigan consulted some of the most recent scholarship, and nonetheless, went against it. Subsequently, scholars took a similar line, but Rattigan's approach has been ignored in the sanctified "history" that scholars construct for their fellow professionals. Rattigan also anticipated aspects of Stone's own interpretation: I will next consider a dynamic on which the two of them drew.

Sources and Historiography in
Alexander and *Adventure Story*

The locations of Rattigan's two-act play give a sense of its structure and selection. There are six, four of which overlap with four main locations of Stone's film: the palace in Babylon, Alexander's tent before Gaugamela, the site in Media where the dead Darius was discovered, and "headquarters" in Bactria (for Rattigan, Alexander's tent, without Roxane's father, who was leading a rebellion elsewhere; for Stone, the castle of Roxane's father, who is, correctly, present). Quite independently the two dramatists were drawn to a similar core, and both place major emphasis on the palace in Babylon. Unlike Stone, Rattigan uses the palace for two scenes of the Persian court before Alexander's conquest. He also has a scene in the temple at Delphi ("built into the face of a mountain") and another in the tent of the Persian king when it has just been captured at Issus.

Unlike Stone, he has no scene in Macedon. He also leaves out India and any references to the march through the Gedrosian desert. There is a council of war before Gaugamela, but naturally no battles are shown on stage. The drama is quite tight, but only by stringent omission. It could not possibly accommodate Stone's stunning Gaugamela, for which the large contingent of trained combatants was multiplied by "special effects" to precisely 47,000 men on Alexander's side (Ptolemy's figure) and about 170,000 on the Persian side (the figure I suggested to convey the vast scale of the enemy army, put by Greek sources at a million or so). Nor could it contain Stone's visual and logistical masterpiece, the Indian battle against real war-elephants (armed with tusk extensions), which one historian, Ptolemy, struggles to recall more than forty years later, and another historian, myself, assisted on horseback as Stone's historical consultant and Companion cavalryman.

It is remarkable, then, that both scripts begin in the same way, asking to whom the dying Alexander will leave his kingdom. Like Stone, Rattigan shows a selection of officers and Roxane by the bedside, but unlike

Stone he includes the Persian queen mother, who will be so important for the drama, and omits the eunuch Bagoas. Only a year before, in 1948, William Tarn's authoritative book had tried to dismiss Bagoas from history, erasing an uncomfortable reality. Rattigan, we shall see, was not just a follower of Tarn, but even had he wished, he could never have reinstated Bagoas on the London stage of 1949. The Lord Chamberlain would have censored him. If Richard Burton looked too homoerotic as Hephaestion, the author and producer would take no chances with a controversial eunuch. Some of those attending the first trial screening for Stone's distributors, Warner Bros., would have agreed.

Why do both plays begin similarly at the end of Alexander's life? Stone had read Mary Renault's *Persian Boy*, and by letter in 1974 Renault told me that she had found good things in Rattigan's drama. The similarity, then, may be due to this indirect link. Rattigan's style, of course, is his own: "Sir? Sir? This is Perdiccas. Can you hear me?" As in Arrian's history, soldiers then file past their dying king's bed, "underofficers" in Rattigan's view, "two from each company." In December 2003 at Pinewood Studios, Stone filmed a lengthy scene of men and officers filing past the dying Alexander but never used most of it in the first versions of the film: it can be seen, most effectively, in the excellent Final Cut. Stone's Alexander only appeared to speak: did he say "Craterus," onlookers wondered, or "to the strongest?" Here again Stone's script links up to an idea once expressed to me by Mary Renault. In Greek "to the strongest" is *toi kratistoi*. Did Alexander start to say *"toi Krat—,"* she wondered, and either stop or be stopped before he could finish the unwelcome word? By contrast Rattigan allows Alexander a significant whisper. "Why did you never let me see it would end in this. . . . In bed, not in battle. . . . Where did it first go wrong?" The "adventure," we realize, is to be a misadventure.

Quite unlike Stone, Rattigan then moves to Delphi in late autumn 336 B.C.E., when Alexander has just become king. The scene is significant on several levels. A courteous Hephaestion solicits the Pythia for permission for Alexander to put a question to the oracle. A brusque and peremptory Philotas then enters and starts to threaten the priestess. The Pythia refuses, whereupon Alexander enters, having climbed over the parapet wall. He poses a written question to the Pythia, who reads it almost in disbelief: we realize from her comments that it must be a question about conquering the entire Persian empire. She treats it almost as a boyish joke: "Thirty-five thousand against a quarter of a million?" Alexander gives his military plan in outline, including a quick march through the Cilician Gates, "where only three men can walk abreast." The reference is important evidence of Rattigan's range of sources. He would not have found it in Arrian, Tarn, or Plutarch's *Life*, but he would have found it in Curtius (3.4.11), where the "road would take hardly four men, armed, side by side." Curtius, part of Tarn's "vulgate," will reappear again in the play, to even greater effect.

Alexander then gives an outline of his political plan: a "new order in Asia" that will be a "Hellenic world" where city-states will persist but "national sovereignties" must be given up in a "world state." The Pythia is still skeptical: "Why must you do this madness, Alexander?" One answer, as we will see, lies in the modern sources on which Rattigan had fastened. Alexander's answer, however, is that the plan goes back to a boast he made when insulted by Attalus and challenged by his drunken father, Philip, at the latter's "marriage after divorcing my mother." This "boast" must be fulfilled, even though, as the Pythia observes, Philip is now dead. Here, Rattigan put important psychological weight on the scene of Philip's remarriage, which Stone also exploits. Stone uses it directly and much more memorably in a complex mental context.

The Pythia refuses to put the question to Apollo because questions have to be submitted first to the Council (in Rattigan's view) and can only be passed on when the Council has agreed to them. But Alexander is insistent, with words about his "hopes" that derive directly from Plutarch. The Pythia laughs and calls him "invincible": Alexander "stiffens into rigid silence" and takes the word as an oracle from the god. The Pythia denies that it is, but Alexander is adamant. She warns him that one conquest must precede all others: he must first know himself. Alexander says that he does, but the Pythia is doubtful. "Remember, Alexander, there is always the last battle." Alexander departs: "I shall win it: I am invincible." But the audience should have doubts.

Those who saw the play still remember this scene. It was far more dramatic, evidently, than is suggested by the impossibly polite English on the page: "Goodbye, Pythia. Are you quite, quite determined not to answer my question?" The words (like the entry by climbing over the wall) have a schoolboy tone. Beneath it, nonetheless, are matters of major dramatic and historical importance. Alexander's visit to Delphi is described in chapter 14 of Plutarch's *Life*, but is it historical? In 1948 Tarn had accepted it, putting the visit in late 336 B.C.E. and adding that the "accounts of the *tamiai* at Delphi show that subsequently to the autumn meeting of 336 somebody presented toward the building of the temple 150 gold 'Philips' which were expended in the spring of 335; and it does not appear who this could have been but Alexander." Although 150 gold Philip coins is not a big gift, Tarn observed that Alexander was short of money in 336 and would be traveling with few funds.

The Delphic accounts have now been studied more closely, and Tarn's argument can be refined. By the autumn of 336, the Spartan king Cleomenes II had given the temple a mere 510 drachmas, even though his chariot team had just won a victory in the Pythian games: by these standards, a gift of 150 Philip coins (2,000 drachmas) was not so insignificant. More importantly, one of the treasurers' lists has now been convincingly fixed just after the news of Philip's death, itself (on other grounds) now datable to the autumn of 336. This list mentions no Philip coins. The next list, from the spring of 335, does mention them: they come from "the treasurers" and are to be spent on cypress wood from Sicyon for the new temple. There is no calculation to imply that the coins have been bought in by exchange at a higher rate. They surely arrived as a gift, precisely between late 336 and early 335; the "treasurers" may even have received more, of which only these 150 are mentioned for a particular purpose. A Macedonian donor, surely Alexander, is still a very likely guess.

The Delphic visit is widely credited by modern historians, but the encounter with the Pythia is more questionable: it reads like a hostile bit of rumor. According to Plutarch Alexander "dragged" her "by force" until she called him "invincible." Memorably, Tarn rephrased the words to mean that "Alexander probably took her arm and said 'O come along' or something of the sort. . . . Any display of real force is out of the question. No one can imagine Alexander using force to any woman, let alone a priestess." It is as well that he did not see Stone's scene of Alexander assaulting Roxane. Rattigan, too, was not persuaded by Plutarch. His Pythia calls Alexander "invincible" with a laugh, meaning that he is "invincible" about the matter in hand. It is her own spontaneous remark, but is it a divine omen? Alexander has no doubts, but we are left to wonder.

The avoidance of force or roughness is typical of Rattigan's hero throughout act 1. Philotas is much ruder, as we will see again in act 2: we gather that he is twenty-seven, quite old in the opinion of Hephaestion, who explains that he himself is twenty-one. This observation neatly emphasizes the extreme youth of the protagonists. As for Hephaestion, is he "afraid of Alexander? Good heavens, no. He is my best friend." The Lord Chamberlain would certainly not be troubled by him. He has never failed Alexander, at least until this business of putting a question straight to the Pythia.

As for Alexander, he is the newly elected "Captain-General" of the Greeks. The title is not Tarn's, but it had had a long popular life. Back in 1897, D. G. Hogarth (later the historical advisor to T. E. Lawrence) had applied it to Philip and to Alexander: it had also featured in the popular 1934 book by F. A. Wright (Professor of Classics at the University of London) and more recently in A. R. Burn's *Alexander the Great and the Hellenistic Empire* (1947), a short book that Rattigan did not choose to exploit. I suspect that Wright was his source. The Greek title *hegemōn* would translate as "Leader," a title impossible to use so soon after Hitler.

Alexander's supposed plan for a "world state" is central to the "adventure," and its source is even more interesting. Contrary to what we might suppose, it does not come from the idealistic Tarn. He had argued forcefully for years against the idea that Alexander had planned world conquest. His argument began in 1926, after one world war, and was repeated, unchanged, after another war in which "world conquest" had acquired even more sinister associations, both Nazi and communist. Nonetheless the aim had first been credited to Alexander by J. Kaerst's German study in 1901, and in 1931 even Ulrich Wilcken's excellent biography accepted it. Words like "Weltherrschaftsideal" or "Weltreichsgedanke" gave the aim a theoretical (but vague) tone.

Rattigan was clearly not convinced by Tarn's contrary arguments or by his alternative suggestion that Alexander hoped for a "brotherhood of man." He found his cue in America, in the recent book by C. A. Robinson, professor at Brown University, which was published in New York in 1947. It was Robinson (not Tarn) who made Alexander's "world state" current in English: "Alexander's goal was a new and better world . . . there could be little doubt about his ideas on world conquest and his own relation to a world state"; he was concerned with "giving a sense of unity to a world state. Would brotherhood be the answer, but how to achieve it?" Ultimately Robinson's Alexander was aiming for the "remarkable idea of a common culture for the world." Robinson knew Tarn's earlier work, and surely he also knew Wilcken's (translated in 1932), which linked "world-rule" to the aim of a fusion of Macedonians and Iranians. "World-rule laid hold of Alexander even more strongly in his later years . . . ," Wilcken wrote. "Only a world-ruler before whose eyes people lose their national significance is capable of conceiving such a scheme" as the fusion of conquerors and conquered. In 1946–47, Robinson wrote at a time of revulsion against nationalist war, when hopes were high, in some quarters, for a United Nations.

Rattigan found in Robinson the high ideal that his "adventure" story needed and that would make the drama poignant: it appealed to him, perhaps (ill-advisedly) as a historian, and above all as a dramatist. One problem with a modern drama about Alexander is how to make the conqueror's main aim sympathetic to a modern audience. Stone's film laid emphasis, rightly, on the ambition for personal glory, the rivalry with the ancient heroes, and the fame to be won through deeds. His Alexander's aim was indeed to conquer as far as the outer Ocean, the eastern edge of the world. Rattigan's Alexander is not even sure who will rule his eventual "world state": he will have to be a Greek, but perhaps not Alexander himself. Stone's Alexander, by contrast, wants personal glory won by conquest—but such glory is not unquestionable greatness for many modern viewers, whether in 1949 or 2004. What else was Alexander's aim? Initially, the answer is probably "nothing," and in Stone's film it is only the aged Ptolemy who reflects with hindsight on Alexander's bringing about a "Hellenic civilization," an "empire of the mind," through his many new Alexandrias in Africa and Asia. The notion is quite a plausible one for the elderly ruler of one such Alexandria, who had shown himself to be a conspicuous patron of Greek culture, including a Greek Library and a Museum. On the balcony in Babylon, however, Stone's Alexander talks to Hephaestion of "freeing the peoples of the world" and "connecting up" what had previously been separated and in places, decidedly uncivilized. Stone's script changed here quite late on, and although echoes of this theme can certainly be found at various points in the ancient Alexander historians, I have never felt that the script was as sharp as it could have been. Hephaestion's warning counterbalances Alexander's words ("slavery," "they suffered greatly"), but the problem is that we do not know what general good, if any, Alexander saw in his continuing conquests from Babylon onward. Personal glory and ever more conquest leave a gap for many modern viewers, even if they are the hard, pre-Christian truth. Unlike Rattigan, Stone at least held back from talk of a "world state."

Rattigan's Alexander has been taught about this state by his tutor, Aristotle. Here, other sources come into play. Rattigan's Aristotle has also told his pupil that a man can become a god only "by doing what is impossible for a man to do." He disapproves of Alexander's use of Homer as a military manual (Rattigan never once mentions the role model Achilles: "a deeply selfish man," warns Stone's Aristotle). Why has Rattigan linked Aristotle with these ideas?

Direct use of Aristotle's surviving writing is not the answer. On the topic of "becoming a god," Aristotle's *Nicomachean Ethics* book 7 and *Politics* book 3 (1284a) are the important texts. Gods can come into being from men "because of an excess of excellence"; if an individual of superlative virtue were to exist, beyond comparison with all other men, then he would be "like a god among men." A year after Rattigan's play, an important scholarly study by J. P. V. D. Balsdon (another exponent of common sense and plain language) rightly concluded that Aristotle was engaging here in "the quasi-metaphysical grading of a humanly inconceivable paragon." Even then, he would be "like a god," not a god outright. Rattigan has changed Aristotle's words ("become a god by doing what is impossible for a man") so as to give Alexander the sort of riposte that his scriptwriting very much likes: "If I do the impossible it won't be because I've become a god but because I was born Alexander." In Stone's film, Alexander's belief that a god was his father is reflected on by Ptolemy ("it was a myth . . . or at least it began as a myth"), as is Alexander's own eventual status as a god. Stone felt that showing the offering of divine honors would be confusing to most modern viewers (Alexander liked them, but in real life did not demand them). Rattigan seems to have felt the same, and they would not suit his boyish king. They remain peripheral to both dramatists, although in history they are one of Alexander's major legacies.

The "world state" attaches to a second Aristotelian difficulty. The only text that is relevant to the topic is *Politics* book 7 (1327b) : "The Greek race lies midway between Asia and the north and has the double quality of being both 'spirited' and 'intelligent,' and so it continues being free and having the best political organization and being capable of ruling everyone if it attains a single political form." The text had been reinterpreted, unconvincingly, by Victor Ehrenberg in an important study of Aristotle and Alexander that was translated in 1938. Rattigan either rejected or ignored Ehrenberg, preferring the views of Werner Jaeger, whose book on Aristotle had just appeared in a second edition in 1948. Jaeger, writing from Harvard, stated bluntly that "it was a matter of faith with Aristotle that Greece could rule the world if it were politically united," and that Aristotle passed on this lesson to Alexander. The old "antinomy" between "patriarchal, agricultural kingship and the freedom of the democracies" could only be overcome by "the outstanding personality of a real king in whom Greece could see its own embodiment. Aristotle knew that such a man is a gift of the gods."

Jaeger's inaccurate (and politically alarming) view was plainly the source for Rattigan, who was also writing in 1948. Stone's film presents Aristotle in a rather different light. It places the philosopher beside some old architecture, shown partially ruined to symbolize an older fading world, and then makes Aristotle talk about the possibility that Greeks would rule the world if only they would look outward beyond what Plato had described as their "frog pond" around the Mediterranean. There was no talk from the old man about the need for world kingship (the view has had far too much of a life in Germany). Instead this fine scene shows that he is still thinking in terms of the virtues needed for founding a city-state. Meanwhile, the first glimmer of a conquest as far as the eastern Ocean, the world's end, has surfaced in the young Alexander, stemming not from Aristotle's political theory but from his exposition of a grossly inaccurate map.

At one point after 1949 it almost seemed, for a moment, as if Rattigan's Aristotle had been rightly represented after all. In later Arabic sources a letter survives that is ascribed to Aristotle and addressed to Alexander. Only a few scholars ever considered it genuine, but in the 1960s the fine scholar S. M. Stern rediscovered a much longer version of it in manuscripts in Istanbul. The texts varied, but Stern ably reconstructed "Aristotle's" advice. For a start, "Aristotle" advises, Alexander should simply deport the inhabitants of Persia (or at least their ruling class) and settle them as a punishment in Greece. He should then encourage prosperity and "just behaviour." The result will be "concord," and happy is the man who "sees the glorious day when men agree to constitute one rule [in Arabic, *amr*] and kingdom [*malikat*]. They will cease from wars and struggles. . . . I would love to remain alive and see that age—if not all of it, at least a part."

In Stone's film, Aristotle speaks for an old worldview, soon to be refuted, but in this letter he hopes for a new one that Rattigan (and Jaeger) had ascribed to him. Is the letter genuine? Behind the Arabic translation lies a lost original in Greek, but Stern rightly recognized that "if the idea of Greek unity was of such importance for Aristotle he succeeded in hiding it remarkably well in a participial clause" in *Politics* book 7, the only other source for it. Nonetheless, Stern suggested that Aristotle may have accepted "some kind of universal state, but we do not know exactly what he meant." Would this world-state absorb small city-states completely (Rattigan implied that it would not)? More controversially, Stern also suggested that Aristotle might have written some such words of hope in a letter to Alexander between 331 B.C.E.

(the victory at Gaugamela) and 327 (the murder of Callisthenes, Aristotle's kinsman). In Stone's Director's Cut and Final Cut, the old Aristotle does write a letter of warning to his pupil at this very time, but it stresses the need for moral restraint and self-control. Alexander rejects this advice: in the film, should Aristotle's advice have been politically idealistic instead? In fact, the Arabic "letter" contains one patent reference to post-Aristotelian Hellenistic history that Stern misunderstood and therefore tried to emend. Even the longer text of this letter is patently a late Hellenistic fake. It does not correct Stone's film.

World conquest and idealistic aims are parts of Stone's film, but despite Aristotle, not because of him. In Rattigan's play they are present because they exist in books written in 1947–48 by scholars in America for a wider public. They represent views that Alexander historians now routinely rubbish, but they are not, quite strikingly, the views of William Tarn. Tarn believed that "it was left to Alexander himself to rise to a higher level than Plato or Aristotle" (who considered the barbarians in Asia to be "slaves by nature" and fit only for despotic rule). Here Stone's film, correctly, agreed with Tarn's line. As for Alexander, "legend strove to give him that world-kingdom which he never sought in life." Here, Stone's film, in my view rightly, disagreed. Within a year of the publication of the revered Tarn's conclusions, Rattigan was also going against them. In interviews he said that he recognized that books differed widely about Alexander and that the wiser ones "sat on the fence": he chose views that suited his drama, and found them outside Britain's leading authority on Alexander.

The Pythia in his play gave advice too: "Know yourself." Rattigan traces the roots of Alexander's ambition to a quarrel with his drunken father: the Pythia seems to see that it will lead to serious problems. The quarrel is described in Plutarch's *Life,* and is therefore in Stone's film too, where it ended up being cut in as a "parallel story'" after the murder of Parmenion, an onlooker at the fateful wedding feast in 337/36 B.C.E. This feast is one of the film's brilliant party scenes (with a first glimpse of Pausanias, Philip's future murderer, who is being sexually abused behind a pillar among the wedding guests). The film replays Plutarch's words to and from Philip, but there is no boast by Alexander, Rattigan's invention. Rather, the episode is a source of anger, then pained disdain, in an Alexander who must now grow up by himself. Unlike Rattigan, Stone cuts dramatically to Olympias, who is looking down through an upstairs window at the tensions that she had already predicted to her son.

"Know yourself, Alexander," Rattigan's Pythia warns after hearing his ambition and its origins. "I know myself, Pythia." "Do you, Alexander? Are you sure?" I have tried to know the sources of this scene because the scene is at the root of Rattigan's entire drama.

Structure and Story in Act 1 of *Adventure Story*

The remaining four scenes of act 1 add two particular drives to the Pythia's fears: the effects of conquest and the dynamic between Alexander and his dead or absent parents. The effect of Alexander's parents much concerned Stone, but the dynamic is differently grounded. Rattigan's scene 2 shows us the Persian court in Babylon with Darius, the queen mother, and, among others, a "burly" Bessus (about fifty years old). Reports of Alexander's progress through Asia Minor are discussed by the queen: "antics of a lunatic schoolboy" (the Pythia would agree). For both Stone and Rattigan, Alexander's risk taking, rightly, looms large. The queen mother commends the exiled Greek Charidemus's strategy: "Leave the boy to rot in Phrygia: he can't get through the Cilician Gates." Charidemus is not mentioned in Arrian or Plutarch: Rattigan's queen must be adapting what she has read in the vulgate Diodorus 17.30 or more probably Curtius 3.2.10–19. At Delphi, Rattigan's Alexander had observed, "Speed is the main thing. Asiatics don't understand speed." The scene in Babylon ends with Darius reading, incredulously, that Alexander is already through the Cilician Gates. Not, however, before Darius has passed a wry comment on the Greeks' "democracy." They keep fighting themselves every year, whereas the Persians left democracy behind centuries ago: did Rattigan think here of the spurious Persian debate about democracy in Herodotus 3.80–82? The Persians now have a "world-empire" instead, which is "so far beyond a Greek's ken that they have to dub us 'barbarians' to save their political self-respect." There are no villains in Rattigan's play, least of all in Asia (the play's "Orientalism" is many-sided). The Persians behave like wise, older gentlefolk. We are to remember, of course, that this same world-empire is Alexander's professed aim.

In scene 3 we move to Darius's sumptuous tent, just captured at Issus. For obvious reasons Stone did not show this battle. The rule-of-thumb for audiences of action movies, aged sixteen to twenty-four especially, is that a big battle must come within the first twenty-five minutes. Only one of the big battles was affordable or dramatically possible, and when Stone took over the scriptwriting in 2002, it had to be

Gaugamela. One of the successes of the Final Cut is that the battle is brought even closer to the beginning of the film, an idea that was tried out by one of Stone's fans and then sent to him for further experiment.

At Issus, Rattigan plays games with the captured luxury of the Persian court: "The Great Kings of Persia, even while on active service, lived in a style and a grandeur which have hardly been seen in the world since." We meet Cleitus the staunch Macedonian, an orderly Parmenion ("Where are King Darius's documents?" Answer: a Persian servant has just burned them), and, again, a corruptible Philotas: "The wealth of those barbarians! It makes one vomit!" "Not me, it doesn't." Rattigan also includes a dispute between the officers about their relative merits in the recent battle. So, remarkably, does Stone, but his takes place six years later in the Bactrian castle.

The important turn in the drama begins when Alexander returns, limping and wounded, from pursuing Darius. Cleitus begins to bathe the wound, kneeling before him but resenting the position (significantly, in view of the future), while Alexander keeps on moving around. Stone also shows Alexander refusing help for his wound, but this time in the "hospital" tent after Gaugamela: it is one of his several understated scenes showing Alexander's nobility, too underplayed, perhaps, for those critics who could not understand how an Alexander like Stone's could ever have been a leader of men. In Rattigan's script, the king's nobility is brought out by direct echoes of Plutarch. "So this is what is to be a king": at this stage Alexander will not touch wine; he will not touch captive women, either ("sex and sleep," as in Plutarch's *Life*, remind him that he is mortal). Here, Rattigan omits Alexander's sexual affair with the noble Barsine, captured after Issus, no doubt because William Tarn had just tried to expunge her from history. Stone also leaves her out, but only because she would blur the dynamic he wanted between Bagoas and then Alexander's "first" woman, Roxane.

Before Alexander enters, we have learned that he calls old Cleitus "father" because Cleitus had saved his life in battle. Stone's Cleitus, too, is commended by Alexander's father (albeit in a "parallel story"), though he is never called "father." The rescue is transposed to Gaugamela because Stone, too, saw a connection between it and Cleitus's murder a few years later. Rattigan's Alexander duly calls Cleitus "father" and then refers, significantly, to his real father. He questions old Parmenion about Philip's behavior after victory, implying that Philip would probably be drunk anyway. Significantly, he then "stiffens" and invokes Philip's reactions to his own success: "Let him see me now—in

Darius's tent, wearing Darius's mantle—let his eyes burn with the sight." It is the first hint of an underlying psychodrama. Stone, too, makes Parmenion comment on Philip's pride at his son's successes, but not until Alexander's entry into the palace at Babylon: there he receives a rather cryptic response ("my anger and my pride . . . blind me"). In the film the first warning signs that trouble is looming for the adult Alexander are different, and differently placed. In the Director's Cut and the Final Cut, Stone flashes back to Philip just as Alexander is leaving the field of Gaugamela. Torch in hand, Philip is telling his young son the arcane story of Zeus's mixing of the ashes of the wicked Titans into the nature of subsequent humans. Particles of these turbulent monsters are in each one of us. This ancient myth was ascribed to Orpheus and might well have been known in Macedon. In 2003 I drew it to Stone's notice, believing it to have featured in the Derveni papyrus, the oldest known Greek papyrus, which was found with funerary offerings in a grave in southwest Macedon. A mention of this myth in the papyrus now seems less likely as more of the text has been published, but the story is an apt evocation of the elemental forces in man. Ptolemy's later references in the film to Alexander as a "Titan" belong in this ambivalent context. Rattigan omits Greek myths entirely.

Rattigan's deployment of Alexander's rivalry with Philip leads to his first (and almost only) allusion to Olympias. "Hephaestion," Alexander asks, "do you ever think I'm mad?" (On the balcony in Babylon, Stone's Alexander asks, "Which am I, Hephaestion, weak or divine?"— a hard bit of dialogue for us to swallow.) He wonders what to send "my mother" (her name, Olympias, is never used) and opts for the "basin" in which Cleitus has just bathed his "scratch" of a wound: "She'll find an historic association in that." I suspect that Rattigan is thinking here of Olympias's dedication of a phiale (more of a cup than a basin) to the goddess Health in Athens at a date soon after Issus. We only know of this dedication from the Athenian Hypereides' speech *For Euxenippus*, but somehow Rattigan had picked it up, perhaps from sources about Olympias in a handbook.

The gift is presented rather dismissively: only a "basin" for mother at home. For Rattigan, but not for Stone, Philip's impact on Alexander is much more potent than Olympias's. Rattigan also hints at a new danger: luxury and its ability to corrupt. In Stone's film Alexander himself comments on this danger, regarding it as a danger for his men, not himself. He tells them in his speech by the Indian riverbank when they refuse to go on: "You have fallen in love with all the things that destroy

you." Stone's Alexander wears pseudo-Oriental clothes and sits on the
Persian golden throne, but luxury is never emphasized as part of his
own decline. Ptolemy's summing-up confirms the film's emphasis here.
It stands aside (in my view, rightly) from the widespread stereotype
about the corrupting effects of "luxury" found in the Greek and especially the Roman sources: Rattigan, however, will emphasize the change
in Alexander hinted at here by reinstating Persian splendor in later
stage settings. For the moment, though, Alexander's divinity is only a
mock-heroic notion with which Hephaestion has some fun. When Alexander first considers the captive Persian throne, he merely reflects on
its "loneliness," not its splendor. Here he anticipates the theme of the
"loneliness of power" that Ernst Badian was to develop in a widely read
essay on Alexander published with other studies by him in 1964.

The captive Persian queen and her family are then met, much as in
Plutarch's *Life*, and their persons are courteously honored. Omitting
Issus, Stone transposed this scene to the Babylon palace and its harem,
prefacing it (in the cinema version) by a significant gaze from Alexander. It falls not on any of the Persians' surrounding women but, in preference to them all, on the newly encountered eunuch Bagoas. It was a
pity that the experienced actress Jeanne Moreau withdrew from a role as
Stone's Persian queen. The scene with her younger substitute is weaker
for her absence. In Rattigan's scene, the Persian ladies are entrusted to
Hephaestion, "my closest friend and wisest counsellor. He will see that
you come to no harm." The "harm," rather, is to be Alexander's. He restores Darius's cloak to the queen mother, but he then sits briefly on the
Persian throne, whereupon a Persian servant grovels before him in
non-Greek obeisance. An onlooking Hephaestion disapproves. When
Alexander invites him "to come and watch me take my imperial bath,"
significantly Hephaestion "does not move." In Stone's film it is Bagoas
in Babylon who is told, just once, to give Alexander's bath night a miss.

Rattigan's scene 4 returns to Babylon, where King Darius hears from
Philotas, Alexander's envoy, that his latest peace offer has been rejected. Otherwise Rattigan follows Plutarch, who places a peace offer in
331 B.C.E. and connects it (wrongly) with news of the death of Darius's
wife in captivity. Correctly, Rattigan does not follow the suspicions of
modern scholars who note that the wife died in childbirth and then intimate that Alexander impregnated the lady himself despite his reported attitudes to "sex and sleep." Her death and a peace offer actually belonged in mid- to late 332, and the paternity of the unborn child
was Darius's. By combining the two, Rattigan stresses Alexander's

gentlemanly respect: "He was crying dreadfully," Darius's daughter writes to her father, "and he came every day for a week with a different present for me." He is "so gentle and kind." Rattigan is playing on this line excessively in order to heighten the subsequent misadventure.

The final scene of Rattigan's act 1 dwells on a moment that is climactic for Stone too: the council of war before Gaugamela. Like Stone's, Rattigan's Alexander explains the tactics: "I shall replay Darius's own tactics against him and launch the entire Companion cavalry straight at the hinge ["crack," in Stone's script] in his line." Unlike Parmenion, he says he will not "steal a victory," the famous remark recorded in Arrian, by attacking at night. He concludes swiftly and urges his commanders in turn to speak briefly to their own units. Rattigan's Alexander sounds like the young Guy Gibson addressing the Dambusters on the night before operations.

In Stone's cinema version, Alexander explicitly declines to sleep the night with Hephaestion. By the time of Gaugamela, we are to infer, sex was not the main force in their relationship. Rattigan's Alexander merely asks, "Are you prepared for another all-night vigil? . . . I wonder how many hours of sleep I might have robbed you of in your life, Hephaestion." Behind these words one can sense the only innuendo that Rattigan, a homosexual, allowed himself about the two "best friends" in the script.

Whereas Stone concludes the night with the parting between Hephaestion and Alexander, Rattigan adds two remarkable scenes. First, his Alexander is alone, watched only by the same Persian servant who had groveled to him after Issus. "He is shivering and his hands begin to shake." The starting point for this scene was chapter 31 of Plutarch's *Life*, where Alexander "spent time with his seer Aristander in front of his tent, carrying out certain secret rites and offering blood-sacrifices to Phobos (Fear)." During his writing of the script, Stone repeatedly asked me what these rites might have been (human sacrifice, or what?) and whether they were significant. In his mind they linked up with that final "freedom from the fear of death" that Ptolemy praises in Alexander. In the film, therefore, we see a sculpted mask of Phobos in the camp by night. In real life the offerings, I assume, were intended to avert a panic in Alexander's camp. The recently published Babylonian "diary" has shown us, from the non-Greek side, that the Persian army had been beset by fear only a few days previously.

Rattigan's Alexander struggles here with an almost Christ-like suffering. "God, God! Take this fear from me. . . . I am invincible. . . . Take this agony from me." The cure for it is an appeal to "father Philip." "Look down now and sneer. Say 'what a weak and effeminate coward I have for a son.'" The invocation (echoing Philip's words at his remarriage) provokes anger in Alexander, and anger alone "conquers fear." Thanking Philip for this therapy, Alexander recovers, but the drive within him is now clear to us. His ambition began, we have been told, with a boast at Philip's remarriage; after Issus it turned out to be fueled by competitive rivalry and exultation; now it is supported by the surging anger that his father's taunts can still provoke in him. The Pythia had indeed seen into hidden depths.

A mother figure then intervenes. Parmenion warns Alexander of imminent personal dangers, one of which is that the Persian queen mother intends to poison him that very night. Here Rattigan transposes from three years earlier a famous scene with Alexander's doctor, the Greek Philip. The queen mother, we learn, has been in the way of bringing Alexander a warm drink in the evening. Hephaestion may have refused to play kings and queens in the Persian bathtub, but Mother has taken over with a soothing cup of mulled wine. Tonight the drink will be poisoned.

Alexander drinks it nonetheless, betting that the queen mother might have said that she planned to poison him only to forestall an attempt by someone else. She would never do it, he believes—and indeed she admits as much. The first act ends with the Persian queen mother offering to walk across the lines and beg her son Darius not to fight. But Alexander says he must fight: "Don't cry, it's I who want to cry tonight." Like Stone, who was much criticized for this aspect, Rattigan does not hesitate to connect his hero with tearful emotion. "No, Mother," says Alexander, "I won't let you." His "own mother," he says, "is very far away, you know," and the queen is now taking on a maternal role. Alexander has surmounted his anger at his dead father's taunts, but he has transferred his need for a mother to the mother of his enemy, Darius. Rattigan saw a drama in this transference, and his act 2 will develop it strongly. But he took his cue, even here, from an ancient source. The vulgate Diodorus 17.37.6 and Curtius 3.12.17 expressly state that Alexander called the captive queen his "mother" when they met after Issus.

The two of them now bond as human beings, as even Darius in Babylon had said that he might with Alexander. Class solidarity spans the hostility of war, as in the masterly film *La Grande Illusion*. "Did Darius hate his father?" Alexander asks. "And did *you* . . . ?" The queen says that they both loved him "very dearly." "Strange," says Alexander, with the implication that he hated Philip. The scene ends with his head, childlike, in his newly found mother's lap. Thankfully, Stone's scene in Babylon ends differently. After another superb scene of partying, Alexander retires with Hephaestion (not, significantly, with Bagoas for bath time tonight) in order to read a letter he has received from Olympias. She warns him of plots and disloyalties all around him: "dark suspicions, but they *are* dark, Alexander," as Olympias–Angelina Jolie so dramatically tells him. Her love is for her son, but, as Hephaestion has shrewdly hinted, is it from her and the strains that she can cause that Alexander is running away?

Stone's Alexander rivals the ancient heroes in his search for undying glory, but the fears and pressures of his mother are propelling him eastward in pursuit of it. Rattigan's Alexander has found a second mother in Asia, but there is a "demon" in him that is not a legacy from Zeus's Titans. It is the scar of his father's insults, and it will drive him on into act 2.

Act 2 of *Adventure Story*

Rattigan's second act shows these tensions playing themselves out, from a long and remarkable scene with Philotas (the best in the play) to Parmenion's murder and the murder of Cleitus too. This act covers the same ground as most of the second hour of Stone's film, but it lacks its variety. It is here that Stone exploits the "parallel stories" of earlier tensions in Macedon to lift the linear story into a drama. He is exploiting what he sees as a repeated pattern in Alexander's adult career. He also exploits the symbolic power of dance, by showing two carefully contrasted dances with contrasting music and contrasting sexual overtones. For Stone, dance is an important form of social expression that is underexploited by historical films. He still regrets that he lost the chance in the early 1990s to direct a film script on Evita Perón for which he had planned a dramatic use of dance. His *Alexander* stretched to the limit a supporting cast of dancers from international *corps de ballet.* Critics did not even mention the implicit meaning of these unusual scenes.

For Rattigan, the wise queen mother is the unifying figure who draws the threads together and understands what has happened, like a school matron dealing with a distressed English boy. The action scenes conclude with an unusual choice: the burning of the army's baggage before the Indian invasion. There was a personal reason, I will argue, for Rattigan's choice of this concluding action. Then we go back, finally, to the deathbed at Babylon: who, now, is to be Master of the World? At Gordium, so King Darius had heard, Alexander had solved the riddle of the ancient knot by cutting it with his sword. Alexander begins act 2 by reflecting that the cutting was no solution. He has found Darius dead "in a farm-cart," picking up Gordium's omen of "the empire of the world in a farm-cart," a parallel that only Rattigan, I think, has ever drawn between the two events. "After all, Hephaestion, I never did solve that puzzle, did I? How can one solve a puzzle with a sword?" Once again, Hephaestion does not reply: the question is to be answered by the rest of the play.

Act 2 begins by showing the fugitive Darius being murdered and then discovered by his pursuer. Unlike Stone, Rattigan upholds the tendentious legend found in Plutarch that the dying young Darius "hereby names Alexander of Macedon as my lawful and true successor." This fictional story ties up with the respect Darius has previously expressed for his enemy. It also ushers in Alexander's new role as the successor king of Persia, with all the tensions that that role's pomp and despotism bring. Since the 1980s Pierre Briant has been suggesting that we can usefully look on Alexander as the "Last Achaemenid." In my judgment that emphasis distorts Alexander's aims and image, but in 1949 Rattigan had already anticipated Briant's point of view.

Scene 2 establishes the new Persian kingship by showing Alexander condemning the pretender and murderer Bessus to death in the Persian fashion. Bessus begs for a military execution, knowing that a Persian court will have his nose and ears cut off. Alexander refuses, much to Cleitus's disgust. But Alexander explains that they must consolidate their conquests by ruling as the Persians expect. They cannot simply be merciful and go home. "I'm sorry," says Cleitus, putting an arm round Alexander, "I'm a tactless old fool." "You're father Cleitus," says Alexander, to remind us of this role before their imminent disaster unfolds.

"Consolidation" does not exclude a march to India, Alexander's new plan. Ptolemy has doubts about it and also worries about the continuing "insurgency" around Herat, in modern Afghanistan. Its leader, unhistorically, is Roxane's father: what, then, about the girl? Should they send her head to her father to teach him a lesson? Alexander's way with insurgents, after all, is to terrorize and kill them. It is now that we meet Roxane and learn that Alexander has already spent a casual night with her (how different from the Alexander we saw at Issus). Ptolemy then suggests that Alexander should marry her "if you want to pacify Bactria in a few days." Alexander is incredulous.

Stone's Ptolemy introduces Roxane with a continuing note of uncertainty: why did Alexander marry her? What *was* she really like? For Stone the marriage plan is Alexander's own, provoked by the love and desire on which Arrian's sources (including, I think, Ptolemy) insisted. In Stone's view, which is worth pondering, Alexander also wanted a son. In Roxane, we come to realize, his Alexander sees a girl who has a look, even the attributes (the snaky ones, that is), of Olympias. The implicit sexual psychology is quite unlike Rattigan's. For the playwright, Alexander's substitute mother figure is the Persian queen back in Babylon. By a neat deflation Rattigan denies that love ever came into the Roxane affair. His Ptolemy tells Alexander that they can always make up a love story and publicize it to the world (as Ptolemy in fact did). Here, Rattigan was building on his modern authorities. For Robinson, "Alexander fell in love with her, so the *legend* goes, and married her but in reality it was a political marriage" (italics in original). For Tarn, unforgettably, "it was a marriage of policy. . . . Tradition naturally represents Alexander as in love with her, but it is doubtful if Alexander ever cared for any woman except his terrible mother." Rattigan artfully accounts for the so-called legend, whereas Stone accepts the "love" because it is actually in the sources. He then links it, memorably, with Tarn's "mother-love" by a snaky link between Olympias and Roxane. He warns implicitly of the dangers by exploiting the dance that ancient sources ascribed to Roxane at her first meeting with the king. Stone and the choreographer Piers Gielgud worked initially with east Iranian dance steps and then opted for arm movements by Roxane and her accompanying dancers that evoke modern notions of the Indian Kālī, a goddess linked with death. Significantly, the dancers carry knives so as to add a note of ill-omen to the simple flute music. Roxane, the dance implies, will prove to be lethal (by killing Alexander's greatest love, Hephaestion) despite her sexual allure.

At first, Rattigan's Alexander hesitates and appears to refuse the marriage plan, much to "father" Cleitus's relief. But Ptolemy still hopes, and on checking Roxane again, Alexander finds that she has "one valuable asset as a wife"—she "can't talk." In contrast Stone raises the drama by beginning his sequence of "parallel" stories here, as best seen in his Director's and Final cuts. The choice of Roxane sends Alexander's mind back to the time when Olympias was advising him to marry a good Macedonian girl and secure his preeminence at Philip's court. Ten years later, he has done the opposite.

Meanwhile, Rattigan's Philotas, unlike his Roxane, can talk very well. Like Stone, Rattigan postpones Philotas's trial, giving it an unhistorical context. Stone combined it (for lack of space) with the Pages' Plot and took a line closer to Plutarch's: that Alexander's officers disliked Philotas and urged his execution. Rattigan, however, departs strikingly from Plutarch, who is usually his main source. What he gives us is a subtle moral challenge, based on bits of the long description of the affair by Curtius. For a start, his Alexander accepts that Philotas is completely innocent. In 1949 Rattigan's notable interpretation was not at all the professional line. For Wilcken, in 1931, "whether the sentence was just or not we cannot tell." Alexander "prosecuted in vehement language," but if "the condemnation of Philotas was a judicial murder, it is not the fault of Alexander but of the assembly of the Macedonian army." For Robinson, Philotas was not an innocent party, although there were grounds for resenting Alexander at the time. For Tarn, there was indeed an "action" of Philotas's to be explained: Ptolemy "stated" that the proofs of the treason were perfectly clear," and Philotas was "properly put on trial. . . . It was rough and ready justice but the army gave a fair trial according to its lights."

Rattigan's Alexander has already shown his distress at Philotas's dangerous predicament: yet again he has "wept over him," albeit only once. These "tears," so alien to English and American preconceptions, were picked up from Curtius (6.7.28). What follows, however, is Rattigan's neat redirection of another cue in Curtius, whose description of the "trial" is notoriously prolonged and complex. Rattigan's Alexander states expressly to Hephaestion that Philotas is innocent of the conspiracy, but there are other charges that the "High Council of the Army" believes to be serious. Alexander will not disabuse them, for he will not be there in person for the trial.

Here, Rattigan plays cleverly with Tarn and Wilcken's ascription of the sentence to the "army" or the "assembly," while also picking up the idea of a "Council" from Curtius: Curtius refers to this Council both here and in the Pages' Plot (a *consilium* as distinct from a *contio*). Not even in recent scholarship has a "Macedonian Council" been given such independent power. The dramatic result is a callousness that shocks Hephaestion and leaves Alexander with room for a cool compromise. Philotas must recant the letters that record his discomfort about Alexander's divinity, despotism, and conceit. If he does so, Alexander will not send these incriminating charges on to the Council. The turning point thus occurs in private before any trial at all. Philotas refuses, remarking that the demand to swear that he will never again repeat such charges is itself a proof of the despotism he resents. "I didn't try to kill you, you know; but if you should be fool enough to pardon me now, I would."

Significantly, Philotas has belittled Alexander "not by what he does, but what he is": Alexander reverses him, saying, "What a man does is everything." Remarkably, Stone also presents the view that "we are what we do," but presents it quite independently, as a hero's ideal of fame and immortality. Rattigan will return to this theme in scene 5, just as he returns to it in several of his later plays. Meanwhile his Alexander goes a step further: he orders that Parmenion must now be killed back in "Babylon," that Hephaestion must be the one to see to it, and that he also give out that Parmenion "had been" plotting. "Had been?" "He must die resisting arrest."

Hephaestion refuses, even proposing that Alexander kill him first. Alexander retorts, "This is the moment that Alexander first discovered he had no friend in the world. . . . Leave me now." He has just told Philotas that this "vast empire" can only be ruled by despotism, not "like Athens, with a democratic revolution every year." He has also harked back to Aristotle: "The true King is a god among men" (not "like" one, as stated in *Politics* book 3). "He himself is the law" (as Aristotle had indeed written, but only of a superhuman paragon). In his present "loneliness," anticipating Badian's "loneliness of power," Alexander asks only that he be forgiven for comforting himself with thoughts that he is "son of a god." His new role, we are to realize, has obliged him to be despotic. But we also notice that from this scene onward, he is drinking repeatedly, as he never did at Issus. As Hephaestion leaves, Alexander's hands shake, just as they shook before Gaugamela. He diverts himself by playing games with the returning Roxane. He hides a ring in one hand and a dagger in the other, and tells her she must choose one of the two. Stone's Alexander was already married to Roxane by the time of the Parmenion affair, and his Alexander diverts the strain of the occasion quite differently, by taking Bagoas to bed. Stone's Roxane had already found the "dagger and copy of Homer" that Onesicritus tells us Alexander kept under his pillow. In contrast, Rattigan's Roxane now chooses the ring and marriage. The choice is a proof of the luck Alexander enjoys. The encounter is a neat, drunken end to the play's most successful scene.

Back in Babylon Rattigan's Persian queen entertains the officer whom Alexander has sent to deal with Parmenion in Hephaestion's place: Perdiccas. She hears of the "conspiracy" and promptly offers to go to Alexander, referring to him, pityingly and knowingly, as "poor Alexander." A good scene develops nonetheless in which Parmenion meets the queen and is helped to see his imminent danger. Undeterred, he goes to meet it: our sympathies are aligned with Parmenion, as previously they were aligned with Philotas.

Up in Bactria, we move next to Roxane's wedding, in which Hephaestion is to carry Alexander's crown while Cleitus will carry Roxane's. Wine is now Alexander's prop, and the "props" in his tent include the reinstated Persian furniture. Ominously, "father Cleitus" is hurt by a slighting remark from Alexander about his Macedonian homeland. After their last scene together, Hephaestion, too, has to be won around. "Despot I am," Alexander tells him, "because I must be": the world-state requires it, "ruled by the man-god whose word is law" (Aristotle's *Politics* again). "No more war, no more oppression. A universal peace, blessed by the Almighty Gods. It's not an unworthy vision?" "No, Alexander." (It was C. A. Robinson's vision in 1947.) "It's now or never, Hephaestion. If I fail, who else shall succeed?" One can only hope that the lines were spoken with a wine-induced slur. On hearing that he must grovel in honor, Cleitus, thankfully, diverts the drama.

Stone, by contrast, sets the fateful quarrel in India, linking it not to Roxane's wedding but to the remarkable dance by the eunuch Bagoas (known in one source for a public dance, but not until 325). Under strain, Stone's Alexander has turned to Bagoas, not to Roxane, for sexual comfort during the Parmenion crisis. Bagoas now outdances Roxane's debut by emerging in a dazzling whirl of agility and sexual provocation. The dance is set not to Roxane's flute-music but to a driving, elemental drumbeat devised by the musical director, Bud Carr, to emphasize its sexual force. On an unpolished floor at Pinewood, Francisco Bosch (Bagoas) and a supporting circle of ballet professionals capped even Rosario Dawson's (Roxane's) first big Hollywood screen moment, which she executed on a rough stone floor in Morocco with an unfilmed mountain precipice just to one side. Bagoas's dance, its lighting and the subsequent scripting make this scene quite remarkably queer.

Provoked by the prospect of Persian groveling, Rattigan's Cleitus speaks out. Alexander observes to him that the Iranians are not barbarians but "a hundred times more civilized than he is": Stone's Alexander has already thrown this very lesson at an unwilling Cassander. Tension mounts, and Rattigan's Cleitus invokes Philip's "shame" at his son's new style; he leaves the tent shouting, "Unlike his son—Philip, at least, was a man." Alexander calls on the guard to kill him, but there is no word of their refusal or of Alexander's hasty fear of a "conspiracy." Instead, he hurls a spear out through the tent and transfixes Cleitus before he reenters. Alexander's reaction is eloquent: "This has happened before. The wedding banquet. I've killed my father. . . . Parricide! I'm a parricide. I must die." In a most remarkable overlap, Rattigan (like Stone) has flashed back here to events associated with Philip in 337/36 B.C.E. For Stone, too, the "parallel story" here becomes the murder of Philip himself just after he had expressly told Alexander always to trust and value Cleitus. Rattigan, rather, links Cleitus's murder with Roxane's wedding in order to make the same link: two quarrels, with Cleitus and Philip, each at a wedding. For Stone, Philip's wedding had already been shown as a "parallel story," after Alexander's "necessary" killing of Parmenion. During that wedding his Alexander had indeed spoken in pride and acted in anger, and now we understand why in Stone's film he had spoken of these emotions so cryptically to Parmenion in Babylon. Nonetheless, like Rattigan, Stone superimposes Cleitus's death on Philip's. In the aftermath of Cleitus's murder, we see Stone's Philip spitting blood, just as when he himself was killed.

For Rattigan, there was no act 3—none of Stone's third hour in India with the parallel story of Olympias and her encounter with Alexander after Philip's killing, or her reappearance on the flickering surface of Alexander's final wine cup in Babylon. Instead, Rattigan shows us the king's and the army's baggage being burned to lighten the Indian march. His scene 5 is a neat, but most unusual, end point. Rattigan had found it in Plutarch, but he had picked up on its potential, I suggest, because he himself had taken part in a similar scene. In 1941 he had been in the gun crew of a heavy-laden bomber bound for West Africa that had put down when short of fuel. It had to be lightened of its baggage, and, like his Hephaestion in 1949, Rattigan was put in charge of the baggage destruction. He carried it out meticulously, down to the very frames of the men's photographs of their girlfriends. He made only one exception in his own favor, an exercise book filled with one of his plays-to-be.

Before the baggage burning, the Persian queen mother arrives for a last sympathetic interview. Alexander's orders for India are bold now to the point of folly, and he will "ride Bucephalas tomorrow—as if we were going into battle." But first he begs her, "Look at me, Mother. Am I so very changed?" No, the queen replies, there was never any turning back, at least not since the night before Gaugamela, when Alexander overrode her offer to walk to Darius and plead with him. The "devil" in Alexander would never have let him rest, unless "I had been your real mother, I could have killed him for you." The "devil," we infer, is the continued dynamic that swirls round Philip and was never quelled by Olympias, absent and still unnamed. The end "will be bitter," but Alexander insists, "I shall be remembered not for what I am but for what I do." A lifelong theme of Rattigan's drama returns here. "But, Alexander, what you do makes you what you are."

Once again, the insight comes from an older woman: first the Pythia, now the Persian queen. "The first conquest is yourself—only after that, the world." The queen blesses Alexander with a kiss, and then, chastened by her words, Alexander orders Hephaestion to burn his own baggage along with the men's. To Hephaestion's relief, the gold Persian throne must be included.

"But it didn't burn," the epilogue begins dramatically; "there is no way of burning a conquered throne." Alexander lies dying (of a "chill"), and he evades the question of who is to be his successor. He foresees the consequences: "Who shall I condemn to death?" The play might have ended with these words, but Rattigan somehow had to add, "Goodbye. The adventure is over and the adventurer would like to go to sleep."

Contrasting *Adventure Story* with *Alexander*

Rattigan once remarked that the film camera is the death of drama because it "excludes inference; and inference is drama." He went on, nonetheless, to write many film scripts for Hollywood, where perhaps he learned to revise his superficial view. Stone's *Alexander* has more threads than Rattigan's play, many of which indeed need to be inferred: cross-references in the script and images, movement, including dance, and facial expressions all help to convey them.

Rattigan's weaknesses are all too explicit: the style, the schoolboy tone, the army officer manner, and the immensely implausible themes of surrogate mothering and Alexander's aim to found a world-state. Most of them are weaknesses of his time: some derived from his English ambience and social class, others from scholarly books that appeared in 1947–48. How accurate did he intend to be? Even while writing, Rattigan was disinclined to claim the support of history. He wrote to a historically minded older friend, "I haven't really tried to create a fair and faithful portrait of the man. The play isn't meant to be a character-study of Alexander—I think that would be impossible anyway. . . . Instead of writing a play about Alexander the Great, I decided to write a play about a man called Alexander who gained the whole world and lost his soul. I realize perfectly that it is highly debatable whether the real Alexander did indeed lose his soul, or even whether he had any soul to lose." However, he added, importantly, "But there is, I know you will admit, at least some evidence on my side." This admission undercuts his avowed aim.

I have pointed to a use of ancient sources in *Adventure Story* that is much wider than Plutarch's *Life*. Rattigan read the texts carefully and developed hints that caught his dramatist's eye: the result cannot simply be taken as a "play about a man called Alexander." Stone, also writing an "Alexander," would never claim that his film was only that. He was amply aware of the ancient sources' contradictions and the times where his own film contradicted them. His aim was to make a dramatic and watchable film, but it was also (I suspect like Rattigan's) to reach after the "essence" of the events of a known life. Necessarily, fiction was built into the enterprise: we have next to no idea of anything that Alexander ever said or that was said to him, and yet a film must have a script with dialogue. The aim was to present a sustainable interpretation related to a pattern of things that Alexander did. It was not just "a film about a man called Alexander." Where we do not know the truth, Stone aimed to ascribe drives and motives to characters that he (and we) could consider credible.

Rattigan sought credibility through three themes: the aim for world rule and the impossible strains it imposed on any aspirant; despotism and the hard choices that Persian conquest imposed on a Persian king's heir; and, at a deeper level, the dynamic of father and mother, accounting for Alexander's ambition and for the "demon" in him: this was visible in his acceptance of a surrogate father in Cleitus and a surrogate mother in the Persian queen. Rattigan avoided any scene in Macedon and any scene in battle. His Alexander, then, could float free of the very contexts that would most rapidly have exploded his theme of boyish gentleness. Personal glory, force and violence, the psychological effects of combat and killing—Rattigan shut them all out.

Like Rattigan, Stone began with a high admiration for the young Alexander, which traced back (like Rattigan's) to his own youth and reading. The antiheroic minimalism of many books published in the last thirty years was known to him, but it did not convince him, and it certainly did not attract his support as a film dramatist. The story, he felt, was more interesting, and more like many Greek myths: a young man who aimed too high and thus had so very far to fall. His film, therefore, gives space to values that Rattigan omits. The ideal of fame won by deeds of war, the ambivalent example of the ancient heroes, the brutalities of Macedonian life (whether at parties or at the execution of Philotas)—all these themes were part of Stone's much wider picture. It is natural for modern readers to ask, too, whether killings in combat always breed a taste for yet more combat and killings. Interestingly, Stone only touched on this theme (in the Indian battle), and despite his Vietnam experiences did not follow it through in any detail. His own personal experience of battle emerges, rather, in Ptolemy's unexpected summing up. When Ptolemy pulls back from his denial of the value of Alexander's "dream" (implicitly refuting Tarn), he praises Alexander instead as the "freest man" he ever knew because he was free from the fear of death. Alexander himself has already sounded this note in his pre-battle speech at Gaugamela ("Conquer your fear, and you will conquer death"). Surprisingly, this very quality was picked out by Curtius in his summing up: Alexander showed "a perpetual contempt for the fear of death" (Arrian merely praises Alexander's "obliteration of the fear of death in his men by his own fearlessness"). Stone's Ptolemy ends, then, with a theme that the ancients themselves emphasized. Even modern minimalists would be unwise to deny this quality in Alexander, but it is Stone the war veteran who has brought it back into prominence.

Beside the main action Stone runs two parallel dramas: a sexual one and a parental one. His treatment contrasts tellingly with Rattigan's. Rattigan was himself a homosexual, but in England of the 1940s and 1950s homosexuality was censored on stage and was still a criminal offense. Nobody attacked Rattigan's *Adventure Story* as queer: I have suggested, at most, a concealed allusion (those all-night vigils with Hephaestion), but Bagoas is totally absent from the drama. For Stone, sexual relations are a main theme. The young Alexander directs his gaze in Babylon to a eunuch, not a female harem, and when he marries, the bride Roxane resembles his mother in looks. Under stress he turns to the eunuch and then publicly embraces him after a sexual dance in which the eunuch has outdanced Roxane. Then Alexander loses his greatest love, Hephaestion, to Roxane's jealousy, which has become an even harsher force than his mother's dark fears and passions. In a rage he assaults her while the scene of his father assaulting his mother flashes back through his mind. *Adventure Story* neither risked nor imagined any of this dark parallel story.

What Rattigan does imagine is the parallel story of a father complex. A drama of a conqueror of the world who loses his soul does not require one: why, then, did Rattigan add this level to his play? His eye saw it in the sources, but it came home and made particular sense to him personally. His own father had humiliated his mother by a series of extramarital affairs, above all by one in Romania that cost him his diplomatic career and impoverished the family: Terence's schooling at Harrow had depended on his winning a scholarship. As a boy he lived with the resulting quarrels between his parents. Remarkably, his youth had many of the tensions that Stone ascribes to Alexander's. He grew to blame his own homosexuality on his father's evasions and distance from him: "He said he never gained his father's love," a later collaborator recalled, "and he was very self-analytical." His mother, by contrast, remained the support and guiding love of his life, his very own "Persian queen."

It is not gratuitous to read *Adventure Story* in this context, because Rattigan went straight on in the spring of 1949 to dramatize it directly. His next play was *Who Is Sylvia?*—a thinly disguised tragi-comedy about his own parents' troubled marriage, dedicated "to my father, with love, with gratitude and in apology." During rehearsals his father, aged seventy, fell terminally ill but not before he and Rattigan's mother could enjoy what had remained a sufficiently mild reworking of their lives.

Rattigan projected onto Alexander a dynamic that he himself could recognize. What of Stone's Alexander? The film is dedicated both to his mother and to the mother of its producer and coordinator, Moritz Borman. Stone's one published novel concerns the "night dreams" of a boy's tormented childhood. In interviews for *Alexander*, he spoke of his father's pessimism and the high standards and expectations set for him by his optimistic mother, a stern critic. Like Rattigan, he grew up aware of his parents' serial affairs and eventual split. "Men hate the gods," Philip the pessimist tells his young son at the end of a bleak lesson about the mythical heroes. Mothers, Alexander also learns, are the most dangerous people, like the snake that slips past him in the cave at Pella. But his mother, the optimist, wants only the best for him: it is she who urges him to seize the kingdom and secure it with the necessary killings. She loves him, just as she still loves Philip ("I never stopped"). Yet when her reaction to Philip's murder returns to Alexander's mind ten years later, his ambition is finally broken, and he announces to his army the return from India.

Behind both Rattigan's and Stone's psychodramas lie important aspects of their own experience: Stone emphasized the mother, with important balancing flashbacks to the father's teaching and approval. Rattigan emphasized the father and the effects of his insults, suppressing the real mother entirely (he never staged a scene in Macedon) and replacing her with a substitute, the mother of Alexander's royal opponent. Even in 1949 critics rubbished this psychodrama of "an Oedipus complex in the ruthless destroyer of Oedipus's own city Thebes," a "sexually neuter" Alexander. It was absurd to see him in the style of Freud, "weeping over his mother's knee." In 2004 Stone showed a weeping and agonized Alexander, in thrall to the pull of his mother, and was greeted with exactly the same criticisms. Rattigan's shrewdest critic remains the acute T. C. Worsley: "His play is not mature enough to satisfy those who have responded emotionally to the figure of Alexander, nor is it sufficiently crude to appeal to that large public who enjoy seeing history reduced to a sort of contemporary slip-slop." *Plus ça change . . .*

Anglo-American audiences were most resistant to the film's image of an Alexander under his mother's thumb, whereas audiences in Brazil, Spain, and Italy were much more empathetic, making the film a big box-office success in those countries. Historians will certainly question whether this element is defensible, not just in the absence of ancient evidence but also in the light of what they think about the stages of adolescence and maturity in ancient society, let alone the rough Macedonian world: surely Alexander was tougher and less hesitant when he was sixteen to eighteen? But after years of thinking about these problems, I must emphasize that we do not know what Alexander was really like. We know what he did: with Rattigan, can we then work back to what he was? We know how he was remembered, or sometimes wished to be seen. Rattigan's Alexander is implausible in language, character, dynamic, and aim because we can place him in a particular context of English social class and contemporary scholarship, not ancient Macedonian society. Stone's Alexander is much more varied, and he certainly cannot be reduced to a simple mother complex. Yet his Alexander, too, is often not my historian's Alexander. Can historians say for sure that their Alexander is the real one? We do not know, but we can look at Stone's remarkable film as a springboard to take us back to much of importance that we do know. We may reject parts of Stone's hero, but we need, in turn, to analyze and account for our Alexanders too.

Postscript and Bibliographic Notes

I am grateful to my godfather, Sir John Hogg, for first bringing Rattigan's play to my notice and to David Raeburn for reawakening my interest in it, lending me his copy, and sharing his own memories of its performance in 1949. Details of Rattigan's life leading up to the first night are discussed in Michael Darlow, *Terence Rattigan: The Man and His Work* (repr., 2000), 229–43, and in further detail by Geoffrey Wansell, *Terence Rattigan* (1995), the biography that has helped me most. Charles Duff's *The Lost Summer: The Heyday of the West End Theatre* (1995) is an excellent account of Rattigan and his West End contemporaries, with valuable personal material from the director Frith Banbury. On BBC Radio in 1976, I was fortunate to hear the distinguished reviewer Anthony Curtis quote from a letter by the dramatist David Rudkin that Darlow also quotes on his page 12: "I detect in [Rattigan's] plays a deep personal, surely sexual pain, which he manages at the same time to express and disguise. The craftsmanship of which we hear so much loose talk seems to me to arise from deep psychological necessity, a drive to organize the energy that arises out of his own pain."

That observation is relevant, too, to the Alexander dramas I discuss. The two of them are also an interesting warning against assumptions of "intertextuality" by scholars where none, in fact, exists.

I quote also from *"Chips": The Diaries of Sir Henry Channon,* edited by Robert Rhodes James (repr., 1996), 433. The details about Richard Burton are from Wansell, *Terence Rattigan,* 185–86. Kenneth Tynan's criticisms are reprinted in his *Curtains . . .* (1961), 74. The attacks from the Royal Court's clique on the contemporary West End, including Rattigan, are well described by Duff, *The Lost Summer,* 191–97.

On matters that concern Alexander and his historians, the visit to Delphi was discussed by W. W. Tarn, *Alexander the Great,* vol. 2 (1948), 338–46, and reopened by François Lefèvre, "Alexandre et l'Amphictionie en 336/5," *Bulletin de Correspondance Hellénique* 126 (2002): 73–81, especially 78–79 on the historicity of Alexander's gift ("reste à démontrer") and his visit to the oracle ("on n'écartera pas définitivement"); and Patrick Marchetti, "En relisant les comptes de Delphes autour de l'archonte Palaios," ibid., 59–72. His reported dealings with the Amphictiony are reassessed by Pierre Sanchez, *l'Amphictionie des Pyles et de Delphes* (2001), 245–58.

J. P. V. D. Balsdon, "The 'Divinity' of Alexander," *Historia* 1 (1950): 363–88, discusses the main relevant passages from Aristotle. So does Victor Ehrenberg, "Aristotle and Alexander's Empire," in his *Alexander and the Greeks* (1938), 62–102, at 69–70, but less persuasively. I quote from Werner Jaeger, *Aristotle: Fundamentals of the History of His Development* (2nd ed., 1948), 121–23. W. W. Tarn, *Alexander the Great,* vol. 1 (1948), 146, claimed that Alexander "found the Ideal State of Aristotle, and substituted the Ideal State of Zeno." S. M. Stern, *Aristotle on the World State* (1968), was too optimistic about a Hellenistic fiction. On page

6, lines 22–23, he emended the Arabic text *ahl faranja* ("people of the Franks," i.e., Gauls) into *ahl farija* ("people of the Phrygians") and tried to relate it to the supposed early links of Macedonians and Phrygians. But line 22 also names "Atalūs," the decisive point. The author is alluding to Attalus of Pergamon and the Gauls and therefore he is himself a Hellenistic writer, not the real "Aristotle" at all.

The Titans in Orphic texts are discussed by M. L. West, *The Orphic Poems* (1983), 164–66. Olympias's dedication in Athens is in Hyp. *For Euxenippus* 19; see David Whitehead, *Hypereides: The Forensic Speeches* (2000), 215–16. Ernst Badian's "Alexander and the Loneliness of Power" was reprinted in his *Studies in Greek and Roman History* (1964), without mentioning Rattigan.

The panic in the Persian army in mid–September 331 B.C.E. is discussed by Paul Bernard, "Nouvelle contribution de l'épigraphie cunéiforme à l'histoire hellénistique," *Bulletin de Correspondance Hellénique* 114 (1990): 513–41, at 516–18. I have discussed Alexander's Persian customs thoroughly in "Alexander the Great: The Last Achaemenid?" in *Persian Responses*, ed. Christopher Tuplin (2007), 267–312.

Rattigan's remarkable scene between Alexander and Philotas draws on Curtius, especially 6.7.8 (Alexander's initial weeping), 6.8.32 (the preliminary hearing between the two), 6.8.1 (the "Council"), 6.10.3 (Alexander's absence from the Assembly), 6.11.4 (the "Council" again). Rattigan weaves his drama cleverly around these pieces.

The dagger and the scroll of Homer under the pillow (found by Rosario Dawson in the film) are from Onesicritus, cited in Plutarch's *Life: Alex.* 8.2. Roxane-Rosario's dance at a drinking party is in *Alex.* 47.7. Bagoas's dance is at 67.7, with Dicaearchus, ap. Athenaeus 13.603 A-8. The comment that Alexander was "madly keen on boys" (*ekmanōs philopais*) is that of Athenaeus and his speaker in the third century C.E. and is merely illustrated by the anecdote from the Peripatetic Dicaearchus (ca. 300 B.C.E.).

Rattigan's own experience baggage-burning is described by Darlow, *Terence Rattigan*, 147–48. Alexander's is in Plut. *Alex.* 57.1–2, and misplaced in Curt. 6.6.15 so as to accentuate his theme of the soldiery's resistance to luxury. Rattigan's remark about "a play about a man called Alexander" occurs in an interesting letter of 1948 to E. V. C. Plumtre, a distinguished classics master at Rattigan's old school, Harrow. His comment about "the camera as enemy of the screenwriter's art" dates to 1949, in a short article for the anthology *Diversion*, published before his own prolonged dealings with Hollywood began.

Rattigan's relationship to his father is best documented by Wansell, *Terence Rattigan*, especially 42–43, 92–93, 107–9, 140–41, 149–50, 194, 199–215, 293–94, 325–26, 370–71, 383–84. His second (unperformed) version of *Adventure Story* in 1954 laid much more emphasis on Alexander's problematic relationship with Philip: "All my life I hated you so much that now, at the last, I have become you [Philip]," Alexander says at the end of act 2. The emergence of the Persian queen as a surrogate mother is picked up in a florid work by Princess Marthe Bibesco, *Alexander of Asia,* translated (in 1935) by Enid Bagnold: "The mother of Darius called him by no other name than 'son' and 'beloved son'" (17). I wonder if this text might have lingered in Rattigan's mind. He knew Bagnold, eventually a fellow playwright, and she might have given it to him, as later she gave it to me. The acute T. C. Worsley's comments about Alexander were published in the *New Statesman* in 1949; Wansell, *Terence Rattigan,* 192, summarizes them. Curt. 10.5.29 already remarked, like Stone's Ptolemy, on Alexander's "contempt for the fear of death."

Oliver Stone's novel *A Child's Night Dream* was published in the United States in 1997. He has alluded to his parents' differing natures in various interviews: see *Ciné Live,* no. 86 (January 2005): 38.

I am particularly grateful to Oliver Stone, Moritz Borman, and Thomas Schühly for allowing me to participate in *Alexander* with such good humor throughout.

The Appearance of History

Robert Rossen's Alexander the Great

KIM SHAHABUDIN

HERE ARE TWO sides to Alexander's story—the history (what he achieved) and the myth (what he became). The two are fatally linked, with the incredible feats found in the former driving the embellishments and inventions found in the latter. This awkward mix makes biographical treatments of Alexander especially difficult to achieve and may have contributed to the scarcity of dramatic retellings of his life, in the theater and also on the screen. Until the recent flurry of interest that culminated in Oliver Stone's *Alexander* (2004), there had been only three serious attempts to film his story in English. Two of these attempts were unsuccessful: a film version of Terence Rattigan's play *Adventure Story* got no further than the casting, while a proposed television series with William Shatner remained unsold (the pilot episode was screened in 1968).[1] Only one film prior to *Alexander* achieved a theatrical release: *Alexander the Great* (1956), produced, written, and directed by Robert Rossen and starring Richard Burton as the Macedonian king.

Rossen takes a biographical approach to Alexander's story, selecting and arranging his material to present a personal interpretation of his hero's character and psychological development. A summary of the film's plot and characters will be useful before looking more closely at Rossen's work. Its narrative begins before Alexander's birth, with the orators Demosthenes (Michael Hordern) and Aeschines (William Squires) debating the Athenian response to the conquests in Greece of his father, Philip. Receiving the news while on campaign that Olympias (Danielle Darrieux) has borne a son, Philip (Frederic March) is somewhat skeptical. However, he is persuaded to accept the child, whom we next see as a young man at Mieza under the tutelage of Aristotle (Barry Jones), surrounded by the Companions who will remain with him until his death. In a series of meetings, Alexander and his father are shown to be in conflict over two issues: Philip's estrangement from Olympias (putting into question her son's legitimacy) and what Alexander sees as his father's jealous hoarding of glory. Nevertheless, Philip invests some power in his son, and following the defeat of Athens at Chaeronea, Alexander visits the city to negotiate terms. There he meets Barsine (Claire Bloom), the half-Persian wife of the Athenian general Memnon (Peter Cushing), who will later become his mistress.

Following Philip's murder by the Companion Pausanias (Peter Wyngarde), Alexander is acclaimed as king by the Macedonian army and embarks on his father's plan to conquer Persia. Memnon has joined forces with the Persian king Darius (Harry Andrews), but his advice to take Alexander seriously is ignored, and during the defeat of the Persian army at Granicus the Athenian general is killed. Alexander continues to advance through Persia, on his way solving the problem of the Gordian knot, and is reunited with Barsine at Miletus, where she criticizes his brutish style of command. Alexander refigures his mission as a kind of holy war against Asia, freeing all captives and sending home those who do not wish to follow him. In the successful battle against the Persian forces that follows, Darius flees and is eventually murdered by his own nobles, leaving a letter asking Alexander to marry his daughter Roxane (Teresa del Rio) and unite Persia and Greece. However, with this second father-figure dead, Alexander begins to overreach. At Susa, he halts the Macedonian destruction of Darius's palace and declares his intention to conquer to the ends of the earth. The armies reach as far as India, but unrest grows among the Macedonians; Alexander's Companion Philotas (Ruben Rojo) and his father Parmenio (Niall McGinnis) are both put to death for treason. Finally a drunken Alexander quarrels with and kills his friend Cleitus (Gustave Rojo). Realizing that his dream has turned sour, he orders a retreat, and at Susa a mass wedding takes place between Persian brides and Greek grooms, including Alexander and Roxane. At the wedding feast, though, Alexander falls ill and dies, telling Barsine to have his body cast into the Euphrates and leaving his empire "to the strongest."

Rossen's film gives us, on the one hand, the military and political conquests of the soldier-king and, on the other, the romantic heroizing of the man. In any retelling of Alexander's story, but especially in those which attempt a biographical narrative, the balance between these two elements is key. Popular fiction writers, including Mary Renault, have approached the problem by creating domestic narratives that focus on the latter aspect, the man and his myth. However, the scale of epic film-making dictates a similar grandeur in narrative and scope, putting the emphasis on the effect of the individual on the canvas of history. The best epic films are perhaps those which make explicit their balance between history and myth: Anthony Mann's *El Cid* (1961), for instance, or David Lean's *Lawrence of Arabia* (1962); among films set in the ancient world, there is Stanley Kubrick's *Spartacus* (1960), cited by Oliver Stone as a model for his *Alexander*.[2] In films like *JFK* (1991) and *Nixon* (1995), Stone has often sought to discuss the ways in which (even recent) history may shade into myth: *Alexander* also demonstrates this concern. The following discussion considers the uses of history and myth in Robert Rossen's *Alexander the Great*, and how these may have contributed to the film's problems with both critics and popular audiences.

An Honorable Failure

On its release in 1956, *Alexander the Great* was given the grand Hollywood treatment, with a reputed one million dollars spent on promotion in the United States alone. The trade publication *Motion Picture Herald* (April 14, 1956) lists some of the highlights of this campaign: an unprecedented thirteen-page publicity spread in *Life* magazine; a tour by "Dave Ballard, the seven-foot five-inch 'Alexander' giant"; floats and parades featuring "Macedonian maidens," "spear-carrying warriors," racing chariots, and elephants (real and mechanical); 300 radio spots and multiple double-page newspaper advertisements. Merchandising link-ins included a Dell Comics adaptation, fashions and jewelry inspired by the film, and promotions by American Airlines; in a neat combination of film promotion and merchandising, six models toured Broadway wearing Wat-A-Kote rainwear decorated with the legend, "Snow or rain, I'm going to see 'Alexander' at the Capitol Theater."

The massive publicity reaped rewards initially, with record box-office takings and holdovers in all the major U.S. cities. Many reviews in the popular and trade press were enthusiastic, with the *New York Times* (March 31, 1956) describing it as "eye filling and spectacular" and *Variety* (April 4, 1956) declaring it likely to "reap handsome box-office spoils." A more cautious note was sounded by *Motion Picture Herald* (March 31, 1956), which warned that "mixed critical reaction may be anticipated." This prophecy was duly borne out by more negative reviews such as that in the British *Monthly Film Bulletin* (May 1956), which condemned the film's "unimaginative" scripting and "generally pedestrian style and approach." Audience figures tailed off rapidly after the initial publicity-led surge, and in 1962 a retrospective of Rossen's work named the film "one of his least successful."[3]

Alexander the Great's box-office problems seem likely to have been partly caused by a mismatch between the film itself and the kind of expectations promoted in its audiences by United Artists' publicity campaign. Released at the height of popularity for Hollywood historical epics set in the ancient world, the brash glamour of the studio's publicity "ballyhoo," with its maidens and warriors, elephants and giants (neither of the latter appeared in the final film), directed viewers to anticipate a spectacular extravaganza taking its cue from cinematic visions of antiquity like *Samson and Delilah* (1948), *Quo Vadis* (1951), and *The Robe* (1953), the last of which also starred Richard Burton. Such hopes were doomed to disappointment. Rossen's vision lacks three major ingredients of this type of commercially successful historical epic: first (and perhaps fatally) its spectacle; second its humor; and third what Derek Elley has described as its "calculated vulgarity."[4] The latter two are essential to defuse the pomposity of epic film's grand ambition. Here visual style, dialogue, and musical score are all typified by an air of portentous seriousness. The popular cinemagoer who hopes to find trivial pleasures is swiftly disabused.

This denial of pleasure was a significant problem for a hugely expensive historical epic film. One particular reason for the popularity of the ancient world in Hollywood cinema after 1930 was its ability to justify spectacular and luxurious visions of excess, eroticism, and violence that were otherwise excluded by the moral strictures of the Production Code.[5] Such highly pleasurable images guaranteed box-office takings, thus recouping expensive production costs. The films also produced pleasure in their audiences in other ways. Psychoanalytic theories of film viewing have proposed that viewers identify with the characters and situations onscreen, "putting themselves in the picture." This is especially true with epic films, where our senses are bombarded with

stereophonic sound and widescreen Technicolor images; we are literally engulfed by the cinematic experience.[6] Other critics have argued
that using antiquity as a setting for epic films allowed the Hollywood
studios to demonstrate their own potency in recreating chronologically
and culturally distant worlds. In this schema the viewer gains pleasure
from the control demonstrated by man, even over history itself.[7]

In *Alexander the Great*, in contrast, decoration and beauty are down-
played, distancing strategies deny the viewer the opportunity to identify with characters, and rather than man demonstrating his control
over history, history is allowed to control the film. Many of the features
one would expect to find in epics as sites of spectacle are included:
dancing girls, a single combat scene, battles, royal palaces. Yet in each
instance an austere denial of pleasure attaches to the scene. A party sequence in the earlier epic *Quo Vadis* illustrates the more conventional
style. Dancing girls are placed in the foreground of the frame, dominating the screen; their movements are followed both by the camera and
by the eyes of the emperor Nero and his party guests. They are presented to on- and offscreen audiences as a voyeuristic spectacle to be
enjoyed, with the former offering comments on their beauty as a cue to
the latter. In *Alexander the Great*, dancing girls appear at Philip's marriage to Eurydice. However, they are present only briefly as part of a
larger crowd at the party, and rather than taking center stage are often
obscured by other cast members. Not only do they go entirely unre-
marked by their onscreen audience; they are even physically brushed
aside, pointing to their role as a trivial distraction from the serious business of the narrative rather than an opportunity for visual delight. A
similar approach marks the single combat scene, which plays out rather
as a conflict of ideals between the noncombatants Alexander and Cleitus. The camera skips briskly over the violence of the combat itself,
and its loser's death is incidental to Alexander's murder of his friend,
which follows. This puritanical outlook extends also to the overall color
scheme of the film. Despite having the advantage of Technicolor, the
color palette of both set and costume designs is muted, using mostly
blues, browns, and yellows rather than the extravagant pinks, greens,
and reds of earlier films. Even the weather is subdued, with the skies
cloudy rather than a clear Technicolor blue.

If there is little for the eye to enjoy, there is even less chance of
finding a character to identify with. Possible candidates are swiftly
discounted: Philip is a drunk and an adulterer; Olympias conspires
against her husband to gain power; the cuckolded Memnon becomes a

mercenary; Eurydice is colorless, and Barsine a high-minded prig. We are not even permitted to empathize with the hero, Alexander himself. From his first mention in the script to his deathbed scene, the legend of his divine parentage is foregrounded, keeping the film audience at a mortal distance. The effect of these distancing characterizations is to induce the viewers, not to passively empathize, but to actively criticize; to become aloof and disinterested, stern judges rather than human beings with similar feelings and dilemmas. This is cinemagoing as duty, not pleasure.

While earlier epic films had exploited the vagueness of popular historical knowledge to recreate history as Hollywood might wish it to have occurred, Rossen insists on a more authentic vision. Battle scenes are staged in settings that replicate those described in the historical sources: cramped locations such as river crossings and mountain passes that restrict the scope of their cinematic impact; they are characterized by a pervasive atmosphere of chaos and confusion. While this may better evoke the historical reality of ancient warfare, it does not translate well to popular cinema. The disarray was sometimes ascribed to ineptness rather than intention, with one reviewer complaining that "the battle scenes are so carelessly shot and edited it is not always possible to know who is killing who."[8] For comparison, *Quo Vadis* contrasts sharply with this approach, with the tight choreography of the cinematic Roman army epitomizing the control, power, and grandeur that fueled audience enthusiasm for historical epics.[9]

Rossen's subverted use of the conventions already well established for the historical epic genre resulted in the production of an odd hybrid, an expensive epic film that snubbed spectacle—the very thing expected by both audiences and (hopeful of recouping its costs) the studio. Having failed in terms of this commercial imperative, the director might still have hoped for critical praise. However, this was no more forthcoming. The judgment of critic Andrew Sarris, for instance, in *Film Culture* (April 1956), was that "Rossen has aimed for greatness . . . and has missed honourably." The problem may lie in a misapprehension about how audiences interpret films. Through various cinematic cues the director's preferred reading of the film is presented as an earnest attempt to retell history through cinema. There seems to be a tacit assumption that the seriousness of this approach will validate the film as qualitatively superior next to the trivial fictionality of previous historical epics. However, the cool audience reception suggests that a film's achievements are more often measured by its success in cinematic genre terms, and that in the epic film genre selected for this retelling, "greatness" and "seriousness" are not equivalent.

Historical epic films that have been critically acclaimed, like *El Cid*, *Spartacus*, and, more recently, *Gladiator* (2000), are not primarily interested in high cultural concerns about historical authenticity. Rather, they openly acknowledge the popular cultural incarnations of their historical characters, and especially the processes by which they become mythicized as heroes. Using the popular medium of film, they show how earlier popular transmissions of narrative (oral storytelling, popular fiction, visual culture) have enabled the mythmaking through which those traditionally excluded from high culture may find ways to "own" heroic figures, independent of elitist and exclusive written history. Thus great epic cinema operates simultaneously on two levels: it interrogates old myths, and it makes new ones.

In fact (as I shall show), despite its apparent commitment to history, myth has a strong presence in *Alexander the Great*. However, the film's "serious" historiographic agenda disallows the usual strategies of epic films that use popular storytellers within the narrative to openly differentiate between mythic and historical modes; rather than being an object of enquiry, myth is enmeshed in the historical framework. Thus the film misses its ambitious goals in all three fields: as historiography, as an epic film, and as a commercial product. Nevertheless, it is an honorable failure, having at least tried to use antiquity as more than just a vehicle for commercial profit, as a closer examination of its narrative will demonstrate.

Narrative Themes

The narrative agenda of the film is dictated by Rossen's desire to explain Alexander's motives for his unprecedented campaign of expansion. This is especially evident in his examination of the rivalry between Alexander and his father. Rossen confirmed this as his main narrative theme in an interview, claiming that the film had failed because cuts forced on him by the studio abridged its explanatory force.[10] In fact, it is illustrated in such a variety of ways that the importance of the issue is almost overdetermined. Power conflicts between Philip and Alexander are foregrounded from early in the narrative. At Mieza, the young Alexander is shown to be jealous of Philip's exploits on the battlefield, which he longs to emulate. When Cleitus returns from the campaign without instructions to return with the prince, Alexander's frustration is made clear. However, when his father does give him power of regency, he disobeys his orders, sacks a rebelling city, and orders it to be rebuilt under the name Alexandropolis. The rivalry between the two becomes more pronounced when Alexander saves Philip's life at Chaeronea. On the one hand, the son's ambitions for the throne are overtaken by protectiveness for his father; on the other, by taking the role of protector, he usurps his father's position in the familial hierarchy.

More retro-psychoanalysis is found in the interactions between Alexander and Philip and two women: Olympias and her rival, Eurydice. Though Alexander's relationship with his mother does not display the same erotic undertones seen in Stone's film, certainly the bond between them is presented as a threat to Philip. Olympias flirts with young men of a similar age to her son, in scenes that situate such potential erotic activity as perverse and indicative of her amoral nature: for instance, when she is discovered throwing a decadent party in the palace while disorder rages outside in Pella, or when she plies Pausanias with drink and implants in him the idea of assassinating Philip. Thus Alexander's closeness to his mother is figured not as a healthy mother-son relationship, but as a power-driven attachment to a perverse and dangerous female. Philip's relationship with the young Eurydice, on the other hand, is presented as "normal" despite the age gap and (in modern terms) its adulterous status: it is a love match, designed to produce legitimate children. Alexander's scenes with Eurydice see him rebuffed because of her sincere love for Philip; in both cases, the son threatens the father's erotic partnerships.

In a more pragmatic sense, paternity is significant also for Alexander's political ambition to succeed Philip as king. From the first news of Alexander's birth, suspicions about his paternity are raised. Parmenio persuades Philip not to kill the Egyptian priest present when he returns to Pella, but their discussion makes it clear that Philip believes the priest to be the boy's father. Olympias muddies the waters by declaring the child a "little god." Stories of mortal women made pregnant by visitations from the gods in various forms are rife in Greek myth: Philip himself claimed to be a descendant of Heracles, fathered by Zeus on the mortal Alcmene. However, the cachet of divine parentage might be somewhat offset by the stigma of illegitimacy that accompanied it. In the film, Macedonian court politics are seen to take advantage of this dishonorable status when Attalus celebrates his niece Eurydice's marriage to Philip by invoking the hope for "a legitimate heir."

The narrative placing of Philip's death and Alexander's accession at the exact halfway point of the film structurally indicates the significance of this father-son theme. However, the rivalry does not cease with

Philip's death: as Olympias points out to Pausanias, the way to achieve fame is to kill someone famous. Alexander must metaphorically "kill" his father, first by conquering Persia and thus surpassing Philip's achievements, and then by defeating the Persian king Darius, drawn as a Philip-substitute. This latter pseudo-parental relationship is especially conveyed in the sequence showing the exchange of letters between the two kings, drawn from the mythicizing *Alexander Romance*. Darius tells Alexander to "go back to the bosom of your mother Olympias," calls him an "impudent and shameless boy," and sends him "a whip, a ball, and a bag of gold" so that he may "play with boys of your own age." After this, Alexander's pursuit of Darius becomes obsessive and personally motivated. When the Great King's corpse is discovered, his dying letter addresses Alexander as "my son" and urges a formalization of this relationship in the Macedonian's marriage to his daughter Roxane.

After Darius's death there is a return to a related theme first introduced at the very start of Alexander's story: that of divinity. Chided for his compulsion to outdo his father, he displays an anachronistic monotheism, telling Barsine, "I am not Philip's son. I am the son of god." In the next scene, Aeschines tells the Athenians that Alexander has asked them to proclaim him a god—"son of Zeus Ammon." Ammon was an Egyptian deity, though identified by the Greeks with Zeus. The historical Alexander's conquest of Egypt (not shown in the film) resulted in his acclamation as pharaonic god-king—"son of Ammon"— on his visit to the oracle at Siwa (also omitted from the film). However, the references to Ammon, taken in conjunction with the presence of the Egyptian priest at the start of the film, point to a particular source for this story: the *Alexander Romance*, which also provided the story of Darius's letter.[11] In this mythicizing (and often fantastic) narrative, Nectanebos, the last Egyptian pharaoh, is forced to flee his own land. Arriving in Macedon in Philip's absence, he disguises himself as a priest and seduces Olympias by a combination of magic and trickery, telling her that the god Ammon will appear to her "with golden hair" (1.1–7).[12] The seduction results in the conception of Alexander. In the film, this narrative is played out both verbally and visually. Philip's suspicions of the Egyptian priest have already been mentioned, as have the intimations of Alexander's illegitimacy. Olympias's description of the baby as a "little god" is a response to Philip's "Little lion!" The two sets of imagery, god and lion, meet in the demigod Heracles, who is identified with Alexander on the coin that appears in the opening frame of the film. Alexander's physical appearance in the film also appeals to these leonine and divine associations, with gold-toned makeup and a brushed-back mane of tawny hair—like the "golden hair" of the god Ammon prophesied to Olympias.

Rather than using the mythmaking transmissions of folk narrative, Rossen shows stories of the king's divinity being disseminated by Alexander himself. Rulers of the ancient world who believed themselves to be gods were a familiar theme in the cinema of the time: Nero in *Quo Vadis* and Caligula in *Demetrius and the Gladiators* (1954), among others. In these Roman films, the belief is a sign of the insanity induced by the acquisition of power, a warning from antiquity that appealed directly to the postfascism, Cold War audience. Here, however, Aristotle warns Philip that the boy "believes himself to be a god" long before he is able to exercise power, suggesting that it is the reason for his unprecedented conquests rather than a consequence of them. In another significant scene for this theme, Alexander declares the mission against Persia to be "a holy war." However, his death scene finds him accepting "man's fate" of mortality, and asking Barsine to cast his body into the Euphrates, so that "it will disappear, and men will believe that from the gods I came, and to the gods I returned." This final scene has the king complicit in his own mythopoesis. Has Alexander always doubted his own divinity, or is this a new realization? The narrative leaves this question unanswered.

The character of Barsine literally embodies the third major narrative theme of the film: the unity of Greece and Asia. Barsine tells Alexander when they first meet in Athens that she is "half-Persian, half-Greek." Alexander comes to realize that just as Barsine combines Greek and Persian, so must his empire; and just as victory is achieved in the personal sphere by winning Barsine's heart rather than treating her as a captive, so in the public sphere he must win the hearts of men to rule rather than physically conquering them like his father. This revolutionary approach to imperial governance explains the inclusion of the story of the Gordian knot despite the omission of other, perhaps more cinematic, episodes from Alexander's life (for instance, the taming of Bucephalus, his visit to Achilles' tomb). In this sequence, Alexander is told that it has been prophesied that he who succeeds in untangling the knot will become "ruler of Asia." He slashes the knot with his sword, foretelling his military success and cinematically schematizing himself as an original political thinker.

The theme is further enacted in Darius's deathbed letter, which asks Alexander to marry his daughter Roxane, so that "the seed of Darius and Philip may be mingled in her, and our worlds may become as one." This marriage is (unhistorically) included in the mass wedding between Persian brides and Greek grooms at Susa that takes place at the end of the film, just preceding Alexander's death. By using Barsine and Roxane to carry this theme of East/West unity, feminine virtues of cooperation are lauded above masculine competitiveness. While Stone's Alexander relates his ambitions for unity to his beloved Hephaestion (thus reworking the theme to incorporate inclusive sexuality), Rossen's Alexander lacks support from his male Companions. Cleitus embodies the masculine competitive attitude when he enacts the issue as a combat for Alexander's entertainment: "a contest . . . between a Macedonian and a Persian." The contest ends in the defeat of the Macedonian, symbolic of the old order, and is followed by the death of Cleitus at Alexander's hands, which marks the end of Alexander's personal journey and the beginning of the Macedonians' journey home.

The narrative theme of Alexander and the unity of mankind was almost certainly inspired by the writings of the historian Sir William Tarn. In 1933 Tarn gave a paper at the British Academy that argued just this: that the Macedonian king had originated the idea that "all mankind was one and all men were brothers."[13] He restated this view in his 1948 two-volume history of Alexander, likely to have been among the "modern histories" cited in the film's British pressbook as consulted by Rossen during "three years' research" for the film.[14] Tarn's extended discussion of this theory in the second volume of his work was headed "Brotherhood and Unity"; its influence on Rossen's script may be discerned in Alexander's cries of "Cleitus, brother!" both before and after the Companion's murder. Published shortly after the Second World War, Tarn's theory must have been attractive to a world that craved peace.[15] Rossen had his own reasons for using his biography of Alexander to deliver a message of cooperation, and it is to Rossen's own biography that we turn next.

Rossen, HUAC, and Alexander

In 1951, against the background of the Korean War and the start of McCarthyite paranoia, Robert Rossen was among the Hollywood figures subpoenaed to appear before the House Un-American Activities Committee (HUAC). He testified to the committee that he was not presently a member of the Communist Party but refused to discuss his past activities or to confirm any other names put to him. As a result, he found himself blacklisted and for the next two years was unable to find work in Hollywood. In 1953 Rossen returned to the committee, and this time testified that he had been a Communist Party member from 1937 until 1947, but now opposed the party and its aims. He also confirmed fifty-seven names of film industry figures with Communist sympathies or affiliations.[16] This recantation allowed him to resume work in the U.S. film industry, though the fact that he never again visited Hollywood indicates his feelings. It was during the two years of enforced inactivity preceding his recantation that he began to develop his script for *Alexander the Great*.

Like Oliver Stone, Rossen was both director and scriptwriter for his Alexander film. He also produced the film and did his own research, giving him an unusual degree of personal involvement in the project. Based on his previous record, Rossen would have been an unlikely choice to direct a historical epic. He began his career with Warner Bros. studios as a scriptwriter of social problem films, and his early (and critically acclaimed) films as director focused on the American drive for success at any cost, and the corruption that inevitably accompanied that success. For instance, *Body and Soul* (1947) follows a young man who escapes the slums through his talent for boxing. Along with his success comes the erosion of moral values and personal relationships, though he is finally redeemed by his rejection of the corrupt system. *All the King's Men* (1949) featured an idealistic political activist who rises from the rural working classes to become governor but then cynically exploits his former peers to maintain his position.

This latter film was especially praised by critics, receiving many awards, including the Academy Award for best film. However, Rossen had no background in making films with a historical setting, or experience with the logistics involved in creating a spectacular epic. In addition, all his earlier (and subsequent) films were adapted from books. Nevertheless, Alan Casty argues that *Alexander the Great*, as an account of the personal motivations and character development of a young man whose world is changed by the acquisition of great power, continues Rossen's earlier concerns.[17] His prior films were distinctively American in their narrative themes (success in politics and sport, corruption and graft in public life). By setting the same concern about corrupted idealism in the ancient world, Rossen seems to be at the same time universalizing the issues and consciously distancing himself from the kind of "Americanism" that had inspired the HUAC hearings. Nevertheless, in his testimony to the committee Rossen professed a passionate belief in

America as "a growing society." Set against the backdrop of his enforced radical reassessment of political ideals during the time the film was being developed, Rossen's account of Alexander's life and its relevance to America's capacity to grow may be read as a plea for a more tolerant and inclusive society, with governance directed by cooperation and not warfare.

An examination of the film's casting demonstrates this agenda. Casting choices in films set in the ancient world (as in other cinematic subgenres) were subject to certain conventions and audience expectations. Many of the leading roles in *Alexander the Great* were played by actors who had previously played in films with a similar historical setting: Richard Burton (*The Robe*), Frederic March (*Sign of the Cross* [1932]), Barry Jones (*Demetrius and the Gladiators*), Niall McGinnis, Stanley Baker, and Harry Andrews (*Helen of Troy* [1956]). Their appearance would have reassured cinema audiences that the film was set in an "authentic" version of the cinematic ancient world: a more relevant concern for the average cinemagoer than historical accuracy. British actors were popular choices for major supporting roles in these films, their accents being seen as specially suited to the "highbrow culture" associated with the ancient world. However, the hero was usually played by an American, with the villain's part falling to a British actor. This appealed to the common Hollywood subtext of America as New World proving its supremacy over the old, corrupt world of the British empire.[18]

The main casting in *Alexander the Great* subverts this conventional schema. The absence of American voices in major speaking parts is striking; their only representative is Frederic March as Philip. In the narrative, Philip signifies the old way of conquest by might, which Alexander has to learn is unsuited to the rule of a vast empire, being less durable than "the conquering of men's hearts." However, it is Alexander who is seduced by the possession of power, even (perhaps) into believing that he is divine, the son of the god Zeus. His crisis of idealism matches Rossen's own in his experiences with Communism. Rossen's recantation in 1953 cited "the bankruptcy of Communist Party thinking." He added that "the same reasons you go into the party are the same reasons which make you go out, which is ultimately the discovery that the idealism that you were looking for, the fighting for the ideas that you want, are just not in the Communist Party."[19] Reading the narrative through the filter of Rossen's political experience, Casty concludes that the film should be read as "Rossen's comment on the failure of contemporary political ideals to fulfill their aims as they become

twisted by the corruptions of power and the weakness of men."[20] However, this judgment might equally fit his earlier American films. It is certainly reasonable to see the film as condemning equally the failure of
Communism and the bullyboy tactics of HUAC. But it also offers a hint
of optimism—the capacity of a growing society to recognize, as Alexander does, that the unity of mankind cannot be achieved by might, but
only by winning the hearts of men.

History and Myth

The political and moral messages in Rossen's account of Alexander's
life also dictate the material he selects for his narrative. What we know
about the life of Alexander is a colorful mixture of history and myth.
The major extant written sources are all second-hand: the military
historian Arrian, who draws from Ptolemy and Aristobulus, both of
whom traveled with the king; the biographer Plutarch, who uses the
same sources but also claims to have had access to Alexander's correspondence; and the writers grouped together as the "vulgate tradition"
(Diodorus of Sicily, Quintus Curtius Rufus, Pompeius Trogus), who follow Cleitarchus, also thought to have been present for at least part of
the journey. These writings claim some authority via their foundation
in eyewitness accounts.[21]

However, during the Wars of the Successors that followed Alexander's death and failure to name an heir, various dubious stories, events,
and documents appeared: for instance, Alexander's "Will" and "Last
Plans"; the rescue of his diadem by Seleucus; and the mysterious appearance of a previously unknown "heir" fathered on Barsine. Each
fortuitously supported the entitlement of one or another claimant to
power. The most fantastic embellishments to Alexander's biography
found their home in the *Alexander Romance,* which is thought to have
first appeared less than a century after the king's death. Any new retelling of Alexander's story must start by making a critical selection from
the complex tangle of source material, and both Rossen and Stone comment on this confusion of myth and history. In the preface to Robin
Lane Fox's 2004 book on the making of the film, Stone notes the continuing transmission of many of the more fantastic stories: "Thus the myths
grow, apart from the truth and yet with a kernel of truth to them." Rossen, too, admits to difficulties; he is quoted in the British pressbook as
saying, "For centuries, myth and fact have been intricately confused,"
describing the sources as a "maze of often contradictory statements."[22]

Given this agreement on the problem, it is interesting to compare the approaches taken by the two filmmakers.

In fairness to both, it should be noted that while historians are bound by standards of evidence when selecting material, the first concern of a commercial filmmaker is rather the demands of the dramatic narrative. The manifold incidents and events in the biographical legacy of Alexander would make an unwieldy (and expensive) cinematic narrative if simply presented in succession. Selections must be made for the sake of both dramatic impact and narrative economy. Both Rossen and Stone select the incidents from Alexander's life that best convey their interpretation of his story; both omit incidents that do not make a large enough contribution to the narrative themes to justify their inclusion; both reengineer the chronology of events for economy of storytelling; both use images from material culture in their credit sequences, and the figure of Ptolemy to validate their on-screen narratives as historiography. However, there are crucial differences in the ways in which they negotiate history and myth. These are cued to the viewer in the opening and closing sequences that provide the frameworks for reading the narratives.

Rossen's film opens with the somber sound of a military drumbeat, and Richard Burton's voice as Alexander declaiming lines taken from Arrian: "It is men who endure toil and dare dangers that achieve glorious deeds, and it is a lovely thing to live with courage and to die with everlasting renown" (5.26).[23] The screen lights up to reveal a single centered image—a cast of a coin, depicting the head of a male wearing a lionskin. Across the center of the cast the film's title appears, making it clear that we are to understand the image as a portrait of "Alexander the Great" himself. These opening references suggest that this film will involve the audience in a close engagement with the ancient sources from the start: they will hear Alexander's own words, and see his face as it was captured during his lifetime.

Such a focus on historical source material contrasts with credit sequences in other contemporary historical epics, which feature cinema itself and its re-creation of historical worlds. *The Robe*, for instance, plays its credits over a red curtain, which draws back as the sequence ends to reveal the film's cinematic Rome. The onscreen image here uses the invented reality of the film to repeat the physical reality of the cinema: the actual red curtains that the audience would have just seen drawn across the screen to mark the start of the film. *Helen of Troy* employs a similar strategy, beginning the film with two Greek soldiers hauling open heavy doors to disclose a painted backdrop of pillars and statuary over which the credits play. In both of these films, artifice takes center stage. Attention is purposely drawn to the essential fictiveness of onscreen antiquity: cinema has the power to invent worlds. By contrast, Rossen's film foregrounds the sources of his narrative rather than the means used to communicate it. *Alexander the Great* is immediately marked out as being primarily concerned with retelling history rather than entertaining its audience.

This opening engagement with the sources is matched at the end of the film with an explicit reference to the transformation of historical events into historiography when Ptolemy takes on the role of narrator. The importance of Ptolemy's history to our sources for Alexander has already been mentioned. After the king's death, Ptolemy laid claim to Egypt, founded the dynasty of pharaonic monarchs that ended with Cleopatra VII, and wrote an account of Alexander.[24] This was the source for Arrian's history, while Arrian is in turn quoted by Rossen in the precredit sequence. Thus a linear transmission of knowledge is demonstrated, from the eyewitness Ptolemy, through Arrian, to Rossen himself and his audience. This narrative strategy appeals for Rossen's cinematic account to be considered as part of the continuing historiography of Alexander.

In *Alexander,* Oliver Stone also opens with images drawn from the material sources: the Alexander Mosaic; a third-century head of the king from Alexandria (now in the British Museum); and an Egyptian cartouche of his name. The images are continually changing, successively fading in and out through a swirling blue overlay that visually enacts their ephemeral status. This is visually the reverse of the impression of solid unchanging historical fact given by the credits sequence in the earlier film. A similar contrast applies to Stone's use of Ptolemy. Like Rossen, Stone casts Ptolemy in the role of narrator and biographer. The main body of the narrative is framed with scenes at start and end, showing the older Ptolemy in Alexandria dictating his history to his scribe. Rather than suggesting historical validity, though, the sequences show how our knowledge of Alexander has been shaped from the start by the whims of those who survived him.

Ptolemy is depicted standing next to a statue of Hermes, god of communication, signifying his function in the transmission of Alexander's history. He describes Alexander as "a god . . . or as close as anything I've ever seen," and asks, "Did such a man as Alexander exist?" He answers his own question: "Of course not. We idolize him, make him better than he was." Such posthumous (but relatively innocuous) heroizing seems to set up Ptolemy's account as the sentimental recollection of a friend. However, the tone darkens in the last scenes of the film when Ptolemy falters and declares, "The truth is, we did kill him," adding: "The dreamers exhaust us. They must die before they kill us with their blasted dreams." However, he then tells his scribe to discard these musings, calling them "an old fool's rubbish." There are echoes here of Stone's familiar concerns, in films like *JFK*, with political conspiracies and coverups and the corruption of ideals. The audience is left uncertain of what the true story is, of where the history ends and the myth begins.

Thus Stone's narrative structure and dialogue draw attention to the mythicizing process in the retelling of Alexander's story, and Rossen's to the historical. However, examining the content of Rossen's film shows that, through his use of sources, myth retains a strong presence.

Problems with Sources

The pressbook for the British release of *Alexander the Great* appeals to the filmmaker's investment in historical research, noting that Rossen "painstakingly read through all those ancient writers who speak of Alexander, as well as the works of modern authors."[25] Historical validation was especially important in the postwar historical epic genre with which *Alexander the Great* was associated. Borrowing the authority of academic history enabled studios to show images of eroticism, violence, and dubious morality, banned from films with contemporary settings but immensely popular at the box office. At the same time, with commercial imperatives foremost, no amount of historical research was going to be allowed to get in the way of a good story. Consequently studio insistence on a film's historicity was often no more than rhetoric. Studio publicity for *Quo Vadis*, for instance, claimed that historical research for the film filled four volumes, which were to be deposited with an academic library.[26] This did not prevent the film from staging a vast triumph scene in the Forum that would, in antiquity, have been physically impossible (but was highly reminiscent of Mussolini's recent speeches to modern Romans), or from having the empress Poppaea murdered by Nero only moments before his own death at the hands of his mistress, Acte. The chronology and events were at odds with historical sources, but worked brilliantly for drama and narrative economics.

In the case of *Alexander the Great*, studio assertions about the filmmaker's commitment to ancient sources were more than just part of the publicity ballyhoo. In an interview ten years after the original release, Rossen confirmed that he had undertaken "about three years of research personally."[27] His resulting intimacy with ancient sources (both written and material) is foregrounded throughout the film with direct quotes from ancient texts incorporated into the script. Following the quotation from Arrian that opens the film, for instance, the narrative proper commences with dialogue drawn from the Philippic speeches of the orators Demosthenes and Aeschines, more of which appears later in the narrative; lines from Plutarch's *Life of Alexander* are also featured.

In addition to these verbal references, ancient material culture is used to validate the visual representations. The opening coin image has already been discussed. One of the best-known images of the Macedonian king comes from the Alexander Mosaic, discovered in 1831 in the House of the Faun at Pompeii.[28] It apparently copies a fourth-century B.C.E. painting of the battle at either Issus or Gaugamela: two of the surviving portraits have been identified as Alexander and Darius.[29] The British pressbook notes Burton's "uncanny physical resemblance to historians' descriptions and the ancient plaques of Alexander."[30] Placed next to this editorial is a photo of Burton in three-quarter profile with half his face in shadow, eyes wide open, and hair drawn back off his face, a pose clearly borrowed from the Mosaic's Alexander.

The film's historiographic ambitions make it keen to display its acquaintance with the same sources that academic historians might consult. However, this implied rigor is seriously undermined by its equal zeal to show off its use of a less reliable source: the *Alexander Romance*. The *Romance* interweaves historical fact with fictionalizing practices like exercises in rhetoric and outright fantasy elements from folktale and myth. As indicated previously, two scenes key to Rossen's main narrative theme are derived from the *Romance*: Alexander's possible siring by the Egyptian priest Nectanebos, and his exchange of letters with Darius.[31] Both reinforce the theme of father/son rivalry and its effects on Alexander's character development and aspirations. However, nothing in the way these sequences are presented in the film suggests that they might not be equivalent in historical terms to any other incident included in the narrative. The director's uncritical use of the *Romance*'s often fantastic account of Alexander's life puts into question the implication (prompted by the narrative alignment with Ptolemy and opening display of ancient objects and text) that the film might be understood as historiography.

In fact, a closer look at that opening sequence reveals that the very sources offered as validation of the film's historicity illustrate rather the problems of negotiating history and myth in Alexander historiography. The lines from Arrian are taken from his account of the king's speech to the Macedonian army, in revolt and demanding to return home from India. They do indeed appeal to popular knowledge, being perhaps the best-known speech attributed to Alexander. However, Arrian was not himself an eyewitness; his account is second-hand. Recent Alexander historians have raised doubts over the speech's authenticity. N. G. L. Hammond, for instance, asserts that "we can be confident that Arrian did not write the speeches," while P. A. Brunt concludes that they are "an epideictic display by Arrian."[32] Certainly it seems unlikely that we should be hearing the very words spoken by the king.

More uncertainty attaches to the opening visual imagery. The image on the cast of the coin shows a male head, draped with what, on close inspection, can be seen to be a lionskin.[33] That this head is to be identified with a portrait representation of Alexander is clearly implied by the overprinting of the title. This identification chimes with modern experience, especially in monarchies, where a portrait of the monarch is often found on coins. However, this was not the custom with ancient coinage. The most widely disseminated images of Alexander's rule would have been on the coinage issued first by himself and later by his successors, and many of these survive.[34] Much of the silver coinage issued during Alexander's lifetime displays on one side Zeus, and on the other Heracles, claimed by the Macedonian kings as an ancestor and iconographically identified by the lionskin draped over his head like a helmet. It seems likely then that the head depicted on the onscreen coin is that of the demigod rather than the king.

It would be a mistake to simply assume that Rossen's decision to identify a Herculean image with Alexander was an uneducated error. Certainly the image may have been used because (like the incidents from the *Romance*) it supports his narrative concerns, reinforcing the visual identification of the king with both leonine and Herculean (therefore semidivine) imagery. However, Rossen's extensive research is likely to have brought him into contact with the theory among numismatists that, after the king's death in 323, Heracles' representation on coins was a crypto-portrait of Alexander himself.[35] Given the film's explicit determination to prove its historiographical credentials with references to both ancient sources and modern historians like Tarn, it is more than possible that the director actively decided to incorporate this historical debate about Alexander imagery into the visual narrative of the film. At least we can be certain (in this as in all Rossen's decisions about which of the complex tangle of reliable and dubious details to include) that the major motivation was not the commercial imperative to create spectacular entertainment regardless of historical fact. Rather, it confirms the filmmaker's aspiration to present his own reading of Alexander's history through the medium of cinema.

Conclusion

Viewed in the contexts of the director's personal history, claims made about the extent of his research, and narrative cues in the film itself, *Alexander the Great* must be seen as a genuine endeavor on the part of its director to discover the motives that drove the historical Alexander's extraordinary career. In a sense, Rossen attempts to assume the role of historiographer, albeit working in the medium of film rather than written text. The theorist Hayden White coined the term "historiophoty" for this kind of "representation of history and our thoughts about it in visual images and filmic discourse."[36] The critical and commercial failure of Rossen's project seems at least partly tied to his historiophotic ambitions. Attempts to present historical debates and theories (like Tarn's beliefs about Alexander and the "unity of mankind") and accurate representations of historical events (like the battle at Chaeronea) resulted in a dialogue-heavy film that lacked the spectacle promised in studio publicity. This confounded an audience more familiar with seeing the ancient world in epic film as a site for extravagant entertainment.

These issues point to the need for future historiophoters to find imaginative ways of visually communicating debates that are more usually transacted verbally, and events that are not as spectacular as their effect on the canvas of history might imply. Whereas history is the cumulative product of a complex web of causes and effects, cinema reduces it to a single closed, linear narrative with a solitary interpretation.[37] Rossen's film is vulnerable to this charge, as a product of the particular industrial conditions current at the time of its release. The dominant classical Hollywood cinematic tradition, especially strong in the postwar years, insisted on certain visual, verbal, and narrative conventions that combined to produce cinematic realism.[38] This essentially linear narrative style, relying on simple chronology and regularity of cause and effect, remains the most popular form of cinematic storytelling. The multiple versions of Alexander's biography make telling his story in this cinematic style especially difficult. More recently, however, new forms of cinema have appeared that openly display the constructed nature of cinematic "realities" by disrupting conventional linearity. Such sophisticated cinematic texts are now found not only in art houses, but also in the multiplexes: the parallel storylines of Quentin Tarantino's works for instance, the "backwards" narrative of *Memento* (2001), or the multiple realities of *The Matrix* (1999) or *Vanilla Sky* (2001). Such new ways of storytelling might enable cinema to finally do justice to the multiple versions of Alexander we have accumulated in history and myth. Oliver Stone's *Alexander* disappoints in this respect, being keen to demonstrate its postmodern understanding of history as selective narrative, but holding to a conservative style of essentially linear, realist narrative.

Rossen and Stone have more in common than a conservative narrative style; both began as scriptwriters, and have won Academy Awards, for instance. A closer look at their respective careers finds more similarities that are mirrored by similarities in their cinematic Alexanders. Both have been associated with "social problem" films; both have been shunned by the establishment (Stone following the controversy over *JFK*). Perhaps most tellingly, both underwent traumatic experiences that prompted radical changes in their political beliefs (Rossen's blacklisting, Stone's service in Vietnam). Their Alexanders show the effects of these experiences. In each case the king is an idealist misunderstood by his contemporaries. He is visionary in his belief that it is the hearts rather than the bodies of men that must be conquered, and in his embrace of the idea that all races are equal. Finally, in both films, the hero who seemed to believe himself invincible is forced, through the deaths of those closest to him, to confront the truth of his own human frailty.

Ultimately a work of historiography achieves repute when it becomes embedded in the tradition of historical writing about a figure, period, or event: cited by, as well as citing, other historiographers. Rossen's film is not (to my knowledge) cited as a source for further written discussions. However, its influence on Stone's cinematic retelling of Alexander's history is well evidenced: in Alexander's dream of world unity; in the device of Ptolemy as narrator; and especially in Alexander's unambiguously blond hair.[39] For at least two generations of cinemagoers now, it is likely that dark-haired visions of the Macedonian king will seem "wrong," just as Cleopatra will always wear her hair in a shiny black bob. Perhaps this is the lesson about history that cinema teaches best: the ease with which its figures and events may escape the rigidity of academic scrutiny and, accepting the same fate that Rossen's

Alexander asked for his corpse, be swept away by the fast-flowing waters of popular myth.

Notes

Thanks to Alastair Blanshard and Maria Wyke for comments on earlier drafts of this work. This research was made possible by an award from the Arts and Humanities Research Council.

1. There is a video recording of Rattigan's play, filmed at the BBC studios at Alexandra Palace and screened in 1950: the proposed film is mentioned by Raymond Leader in *ABC Film Review* 4 (June 1954): 11. Leader notes that three films about Alexander were being discussed at that time—Rossen's film, the adaptation of Rattigan, and one other mystery candidate. The play itself is discussed at greater length in Robin Lane Fox's chapter in this volume. The pilot for the television series was made in 1964 but not screened until 1968, by which time Shatner and his co-star Adam West (playing Cleander) had come to the notice of audiences for their performances in *Star Trek* and *Batman*. The later cult status of these two series has since prompted a swell of interest in Shatner's Alexander, and the pilot was released on DVD in the United States in 2004. Visually Shatner's golden-haired Alexander resembles Burton's portrayal, though his characterization is perhaps more youthful and impulsive, with less of Burton's brooding sense of destiny. Neither script nor acting is of the highest quality, but many of the key themes seen in other films are included here: Alexander's physical energy and charismatic heroism; his loyalty to his Companions; his desire to surpass his father; conflicts with older advisors over his ambitions for conquest. Having begun his career as a theatrical actor, Shatner had already appeared in a film inspired by antiquity, as a featured member of the Chorus in *Oedipus Rex* (1957). Filmographic details for the *Alexander the Great* pilot are at www.imdb.com/title/tt0326725/; for a very personal scene-by-scene analysis, see www.agonybooth.com/alexander/. In addition to those listed above, there have been various proposals that did not get further than preproduction: Robin Lane Fox has described how his book was optioned twice, with no result, for films involving Gregory Peck and Steven Spielberg (Robin Lane Fox, *The Making of Alexander* [Oxford: R & L, 2004], 19–21). In 2004 Mel Gibson and Baz Luhrmann were both said to have films in preproduction; neither now seems likely to appear following the disappointing box-office results for Stone's *Alexander*.

2. Ian Nathan, "Stand Firm: Hardship and Danger are the Price of Glory," *Empire* (January 2005), 99.

3. Henry Hart, "Notes on Robert Rossen," *Films in Review* 13 (1962): 334.

4. Derek Elley, *The Epic Film: Myth and History* (London: Routledge, 1984), 75.

5. For a discussion of the Production Code and the consequent popularity of the ancient world among filmmakers, see Maria Wyke, *Projecting the Past: Ancient Rome, Cinema and History* (London: Routledge, 1997), 92–94.

6. On identification, see Laura Mulvey, "Visual Pleasure and Narrative Cinema," *Screen* 16, no. 3 (1975): 6–18. On engulfment in cinema, see Thomas Elsaessner, "Specularity and Engulfment: Francis Ford Coppola and *Bram Stoker's Dracula*," in *Contemporary Hollywood Cinema*, ed. Steve Neal and Murray Smith (London: Routledge, 1998), 191–208.

7. On the ancient world as a metaphor for Hollywood, see Vivian Sobchack, "Surge and Splendor: A Phenomenology of the Hollywood Historical Epic," *Representations* 29 (Winter 1990): 24–49; Wyke, *Projecting the Past*, 31–32; Michael Wood, *America in the Movies: Or, "Santa Maria, It Had Slipped My Mind"* (London: Secker & Warburg, 1975), 173.

8. Hartley Ramsay, "Alexander the Great," *Films in Review* 7 (1956): 220.

9. For another example, see Jon Solomon, *The Ancient World in the Cinema* (New Haven, CT: Yale University Press, 2001), 53–55, on the battle scenes in *Spartacus* (1960).

10. Daniel Stein, "An Interview with Robert Rossen," *Arts in Society: The Film Issue* 4 (Winter 1966–67): 49, 52.

11. For a discussion of the Egyptian origins of the *Romance,* see, for instance, Richard Stoneman, "The *Alexander Romance*: From History to Fiction," in *Greek Fiction: The Greek Novel in Context*, ed. J. R. Morgan and Richard Stoneman (London: Routledge, 1994), 122–23. Rossen himself mentions the Egyptian version of the *Romance* in Stein, "An Interview with Robert Rossen," 52.

12. Quotations from the *Alexander Romance* are taken from Ken Dowden's translation of the Greek version in *Collected Ancient Greek Novels,* ed. B. P. Reardon (Berkeley: University of California Press, 1989), 650–735.

13. W. W. Tarn, "Alexander the Great and the Unity of Mankind," *Proceedings of the British Academy* 19 (1933): 123.

14. W. W. Tarn, *Alexander the Great,* 2 vols. (Cambridge: Cambridge University Press, 1948), 1:145–48, 2:399–449. The declaration of Rossen's research is in the pressbook for the U.K. release of the film, published in 1956 by United Artists Corporation Ltd., and confirmed by Rossen in Stein, "An Interview with Robert Rossen," 52.

15. Tarn's theory has been opposed, in particular by Ernst Badian, and is now largely disregarded. Badian's "Alexander the Great and the Unity of Mankind" was published two years after Rossen's film was released (*Historia* 7 [1958]: 425–44). Nevertheless, it persists in popular ideas about Alexander, and reappears in a more general form in Stone's film. See also Thomas Harrison's chapter in this volume.

16. Rossen's testimony can be read in full in the transcripts of the hearings: *Hearings before the Committee on Un-American Activities, House of Representatives* (Washington, DC: U.S. Government Printing Office, 1953), 1457–58.

17. Alan Casty, *The Films of Robert Rossen* (New York: Museum of Modern Art, 1969), 32. This book provides a comprehensive survey of Rossen's career.

18. On this use of casting conventions in Hollywood epics set in the ancient world, see Wood, *America in the Movies*, 184; Wyke, *Projecting the Past*, 23, 71.

19. *Hearings before the Committee on Un-American Activities*, 1458–59, quoted in Casty, *The Films of Robert Rossen*, 9.

20. Casty, *The Films of Robert Rossen*, 33.

21. On the sources for Alexander, see N. G. L. Hammond, *Three Historians of Alexander the Great: The So-Called Vulgate Authors, Diodorus, Justin and Curtius* (Cambridge: Cambridge University Press, 1983); and Hammond's *Sources for Alexander the Great: An Analysis of Plutarch's* Life *and Arrian's* Anabasis Alexandrou (Cambridge: Cambridge University Press, 1993).

22. U.K. pressbook for *Alexander the Great*, 7.

23. All quotations from Arrian are taken from *The Campaigns of Alexander*, tr. Aubrey de Sélincourt, introduction and notes by J. R. Hamilton (rev. ed., London: Penguin, 1971).

24. For Ptolemy as a source for later historians, see Lionel Pearson, *The Lost Histories of Alexander the Great* (New York: American Philological Association, 1960), 188–211.

25. U.K. pressbook for *Alexander the Great*.

26. Wyke, *Projecting the Past*, 139.

27. Stein, "An Interview with Robert Rossen," 52.

28. The Mosaic is now in the Museo Archeologico Nazionale in Naples.

29. For a discussion of the Mosaic's place in Alexander imagery, see Andrew Stewart, *Faces of Power: Alexander's Image and Hellenistic Politics* (Berkeley: University of California Press, 1993), 130–40.

30. U.K. pressbook for *Alexander the Great*, 10.

31. Interestingly, the Romance (in its various versions) has itself been compared to cinema narrative, Richard Stoneman describing it (disparagingly) as "Cecil B. de Mille's Gospel of Alexander" in *The Greek Alexander Romance* (London: Penguin, 1991), 23.

32. Hammond, *Sources for Alexander the Great*, 258; P. A. Brunt, tr., *Arrian: Selected Works: English and Greek*, rev. ed., with intro. and notes by P. A. Brunt, Loeb Classical Library, 2 vols. (Cambridge, Mass.: Harvard University Press, 1976–1983), 2:533.

33. Of course, the original cinema audience did not have the opportunity to examine a brief image in detail that is afforded by recent video and DVD technology.

34. For a discussion of the uses of imperial coinage, including that of Alexander and his successors, see for example C. J. Howgego, *Ancient History from Coins* (London: Routledge, 1995), 39–55.

35. Stewart argues against this notion, also listing references for its supporters, in *Faces of Power*, 158–59.

36. Hayden White, "Historiography and Historiophoty," *American Histori-cal Review* 93 (1988): 1193. Read in conjunction with other articles in this issue, a special forum on history and film, White's provides an excellent survey of the debate on this topic.

37. Robert Rosenstone, "History in Images/History in Words," *American Historical Review* 93 (1988): 1174.

38. The authoritative exposition of the classical Hollywood style is found in David Bordwell et al., *The Classical Hollywood Cinema: Film Style and Mode of Production to 1960* (New York: Columbia University Press, 1985).

39. This was seen not only in Stone's *Alexander,* where the dark-haired Colin Farrell had his hair bleached for the part, but also in Baz Luhrmann's proposed *Alexander the Great,* which was to star the fair-haired Leonardo di Caprio. Stone's first choice for *Alexander* was Heath Ledger, also fair.

Part 3

Alexander's Intimates

Sexuality and Gender

Alexander and Ancient Greek Sexuality

Some Theoretical Considerations

MARILYN B. SKINNER

T O CONTEXTUALIZE this chapter, let's revisit the opening scenes of another recent blockbuster, Wolfgang Petersen's *Troy* (2004). Two armies, the Greeks and the Thessalians, are drawn up in battle formation to witness a single combat between their respective champions. In front of the lines the enemy defender is flexing his muscles, while the Greeks are frantically shouting for their man, an unaccountably missing Achilles. He turns up in his tent, not sulking over some insult but sprawled naked in bed with a pair of anonymous girls, sleeping off what had obviously been a grueling night. This Achilles is robustly, reassuringly heterosexual. If he later gets upset when his protégé Patroclus is killed, it's *okay*—they were cousins, after all.

Petersen's heavy-handed attempt to clean up Achilles' act earned censure from viewers, and not just classicists.[1] Consciousness that "the Greeks were different" in tolerating, and even glorifying, some forms of homoeroticism is spreading among a wider movie-going population, or at least those who blog or post reviews on the internet. Presumably, then, no eyebrows should have been raised when, in the theatrical release of *Alexander,* Oliver Stone presented a more or less faithful rendition of the biographical facts as reported by ancient sources, including a quasi-erotic reading of the friendship between Alexander and Hephaestion. Yet the immediate uproar (see the chapters by Joanna Paul and Jeanne Reames in this volume) seems to indicate that a nonspecialist public is happier thinking about the protocols of ancient sexuality only in the abstract; having them realized onscreen, especially in the person of the hero, still elicits discomfort.[2] Contemporary audiences, moreover, know more or less *what* was permitted, but are not sure *why* it should have been acceptable. For that reason, I would like to explain in this chapter just how the ancient Greek sexual code functioned socially. While much the same system was in force throughout Greece from the Archaic period (seventh and sixth centuries B.C.E.) onward, in territories as diverse as Crete and Sparta, I will focus upon its place in Classical sixth- to fourth-century Athenian culture, as that is the era for which we have the most evidence. If we examine it from the viewpoint of an elite male Athenian citizen, we will discover the societal purpose homoerotic bonding appears to have served. Paradoxically, we will also find out that both Achilles' relationship with Patroclus and Alexander's friendship with Hephaestion fell disconcertingly outside the parameters of the norm.[3]

With some variation between the cultures of Greece and Rome, sexuality in the classical world was conceptualized differently than it is in the contemporary postindustrial West, structured as a vertical rather than a horizontal system. In the abstract (that is, setting aside the realities of lived experience), sex was not perceived as reciprocal and egalitarian, with the partners giving each other mutual pleasure. Instead, it was thought to mirror the steeply hierarchical framework of social relations (Foucault 1986, 215). All sexual encounters in which at least one of the participants was a free adult male citizen were expected to conform to a dominance-submission paradigm: the adult male played the active part by penetrating a body orifice of the other person, who in being penetrated assumed a passive, feminized role, no matter what his or her sex (Dover 1978, 100–109). Public standing was thus reaffirmed under the most intimate circumstances, since a virile male demonstrated his intrinsic advantage over members of other groups by making use of their bodies for his pleasure (Halperin 1990, 30–31). Although the broad imposition on antiquity of this "winner-take-all" model of ancient sexuality, commonly referred to as the "penetration model," has been challenged as too simplistic, much current scholarship has accepted it, since it does clarify fundamental distinctions between the ancient and the modern worlds.[4]

Sexual preference is, for us, the defining element of sexuality: it forms an essential component of personal identity, establishes a dichotomy of behaviors, and, for many persons, fixes the morality of a given act. In the ancient penetration model, sexuality is grounded not on preference for one sex as object but on the notional genders of active and passive, which do not quite correspond to our biologically based genders: "active/passive" was not the equivalent of "male/female."[5] In democratic Athens, the active role was coterminous with male citizen status. It was as much a caste as a sexual marker, inseparable from the civic institutions that disguised the realities of economic stratification by insisting that mass and elite householders were equal among themselves in their superiority to others. Absolute bodily integrity characterized that equality: every male Athenian citizen, no matter how poor, was physically inviolable. To lay a hand upon him without his consent was *hybris*, a form of assault that might be punished by death (Halperin 1990, 96).[6] This did not mean, however, that he himself was free to do as he pleased.[7] The head of a household, or *oikos*, the basic unit of the city-state, was legally responsible for the behavior of its other members, including women, children, and slaves; he was therefore expected to display rational self-restraint in indulging his appetites, especially for sex. Intemperance was the mark of the man enslaved by lust and incapable of properly governing himself, much less those subject to him (Xen. *Mem.* 1.5.1–5). Such lawlessness was epitomized in the stereotype of the tyrant, who, emboldened by absolute power, gives free rein to his passions without regard for decency (Pl. *Resp.* 571a–575a; Arist. *Pol.* 1314b.28–36).

Sexual passivity, conversely, was not sex-linked but imputed to categories of persons, male and female, who were perceived as deficient. Citizen women, slaves, foreigners, freeborn male prostitutes, effeminate adult males, and (with qualifications) citizen youths were all "lesser" to some degree. Women were viewed as passive by nature, and there was no intrinsic shame in their sexual submission, but their putative incapacity to restrain their sexual desires made male custody imperative (Carson 1990; Dean-Jones 1992). Slaves, being chattel, were at their owner's disposal. Resident aliens, without the full rights of citizenship, had some legal protection (Arist. [*Ath. Pol.*] 58) but might still be harassed with impunity (Aeschin. *In Tim.* 43). Male prostitutes of citizen status were barred from performing civic functions, since, it was argued, they had voluntarily debased themselves for money (Aeschin. *In Tim.* 19–21; Dem. *Androt.* 22.29–32, 73). The *kinaidos,* or effeminate man who preferred the passive role in sex, was an object of bitter contempt, a moral deviant who breached the essential rules of masculinity (Winkler 1990, 45–46) and whose lust, like that of a woman, was presumed insatiable (Arist. [*Pr.*] 4.26.29–30).[8] Certain social inadequacies that assigned second-class status relative to the citizen male were believed to be determined by congenital factors. Thus Aristotle, in analyzing the composition of the household, can assert that there are such beings as natural slaves, who function best under the rule of a master (*Pol.* 1254b.15–1255a.1), and that those slaves, together with women, do not have full capacity to exercise judgment, a condition that necessitates their permanent supervision by the householder (ibid., 1260a.9–15). Sexual passivity might therefore be notionally aligned with cognitive disability as well as diminished status.

Within this dominance-submission scheme, citizen youths occupied an equivocal place. Poised on the very brink of manhood, the nude figure of the elite adolescent, muscles toned by gymnastic exercise, was the incarnation of human beauty (Ferrari 2002, 112–26). Desire for a boy in his prime (commonly thought of as between fifteen and eighteen, though some leeway was acceptable on either end) was therefore considered as natural as desire for a woman. "Normal" men might be interested in both boys and women, or, alternatively, they might be partial to one or the other; that was considered a matter of taste rather than involuntary bent. However, there was a special romantic and erotic charge attached to courtship of the beautiful youth. Though not yet possessed of full citizen status, he was considered a free moral agent, capable of making reasoned decisions about his conduct. Women's sexual services could be bought or commanded, but *his* affections had to be won (Dover 1973, 65–67). In Greek literature and art, then, the lover's pursuit of the unwilling beloved is a constant theme: songs performed at aristocratic banquets complain of a youth's fickleness, pottery vessels used at Athenian drinking parties depict men and boys engaged in various stages of courtship, and inscriptions on those vessels turn handsome young men into celebrities: *Leagros kalos,* "Leagros is beautiful."

Because the citizen youth was inferior to adults only by virtue of his age and relative inexperience, and because in just a few years' time he would assume his father's place as soldier, householder, and voting member of the assembly, the community took an interest in his welfare

and worried over possible negative consequences of his erotic relationships. While no Athenian law expressly prohibited noncommercial
consensual intercourse between two citizen males, several provisions
guarded the chastity of boys—forbidding relatives to prostitute them,
regulating access to schools, and perhaps punishing such intercourse
when prosecuted by the junior partner's family under the law of *hybris*
(Cohen 1991a, 175–80; 1991b). The existence of a law disenfranchising
men who had earlier prostituted themselves indicates anxiety over the
corrupting effects of money on character. Greeks also feared that im-
moderate sexual submission in adolescence might produce a habitual
craving for the passive role (Arist. *Eth. Nic.* 1148b.27–29; Arist. [*Pr.*]
4.26.33–38). Many sources, finally, express concern over the pernicious
influence of a less-than-virtuous lover who seeks his own pleasure
rather than the good of his companion (e.g., Thgn. 31–36; Xen. *Symp.*
8.19–21; see esp. Pl. *Phdr.* 238e–241d). As a result, Athenian society imposed upon erotic relations between adult men and youths a whole set
of courtship practices intended to distinguish true affection from mere
carnal craving. Love of boys was valorized but also ritualized: "it had to
be accompanied by conventions, rules of conduct, ways of going about
it, by a whole game of delays and obstacles designed to put off the moment of closure, and to integrate it into a series of subsidiary activities
and relations" (Foucault 1986, 196–97). Natural impulses were thus
channeled into a highly artificial system of proprieties, defined in modern scholarly terms as the social institution of boy-love or *paiderastia*.

In the *Symposium,* Plato's treatise on sexual desire (*erōs*), Pausanias,
one of the speakers, explains how this institution purportedly operated
(180c–185c). Instruction in virtue was its rationale, and noble, "celestial"
passion, personified in Aphrodite "Ourania," differed from its vulgar
and promiscuous counterpart (Aphrodite "Pandemos") by its achievement of that objective. Even more than beauty or athleticism, it was the
boy's character, his potential for moral development, that ideally
aroused love in his admirer. The older man (*erastēs,* "lover") sought to
win his beloved (the *erōmenos*) through promises and entreaties, but the
youth was expected to resist such advances until the *erastēs* had proved
his worth. Then, and only then, might the *erōmenos* yield, in the expectation of bettering himself. Once they became lovers, the *erastēs*
assumed responsibility for training his protégé in skills of mind and
body while serving as an exemplar of manly excellence. Throughout
his speech, then, Pausanias is emphasizing the educational features of
the practice. In a society where low life expectancy, late marriage for

men (at approximately thirty), and frequent warfare meant that many
adolescents would have already lost their fathers, such a mentoring relationship with an older male served pragmatic ends in guiding the
transition from youth to adulthood. Institutionalized pederasty has in
fact been characterized as a form of "displaced fathering" (Cartledge
1981, 22).

Concentration upon the virtue and personal honor of both parties
meant that sexual gratification, though permissible, was bounded by
restrictions. During the sexual act, the lover had to show the highest regard for the reputation of the *erōmenos*, behaving with tact and restraint.
Apart from obscene comic jokes, sodomy itself was a taboo subject;
though there are explicit sex scenes on vases, the customary position is
intercrural, which involves no actual penetration (Dover 1978, 98–100).
The boy, for his part, properly felt affection (*philia*) for his partner, but
not sexual desire—nor could he himself experience bodily pleasure
from the act, for that would involve enjoyment of the passive role.[9] Instead, he was said to oblige (*charizesthai*) his mentor by allowing him
liberties, but only out of gratitude and in exchange for instruction. With
the passing of time, as the youth grew to manhood, the sexual aspect of
the relationship might terminate, but a lifelong friendship remain. The
common goal of both parties was therefore advancement in virtue: such
erōs, Pausanias concludes, compels both the lover and his beloved to
devote great care to the achievement of excellence (*Symp.* 185b7–c1).

In practice, *paiderastia* was class-linked. Only the wealthy had leisure
to attend the gymnasium and take part in the drinking parties (*symposia*) that were the venues of courtship. Under the radical Athenian democracy of the fifth and early fourth centuries B.C.E., popular attitudes
toward the custom hardened and its practitioners fell back on constructing high-minded defenses of its value to the community. Explicit
depictions of homoerotic courtship on Attic vase paintings, fashionable
in the late Archaic age when power was in the hands of oligarchic ruling groups such as the Pisistratid dynasty, abruptly disappear during
the decade 480–470 as democratic rule gains impetus (Shapiro 1981;
2000). Old Comedy, strongly biased toward popular interests (Xen.
[*Ath. pol.*] 2.18), never depicts pederasty in a positive light: its conservative apologists, like Just Argument in the central scene of *Clouds* (889–
1114), are shown up as disgusting hypocrites, the boys they pursue as
callous hustlers.[10] In forensic speeches accusations of dissolute behavior involving youths are routinely trotted out against opponents. Yet
whether blatant hostility was merely provoked by class tensions or was

also based upon ethical considerations is a disputed matter, for the evidence is ambiguous: all these ostensible manifestations of displeasure could be explained as censure of the social group or the individuals with which pederasty was associated, not of the institution *per se*.

In addition to its professed purpose of initiating young men into the behaviors and attitudes proper to elites, pederasty was a strategy for maintaining class privilege by establishing social ties across age lines. Closeness that grew out of a pederastic association, for example, might be solidified through a marriage pact whereby the former beloved wedded a kinswoman of his lover. From an outsider's perspective, such alliances between former sexual partners would look like cronyism, the consequence of a disreputable liaison hardly distinguishable from prostitution (Hubbard 1998, 53). Where did expediency stop and comradeship begin? When he examines the ethical aspects of friendship (*philia*), Aristotle is keenly aware of the difficulty of forging an altruistic bond out of a union motivated, to some degree, by sexual desire and self-interest. Still, he concedes that mutual affection can arise if the partners are like-tempered (*Eth. Nic.* 1157a.6–12). Benevolent love between men, in turn, might encourage bravery on the battlefield and harmony in civic life. There was, then, a recognized possibility that the pederastic relationship, as it matured into true friendship, could serve the state as a whole, and not just class interests. For Greek society, that was ultimately its justification.

There are salient points of difference between ancient pederasty and present-day homosexual pair-bonding. First, even though the age difference between *erastēs* and *erōmenos* might be only a few years, the relationship was viewed as cross-generational. Second, physical intercourse ordinarily ceased once the junior partner reached maturity, though we do know of couples who were apparently sexually active in later life. Aristophanes, another of the speakers in Plato's *Symposium*, defines *erōs* as the compulsion to seek out and reunite physically, as far as is possible, with the lost half of a divided self (192b–c), and he singles out Pausanias and his long-time companion, the tragic poet Agathon, as partners who have perhaps found their lasting soulmates (193c). However, the hierarchical construction of ancient Greek sexuality would require the younger man in such a continuing relationship to keep playing the subordinate role of *erōmenos* publicly, as the rules did not recognize the possibility of egalitarian affairs between two adult males. This prescription naturally exposed him to the risk of being branded an effeminate *kinaidos*, as indeed happened to Agathon on the

comic stage (Ar. *Thesm.* 28–265; Ar. *Gery.* fr. 178 K–A). Accordingly, prolonged identification with the position of *erōmenos* was not only hazard-
ous, but strongly discouraged: the early Stoics were ridiculed for asserting that, apparently for instructional purposes, a pederastic relationship
might continue until the "boy" was twenty-eight (Ath. 563e).

The most striking divergence between contemporary ideas of male
same-sex relationships and Greek pederastic affairs is that the latter did
not entail exclusive sexual preference. Gay men who are "out," to our
way of thinking, typically do not have heterosexual involvements as
well; though we recognize bisexuality as one mode of sexual orientation, we view it (perhaps naively) as a minority option. Ancient society
was aware that individuals might prefer members of their own sex, but
imposed upon the male householder the obligation to sire a legitimate
son and heir, his private inclinations notwithstanding.[11] The object of
nonreproductive, "recreational" sex could be a matter of choice, but
marriage was a familial and social duty. In practice, then, an *erastēs*, no
matter how intense his passion for boys, as a married man would still
be bisexual (though he himself might be puzzled by that term). Society
expected him to be sexually aroused by his wife, at least sufficiently for
ordinary marital relations. As sexual predilection had not been crystal-
lized into a defining category of personal identity, ancient erotic attraction was comparatively diffuse, and criteria of beauty for each gender
were more or less homogeneous: in early vase painting, the attractive
young *hetaera* or courtesan is oddly boyish, while later the beautiful boy
is unusually girlish (Dover 1978, 70–73). Modern Western culture exercises a stronger narrowing effect upon innate propensity.

For fifth-century Athenians, the problem of fitting the companion-
ship of Homer's Achilles and Patroclus into this sexual paradigm was a
notoriously thorny one.[12] It was possible to rule out alleged homoerotic
elements altogether: thus Xenophon makes Socrates, defending the
superiority of spiritual to carnal love, pointedly insist that Achilles did
not regard Patroclus as a boyfriend (*paidikois*) but as a comrade (*hetairōi*)
and solely in that spirit avenged him (*Symp.* 8.31). On the other hand,
classical audiences felt it natural to treat Achilles' pursuit of vengeance
on behalf of his friend as a sublime instance of the self-sacrifice inspired
by love. Thus Aeschines ascribes the epic hero's devotion to *erōs* (*In Tim.*
143). This, however, necessitated the assumption that Achilles was, as
erastēs, the elder of the two, as well as the better man in strength and
valor. Some poets indeed portrayed him as such: Pindar casts Achilles as
Patroclus' athletic trainer (*Ol.* 10.19), and Aeschylus, in his lost tragedy

Myrmidons, made the grieving protagonist Achilles frankly allude to intercrural sex in language indicating that he had been the active partner (*sebas de mērōn hagnon,* "the sacred reverence of the thighs," fr. 135 Radt, cf. frr. 136–137). Yet in Homer Patroclus is unequivocally the elder, though it is conceded that Achilles is better-born and physically stronger (*Il.* 11.786–787).[13] Consequently, Phaedrus, a third member of the company in Plato's *Symposium,* sharply criticizes Aeschylus for confusing the relations between the men. In his view Achilles actually gave even greater proof of love through his death because he had been the *erōmenos,* not the god-possessed lover (180a–b).

This uncertainty about the roles the couple played indicates that Greeks of the classical period were imposing a pattern familiar to them upon a text ignorant of it. Modern authorities conclude, then, that the establishment of pederasty as a social institution was *subsequent* to the composition of the Homeric poems (Dover 1988, 130–31; Percy 1996, 37–40). David Halperin instead aligns the epic friendship of Achilles and Patroclus with those of Gilgamesh and Enkidu in Sumerian myth and the Biblical David and Jonathan. Structurally, the three accounts are remarkably similar: each depicts an exclusive, but overtly nonerotic, attachment of two coevals in which the status of the partners is asymmetrical and the subordinate member ultimately dies. The Achilles-Patroclus relationship would consequently not be pederastic, as later Greeks understood the practice, or even proto-pederastic, deriving as it did from a much older non-Hellenic mythic tradition (Halperin 1990, 75–87). For the purposes of the narrative, furthermore, what is emphasized is the intensity of the *affective* bond uniting the men, as it is that which motivates the actions of the surviving partner (Zanker 1994, 15–16). Such passionate comradeship is primarily reinforced through the shared experience of battle, not through physical intercourse. Whether the brothers-in-arms are also lovers is simply beside the point.

As blueprints of homosocial male relations available to an ancient Macedonian Greek, both the "penetration model" and Achilles and Patroclus's friendship should be kept in mind when assessing Stone's portrayal of his hero's complicated but—within its cultural milieu, perfectly normal—sexuality. The historical record implies that Alexander was inclined toward both sexes, and modern biographers generally agree. While his three marriages were doubtless undertaken primarily for political considerations, we are also told of a protracted affair with the Persian noblewoman Barsine (Plut. *Alex.* 21.4), which may have produced a son, and youthful attachments to Macedonian courtesans are the subject of later gossip (Ath. 10.435a; Plin. *HN* 35.86–87; Ael. *VH* 12.34). Since the subject is discussed elsewhere in this volume by Elizabeth Carney, I can be brief about the cinematic handling of Alexander's marriage to Roxane. By investing his desire for her with murky incestuous undertones and neglecting to mention other liaisons with women, Stone makes Alexander's heterosexuality more tenuous than it appears to have been. Our either/or paradigm of sexual orientation may have shaped that depiction: *because* Alexander is known to have had homoerotic involvements, his unexpected attraction to a not altogether suitable woman must be attributed to kinkier drives. Ancient culture, acclimatized to thinking in terms of both/and, could romantically describe it as a case of love at first sight (Curt. 8.4.23–25; Plut. *Alex.* 47.4; Arr. *Anab.* 4.19.5).

The easiest relationship to account for in terms of Greek sexual codes is the one most distasteful to modern sensibilities: Alexander's connection with the eunuch Bagoas.[14] Although Stone ignores Bagoas's reputed behind-the-scenes influence (Curt. 6.5.22–23, 10.1.25–38), he reenacts the incident in Plutarch (*Alex.* 67.4) in which an inebriated Alexander, egged on by the Macedonians, publicly embraces and kisses the youth. Plutarch terms the Persian boy the king's *erōmenos.* Being the inferior in several respects—an Oriental foreigner from a newly subject population, an adolescent, and above all a eunuch, castrated to preserve his childish beauty—Bagoas fits impeccably as passive partner into the dominance-submission scheme. There is therefore nothing theoretically wrong with the situation according to Greek protocols. Yet the Macedonians' mocking demands that Alexander affirm his feelings for the boy exhibit contempt for his infatuation with such an exotic Eastern creature, and his drunken compliance indicates that he has abandoned considerations of *aidōs,* respect for decorum. Whether the story is historically true or not, Plutarch's Alexander is assimilated to the stereotype of the tyrant mastered by his passions. That their object is "unnatural," the product of a foreign knife, simply makes matters worse.

In Stone's film, the intimacy between Alexander and Hephaestion—which, in its equality and reciprocity, resembles the ideal for a contemporary gay couple—serves as the positive homoerotic foil to the king's sinister dealings with Bagoas. In ancient terms, however, their relationship is much more difficult to categorize. Since they were of the same age (Curt. 3.12.16), and since Alexander, despite his kingly rank, treated Hephaestion as a peer, they do not fit the Athenian pederastic model. Evidence indicates, however, that institutionalized pederasty was practiced among the aristocratic youths associated with the Macedonian court.[15] Thus some Alexander scholars (e.g., Reames-Zimmerman 1999, 93; Cartledge 2004, 228) believe they were physically intimate during adolescence, though probably not in later life. Stone (perhaps influenced by Lane Fox 1973, 57) implies, particularly in the general release version, some ongoing, if intermittent, carnal activity as adults.[16] In that he is more forthright than any of the leading ancient sources. As Jeanne Reames-Zimmerman observes (1999, 90–91), none of Alexander's extant biographers, Greek or Roman, ever refers to Hephaestion as anything but Alexander's "friend" (Greek *philos,* Latin *amicus*), conforming to Alexander's own epithet for him, *philalexandros* (Plut. *Alex.* 47.5; Diod. Sic. 17.114.2). Use of the term *erōmenos* (Ael. *VH* 12.7) or insinuations that there was something inappropriate about their closeness (Lucian, *Dial. mort.* 14.25) are relatively late and anecdotal.[17] Though deemed excessive even by his admirers (Arr. *Anab.* 7.14.2), Alexander's paroxysm of anguish after Hephaestion's death does not necessarily imply that they were lovers, unless one insists that any attachment capable of producing such grief must be based on sex—an argument that surely goes much too far. From a historical perspective, the precise character of their relations, either in youth or in adulthood, is impossible to determine.

What we do know, however, is that the friendship of Alexander and Hephaestion was readily assimilated—if not originally by the principals themselves, then by the ingratiating court poets who accompanied the expedition (Curt. 8.5.8; cf. Tarn 1948, 2:55–62)—to that of Achilles and Patroclus. The second-century C.E. historian Arrian dismisses as a *logos,* or mere report, the episode at Troy at which Hephaestion purportedly laid a garland at the tomb of Patroclus to manifest his own attachment to Alexander (*Anab.* 1.12.1). Arrian's verdict implies that he did not find it in the writings of Alexander's contemporaries, on which he drew. By his time, however, the correspondence between the two pairs of friends, both coevals and both engaged in a heroic military enterprise, was firmly established, so that tales could be invented to illustrate it. Since the connection between Achilles and Patroclus had long been redefined as frankly pederastic, the bond of Alexander and Hephaestion would be viewed in that light as well. Pronouncements upon their association by ancient sources writing several centuries afterward are therefore not exact reportage; indeed, they are subject to the same caveats against anachronistic distortion as modern discussions of whether Alexander was "gay."

Interpreting Alexander's sexuality as viewed by later Greeks and Romans is an exercise in studying reception of the past. As opposed to the highly structured paradigm of pederasty, the loose and equal arrangements in the Achilles-Patroclus and Alexander-Hephaestion partnerships hypothetically permitted several possible modes and degrees of homosocial bonding and left room for the romantic Greek imagination to exert itself. What is most interesting from our standpoint is that, despite his varied proclivities, biographers depict Alexander as essentially moderate and disciplined in his appetites (at least up until his final years), and particularly self-controlled regarding sex. After quoting his apocryphal remark that sleep and intercourse, more than any other things, reminded him that he was mortal, Plutarch astutely construes it to mean that Alexander thought that the two experiences of sexual enervation and fatigue arose "from the same limitation on human nature" (*apo mias . . . astheneias tēi physēi* [*Alex.* 22.3]). For contemporary audiences accustomed to consider intercourse as both wholesome and life-affirming, that disinclination may be the hardest aspect of Alexander's sexuality to grasp.

Notes

1. See Peter Bradshaw's sardonic remarks in the May 14, 2004, online edition of the *Guardian* (http://www.guardian.co.uk/arts/fridayreview/story/0,12102,1215732,00.html#article_continue). Andrew Stuttaford singles out the bowdlerization of the Achilles-Patroclus relationship as one of the film's major flaws (http://www.nationalreview.com/stuttaford/stuttaford200406020832.asp).

2. Gideon Nisbet (2006, 87–35) notes that contemporary impressions of Alexander at the time of the film's release had been shaped by numerous factors—among others, memories of earlier screen treatments (most notably Robert Rossen's 1956 *Alexander the Great*), popular appropriation of the hero as a gay icon, the political claims of ethnic groups, and the rhetoric of those involved in competing film projects.

3. Konstantinos Nikoloutsos (2008) observes that Stone's representation of Alexander, which teases the viewer by romanticizing the emotional bond between Alexander and Hephaestion in conventional Hollywood style while steering clear of any overt expression of sexual desire, is equally false to ancient sexual protocols. My thanks to Nikoloutsos for providing me with a prepublication draft of his article.

4. For a summary of the debate over the applicability of the "penetration model," see Karras 2000. Opposition to its monolithic features has been voiced

by Hubbard 1998 and 2000b and by Davidson 1997, 2001, and 2007, 101–66. After an exhaustive survey of evidence for same-sex erotic behavior in Greece as a whole, Davidson concludes by stressing the complexity of its manifestations (2007, 467–68).

5. The assumption that gender systems are universally structured around the biological division of the sexes is erroneous. Gender categories are not necessarily dichotomous and in some cultures may readily cross sex boundaries (Parker 2001).

6. Although the body of the Roman citizen male was likewise notionally inviolable, less attention was paid to maintaining a fictitious equality of persons (Walters 1997). On the contrary, social asymmetry was institutionalized through a patronage system in which goods and services were exchanged between those of higher and lower standing. In calibrating social position, money might confer economic power that trumped all other factors, including birth, rank, and respectability—or so the satirists would have us believe (e.g., Hor. *Sat.* 2.5; Juv. 1 and 3; cf. Trimalchio in Petronius's *Satyricon*). Free citizen males of limited resources, dependent upon the caprices of a patron, were always vulnerable to humiliation if not physical injury, and might well consider themselves effeminized, since in the Roman *mentalité* "social subordination always implies the possibility of sexual submission" (Oliensis 1997, 154). By the second century C.E., a division between the more and less respectable orders of society was enshrined in criminal law, where harsher penalties for the same offense, involving corporal punishment, were reserved for those of lower status.

7. For example, sexual access to women, minor children, and slaves under the authority of another adult male was forbidden, and such trespass was severely punished. This, too, was a violation of the autonomy, and indeed the honor, of their guardian.

8. Davidson (1977, 167–82) has challenged the notion that the *kinaidos* is characterized by a specific desire for anal intercourse, arguing that he is instead a type of overall sexual excess.

9. Plato (*Phdr.* 240d–e) represents Socrates pointedly asking what pleasure (*hedonē*) the besotted *erastēs* can give to his companion and suggesting that intercourse with an aging and unattractive lover will ultimately bring the boy to "the pitch of disgust." Cf. the Socrates of Xenophon's *Symposium* remarking: "A youth does not share in the pleasures of sex with the man, as a woman does, but soberly looks upon the other drunk with passion" (8.21). In vase paintings, the boy is shown as standing upright, unaroused and often curiously detached, while his lover bends his knees and lowers his head, a scheme implying that the passive partner is, paradoxically, in control (Golden 1984, 313–16).

10. The plot of *Knights* takes such comic unpleasantness to its extreme. Satirizing the popularity enjoyed by the demagogue Cleon, Aristophanes represents political opportunism as the fawning courtship of a wealthy, stupid old man labeled Demos (*dēmos*, "the citizenry"). Throughout this play, frank references

to buggery are underscored by fecal imagery, so that the ironic depiction of Demos as a pretty *erōmenos* is surrounded with constant reminders of the forbidden subject of anal intercourse (Skinner 2005, 121–23).

11. In Athenaeus's *Deipnosophistae* (603f) we are told that the tragedian Sophocles was fond of youths (*philomeirax*), while his colleague Euripides was fond of women (*philogunēs*). Pseudo-biographical anecdotes contrasting the sexual tastes and behaviors of the two dramatists circulated in antiquity (ibid., 604e–f). According to an ancient biography, Sophocles nevertheless had sons by two different women (*Vit. Soph.* 13).

12. On the enigma of the Achilles-Patroclus relationship for classical Greeks, and its consequent equivocal relevance for Alexander and Hephaestion, see Ogden 2007, 84–88.

13. The tondo of the well-known kylix by the Sosias Painter (Berlin F2278, *ARV*² 21.1 1620) pictures Achilles bandaging the arm of Patroclus, who has been wounded by an arrow. As Steven Lowenstam remarks, the scene—which has no counterpart in surviving literary sources—invokes the motif of Achilles' medical expertise, a tradition already well established (1992, 184–85). However, the fact that he is portrayed as smooth-cheeked, while Patroclus is bearded, indicates that he is regarded as younger, despite his specialized knowledge and ministry.

14. W. W. Tarn, Alexander's apologist-biographer, famously attempted to argue Bagoas out of existence as a malicious invention by a hostile source (1948, 2:319–26) but was convincingly refuted by Ernst Badian (1958).

15. Homoerotic liaisons are a common motif of Macedonian regicide accounts. The assassin may be a former *erōmenos* of the king with a personal grievance (e.g., the murderer of Archelaus; see Arist. *Pol.* 1311b.8–20). Larger conspiracies, such as that of Hermolaus, may involve one or more pederastic couples. Carney 1983 studies the recurrence of this motif and its similarities to the tale of the Athenian tyrannicides Harmodius and Aristogeiton.

16. In the scene following his triumphant entry into Babylon and meeting with Darius's daughter Stateira, Alexander is visited by Hephaestion as he lounges on the royal bed reading a letter from Olympias. The voiceover by Olympias informs us that three months have passed. In the general release version (scene 18), Alexander says, "Stay with me tonight, Hephaestion." The latter glances meaningfully at Bagoas, who is standing in one corner of the room, and Alexander adds, "I'll take my own bath. Thank you, Bagoas." The exchange is missing in the Director's Cut DVD (now scene 15), except for a quick, and in the context rather unmotivated, cut from Alexander and Hephaestion reading the letter together to Bagoas and back. The inclusion of Bagoas here is explicable only in retrospect.

17. For a list and discussion of these texts, see Ogden 2007, 76–80. The one noteworthy exception is a casual allusion to him as Alexander's *erōmenos* in Arrian's transcriptions of the teachings of the philosopher Epictetus (*Epict. diss.* 2.12.17–18). Arrian's authority as Alexander's biographer gives this testimony

weight (Reames-Zimmerman 1999, 90), but, if the language is instead that of Epictetus, it might well be tendentious.

References

Badian, Ernst. 1958. "The Eunuch Bagoas." *Classical Quarterly* n.s. 8:144–57.

Carney, Elizabeth. 1983. "Regicide in Macedonia." *Parola del Passato* 38: 260–72.

Carson, Anne. 1990. "Putting Her in Her Place: Woman, Dirt and Desire." In *Before Sexuality: The Construction of Erotic Experience in the Ancient Greek World*, ed. David Halperin, J. J. Winkler, and Froma Zeitlin, 135–69. Princeton, NJ: Princeton University Press.

Cartledge, Paul. 1981. "The Politics of Spartan Pederasty." *Proceedings of the Cambridge Philological Society* 27:17–36.

———. 2004. *Alexander the Great: The Hunt for a New Past.* Woodstock, NY: Overlook Press.

Cohen, David. 1991a. *Law, Sexuality, and Society: The Enforcement of Morals in Classical Athens.* Cambridge: Cambridge University Press.

———. 1991b. "Sexuality, Violence, and the Athenian Law of 'Hubris.'" *Greece and Rome* 2nd ser., 38, no. 2: 171–88.

Davidson, James N. 1997. *Courtesans and Fishcakes: The Consuming Passions of Classical Athens.* New York: Harper Perennial.

———. 2001. "Dover, Foucault and Greek Homosexuality: Penetration and the Truth of Sex." *Past and Present* 170:3–51.

———. 2007. *The Greeks and Greek Love: A Radical Reappraisal of Homosexuality in Ancient Greece.* London: Weidenfeld & Nicolson.

Dean-Jones, Lesley. 1992. "The Politics of Pleasure: Female Sexual Appetite in the Hippocratic Corpus." *Helios* 19:72–91.

Dover, Kenneth. 1973. "Classical Greek Attitudes to Sexual Behavior." *Arethusa* 6:59–73.

———. 1978. *Greek Homosexuality.* London: Duckworth.

———. 1988. *The Greeks and Their Legacy: Collected Papers.* Vol. 2, *Prose, Literature, History, Society, Transmission, Influence.* Oxford: Blackwell.

Ferrari, Gloria. 2002. *Figures of Speech: Men and Maidens in Ancient Greece.* Chicago: University of Chicago Press.

Foucault, Michel. 1986. *The History of Sexuality.* Vol. 2, *The Use of Pleasure.* Tr. Robert Hurley. New York: Vintage. (Orig. pub. as *L'usage des plaisirs* [Paris: Gallimard, 1984].)

Golden, Mark. 1984. "Slavery and Homosexuality at Athens." *Phoenix* 38:308–24.

Hallett, Judith P., and Marilyn B. Skinner, eds. 1997. *Roman Sexualities.* Princeton, NJ: Princeton University Press.

Halperin, David. 1990. *One Hundred Years of Homosexuality and Other Essays on Greek Love.* New York: Routledge.

Hubbard, Thomas. 1998. "Popular Perceptions of Elite Homosexuality in Classical Athens." *Arion* 3rd ser., 6, no. 1:48–78.

————, ed. 2000a. *Greek Love Reconsidered*. New York: Wallace Hamilton Press.

————. 2000b. "Pederasty and Democracy: The Marginalization of a Social Practice." In Hubbard 2000a, 1–11.

Karras, Ruth Mazo. 2000. "Active/Passive, Acts/Passions: Greek and Roman Sexualities." *American Historical Review* 105:1250–65.

Kassel, Rudolf, and Colin Austin, eds. 1984. *Poetae Comici Graeci*, vol. 3.2. Berlin: Walter de Gruyter.

Lane Fox, Robin. 1973. *Alexander the Great*. New York: Dial Press.

Lowenstam, Steven. 1992. "The Uses of Vase-Depictions in Homeric Studies." *Transactions of the American Philological Association* 122:165–98.

Nikoloutsos, Konstantinos. 2008. "The *Alexander* Bromance: Male Desire and Gender Fluidity in Oliver Stone's Historical Epic." *Helios* 35:223–51.

Nisbet, Gideon. 2006. *Ancient Greece in Film and Popular Culture*. Exeter: Bristol Phoenix.

Ogden, Daniel. 2007. "Two Studies in the Reception and Representation of Alexander's Sexuality." In *Alexander's Empire: Formulation to Decay*, ed. Waldemar Heckel, Lawrence Tritle, and Pat Wheatley, 75–108. Claremont, CA: Regina Books.

Oliensis, Ellen. 1997. "The Erotics of *Amicitia*: Readings in Tibullus, Propertius, and Horace." In Hallett and Skinner 1997, 151–71.

Parker, Holt N. 2001. "The Myth of the Heterosexual: Anthropology and Sexuality for Classicists." *Arethusa* 34:313–62.

Percy, William A., III. 1996. *Pederasty and Pedagogy in Ancient Greece*. Urbana: University of Illinois Press.

Radt, Stefan. 1985. *Tragicorum Graecorum Fragmenta*, vol. 3. Göttingen: Vendenhoeck & Ruprecht.

Reames-Zimmerman, Jeanne. 1999. "An Atypical Affair? Alexander the Great, Hephaestion, and the Nature of Their Relationship." *Ancient History Bulletin* 13, no. 3: 81–96.

Shapiro, H. A. 1981. "Courtship Scenes in Attic Vase Painting." *American Journal of Archaeology* 85:133–43.

————. 2000. "Leagros and Euphronios: Painting Pederasty in Athens." In Hubbard 2000a, 12–32.

Skinner, Marilyn B. 2005. *Sexuality in Greek and Roman Culture*. Oxford: Blackwell.

Tarn, W. W. 1948. *Alexander the Great*. 2 vols. Cambridge: Cambridge University Press.

Walters, Jonathan. 1997. "Invading the Roman Body: Manliness and Impenetrability in Roman Thought." In Hallett and Skinner 1997, 29–43.

Winkler, John J. 1990. *The Constraints of Desire: The Anthropology of Sex and Gender in Ancient Greece*. New York: Routledge.

Zanker, Graham. 1994. *The Heart of Achilles: Characterization and Personal Ethics in the* Iliad. Ann Arbor: University of Michigan Press.

Olympias and Oliver

Sex, Sexual Stereotyping, and Women in Oliver Stone's Alexander

ELIZABETH D. CARNEY

SINCE MY graduate student days, I have occasionally played a kind of parlor game with other Alexander historians in which we cast the major characters in the saga of Alexander the Great for an imaginary movie. When we invented the game in the 1970s, most of us had seen Robert Rossen's 1956 *Alexander the Great* years earlier, but recalled it only dimly (in the days before video and DVD) and somewhat dismissively as a typical fifties blood-and-sand outing, chiefly memorable for a wooden portrayal of Alexander by an astonishingly young and bleached-blond Richard Burton, complete with a Doris Day–style hairdo.[1] I doubt that any of us had seen or even knew of the existence of William Shatner's 1968 television movie/pilot about Alexander.[2] So we were able to make our choices largely unaffected by earlier images. The argument in this game was always about the casting of Alexander himself—whoever was suggested was always too old and too tall. When, however, I nominated Anjelica Huston for the role of Olympias, mother of Alexander the Great, I usually got a lot of support.

Even allowing for the passage of time (I believe Huston was still

135

in her thirties when this notion first struck me), my imaginary casting of Anjelica Huston versus Oliver Stone's real one of Angelina Jolie suggests something basic about my understanding of Olympias and her role in Alexander's life, as compared to Stone's, as realized by Jolie. Nuance, subtlety, and intelligence generally describe the first actress's characterizations, whereas the second has often allowed her beauty and powerful physical presence to substitute for acting.

Creating a believable, compelling, and yet roughly accurate image of Olympias on screen could never be an easy task. Controversy and hostility surrounded her in her own day (ca. 375–316 B.C.E.).[3] Our extant ancient sources preserve many traces of this contemporary animosity against an atypical, political woman. They must, therefore, be read with caution and care. The problem with characterizations of Alexander is the essential mystery, the unknowableness of his character—what John Keegan has termed his "Mask of Command."[4] The difficulty with Olympias, on the other hand, is that the heavily anecdotal sources can easily trick us into believing that they (and we) know more about her than they really do. Scholars have often treated personal judgments of her by individuals as unquestionable facts. More than anything else, what the hostile tradition about Olympias really allows us to "know" is how appealing sexual stereotypes about women, particularly political women, not to mention older women, continue to be.

Olympias's actions and goals need to be understood in the context of the intensely competitive nature of Hellenic culture in general, and more specifically in terms of the realities of royal marriage in a place where the king practiced polygamy and no consistent method of selection existed for choosing a royal successor. Virtually any male member of the royal Argead dynasty could attempt to reach the throne. Royal mothers therefore often served as advocates for their sons' succession. Kings' sons could trust their mothers in ways they could not trust their fathers, who might always prefer another son.[5] Olympias was the daughter of the king of Molossia (today northwestern Greece and parts of southern Albania), and she became the fifth, or possibly fourth, wife of Philip II, king of Macedon, father of Alexander the Great, and conqueror of the Greek peninsula. In the northern kingdoms of Molossia and Macedon, competition often took the form of blood feuds and assassination attempts. Although these activities had been, up until her lifetime, largely male pursuits (so far as we know), Olympias, determined to safeguard the succession for her son (and later grandson), was an enthusiastic participant in both.

A judicious reading of the ancient sources suggests the following character sketch. Olympias was a woman of intelligence, proud of her heroic lineage, indomitable, and physically brave. Like her husband and son, Olympias could be and often was ruthless and literally murderous. Certainly she was responsible for the death of Philip Arrhidaeus (Alexander's mentally limited half-brother, who was, along with her infant grandson Alexander IV, recognized as king after the death of Alexander the Great), as well as the death of his wife, Adea Eurydice. During the same period, she ordered the deaths of a number of adherents of a hostile political faction. Years earlier she had probably arranged the murder of Cleopatra, her husband's last wife, along with Cleopatra's newborn child. It is not by any means certain that Olympias and her famous son had a role in the assassination of her husband and Alexander's father, Philip II, but it is a real possibility.[6] Succession politics became particularly bloody after the death of Alexander, and Olympias played them like a man.

On the other hand, in keeping with the Greek maxim, Olympias not only did harm to her enemies but also helped her friends. She was loyal and seems to have inspired considerable loyalty in others.[7] According to our sources, she was a loving, even doting mother to her son. We know less about her dealings with her daughter, but they remained close and acted together long after her daughter reached adulthood. Olympias was proud of the lineage of the dynasty of her birth, the Aeacids, and apparently maintained close ties with her kin throughout her long career. To some considerable degree, despite the patrilineal nature of the Greek world, she passed her Aeacid identity on to her children—even, and most surprisingly, to her son. Alexander's identification of himself as an Aeacid (and the tendency of our sources to so identify him) is striking. Arrian (*Anab.* 1.11.8), for instance, has Alexander say that he was descended from the *genos* (clan, family) of Neoptolemus.[8]

Olympias played a prominent role in female Dionysiac cult in Macedon, as well as in the dynastic cult of her husband's family (Plut. *Alex.* 2.5–6; Ath. 14.659f–660a). Her predilection for keeping snakes around the house probably related to her known use of them in cult. Ancient sources disagree as to whether she was the source of her son's belief that he was the son of a god, Zeus-Ammon. Plutarch (*Alex.* 3.2) preserves opinions on both sides. He cites Eratosthenes for the story that as Alexander departed for Asia, Olympias told him alone something secret concerning his birth and urged him to do nothing unworthy of his origins, obviously implying that she had confided that his birth was divine. Others, as Plutarch observes, insist that she denied any part in the idea and wittily urged her son to cease slandering her to Hera. Plutarch, implicitly and explicitly (*Alex.* 2.4, 3.1), connects Philip, but not Olympias, to acceptance of the idea that a god, not Philip, had fathered Alexander. Arrian (*Anab.* 4.10.2), however, claimed that Callisthenes, Alexander's official historian, referred contemptuously to Olympias's lies about her son's birth. Many scholars have concluded that Alexander's divine paternity was indeed originally her idea. I do not concur, primarily because many of them base their conclusions on their stereotypical reading of her character. Doubtless Olympias went along with her son's assertions once he made them, and she may have found them attractive, but no woman in the Hellenic world would voluntarily have suggested that she was less than faithful to her husband, and least of all Olympias, in the period just before and just after Philip's murder.

Olympias became the first woman in the Greek world to exercise political influence on a grand scale, primarily because she served as succession advocate for her son, Alexander III (the Great), and later for her grandson, Alexander IV. Philip II's last marriage precipitated a quarrel between him and his son Alexander that led to the self-imposed exile of both Olympias and Alexander. Plutarch (*Alex.* 9.3–10.3) claims that in the period leading up to the quarrel, Olympias exacerbated tensions between Philip and Alexander and that, even after the public reconciliation of the two, she and some of her son's other intimates encouraged behavior that once more put him at odds with Philip. Soon after, as we have seen, she was suspected of complicity (with or without her son's knowledge) in her husband's murder. Although Olympias did not accompany Alexander on campaign (such was not the Macedonian tradition, or at least not Philip's practice),[9] during Alexander's reign she played a public role in the Greek peninsula whose nature is now difficult to define. She received plunder from her son and made splendid offerings at Delphi. She and her daughter both received grain to distribute in a time of shortage. The inscription that commemorates this role (*SEG* IX 2) treats them like heads of state. Olympias also played politics in Athens, where some Athenian politicians seem to have assumed that she had a part in Macedonian public policy and perhaps Molossian as well (Hyp. *For Euxenippus* 19–20, 25). Her actions and her understanding of her position put her in conflict with Antipater, the man Alexander had left in general charge of affairs when he departed for the Asian campaign. At some point, presumably because of this conflict, she left Macedon for Molossia. Throughout his absence, tradition says she sent

Alexander letters warning him against not only Antipater, but also others at court she believed to threaten her son's best interests. She and her daughter worked together against Antipater, somehow challenging his public authority (Plut. *Alex.* 68.3). Her complaints about Antipater, as well as Antipater's about her, almost certainly damaged the relationship between the king and his general, bringing it nearly to the crisis point at the time of Alexander's death. Indeed, it was the obviously convenient timing of his death that led to charges that Antipater's family had been involved, just as the convenient timing of Philip's death led to suspicions against Olympias and Alexander.[10]

Such advocacy was hardly selfless on her part: it certainly brought her power, wealth, and acclaim. But her role also put her at risk. In her fifties, she left her safe "retirement home" in her native Molossia in order to return to Macedon at the head of (if not exactly in command of) an army meant to eliminate threats to her grandson, Alexander IV, and allow him a reasonable chance to live long enough to rule in fact as well as in name. The attempt failed, primarily because the general supporting her proved inept. Olympias endured a brutal siege before her enemy Cassander captured her. Wily to the end, nonetheless, when her executioners appeared, she faced them calmly, like a queen in tragic drama (and quite possibly using tragedy as a model for her conduct). Cassander forbade her burial, but her kin built her a tomb and venerated her memory for generations. In subsequent centuries she became the heroine of the immensely popular *Alexander Romance*, an ancient historical novel whose many versions retained popular appeal until early modern times. More than anything, the historical Olympias was a dynast. In the years after the death of Alexander the Great, she came to symbolize the Argead dynasty into which she had married. Her death, for practical purposes, meant the end of the dynasty.

Somewhat to my surprise, development of the character of Olympias and what proved to be the limitations of the portrayal of that character lay at the heart of Stone's film and (I believe) its commercial and artistic failure. This is not to say that *Alexander* had no other significant weaknesses.[11]

Like Rossen before him, Stone struggled with the problem of how to tell and unify a story that included early family strife, a long and adventurous military campaign, a large number of major characters, complicated political intrigue, and what many ancient and modern writers have understood as the moral deterioration of the main character.[12] Both Rossen and Stone clearly concluded that the conflict between

Olympias and Philip, particularly at the end of Philip's reign, shaped the character and career of their son in a fundamental way. In Stone's view, expressed in the commentary on his film's theatrical release DVD, Rossen's film spent too much of its time and virtually all of its energy on this early conflict. Stone's solution, a structure that combined flashbacks with linear narrative, unfortunately confused and alienated general audiences.[13] A straightforward linear narrative of Alexander's career (Stone's first draft of the script was so organized)[14] might have been clearer, if less likely to suggest anything about the central character's motivation.[15] I can keep my elite Macedonians straight—it is more or less my job—but ordinary viewers had trouble, and the great length of the film intensified the confusion generated by chronological complexity. Stone, however, has often had trouble with narrative construction,[16] yet he has managed nonetheless to produce compelling cinema, primarily by creating vivid scenes (as he did, to some degree, in *Alexander*) and memorable characters (*Alexander*'s weakness).

As popular history, something films with historical settings inevitably become,[17] *Alexander* is a mixed bag. Clearly playing on Plutarch's famous statement (*Alex*. 1.2) that he "wrote lives not history," Stone has said that he makes "film not history."[18] A film dealing with a historical topic, much like a historical novel, must sometimes put storytelling above concerns about historical correctness, particularly in terms of detail; one should expect and not cavil at some combining of incidents and reduction in and conflation of characters.[19] A screenwriter may choose to make an incident that historians consider minor pivotal and may neglect or omit something we scholars think is of fundamental importance. On the other hand, when the order of events is significantly altered, as is the case in Stone's *Alexander,* fundamental falseness in motivation and the chain of cause and consequence is the likely result.[20]

Like academic historians, writers of historical films must have sources, and both Rossen and Stone clearly knew at least some of the ancient sources fairly well. Perhaps it is no accident that Rossen and Stone sometimes seem significantly influenced by the greatest of novels about Alexander, the *Alexander Romance*.[21] In terms of the more sober ancient sources, the authors most interested in character (Plutarch) and lurid storytelling (Justin and to some degree the Vulgate authors generally) attract both filmmakers more than the sometimes dry narrative of Arrian. (In the case of Stone's film, this is ironic: its narrator is the aged Ptolemy, whose history of the campaign was a major, perhaps the major, source for Arrian.)

Filmmakers, despite lack of evidence, must show specific details about past worlds[22] and must choose when historians can avoid choice.[23] For instance, our sources make it difficult to determine the physical location of Olympias and other royal women and the degree to which they appeared in public and spoke to nonrelated males. Stone, of course, must put Olympias in some physical setting and makes the plausible choice to have her appear in public on some occasions, but to spend much of her time in her rooms.

No real point is served by offering up a list of factual errors in *Alexander*. Although Stone did make some actual mistakes—things that he thought he understood and intended to be historically accurate, but that are not[24]—his commentary and that of his historical advisor Robin Lane Fox make it clear that most differences, large and small, between what most of us would consider historical fact and the "facts" of the movie were the result of conscious choices by Stone. Moreover, particularly in matters relating to material culture, his re-creation of the Macedonian past (the palace, for instance) can be quite accurate, down to small details like the drinking cups at Macedonian symposia.[25] (The contrast with the sets of Rossen's film with its Art Deco "Greek" statuary and primitive production values is obvious:[26] Stone was able to take advantage of computer-generated imagery and thirty years' worth of new archaeological discoveries in Macedon. Clearly he made the effort to do so.)

My objection is not that the film's depiction of Olympias in particular and royal women in general is inaccurate or unhistorical (although sometimes it is). No, the trouble or the devil is not in the details of this film but rather in its stereotypical and unsubtle depiction of its two central characters and their dealings with each other.[27]

The central problem of *Alexander* is that Stone chose to make the relationship of Alexander and Olympias the center of the movie (and of his interpretation of Alexander's character and motivation), yet he created an unconvincing and confusing portrayal of this central relationship. The representation of women in Oliver Stone's biopic manages to compound the sexual stereotyping of women in general and Olympias in particular that is already present in virtually all of the ancient sources (and often uncritically accepted in modern scholarship) by introducing new sexist elements into the saga. Alexander and his mother were, judging by the ancient sources, not very sexual people (desire for power rather than sexual experience seemed to drive both), and yet Stone insists on the centrality of their sexuality in understanding why they acted as they did.[28] The result is a simplistic and hopelessly contradictory reading of the character and motivation of the major figures in the drama that was Alexander's life.

Stone's decision to make Alexander's relationship with Olympias the pivotal element in his saga, seen in the context of his entire body of work, is courageous but somewhat surprising. His lack of success in presenting a convincing picture of that relationship is not. Most of Stone's film work has focused on largely male worlds. Critics have often observed that his female characters are not only peripheral to the plot (hardly unreasonable in situations where women really were not present or barely so), but are usually stock figures serving male fantasy,[29] "eye candy."[30] Although Stone has rejected these judgments, apart from the evidence of his films, his own statements suggest the nature of the problem. For instance, he has remarked, "I think women dispense grace,"[31] an assertion that, essential silliness apart, speaks to his tendency to see women as decorative yet mysteriously incomprehensible Others.[32] Moreover, in a number of films, female characters threaten the creative drive of major male characters: they are not merely pretty but actively destructive.[33] In *Alexander*, Olympias is clearly the destructive force.

In *Heaven and Earth* (1993), Stone's only film with a female protagonist (based on a real person), his narrative focused on her victimhood (particularly her role as sexual victim) and paid scant attention to aspects of her life in which she took control and acted aggressively.[34] Stone highlighted her suffering at the hands of others and played down her coping and survival skills. His casting of a very young and inexperienced actress in the central role, in preference to the older and more commanding screen presence of Joan Chen, tended to intensify the focus on the helplessness of the lead character.[35] Thus, despite its apparent interest in a woman's experience, the film demonstrates a pervasive "masculine subtext."[36]

Given his past lack of interest in female characters and comparative lack of critical success with those he did create, Stone's decision to make Olympias and, to a lesser degree, Roxane important characters surprises. He could so easily have all but omitted them and paid attention only to the male military world in which Alexander spent his entire adult life. Instead, Stone gave Olympias a larger and more memorable role in the film than any other character except Alexander himself. (His focus on the relationship between mother and son may have been influenced by the prominence of their relationship in the *Romance*.) Olympias is not only the most prominent female character. Many aspects of her depiction are mirrored in the portrayal of other, less prominent women in the film, particularly in the characterization of Roxane. The figure of Olympias seems to function as a model for all the movie's female figures. One suspects that Stone, sensitive to criticism of his depiction of women, made Olympias so central as a bold response to a perceived challenge. In addition, as we shall see, Stone clearly read his own experiences into his depiction of her relationship with Alexander.

Unfortunately, his attempt to present powerful and aggressive women is unconvincing. A number of the aspects of Stone's depiction of women in earlier films recur in *Alexander*. Perhaps the most striking feature of the film's characterization of Olympias is the relentless focus on her sexuality. In the *Alexander Romance*, too, she is so sexually attractive that she inspires the nefarious Nectanebos to trick her into adultery (1.4) and Pausanias (or Anaxarchus)[37] to kill her husband (1.24). Moreover, the *Romance* makes it clear that Olympias enjoys sex (1.7), and Alexander angers his father by telling him that, when he marries his mother to another king, he'll ask Philip to the wedding (1.20). Interestingly, Stone's Alexander says exactly the same thing in the context of his violent brawl with Philip and Attalus at his father's latest wedding feast.

On the other hand, the characterization of Olympias's sexuality in the *Romance* differs significantly from that of the film. In the former, Olympias has and is shown to have an active sex life, whereas *Alexander* pictures a woman who is very sexual but never seems to have sex (even the rape is not completed) and, in Stone's mind, consciously avoids it.[38] The consequence is that Jolie's Olympias's repressed or denied sexuality informs all the scenes between her and her son, particularly since the actress and actor playing these scenes are nearly the same age. Moreover, the ancient novel does not make Olympias much of a victim: she berates herself for allowing herself to be tricked by the Egyptian conman (1.14), and her son/protector saves her from rape (1.24), kills Nectanebos for tricking her (1.14), and helps Philip kill Pausanias in punishment for his attempted rape and murder (1.24). Even her seduction by Nectanebos turns out well for her and does not long leave her in jeopardy. The *Romance*'s Olympias is often a damsel in distress, threatened, but not really victimized. As a consequence, revenge does not consistently motivate her, and her son is able to reconcile her with Philip. In the film, in contrast, her supposed victimhood leads to a reductive analysis of her personality and actions. While Stone insists that he wanted to portray an aggressive woman who played an active role in events, he emphasizes Olympias's passive suffering and understands her primarily as the object of Philip's bad acts.

In keeping with his emphasis on the passivity of women, Stone insists (in his commentary on the Director's Cut DVD) that Philip and Olympias's contemporaries believed that only the male functioned as a parent, whereas women were mere "receptacles."[39] Clearly he has read the *Oresteia* and remembered Athena's famous assertion that the father is sole parent, but he fails to recognize that Philip, Alexander, and Olympias herself (as well as many others) did not share this view. As we have seen, Alexander spoke of himself as of his mother's *genos* (clan) as well as his father's. Philip encouraged this Aeacid identification, at least early on, by choosing a relative of Olympias as Alexander's tutor, and later a man who actually called Alexander "Achilles" and Philip "Peleus" (Plut. *Alex.* 5.4–5), thus transforming Philip himself into an honorary Aeacid. After the death of Alexander, Cassander, the man who ultimately became the next king of Macedon, married Alexander's half-sister Thessalonice in order to have half-Argead sons. The names he chose for his sons—Philip, Alexander, and Antipater—demonstrate that he, like the rest of the Macedonian elite, did not share Athena's view. Olympias, like other young women of high birth, brought to her marriage and descendants the prize of noble and heroic lineage.

Jolie seems to have believed that Olympias was a captive taken by Philip in a war of conquest, so that her entire marriage itself was a kind of rape.[40] The historical Olympias married Philip by arrangement with her guardian, her uncle, who was king of Molossia. Plutarch (*Alex.* 2.1) even claims (wrongly I believe) that erotic passion motivated Philip's desire to marry her. Like Philip's other marriages, this one certainly had a political context, a Macedonian-Molossian alliance. Olympias would never have expected to be able to choose her own husband. In the Hellenic world, a young woman's male guardian usually made such decisions. Since her father was dead, her uncle acted as guardian. Some royal Macedonian women, it is true, tried to arrange marriages for their daughters, and Alexander's sister Cleopatra attempted to arrange her own marriage, but these were all older widows who lacked a close male relative.[41] Olympias may have had reasons to wish herself gone from her uncle's court (he had forced her father, originally sole ruler, to co-rule with him). Moreover, this was a prestigious marriage (probably the most glamorous yet achieved by a member of her dynasty) to a young ruler on his way up. All things considered, it is likely that she welcomed it.

While the historical Olympias may well have seen her marriage as an opportunity to exercise power and achieve acclaim in a wider world than the remote Molossian court, Stone and Jolie imagine her, from the start, as the suffering object of others' actions and betrayals. Indeed the film graphically insists that the marriage that began as rape continued in the same vein. Philip's attempted rape of Olympias in the presence of her young son is more than yet another film rape fantasy masquerading as discourse about the evils of violence against women (though it is surely that). Borrowing from the "cinema of exploitation," Stone has often used rape as motivation and motif in his films.[42]

This rape scene is also an episode that narrows Olympias's motivation (and that of her son) to matters entirely sexual. By word and deed, the film argues that she is consistently motivated by a desire to take vengeance, apparently for the supposed rape, not for political reasons. Indeed, partially echoing the *Alexander Romance,* Stone's Olympias tells Philip that "in my womb I carry my avenger." In the ancient novel, however, although Nectanebos promises that the child she bears will be "your avenger for the wrongs Philip has done you,"[43] the wrongs in question are not spousal rapes but rather Philip's supposed intention to divorce her on account of childlessness. While the historical Philip was sometimes drunken and violent (and may have countenanced sexual violence by others, if the story that he failed to punish Attalus for the gang rape of Pausanias is true),[44] we do not know that he himself was guilty of sexual violence, least of all against Olympias. While our sources tell us virtually nothing about their relationship except for the troubled last two years of his reign, they certainly indicate that Philip's objections to Olympias and hers to him were political and centered on the issue of the succession (Plut. *Alex.* 9.3).

The prurient treatment of Olympias's complex relationship to Philip is sometimes implausibly combined with the presumption that her marriage worked in the same way as modern bourgeois marriages. Despite the fact that virtually all marriages in the Greek world were arranged, the film implies a marriage created by romantic love (obviously a contradiction of the idea of Olympias as sexual victim).[45] Jolie's Olympias tells her son, echoing virtually every soap opera heroine one can recall, that she has "never stopped loving" Philip. This seems a particularly odd statement given that he has been portrayed as her serial rapist and that no scenes showing affection between the pair appear. This typifies the impossibly contradictory depiction of Olympias and her motivation that characterizes the film. Olympias, in terms of the "facts" of the film, had no reason to love Philip, yet we seem to be expected to take her assertion seriously. Stone probably wanted to portray a love-hate relationship but forgot to. The movie sometimes recognizes that Philip was polygamous and that Olympias's status and position derived primarily from her role as the mother of Philip's apparent heir. At other times, however, we are told that Philip rejected his older wife for a younger woman (most sources call her Cleopatra, but Arrian once (*Anab.* 3.6.5) calls her Eurydice, and that is the name Stone's film employs), divorcing Olympias, exiling her, and depriving her of her title. Apart from the fact that Philip's last wife was young and presumably younger than Olympias, none of this is historical.[46] Moreover, since the movie dates Philip's relationship with "Eurydice" as early as Alexander's initial taming of Bucephalus, it chooses to portray the relationship between Philip and Olympias as entirely hostile at least as early as 350 (the date given in the film).

The implication of this scenario is that Olympias's motivation for her supposed involvement in Philip's death is that she is a woman scorned. Olympias, usually so confident, compares herself with Philip's new wife and is made to ask her son, "Do I seem so old?" Yet the actress chosen to play Philip's last bride looks scarcely younger than Jolie and is certainly far less attractive or memorable. Moreover, despite these lines, Jolie hardly looks threatened[47] or worried and indeed seems amused by the young, supposedly pregnant woman. Here again, Stone's choices undercut his own message. From a historical point of view, sexual jealousy seems an unlikely motive at this point in Olympias's marriage: for many years Philip had sexual relationships with a number of men and women, including, possibly, Olympias's brother. Philip acquired at least one and perhaps two wives after Olympias and before his last wedding. Given what happens in the movie, one would think that Olympias would have been glad to see the back of Philip, not angry. Ancient sources portray her as jealous of threats to her son's position but not of Philip's other women or lovers (Plut. *Mor.* 141b–c).

Indeed, the film tells us that Olympias was involved in her husband's murder exactly because of her fear that Alexander would be put aside. If anything, it exaggerates the immediate danger to Alexander and to Olympias, particularly by picturing the baby born to Philip's new wife as male, not the majority view of scholars.[48] In the film, Olympias tells her son that Philip will never let him be king now and implies that both their lives are in danger. The stress the movie has already put on her as peculiar and isolated makes it hard for a viewer to know whether she is right or paranoid. In any event, this motivation confuses and contradicts the tale of an assassination plotted by a sexually jealous, aging (if invisibly) woman.

Stone's film not only makes Olympias responsible for Philip's murder (as did Rossen's)—something people wondered about at the time and something she may really have done—but insists that Alexander knew nothing about it beforehand (much less likely), ignores the powerful motivation of Philip's actual assassin, and generally downplays the possible involvement of any number of other figures at court or away from it. (In the film Olympias mentions all of these possible assassins to Alexander, but it is clear that we are meant not to believe her.) Instead of choosing to leave her involvement (and that of Alexander) a possibility, the stereotype of the scheming political woman is preferred over anything more subtle: witchy, bitchy Olympias did it with no help from her sweet son.[49] She is murderous and he is not, or at least he is not until she warps him.

In keeping with Stone's inclination to put sole blame on Olympias, the film vitiates the motivation of the actual assassin, Pausanias. Tellingly, Stone shows us in considerable detail two fictitious rapes of women (Olympias and Roxane) but provides only a vague hint (a spanking scene with sexual undertones glimpsed at the wedding banquet) at the real gang rape that motivated Philip's assassin. Indeed, all heterosexual sex in the movie is, at best, "rough trade." Sex between men is implicit rather than explicit: for instance, in the Director's Cut we see the eunuch Bagoas getting into bed with Alexander, kissing him once, and repeatedly gazing at him with calf's eyes—gentle, even genteel, and more than a bit bland.

Despite the fact that both films implicate Olympias in Philip's death, Stone's depiction of Olympias's part in Philip's murder differs greatly from Rossen's understanding of her role and situation. Rossen's Olympias, despite the presence of an Egyptian lover (a nonhistorical figure borrowed from the *Alexander Romance*), is essentially a political creature, ambitious for power. "When you're regent, we'll co-rule," she says to her son. Alexander is torn between the conflicting ambitions of his parents, both ruthless and equally self-serving.

Rossen's Olympias, like the real one, is a public figure, whereas Stone's Olympias seems to exist only in the mind and memory of her husband and son, even in the period of her son's reign when, as I have indicated, we know she played a prominent role in public events. She is a lonely and solitary figure who seems to have no adherents, no other family members, and no significant role in public events and rituals. Given her apparent isolation, she has mysteriously good information about court intrigue and continues, via letters we see her dictate, to offer political advice in the years after Alexander's departure. These letter scenes, on the whole following ancient tradition about her correspondence with her son, are perhaps her most effective scenes in the film. Jolie is allowed to show some slight signs of age and does not look so generically scheming. Surprisingly, we learn that she advised Alexander to marry, though not Roxane, since she was not of royal blood. This particular advice is not historically attested, but the film (in this case in accord with ancient sources) also has Olympias warn Alexander about virtually everyone at court, insisting that even those closest to him were plotting against him. Confusingly, although these warnings are played as another example of her paranoia, Olympias (according to the film, probably not in fact) was right: Alexander's closest associates were all involved in his death. In *Alexander* Olympias dictates these warning missives to a usually unseen servant but is otherwise alone, not clearly part of court life in Macedon or Molossia. One can only presume that she has acquired all of this information and political wisdom by means of her persistent lurking. Ironically, despite Danielle Darrieux's mannered and unmemorable rendition of Olympias in the earlier film, Rossen's script presents a more historical and more clearly motivated royal woman.

Stone's focus on Olympias's sexuality extends to her role as mother. Here again the characterization is impossibly contradictory. While many scholars, rightly or wrongly, have detected a sexual element in the relationship between Alexander and Olympias, for Stone it is almost literally incestuous. The myth of Oedipus, pictured in those odd cave paintings that Philip shows Alexander in Stone's film, has played a role in other Stone films.[50] His Alexander, even as an adult, hurls himself into his mother's lap and kisses her full on the lips. Stone has Alexander the child sleep in his mother's bed and witness his father's aborted rape of her (as well as himself experiencing some physical abuse from his father). The film insinuates that Roxane, whose depiction so clearly and intentionally echoes that of Olympias (see below), is simply a substitute for her. Casting Angelina Jolie, only a year older than the actor who plays Alexander, is not simply the consequence of Hollywood's obsession with youth[51] or indifference to verisimilitude. It is a conscious choice made in support of Stone's interpretation of their relationship, one grounded in falseness of history and representation.[52] The story of Oedipus is a powerful one, as Freud recognized, and may well have relevance to the relationship of Philip, Olympias, and Alexander, but one needs to apply it with subtlety. Stone does the reverse. The tone of these scenes between mother and son, scenes filled with sexual overtones, is problematic. One is never clear whether Olympias, whatever her ambitions, was genuinely if unhealthily fond of her son ("a mother loves too much," she comments opaquely) or merely manipulative and actively evil. After all, the film consistently connects Olympias to the myth of Medea (she is also a stand-in for Medusa), making her a child-killer.

Moreover, the portrayal of Philip is so narrow that Stone's would-be familial sexual triangle has no real force. One has little sense of Philip as a powerful personality, great general, or clever diplomat. Instead he struts, drinks, and spends time trying to get his son to like or understand him, only to turn on him when offered affection or support. His uncertainty and need for affection extend to the populace. "I want them to like me," he confesses. One would not easily know from the film that Alexander led the expedition his father had planned, that the invasion of the Persian empire was Philip's idea. Rather than the "emulation and resentment"[53] that characterized the historical Alexander's dealings with his father, Stone's Alexander resents his father but seems to have nothing much to emulate. Plot and history suggest that Alexander grew up in the context of conflicts between two powerful personalities, but the actual film shows a weak and absent father and tensions more talked about than felt or demonstrated. Stone's earlier work often featured an absent father and a problematic mother, apparently reflecting the writer-director's own unhappy early experiences,[54] although Stone himself has refused to accept these characterizations of his parents.[55] In this regard, one must note that he dedicated the film to his own mother.[56] Moreover, his judgment that Alexander "bore all the marks of a wounded only child"[57] is touchingly incorrect: Stone himself was an only child, but Alexander had a full sister, a half-brother (perhaps two), and three half-sisters. Sadly, Oliver Stone seems haunted by issues genuinely relevant to any depiction of relations among the royal mother, father, and son, yet unable to create compelling and believable motivation for the three figures involved in this family conflict.

According to Stone, Olympias was the motivation for Alexander's campaigns and adventures, not only because she supposedly inspired him to seek a short but glorious life but also because Stone understands Alexander to be running away from her. Scholars have long debated what drove Alexander on[58]—what Arrian called his *pothos* (longing, yearning)—but in *Alexander* Olympias is the *pothos*, in a negative sense. In the film, Olympias wants to join her son in the East as she says he promised. Hephaestion, nearly always drearily noble in the film (his rudeness to Roxane at the time of the "mutiny" excepted), advises Alexander to follow Olympias's wishes. When Alexander refuses, Hephaestion wonders if it is not his mother he runs from. Stone himself has problematized Alexander's failure to bring Olympias to Babylon.[59] There is no evidence that Alexander contemplated doing so or that the historical Olympias wanted or expected to go to Babylon. If she had or understood herself to have some public position in Macedon, Molossia, or both—something for which there is evidence[60]—then she probably did not expect to join him in the East. Certainly, as we have seen, she acted as though she was Alexander's personal representative. The film's tendency to isolate Olympias from the rest of the court and society, to limit her role to the personal, makes an issue out of something that probably was not an issue at the time. Pinning Alexander's insatiable desire to conquer, explore, and do what had not been done before to a supposed fear of his mother oversimplifies his motivation and denies the importance of Homer and heroic emulation.

As we have seen, Stone's obsession with Olympias's sexuality leads either to her depoliticization or confusion about her political motives. He also personalizes her motivation in a way that ignores her political goals and her cultural context. Stone's Olympias often alludes to her descent from Achilles, historically a very real part of her dynasty's public image. It may well be true that she instilled Alexander's emulation of the hero, as Stone implies (Olympias calls Alexander "my little Achilles"), but Stone ignores the degree to which she, Philip, and the Macedonian elite shared in an agonistic culture in which one person's success always meant another's failure. As we have seen, Philip seems to have supported the early emphasis on Homer in Alexander's education. These were values and goals on which Olympias and Philip would have agreed.[61] Indeed, the competitive relationship between father and son was grounded in Homeric values.[62]

The world of Homer permeated many aspects of the life of the Macedonian elite,[63] but Stone ignores Homer (instead the film begins with a quote from the much later Roman poet Virgil) and substitutes the mysterious flooded but painted caves under the palace at Aegae—scenes that puzzled theater audiences. Instead of the power and force of Homer's words, we have generic myths, a kind of Edith Hamilton version of Greek values. As a consequence, Homeric values become simply and idiosyncratically those of Olympias.[64] The film actually pictures both Philip and Aristotle as anti-Homer. Oddly, however, the palace at Pella in the film has a large wall painting (or perhaps wall mosaic) showing Achilles dragging Hector around the walls of Troy, an image on which the cameras focus when we are supposed to recall the origins of Alexander's violent and self-destructive tendencies. If Philip had actually been so opposed to Homer, this would be a peculiar choice for domestic interior decoration.[65]

As we have noted, the film suggests that Olympias was really a Medea (a remarkable exaggeration of any possible reading of the historical figures) who killed her own son because she encouraged him to make Achilles' famous choice of a short but glorious life. In his commentary on the Director's Cut DVD, Stone makes the connection with Medea explicit and asserts that Olympias "metaphorically" kills Alexander out of hatred for Philip. Alexander, having recognized her involvement in his father's death, tells her, "You murdered me in the cradle," presumably by embedding in his character the example of Achilles. When a drunken Alexander looks into the cup containing the fatal poison placed there, according to the film, by the consent of all around him, he sees Olympias, but Olympias as Medusa. We do not see that an entire culture shared in the pursuit of glory—that Alexander was unusual not in his values or ideals, but in his ability to realize them.

The comparative absence of religion as a serious force in the life of Olympias or her son (apart from ritual and atmospheric details like the many images in her chambers) weakens the depiction of both. Jolie believed—rightly, I think—that her character "found a power and strength"[66] in her religious beliefs, but the film does not manage to show that in a convincing way. We do see a lot of Olympias's snakes, but they seem just a kinky or crazy (perhaps both) hobby. Plutarch reports that she used them in cult (*Alex.* 2.6), but that does not happen in the movie. Stone's snakes are apparently poisonous and life-threatening, but the ones Plutarch describes are simply off-putting in the way that snakes appear to most people.[67] In a scene with particularly unfortunate dialogue, Olympias seems to use her presumably venomous vipers to teach some sort of moral lesson. She tells young Alexander that the snake is "his friend" and that "snakes are like people." Nonetheless, we know it is a bad sign when, in the aftermath of killing Cleitus, Alexander appears to have begun to imitate his mother's fondness for keeping snakes around the house; perhaps he has become as murderous as his mother.

Dionysus, so important in Olympias's life and her son's, is mentioned (and oddly associated only or largely with women), but the force and appeal of the god are not indicated. Both Philip and Alexander call Olympias a "sorceress," and Stone himself, in his commentary on the theatrical release DVD, denies that she is, but continues to raise the possibility. The film never depicts Olympias using magic, although the ancient sources contain hints that she did or was believed to.[68] The notion that Alexander was the son of a god, whether or not it really was Olympias's claim, as the film insists, is trivialized. The movie's audience, lacking any understanding of the complexity of Greek notions of divinity, inevitably concludes that her belief that her son was fathered by a god is simply crazy. Stone's Alexander actually calls her a "crazed woman." In fact, no ancient source treats Olympias as mentally unstable, although, intriguingly, modern scholars often jump to that conclusion.[69] In terms of Stone's film, understanding Olympias as crazy can function as a convenient explanation for the extremely contradictory portrait of her character presented.

Here I must turn from the portrayal of Olympias in terms of script and setting to Jolie's interpretation of her role. Clearly no firm line exists between a writer/director's decisions and those of the actors who take roles in a film: Stone was involved in casting and in his role as director insisted on or permitted aspects of Jolie's performance. Indeed, any screen performance is presumably the consequence of the interaction of director and actor.

Let me begin with the implications of Stone's decision to cast Angelina Jolie as Olympias. As we have seen, he consciously chose an actress whose age defied and confused the historical situation. While many people, including the Academy, admired Jolie's work in *Girl, Interrupted* (1999), her subsequent performances proved far less impressive and disappointingly repetitive. What was fresh in *Girl, Interrupted* and appropriate for a woman confined to a mental hospital became Jolie's stereotypical performance, whatever the context of the character she portrays. She had become famous for the wild but sardonic gleam in her eye. She herself contributed to the common perception that in the now long list of roles in which she has played beautiful yet unbalanced young women, she has, in essence, portrayed herself.[70] Her celebrity persona—what she chose to let film audiences know or think they know about her—contributed to her own stereotype, particularly by suggesting that she personally was a bit less (or more) than normal, intense in a way many might consider perverse or bizarre.[71] Later she added to her public portrayal of herself the persona of an intensely motherly figure, devoted to her own children by birth and adoption and the world's children (she became a Good Will Ambassador for the United Nations in 2001 and has spent considerable time on activities connected to this role). Stone stressed her motherly role in talking about his selection of her to play Olympias, and Jolie has talked about bringing to the part her own experience of motherhood.[72]

Directors certainly pay attention to the physical aspects of an actor in making casting decisions, and Jolie's physical presence is compelling. In appearance, she is not simply beautiful but commanding and powerful; one would not hire her to play a weak, gentle, or conventional woman. Her age and height in comparison with Colin Farrell's contribute to the film's understanding of them as a pair. From the first moment she appears on screen, Jolie generates an energy and power not seen in Danielle Darrieux's vapid interpretation of Olympias. Certainly Jolie is the polar opposite of the colorlessly pretty but innocuous actress who played Helen in *Troy*. In all probability, Stone hired Jolie to play a beautiful woman and mother so intense in her feelings as to seem, in modern terms, less than sane and certainly less than balanced.[73] This was brand-name casting.[74]

Angelina Jolie herself made choices that contributed to the disappointingly stereotypical characterization of Olympias; the actress could have done more with the part and did not bother to. Most of the representation of Olympias in *Alexander* is clearly that of Stone, since it is embedded in the script and set: for instance, the single window on the second floor of the palace, apparently solely constructed so that Olympias could lurk with ease and visibility, or the red chiton—color-coordinated with the garments of the assassin she has apparently inspired—that she is made to wear on the day of Philip's murder. Yet Jolie heightens what was already an over-the-top interpretation.[75] She could have chosen to play against this predictable role, or Stone could have encouraged her to do so; her performance could have created the subtlety in characterization lacking in the badly written screenplay and could have resolved or explained the contradictions in her portrayal that I have mentioned. For instance, on any number of occasions she could have looked thoughtful or reflective or even sad, rather than repeatedly narrowing her eyes in apparent crazed calculation. This failure is most striking when we see her observing the quarrel between her son and his father from her lurking window. Despite the fact that Philip tries, if ineptly, to kill Alexander, whose ambition to succeed his father is apparently thwarted, Jolie simply repeats her generic look of calculation; her expression and actions convey no sense that her son's life or her own might be on the line.

Unfortunately, Jolie's performance, if anything, exaggerates the sexual stereotyping of the script. Whereas many of the costumes worn in *Alexander* were quite authentic, Olympias's clothing (at Jolie's insistence, rumor has it) was anything but. Instead of the loose, flowing chiton or peplos, securely fastened at both shoulders or down the arms, or both, Jolie appeared in clinging one-shouldered garments, often implausibly bright white and suggesting more than a hint of Lycra. In his commentary on the theatrical release DVD, Robin Lane Fox gamely describes these garments as currently "unattested" in Macedon.[76] More surprising, given the availability of many examples of Macedonian jewelry, much of it delicate and lovely, was her jewelry. Even when the shape of her earrings was roughly correct, they often took the form of oversized shoulder-knockers.[77] One headdress looked more like something that she got in a Happy Meal than what is found in Macedonian burials. Whereas one might attribute Jolie's implausibly body-hugging garments to her vanity or fear of not displaying her spectacular figure, the oddly inappropriate jewelry seems to have been intended to show that she was "barbaric."

Certainly that seems to have been the reason for her odd accent. Stone made the clever decision to give most of his "Macedonians" various accents from the "Celtic fringe," a laudable rejection of that irritating presumption that people in the past spoke with an upper-class English accent,[78] and a plausible equivalent for a Macedonian accent in relation to Attic Greek.[79] However, instead of choosing some real but different accent for Olympias (so as to indicate that she was not a native Macedonian), Stone and Jolie chose to create a fictional accent from no particular place that sounded a bit like that of Russian spies in early Bond flicks. Significantly, Rosario Dawson's Roxane also has a fictional accent, but no male characters in the film do. Although both Stone and Jolie insist that these fantastic accents simply indicate Olympias's and Roxane's status as outsiders,[80] the telling implication seems to be that Stone and the two actresses saw their characters as less real, less historic than the male roles. Moreover, Olympias, apparently, much like her daughter-in-law, was generically barbaric, something clearly related to their many dark looks, suspicious glances, tendency to skulk, and (in

the film) uniquely murderous ways. Thus Jolie, apparently content
with her now familiar rendition of a woman both crazed and sardonic,
failed to bring any subtlety of portrayal to a role that was already over-
written and underconceived.

This pattern of sexualizing and depoliticizing royal women appears
again in the depiction of the Persian royal women. Despite the elaborate and visually convincing mise-en-scène in Babylon,[81] the Persian
women are shown to be simply pathetic. Indeed, the film's depiction of
Persian and other Asian cultures reproduces a kind of old-fashioned
Orientalism that would have made Edward Said livid.[82] Although Alexander scolds his cranky and racist Macedonians for failing to recognize
that the peoples they have conquered come from a "world far older than
ours," he also tells Hephaestion that they have no system, something he
can presumably provide (thus ignoring not only centuries of Persian
imperial rule, but that of the many imperial predecessors of the Persians).[83] Orientalism, of course, often focuses on Asian women and their
imagined sexuality. The harem scene in the film, though visually striking, clearly plays to that sensibility. The mother of Darius, judging by
our sources, played an important role in Alexander's attempt to build
a connection to the Persian monarchy and claim continuity of rule.[84]
In the film, her figure has disappeared, replaced by her daughter/
daughter-in-law. After a long delay, Alexander married the daughter of
Darius and perhaps the daughter of an earlier Persian king as well. His
Persian marriages took place in the context of mass weddings of Macedonians to female members of the Persian elite. In the film, Roxane re-
places Darius's daughter in many scenes, further obscuring the importance of Persian royal women in Alexander's claim to legitimate rule of
the Persian empire.

In *Alexander,* Roxane is simply an exotic and violent beauty who likes
it rough. In his commentary on the Director's Cut DVD, Stone associates her with the mythical Amazons Alexander and Achilles had sex
with, much given to guttural speech and knife play (Plut. *Alex.* 46.1–
2).[85] She too has essentially no political role. The tedious narrator, Ptolemy, remarks that the marriage had "no political significance,"[86] something of an oversimplification. The historical Roxane was not royal, not
an Achaemenid, but she was the daughter of a Bactrian chief, part of the
elite that ran an area Alexander was having difficulty keeping conquered. Rather than plotting to kill Alexander's royal Persian wife, presumably to safeguard the throne for her son—as the real Roxane may
well have done (Plut. *Alex.* 77.4)—Stone's Roxane apparently plots to

kill Hephaestion, not out of a desire for power, of course, but from simple sexual jealousy.

Stone consciously and often heavy-handedly constructs the character of Roxane as a second but lesser Olympias. Both wear snake bracelets (the camera forces us to notice this detail, implying but not explaining its significance), although Olympias's is gold and Roxane's only silver; both, as we have noted, have hokey and imaginary but vaguely barbarian accents, and both, although sometimes demonstrating political acumen and willingness to offer Alexander advice (both Olympias and Roxane want him to give up his Indian campaign and return to Babylon), apparently commit murders out of petty sexual jealousy. Makeup emphasizes the nearly nonexistent physical resemblance between the two actresses and renders them exotic: both wear much more makeup, particularly eye makeup, than the Macedonian and Greek women.[87] And, of course, marriage for both women is really, literally rape, but each one nonetheless loves her abusive spouse. The implication is that in marrying Roxane Alexander has come as close as he could to marrying his mother (Olympias herself tells him not to confuse them), in fulfillment of his Oedipal desires. Alexander removes Roxane's snake bracelet before they have sex, but even then he thinks of Olympias. The film flashes back and forth between the scene of Alexander and Roxane having sex and that of Olympias warning her son against Roxane. In a gloomy postcoital moment, Alexander says to himself that Roxane was "a pale reflection of his mother's heart."

The construction of gender in the film, despite all the prerelease hoopla about how modern it would be, is risibly earnest. The actor who plays Hephaestion, Jared Leto, must wear eyeliner, unlike all of the other male Macedonians, presumably so that we will not miss the sexual tension between him and his friend. Although Stone shows Hephaestion in armor and in battle, Leto's portrayal unfortunately mirrors modern conventional views of "gay men." He is not allowed to seem masculine and macho in the way many of the other Macedonian males are. Stone's Hephaestion is so languid and passive that one simply cannot believe that the Persian queen mistook him for Alexander, as the story told in so many ancient sources says she did. Stone, despite his good intentions, fails to convey the normality of the relationship in the context of the ancient world,[88] managing merely to sentimentalize it. Indeed, the film tends to be preachy about the rightness and goodness of the relationship. Whereas the *Romance* depicts Alexander's relationship with Olympias in cloyingly sweet terms, Stone's film gives that treatment to his relationship with Hephaestion.

The limitations of the film in terms of women, gender, and sexuality relate to the central problem with the work. Stone consistently fails to understand and convey the cultural and personal motivation of people who lived in a world very different from our own. This happens not because the writer/director did not care, but because he proved more interested in his own mythic understanding of the characters than in their reality. Stone's Olympias and Roxane, instead of becoming complicated and believable agents in the events of Alexander's reign, prove two more examples of what Suzanne Dixon has called "the enduring theme: domineering dowagers and scheming concubines."[89] Both women, in keeping with this old but powerful stereotype, are shown to focus largely on the personal, to play favorites, to lack self-control, to act for selfish ends and out of jealousy.[90] *Alexander* could have told the story of the conqueror's life in a way that imagined his mother and wife without the stereotypes that we have inherited from Plutarch and the rest—but it did not.

The film trivializes and oversimplifies Alexander himself, not just his mother and wife. Picturing him as inspired merely by repressed desire for his own mother makes for a bad movie and bad history. The historical Alexander had a royal signet ring, a symbol of his power and ability to rule. When he was dying, he probably gave it to his close associate Perdiccas, indicating that he was his chosen successor (Curt. 10.5.4, 6.4; Just. *Epit.* 12.15.12; Diod. Sic. 17.117.3, 18.2.4). Stone's Alexander has a ring given him as a love token by Hephaestion. In the film, as Alexander dies, the love token drops to the ground. Randomly, it is last seen on the finger of the aged Ptolemy. History's Macedonians—most particularly Alexander and his mother, Olympias—were all about power, while Stone's Macedonians are all about sex.

Notes

1. Jon Solomon (2001, 37, 42) considers the film one "of the most historically faithful" of movies made about the ancient world, despite the fact that Rossen's film was quite unfaithful to history in its depiction of the events surrounding the death of Philip. For instance, there seems to be a civil war going on in Macedon at the time of Philip's death; the Macedonians suffer defeats; Olympias rules Pella; Olympias is sent away before Philip's last wedding because she is sexually unfaithful. Rossen's Olympias is not based on historical sources, but on the *Alexander Romance*. Solomon admires Rossen's refusal to "glorify or whitewash" Alexander; in this area Rossen's movie compares favorably to Stone's. More dubious is Solomon's view (2001, 42) that Burton does an admirable job, a view shared by Nisbet (2006, 91). Roquemore (1999, 8) is far more

critical, terming it "tedious" and complaining about the "cumbersome dialogue." Nisbet considers Stone's film nearly "a scene-for-scene remake" (2006,
128); I see similarities, but some important differences.

2. See Nisbet 2006, 101–11, for a discussion of this pilot; he compares it favorably to the Rossen and Stone films.

3. For a longer account of Olympias's life with full citations of ancient and
modern references, see my biography of her (Carney 2006) and the three biographical sections of Carney 2000, 62–67, 85–88, 119–23.

4. Keegan 1988. Stone recognizes the mystery of Alexander's personality
when he remarks in his commentary on the Director's Cut DVD that we "don't
know anything about Alexander."

5. On the relationship between polygamy and succession and its impact on
Olympias and Alexander, see Greenwalt 1989; Carney 1992. Not all scholars
would agree with our statements about the succession, although many would.
See references in Greenwalt, whose arguments are persuasive.

6. On the issue of the possible role of Olympias and/or Alexander in Philip's
death, there is no *opinio communis*. See Carney 1992 for discussion and references.

7. Eumenes, for instance, was very loyal to her and her daughter, and
Olympias's nephew Aeacides risked and lost his throne because of his efforts to
assist her.

8. Other examples of Alexander as an Aeacid: Arr. *Anab.* 4.1.26; Just. *Epit.*
11.2.1, 12.15.1, 16.3; Paus. 1.9.8; Curt. 8.4.26; Diod. Sic. 17.1.5; Strabo 13.1.27. See
Amelung 1988.

9. Ath. 13.557b.

10. See further discussion and references in Carney 2000, 86–88.

11. Unless otherwise stated, references are to the theatrical release of *Alexander* rather than to the Director's Cut.

12. See Nisbet 2006, 112–35, for an intriguing discussion of the ways in
which popular culture, Greek nationalism, and competing film projects shaped
the making and nature of Stone's *Alexander*.

13. This is particularly true of the theatrical version of the film, but even the
Director's Cut, though somewhat easier to follow, is less than linear.

14. According to the commentary on the Director's Cut DVD.

15. Kathryn Millard (1998, 232) complains about the domination of "heroic
linear narrative" in film biography and its tendency to imply the inevitability of
events but without offering a sense for the main character's inner life. The difficulty, however, is that rejection of linearity also has its problems.

16. Beaver 1994, 188–89. Stephen Lavington (2004, 179), discussing *Heaven
and Earth*, explains that Stone began the film with a nonlinear structure but
changed it to a more conventional one. Lavington considers the result "stodgy."
He also correctly predicted (ibid., 267) that *Alexander* would be told in flashback. As the commentary on the Director's Cut DVD makes clear, Stone refused
to give up on *Alexander*'s antilinear structure, but he did tinker with it in the
hope of creating a clearer and more comprehensible work.

17. Frank Sanello (2003, xii) points out that historical films are often the way young people in a "postliterate" world learn history.

18. Commentary on the Director's Cut DVD.

19. Rosenstone 2000, 29–31; Solomon 2001, 25–27; Winkler 2004b, 17–21.

20. For instance, in *Alexander*, Alexander's near-fatal wound is inflicted in a version of the battle with Porus. The wound seems to inspire his decision to return, rather than the confrontation with his troops on the Hyphasis, the historical reason for the decision. Moreover, a scene that more or less represents that confrontation happens earlier in the film, with no apparent consequence other than bad feelings. Thus what forces his decision in the film—his near death from a wound—could not have affected his decision to return because, in fact, the wound had not yet happened when Alexander agreed to turn back.

21. As we have noted, Rossen actually includes a character from the *Romance*, the nonhistorical Nectanebos. Stone's film, like the *Romance*, is cavalier about chronology and focuses to a much greater degree than the conventional ancient sources on Olympias and her relationship with her son. See below for other similarities to the *Romance*.

22. Rosenstone 2000, 32.

23. Solomon 2001, 32.

24. For instance, in his commentary on the theatrical release DVD, Stone refers to six major Alexander authors (instead of five) and the ten wives of Philip (rather than seven). More worrying is the moment when he confuses his own fiction with historical fact. In *Alexander*, a number of events are moved to a later time period, including Alexander's elimination of Parmenion and Philotas and the murder of Cleitus. In the film, these things happen after Alexander's marriage to Roxane, but in fact they happened before it. Stone, forgetting his revision of the order of events, says that the marriage marked a turning point, implying that Alexander's adoption of Eastern habits begins only then, and that these deaths came as a consequence.

25. Frank Beaver (1994, xii) considers Stone's films generally to be "superbly crafted."

26. Gideon Nisbet (2006, 92–97) sees this as part of Rossen's conscious (but ultimately ineffective) attempt to avoid conventional spectacle. Pursuing the film's general "Art Deco" look, Nisbet compares its images to the quasi-classical sports sculpture of the Mussolini era (ibid., 98).

27. Robert Rosenstone (2000, 34) makes a convincing case that historical films should be judged by different standards than historical writing, assessed not in terms of detail but "level of argument, metaphor, symbol" and the degree to which they engage the viewer in the big issues. It is on this level that *Alexander* fails.

28. Stone insists in the commentary on the Director's Cut DVD that it was his audience that was obsessed with Alexander's sexuality, and that he reduced the sexual element in that version: the more violent parts of the sexual encounter between Alexander and Roxane, for instance, were eliminated. His insistence is,

however, disingenuous, since he makes the central motivation of Alexander, Olympias, and Roxane sexual.

29. Beaver 1994, 10, 13; Michael Carlson (2002, 15) considers the relative absence of women a "trademark" of Stone's films. Stone, of course, went to an all-male prep school and a still all-male Yale, and then into the army, so he had relatively little knowledge of the world of women. These are the reasons Stone himself usually cites (Carlson 2002, 15) for the peripheral role of women in his work.

30. Carlson 2002, 15.

31. Breskin 1997, 40. Similarly, in his commentary on the Director's Cut DVD Stone connects women to the earth and men to the sky.

32. James Riordan (1995, 11) connects this perception to his experiences with his mother, who often withdrew from him.

33. Carlson 2002, 15.

34. Ibid.; Lavington 2004, 184–91.

35. Carlson 2002, 60–61; Carlson suggests that the "helplessness" of the young actress aided in the "voyeuristic pleasure" of her rape scene in the film.

36. Marinelli 1997, 242.

37. The gamma text (see Stoneman 1991, 161–64) has a variant of the death of Philip in which Anaxarchus, the king of the Thessalians, lusts after Olympias and kidnaps her and in the subsequent battle inflicts an ultimately fatal wound on Philip. Alexander leaves his dying father to pursue Anaxarchus; having captured him and saved Olympias, Alexander helps his expiring father kill Anaxarchus.

38. In his commentary on the theatrical release DVD, Stone seems to recall (incorrectly) that the sources say that Olympias purposely kept snakes around to keep Philip away from her.

39. Jolie, presumably influenced by him because she considers Stone "erudite" (Crane 2004), states a similar view (Mortensen and Lewin 2004).

40. In an interview, possibly because of what Stone told her or her misunderstanding of it, Jolie says, "She lived during a time when women had no rights. She was taken from her home. Her land was conquered and she was taken as a wife. And then she was abused in that relationship" (Murray 2004). Another interview indicates that Jolie believed that the ancient sources pictured Olympias's marriage as rape: "I seem to remember the legend of the story is that Philip raped his wife and you're left thinking whether he has raped her through her life, which is probably why she is so adamant that Zeus is the father of Alexander, not Philip" (Mortensen and Lewin 2004).

41. Olympias played a role in the attempted marriage alliance between her daughter Cleopatra and Perdiccas; Cleopatra herself tried, at various times, to arrange marriages with Leonnatus and Ptolemy; Cynnane, Alexander's half-sister, died trying to bring about the marriage of her daughter Adea Eurydice to Philip Arrhidaeus. In the Hellenistic period there are some other examples of

royal or quasi-royal women functioning as their own marriage brokers, but again all are widows: see Carney 2000, 20–21.

42. Carlson 2002, 9.

43. Stoneman 1991, 38, translating from 1.4.

44. Plut. *Alex.* 10.4; Diod. Sic. 16.93.7–8; Arist. *Pol.* 1311b; Just. *Epit.* 9.6.5–6.

45. In his commentary on the theatrical release DVD, Stone says he thinks that "they truly loved each other."

46. No ancient author apart from the frequently mistaken Justin (who does not understand polygamy) suggests that Philip divorced Olympias, and all accounts have Alexander deciding to leave Macedon, not being forced into exile by his father. In most versions he takes Olympias with him into voluntary exile. See Ath. 13.557d; Plut. *Alex.* 9.4–5; Just. *Epit.* 9.7.5–7.

47. Despite the fact that Stone insists in his commentary on the theatrical release DVD that "Olympias was threatened by her [Cleopatra's] age."

48. Ancient testimony is contradictory (Ath. 13.557d; Paus. 8.7.7; Just. *Epit.* 9.7.12, 11.2.3; Diod. Sic. 17.2.3). The view of Waldemar Heckel (1979) that there was time for only one baby, the girl named in the passage from Athenaeus, has won general acceptance.

49. Rossen's film offers a somewhat more ambiguous take on Alexander's guilt but is equally happy to blame Olympias.

50. Carlson (2002, 16) points to the Oedipal motivation of the character Tony Montana in *Scarface* (the 1983 film was directed by Brian De Palma but written by Oliver Stone) and puts this in the context of Stone's fondness for myth. Lavington (2004, 4) discusses Stone's preoccupation with incest in several films.

51. Jolie's absolute age—she was twenty-nine when *Alexander* was filmed—is not particularly unreasonable for an actress who plays Olympias from around 350 to 323. We can only guess at Olympias's birth date and thus her age at marriage, but she was probably in her twenties at the time of the Bucephalus incident and in her late thirties at the time of Philip's murder. Val Kilmer, the actor who played Philip, was about forty-five at the time the film was released, about the right age for Philip at the time of his death. Philip, however, was probably about ten years older than Olympias, whereas Kilmer is sixteen years older than Jolie. Thus the film exaggerated the difference in age between husband and wife and virtually abolished the age difference between mother and son.

52. It is significant that the little effort *Alexander* makes toward aging Olympias happens after Alexander's departure for Asia. In the scenes where she dictates letters to the absent Alexander, she wears gray and is (or becomes) gray. In all the scenes where the two appear together, no apparent effort has been made to age one or make the other look young: we are shown a "couple" obviously close in age. Lane Fox (2004, 54) reports that Farrell and Jolie began a "romance" during the film, an incidental fact that nonetheless probably contributed to sexual tension shown between the two characters on screen.

53. Fredricksmeyer 1990.

54. Beaver 1994, 181–84; Kagan 2000, 221; Carlson 2002, 15. Lavington (2004, 2) contrasts the withdrawn and distant character of his father with the "sensuous" and "exotic" character of his mother, a Frenchwoman. Like Alexander, Stone had a foreign mother, an outsider of sorts. Arthur Pomeroy (2008, 101n22) also notes the similarity between the relationship of Alexander's father and mother and that of Stone's parents.

55. He rejects this description explicitly in an interview with David Breskin (Breskin 1997, 7–9). However, he later concedes that his mother was sometimes distant as well and, intriguingly, calls her "a foreign queen." Eerily, Stone's father actually arranged his first sexual experience with a prostitute (Riordan 1995, 30), just as literary tradition (Ath. 10.435a) says Philip and Olympias did for their son.

56. As Beaver (1994, 192) observes, he also dedicated his only film with a female main character, *Heaven and Earth,* to his mother. It is worth noting that this earlier character became a prostitute and a victim of spousal abuse, among other sufferings.

57. Commentary on the Director's Cut DVD.

58. See recent discussion in Cartledge 2004, 221–22.

59. Commentary on the Director's Cut DVD.

60. Inscriptional evidence makes this quite clear; the difficulty is understanding the nature of her position, where exactly it was exercised, and how it related to the role of Antipater and her rivalry with him. See above and discussion and references in Carney 2000, 86–88, 90–93.

61. Fredricksmeyer 1990, 304n18.

62. Fredricksmeyer 1990.

63. See Cohen 1995 for a general discussion. Alexander was hardly unique in his love of Homer. Cassander, for instance, was also an enthusiast (Ath. 620b).

64. Here Stone's view is a popular version of Walcot 1987, passim and esp. 20–22; Walcot blamed the agonistic nature of Hellenic society on vicariously ambitious mothers and uses Olympias as an example. This "blame it on Mom" interpretation ignores the general values of the society and attributes to women alone norms embraced by all.

65. Lane Fox (2004, 83) reports that the image was located in Olympias's bedroom. While this location makes the choice seem more appropriate, it remains the case that the image was placed in Philip's palace.

66. Murray 2004.

67. Lucian (*Alex.* 6–7) describes snakes in Macedon and alludes to Olympias's practices while making it clear that the snakes were benign.

68. Daniel Ogden (forthcoming) discusses the possibility that both Olympias and a Thessalian wife of Philip employed magic in their efforts to advantage their sons' chances at succession. Plutarch (*Alex.* 87.5) claims that Olympias destroyed the mind of Philip's other son, Arrhidaeus, by the use of *pharmaka,* a term that can signify either drugs or magical spells or charms.

69. See discussion and references in Carney 1993, 30–31, esp. n.4.

70. Dominic Wills (2004) remarks that her character in *Girl, Interrupted,* Lisa Rowe, "really WAS Jolie." Jolie's interviews about her portrayal of Olympias seem to confirm the view that she has begun to play herself, and play herself as an unbalanced person. She claims that Olympias was "probably not unlike how I would be at that time in history" (Mortensen and Lewin 2004), and, elsewhere, "If I were alive at that time, I would have been a very similar type of woman, I think" (Crane 2004).

71. I do not refer to the private moments some paparazzi "stole" from her but rather to her conscious decision to publicize aspects of her life. For instance, she remarked to an interviewer, "You're young, you're drunk, you're in bed, you have knives, shit happens" (cited in Wills 2004), or her famous fondness for wearing a necklace with a vial of the blood of her husband of the time, Billy Bob Thornton.

72. For instance, she has said, "There is no way that I could have done it without having been a mom. It's totally who my character is" (Crane 2004); and, in another interview, "I don't think I could have ever played her if I didn't become a mother" (Mortensen and Lewin 2004).

73. Lavington (2004, 267) comments that Stone's choice of Jolie was "likely to draw heavily on the actress' eccentric reputation." Jolie herself, talking about the boy who played the very young Alexander, says that he had to "be in a room with a psychotic woman singing and putting snakes in [his] face" (Crane 2004). In other words, Jolie understood her character to be unbalanced, not simply passionate or extreme.

74. Carlson (2002, 14) admires Stone's casting skills and willingness to cast against type, but he seems to be talking about his casting of male actors.

75. Beaver (1994, 7) considers Stone a "bombastic blood and guts" author, but not all of his films have suffered from such poor dialogue as *Alexander.* While he rightly refers (ibid., 9) to the general excess of Stone's work, in some cases excess works, and in others it does not.

76. Lane Fox (2004, 127) discusses the decision not to have Olympias wear a veil, apparently based on (the limited) academic evidence. Rumor has it that Jolie's refusal to cover her face for much of the film was the real reason her character does not wear a veil, but Lane Fox's semi-academic argument is not implausible and could be correct.

77. For instance, of all the Macedonian earrings shown in Yalouris et al. 1980, the longest is 3.75 inches (page 171), and the next longest is 3.25 inches (133); others are 2.00 inches (134), 2.75 (135), 1.50 (137), and 1.20 (137). None of these measurements come close to matching the apparent length of the jewelry Jolie frequently wore. See, for instance, the still shots in Lane Fox 2004, 29, 66.

78. For instance, although Russell Crowe wanted to have his *Gladiator* character, who came from Spain, speak with a Spanish accent, he was instead compelled to employ what Sanello (2003, 14) calls the "Old Vic schtick."

79. Nisbet (2006, 129–30) concurs, though he notes problems with the specifics of the choice.

80. In his commentary on the Director's Cut DVD, Stone says that Olympias was not a barbarian but an "outsider." Jolie explains that "Olympias was an outsider and she had to sound different from the other characters" (Crane 2004). None of this explains why either woman had to have a made-up accent. See below on Roxane as mythic.

81. Kathleen Coleman (2004, 50n5) discusses the impact of the painter Lawrence Alma-Tadema's "pre-Raphaelite mode" on Hollywood's representation of ancient Romans. Stone's images of Babylon have a coloring reminiscent of Alma-Tadema's (see, for instance, the still shot of the Babylon harem in Lane Fox 2004, 87), but also seem to owe a debt to Charles Le Brun's seventeenth-century painting and tapestry of Alexander's entry into Babylon and perhaps other artists (for instance, the eighteenth-century Francesco Fontebasso) as well. Stone, with his traditional private school education, is old enough to have seen such images on the schoolroom walls and in textbooks.

82. See Pomeroy 2008, 103–11, for a discussion of the image of Alexander in Asian popular culture and film, although more connection could be made to Eastern versions of the *Alexander Romance*. Though the Eastern version is quite different from the Western one, when it comes to women and the role of Olympias, sexual stereotyping is apparently universal. In *Reign: The Conqueror*, a Japanese animated television series, Pomeroy describes her role as "malevolent," an "Epirot witch."

83. Indeed, Stone's film often seems to ignore the fact of the Persian *empire*, oddly substituting "Persia" by itself: thus, Gaugamela, Babylon, and Bactria are all labeled "Persia" onscreen. Stone's own commentary on the theatrical release DVD is less than politically correct: he characterizes the Persian viewpoint as a "slave mentality" and the empire as a "system of corruption," while describing Alexander's rule as remarkably unexploitative.

84. See references in Carney 1996, 569.

85. Significantly, the Director's Cut eliminated the part of the sex scene between Alexander and Roxane in which she uses his own knife to try to kill him, but retains her dance, in which she employs a knife. Stone is right to say that we know little about the historical Roxane, but that does not explain why he chooses to imagine her as mythic rather than real.

86. Ptolemy contradicts or at least complicates this judgment later when he speculates about Alexander's various possible motives, including the pacification of the hill tribes.

87. See also Pomeroy 2008, 101. Lane Fox (2004, 68) says that Stone wanted to have Roxane resemble Olympias and considered Rosario Dawson to have the "look of Angelina."

88. Sexual relations between males were generally considered normal in Hellenic societies. However, as Marilyn Skinner explains in her chapter in this

volume, a scholarly generation, thanks to the work of Kenneth Dover and Michel Foucault, has assumed that these relationships in classical times involved a younger and an older partner (a passive and an active partner), not two men approximately equal in age, as Alexander and Hephaestion were (and also Achilles and Patroclus, if one assumes that their relationship was sexual); see Ogden 2007 for further discussion. Davidson (2007) has questioned Dover's view of Greek sexuality. In any event, it is not entirely clear that this is the relevant issue. Macedonians did not always do what southern Greeks did, and there is evidence for sexual relationships between males of the same age and for such relationships to continue, without dishonor, past youth (for instance, Theopompus, *FGrH* 115 F 225b); see further Reames-Zimmerman 1999. This could mean that Macedonians saw the relationship as normal, but southern Greeks would have found it odd.

89. Suzanne Dixon (1992) discusses the reasons for the endurance of the stereotype.

90. Dixon (ibid., 212, 214–15) lists these qualities of women in general and particularly political women. See further discussion and references in Carney 1992, 188n60; 1993, 35–36.

References

Amelung, Walther. 1988. "Alexander und Achilleus." In *Zu Alexander der Grosse: Festschrift G. Wirth zum 60 Geburtstag am 9.12.86*, ed. Wolfgang Will and J. Heinrichs, 2:657–92. Amsterdam: A. M. Hakkert.

Beaver, Frank. 1994. *Oliver Stone: Wakeup Cinema.* New York: Twayne.   -

Breskin, David. 1997. "Oliver Stone: An Interview with the Director." In *The Films of Oliver Stone*, ed. Don Kunz, 3–64. Lanham, MD: Scarecrow Press.

Carlson, Michael. 2002. *The Pocket Essential Oliver Stone.* Harpenden, England: Pocket Essentials.

Carney, Elizabeth D. 1992. "The Politics of Polygamy: Olympias, Alexander, and the Death of Philip II." *Historia* 41:169–89.

———. 1993. "Olympias and the Image of the Virago." *Phoenix* 47:29–55.

———. 1996. "Alexander and the Persian Women." *American Journal of Philology* 117:563–83.

———. 2000. *Women and Monarchy in Macedonia.* Norman: University of Oklahoma Press.

———. 2006. *Olympias, Mother of Alexander the Great.* London: Routledge.

Cartledge, Paul. 2004. *Alexander the Great.* Woodstock, NY: Overlook Press.

Cohen, Ada. 1995. "Alexander and Achilles—Macedonians and 'Mycenaeans.'" In *The Ages of Homer: A Tribute to Emily Townsend Vermeule*, ed. Jane B. Carter and Sarah P. Morris, 483–505. Austin: University of Texas Press.

Coleman, Kathleen M. 2004. "The Pedant Goes to Hollywood: The Role of the Academic Consultant." In Winkler 2004a, 45–52.

Crane, Remy. 2004. "Interview: Angelina Jolie: 'Alexander.'" *Cinema Confidential*, November 22. http://www.cinecon.com/news.php?id=0411221.

Davidson, James. 2007. *The Greeks and Greek Love*. London: Weidenfeld and Nicolson.

Dixon, Suzanne. 1992. "Conclusion: The Enduring Theme: Domineering Dowagers and Scheming Concubines." In *Stereotypes of Women in Power: Historical Perspectives and Revisionist Views*, ed. Barbara Garlick, Suzanne Dixon, and Pauline Allen, 209–25. Westport, CT: Greenwood.

Fredricksmeyer, E. A. 1990. "Alexander and Philip: Emulation and Resentment." *Classical Quarterly* 85:300–315.

Greenwalt, William. 1989. "Polygamy and Succession in Argead Macedonia." *Arethusa* 22:19–45.

Heckel, Waldemar. 1979. "Philip II, Kleopatra, and Karanos." *Rivista di Filologia e di Istruzione Classica* 107:385–93.

Kagan, Norman. 2000. *The Cinema of Oliver Stone*. New York: Continuum.

Keegan, John. 1988. *The Mask of Command*. New York: Penguin.

Kunz, Don, ed. 1997. *The Films of Oliver Stone*. Lanham, MD: Scarecrow Press.

Lane Fox, Robin. 2004. *The Making of Alexander*. Oxford: R & L.

Lavington, Stephen. 2004. *Oliver Stone*. London. Virgin Books.

Marinelli, Bryan. 1997. "When Man and Woman Changed Places . . ." In Kunz 1997, 241–56.

Millard, Kathryn. 1998. "Projected Lives: Meditation on Biography and Cinematic Space." In *Screening the Past: Film and the Representation of History*, ed. Tony Barta, 232–37. Westport, CT: Praeger.

Mortensen, Jeannie, and Kev Lewin. 2004. "An Interview with Angelina Jolie." http://www.handbag.com/gossip/celebrityinterviews/angelinajolie2/ (link no longer functioning).

Murray, Rebecca. 2004. "Angelina Jolie Talks about 'Alexander.'" *Your Guide to Hollywood Movies*. http://movies.about.com/od/alexander/a/alexaj1116004.htm.

Nisbet, Gideon. 2006. *Ancient Greece in Film and Popular Culture*. Exeter: Bristol Phoenix.

Ogden, Daniel. 2007. "Two Studies in the Reception and Representation of Alexander's Sexuality." In *Alexander's Empire: Formulation to Decay*, ed. Waldemar Heckel, Lawrence Tritle, and Pat Wheatley, 75–108. Claremont, CA: Regina Books.

———. Forthcoming. "A War of Witches at the Court of Philip II?" *Archaia Makedonia/Ancient Macedonia* 7.

Pomeroy, Arthur J. 2008. *"Then It Was Destroyed by the Volcano": The Ancient World in Film and on Television*. London: Duckworth.

Reames-Zimmerman, Jeanne. 1999. "An Atypical Affair? Alexander the Great, Hephaistion Amyntoros and the Nature of Their Relationship." *Ancient History Bulletin* 13, no. 3: 81–96.

Riordan, James. 1995. *Stone: The Controversies, Excesses and Exploits of a Radical Filmmaker*. New York: Hyperion.

Roquemore, Joseph. 1999. *History Goes to the Movies*. New York: Main Street Books.

Rosenstone, Robert. 2000. "Oliver Stone as Historian." In *Oliver Stone's USA: Film, History and Controversy*, ed. R. B. Toplin, 26–39. Lawrence: University of Kansas Press.

Sanello, Frank. 2003. *Reel v. Real: How Hollywood Turns Fact into Fiction*. Lanham, MD: Scarecrow Press.

Solomon, Jon. 2001. *The Ancient World in the Cinema*. 2nd ed. New Haven, CT: Yale University Press.

Stoneman, Richard. 1991. *The Greek Alexander Romance*. Harmondsworth: Penguin.

Walcot, Peter. 1987. "Plato's Mother and Other Terrible Women." *Greece and Rome* 34, no. 1: 13–31.

Wills, Dominic. 2004. "Angelina Jolie—Biography." http://www.tiscali.co.uk/entertainment/film/biography/artist/angelina-jolie/biography/3 (accessed in 2004; site regularly updated).

Winkler, Martin, ed. 2004a. *Gladiator: Film and History*. Oxford: Blackwell.

———. 2004b. "*Gladiator* and the Traditions of Historical Cinema." In Winkler 2004a, 16–30.

Yalouris, Nicholas, et al. 1980. *The Search for Alexander: An Exhibition*. Boston: New York Graphic Society.

Fortune Favors the Blond

Colin Farrell in Alexander

MONICA SILVEIRA CYRINO

THE TELECAST of the 77th Annual Academy Awards, which aired on Sunday, February 27, 2005, was supposed to be a cele-bration of the film industry's finest productions and perform-ances of the previous year. But instead of lavishing the usual accolades on the glamorous attendees, edgy comedian-host Chris Rock opened the show by mocking the past year's less than stellar cinematic efforts. "Why don't some movies work?" he inquired with a mischievous grin. "Because the studios make them too fast. Okay? If you can't get a star, wait!" Rock helpfully continued with a very specific example. "You want Russell Crowe and all you can get is Colin Farrell? Wait. *Alexander* is not *Gladiator*."

Rock was not the first to disparage Oliver Stone's epic film *Alexander* (2004), a high-profile, independently financed venture that was by any measure a box-office failure (though see Jon Solomon's chapter in this volume for further discussion). Indeed, the negative response to the film was nearly unanimous: "Critics panned *Alexander*—and U.S. audi-ences ignored it."[1] The fact that the film, a long-planned pet project that Stone wrote as well as directed, failed to achieve significant commercial and critical success in the United States has been attributed to many causes. The disjointed storyline intercut with baffling and jumbled flashbacks, the use of ponderous narration as a framing device, and the stilted, often campy dialogue all came in for criticism. Even the casting of the film's main roles provoked derision within the entertainment industry: "It was a dream team of tabloid mainstays—Hollywood practically burst into laughter."[2] Stone, who had previously won "Best Director" Oscars for *Platoon* (1986) and *Born on the Fourth of July* (1989), as well as an Oscar for "Best Adapted Screenplay" for *Midnight Express* (1978), saw his latest prestige film yanked from its expected position on the red carpet during awards season. One critic, frustrated by the many structural and narrative flaws he observed in the three-hour biopic about the great Macedonian general, groused: "Short life, long movie."[3]

One of the most crucial aspects of any film's American success is the popular impact of the actor cast in the starring role, and the degree of that star's personal appeal, both emotional and physical, to the viewing audience. Audience members regularly carry with them into the movie theater highly evolved and often fixed appraisals of an actor's persona, based on two sets of publicly accessible revelations: the exposures of the actor's "self" in his previous film (or television) appearances, and the fragmentary glimpses of the actor's "private life"—some intentionally revealed by the star and some most emphatically not—in the entertainment media.[4] The audience enters the theater essentially anticipating the fulfillment of these pre-formed expectations about the star's familiar image. This predictable and thus gratifying psychological transaction between the celebrity entertainer and the audience occurs inside the darkened theater but also continues in discourses outside the cineplex, so that "when the performance is over, we feel intact, resolute, endorsed."[5] If the actor's representation of a particular role deviates sharply from audience expectation, however, a sense of confusion and even dissatisfaction can develop that colors any extra-cinematic communications the viewers share about the film. Only very rarely does the viewing public allow an actor to expand his or her dramatic range into different types of performances, choosing instead to ignore any deviation by simply staying away from the theater.[6] Thus, viewer satisfaction or disappointment in response to an actor playing a specific role can profoundly affect a film's popularity and profitability.

Understanding how the American viewing public relates and reacts to a star playing a certain role helps to explain the relative success or failure of individual films, and sheds light on the comparative achievement of Stone's *Alexander*. Film scholars and sociologists have become increasingly interested in the interaction between the viewing audience and the stars they pay to watch, to the extent that "the analysis of stars has become one of the most significant areas of inquiry in recent film studies."[7] Ever since Richard Dyer's groundbreaking work introduced the idea of a "star text" that exists to be "read" by the audience,[8] contemporary critics have examined the ways in which a distinct star image can both affect the production of meaning in a film and manipulate the arousal of emotional pleasure for the spectators. The "star text" is defined as a celebrity image that combines the star's acting ability and prior record of acting performances with his offscreen lifestyle, personality, and behavior, and is thus "an intertextual construct produced across a range of media and cultural practices, capable of intervening in the working of particular films, but also demanding analysis as a text in its own right."[9] Critics note that while the star text of an individual celebrity grows very familiar to the viewing audience, who come to anticipate its contours as expressed onscreen, the star text is not necessarily a unified model: "The star image consists of a variety of complex interwoven elements."[10] In fact, the text of a star's image often embraces contradictory elements and discrepancies, and so invites the frequent negotiation of shifting or seemingly opposite terms. Indeed, a key component of the star text is its evolving nature: "The appeal of stardom is that of constant reinvention."[11] Thus, the audience's ability to negotiate and even reconcile successfully the tensions evident within a star's image influences the way they respond as spectators to the star's performance in a specific role. In the dynamics between stardom and spectatorship, the reconciliation of contraries emerges as a vital process.

The question arises, then, how the audience is able to reconcile the apparent fixity of their expectations about a star's familiar persona with the tensions and inconsistencies discernible in the inherently unstable reading of the star text. The principal mechanism available to the audience for implementing this negotiation of contraries is the process of identification. For the American audience, celebrities are powerful symbols of culture: stars model gender roles, set standards of fashion and physical appearance, act as paradigms for the attainment of success, and offer the impression of close personal and communal bonds: "Americans take stars as demonstrators of both how to be and how to belong."[12] Social scientists have coined the phrase "para-social interaction" to describe the affectionate and intimate feelings ordinary people manifest toward personages they have never met, but with whom they desire to identify.[13] Through repeated exposure to the star's "brand identity," the audience experiences the attachment of recognition: "The familiarity of celebrity makes possible a mediated kind of relationship."[14] In the case of film stars, the audience identifies simultaneously with the celebrity persona and the often notably congruous role he or she is playing. Film produces an especially "intense kind of consciousness," where the process of identification assumes the greatest potency and clarity: "No other medium so effortlessly transports us to another world or puts us in tighter proximity to memorable characters."[15] Under the compulsion of identification, the audience most commonly sees the star/character in terms of similarity ("We are alike") or empathy ("I understand you"). Yet feelings of identification can also be compensatory, in that they make up for something lost or deficient in the spectator; they are also frequently aspirational, in that they encourage the emulation or copying of the star's conduct and self-presentation.[16] What emerges from studies of the star-audience relationship is that there is no singular process, but a multiplicity of types of identification.

Scholars have recognized this great diversity in the potential forms of audience identification with stars and their film roles, and have schematized various categories of progressively involved levels of affinity— what one critic calls "imaginative engagement with characters."[17] These categories occur on a rising scale, beginning with simple recognition, moving on to the stronger alignment, and culminating with allegiance, which is the most powerful form of identification.[18] Filmmakers create allegiance in various ways, but mainly by giving the audience access to the character's inner thoughts through the use of camera angles and reaction shots that emphasize his or her point of view: "Film privileges some agents by giving them an emotional life and a past that allows us to interpret their actions."[19] At the level of allegiance, the film also invites the audience to become invested in the victory of a main character over some great adversity: the spectators are permitted to watch the character's trajectory as he rises to triumph and, if necessary for the plot, to witness his suffering or fall. The generation of allegiance between the audience and the star/character is the most common Hollywood film model, since it is the most reliable guarantor of commercial and critical success: "Narratives that violate this expectation often leave audiences uncertain about where to invest the emotional energy they are primed to give."[20] Films with big box-office objectives tend to align their heroes with audience expectations in order to capitalize on the "para-social continuity" that exists between spectators and star.[21] So the process of successful identification implies a convergence between the audience's expectant desire and the star's performance.

The casting of Colin Farrell—the brash, belligerent, and hell-raising young Irish actor notorious from numerous tabloid sex scandals and police blotters—in the title role of Alexander justifiably raises the issue of the effect his performance had on the overall achievement of the film.[22] Farrell as Alexander would have enormous power to influence reaction to the film among the American audience, who would very likely have been familiar with the up-and-coming actor's recent roles in action-themed thrillers like *Phone Booth* (2002) and *The Recruit* (2003). Viewers would likely be even more aware of his raucous private life as it is salaciously detailed in the entertainment media. Farrell's British biographer notes that the actor's naughty behavior has had a rather contradictory effect upon the avid American public: "As the U.S. press watches, genuinely shocked and bewildered at his beer-guzzling, chain-smoking, womanising ways, he has taken on the full force of American Puritanism and has, apparently, won."[23] The actor's bad-boy image was also augmented by his apparently involuntary contribution to the contemporary genre of the "celebrity sex tape," which "contains 14 minutes of seriously hard-core action between actor Colin Farrell and a former Playboy Playmate, punctuated by dialogue like: 'Where's the zoom on this?'"[24] While Farrell's lurid personal backstory would certainly have the capacity to shape audience perception of him, the raw material of his immediate performance as Alexander—including his physical looks and bearing and, in particular, the depiction of the character's sexuality—would also have a compelling effect.

An examination of the extra-cinematic discourse arising out of the entertainment media in this case reveals a complicated set of expectations, desires, and associations at work among members of the press and the American viewing public. Most critics were quick to condemn the director's choice of Farrell. Many cited the actor's lack of *gravitas*: "The hole in the center of this mythic history is Farrell, who looks overwhelmed and diminished by the burden of carrying an epic movie on his bulked-up shoulders."[25] Others noted that Farrell failed to capture the brilliant charisma and the gripping sense of ambition evinced by the legendary conqueror: "It's hard to deny that Colin Farrell's petulant approach is simply the wrong one."[26] And almost everyone was dismayed to see Farrell's dark hair covered by a series of sun-bleached blond wigs of increasing length and dishevelment: "Looking at Colin Farrell . . . we don't see much apart from a gruff young actor with puffy blond locks that don't match his caterpillar eyebrows."[27] About the only positive outcome among critics was the rehabilitation—by comparison—of Richard Burton's awkward performance in Robert Rossen's 1956 *Alexander the Great*, which was released on DVD by MGM in November 2004 to coincide with the opening of Stone's movie.[28] In a match between the two rising young thespians from the British Isles, both with well-deserved reputations for hard drinking, and both taking on the role of the visionary Macedonian general in incongruous blondness, most critics agreed that Burton's old-school portrayal of Alexander as a brooding rebel trumped Farrell's even gloomier modern interpretation.[29]

Although *Alexander* was Farrell's first mega-budgeted "star" vehicle, in the early stages of preproduction Stone and his team had reason to be optimistic. In the few short years before he signed on to play the lead in Stone's epic, Farrell had proved to be a promising box-office draw in a series of important roles showcased in macho action and adventure films. Indeed, three of his recent films had opened at number 1, and each of the three had grossed over $100 million: *Minority Report* (2002), *S.W.A.T.* (2003), and *Daredevil* (2003).[30] The viewing public could fairly be expected to recognize and accept Farrell in the role of the great warrior-leader. When Stone first took a meeting with Farrell, he was surprised and impressed to see the actor's boisterous mythology made real. "'He came in looking like a Dublin street thug,' remembers the director, laughing. 'He broke two or three wineglasses during dinner just making his points and yelling.'"[31] Despite Farrell's noisy intemperance, or perhaps because of it, Stone chose him to play Alexander, recognizing something of his own intense and turbulent nature in the rebellious young actor. "The hot-blooded director found a perfect partner in his fierce star: you could practically see Stone and Farrell falling head over heels for each other on the set."[32] Even after the film's disastrous debut, Stone has continued to defend his choice of Farrell, citing the actor's combination of will, stamina, and independence, which confirmed for him a clear analogy between the star and the ancient adventurer who annexed much of the known world: "I was looking for a young god who could act . . . someone with the confidence of a warrior and a leader. An Alexander who could walk into the room and look in the eyes of any man, and could move them beyond themselves."[33] Stone gambled, somewhat rashly, that the film audience would also appreciate the parallel he saw between Farrell's originality and passion as an actor and the exceptionally bold achievement of the historical Alexander.

Farrell has stated that his desire as an artist to work with Stone persuaded him to accept the role, although he realized the challenges he would face at the hands of the notoriously demanding director: "He wanted to work with Stone for better or worse."[34] Critics later added that Farrell's more practical aspiration to attain leading-man status on the Hollywood A-list of male actors also drove his decision. Because Stone encountered serious financial problems early on, Farrell actually agreed to a reduction in his ever-escalating pay rate, settling for a $10 million salary and an anticipated 10 percent cut of the film's gross profits.[35] Farrell's own testimony about his role suggests some intriguing angles for evaluating his performance in the film. Most actors who play historical figures work hard to find something accessibly human about their characters to give them a more sympathetic focus, thereby engaging the recognition and affection of the audience.[36] But Farrell instead elected to see the self-imposed loneliness and distance brought on by Alexander's state of near divinity. "There is no character like him and no story like his—not even the story of Christ, which I love. Christ was in the limelight for three years. Alexander had it all his life, from 19 to 32, when he died, king and conqueror, very dark in his desperation to find out what his destiny was."[37] Since the release of the film, Farrell has also cited the physical and psychological difficulties he underwent while playing the role: "The emotional stakes were very high and it was also physically draining, a lot of work. I had to put myself through a lot. I was always on a kind of edge and it was upsetting at times because I found the story very sad. I quickly got over seeing it as something glorious."[38] In the aftermath of the film's less than triumphant reception, Farrell has tended to downplay his experience in the role of the globe-conquering god-king.

An aspect of the film that manifestly swayed public opinion is its depiction of Alexander's complicated sexuality within the context of the epic plot, and thus Farrell's onscreen representation of it would also have had an effect. Before the film's release, Farrell was well aware that the reaction to his interpretation of Alexander's sexuality would be based on the audience's knowledge and expectations of him as a publicly traded celebrity: "Because people do bring a perception to the film, because of my personal record, my drinking and my womanizing and my laddishness."[39] The multiple erotic exploits of the Macedonian warrior-king soon became rhetorically entangled with the multiple erotic exploits of the actor set to play him, as the extra-cinematic discourse about the film began equating Farrell with Alexander in terms of their excessive masculine sexuality. The volatile actor from Dublin suddenly became the ruthless ancient general he was supposed to embody, and the language describing the correlation between them revealed a heady dose of male hormonal vigor. Director Stone had no doubts about Farrell's supple sexuality: "There's an amazing adaptability to him. He was a huge shot of testosterone for this thing."[40] When asked by a journalist how he would go about attacking the role, Farrell growled as if on cue: "You need some serious fookin' balls, man."[41] But Farrell also recognized that he was cast as Alexander in large part because of the potentially risky association between his offscreen persona as a hard-drinking and aggressively macho playboy and the similar adventures of the fabled Macedonian warrior-king off the battlefield: "When so much importance is placed on a particular energy that you've become known for, whether it's brooding or swagger or being butch, it's very easy for the human mind to find comfort in being recognized as one thing, which can be a form of self-imprisonment as an actor."[42] Farrell seemed to realize that his star persona inhabits a particular space, bounded by audience expectations, that could limit his ability to expand his artistic expression.

But Alexander's sexuality was evidently much more expansive than the actor's capacity to play him. Stone has said that he wanted to downplay the historical Alexander's polyamorous inclinations: "I treat it as part of the story, not the whole story."[43] But when the press discovered that Stone's 142-page screenplay contained "an honest, fairly explicit treatment of Alexander's famous bisexuality,"[44] this aspect of the film became the contentious focus of much of the pre-release discourse, and the source of much post-release critical bemusement: "Stone is fascinated by two aspects of Alexander: his pan-nationalism, and his pan-sexualism."[45] The furor centered mainly on the historically attested romantic relationship between Farrell's Alexander and his longtime best friend, Hephaestion, played by American teen idol Jared Leto. Controversy about the film's portrayal of the more flexible sexual practices of the ancient Greeks dogged the production from start to finish, with some critics protesting against the presentation of what they called "gay themes" in the film and some decrying the lack thereof. A few critics simply saw the humor in all the fuss: "Jared Leto's Hephaistion is . . . making such lambent puppy eyes that you half expect Mel Gibson to barge in and throw him out the window."[46] The tumult may have contributed to an overall heightening of the sexualized atmosphere on the set in Morocco, drawing the rabid interest of the tabloids, who were constantly reporting on who was sleeping with whom. Farrell was alleged to have had on-set love affairs with both Angelina Jolie, who

plays his mother, Olympias, and Rosario Dawson, who plays his Bactrian wife, Roxane.[47] By the time the production moved to Bangkok,
Farrell "was supposed to have slept with the majority of the Asian subcontinent."[48] The self-possessed Jolie, who was also romantically linked
in the press to Leto and to Val Kilmer, who plays her husband and
Alexander's father, Philip, sniffed provocatively: "The tabloids didn't
come close. They couldn't make up the stuff that went on."[49] While the
press had a field day, the viewing public was left wondering which Alexander, and which Farrell, would eventually appear in the film.

    The ambiguity of Alexander's sexuality, as articulated both in the
narrative of the film and in extra-cinematic discourse about the film's
sexual content, ultimately proved distressing to audiences on both sides
of the aisle. While some desired to see more explicit homoerotic contact
between Farrell and Leto, and others reacted with squeamish alarm to
the merest hint of boy-on-boy interaction, Farrell as Alexander was
caught in an impossible position. How sexy could the famously straight
star be when playing this amorously confused and confusing role? Although Farrell is known mainly for his plentiful female conquests, the
actor stoked the fires of the uproar a few months before the release of
Alexander by playing a sexually ambiguous young man in a small, independent film, *A Home at the End of the World* (2004). Farrell commented
on the commotion caused by a brief same-sex kiss he shared with his
male costar in the indie film, and blithely connected it to the upheaval
currently surrounding his role in Stone's epic: "I know one thing, when
Alexander comes out, I don't have a kiss with Jared [Leto], but I have a
sex scene with the woman who plays my wife. And there will be *blue
murder* as to why do we see him have sex with Rosario Dawson, but we
don't see it with [Leto]?"[50] Critics were also perplexed by the film's almost teasing avoidance of any visual proof of the erotic relationship between Alexander and Hephaestion: "For all their moist glances, the film,
in effect, plays a game of do-they-or-don't-they."[51] Stone exhibited some
of the same oscillation by defending inclusion of scenes revealing Alexander's sexual interest in male partners when first releasing the film,
only to excise some of that very content (eight minutes, to be exact)
from the Director's Cut DVD—"to make the film more accessible,"
he has argued.[52] But both versions of the film still display a frank
awareness of male homoeroticism, even though Alexander's mildly
suggestive line, "Stay with me tonight, Hephaistion," is axed from the
DVD, while the much more graphic voiceover, "It is said that Alexander was never defeated, except by Hephaistion's thighs," is retained.

Like its director, the film vacillates between its desire for Alexander to be a sexy, enticing, fully actualized erotic character and its timid refusal to allow him to express that inclusive sexiness.

Even Alexander's peculiar relationships with women in the film frustrated the audience and the critics: "His sexuality is made murky by the film's shyness about gay sex and its ambiguity about Alexander's relationship with his 'barbarian' bride and his tigress mother."[53] Early in the film, the audience is made aware of Alexander's highly eroticized conflict with his mother, Olympias (played by Jolie). As a boy, he watches as his drunken father attacks and rapes her. Later, after Philip's murder, Alexander accuses her of complicity in the crime, but then kisses her full on the mouth: she responds by spitting on him, as the iconic image of the filicidal Medea flashes on the screen. And while the film is skittish about Alexander's love affairs with men, it indulges in a vivid and extended sex scene involving his wife, Roxane (played by Dawson). On their wedding night, Roxane flies into a jealous rage when she finds Alexander entwined in a trembling embrace with Hephaestion ("they hug a lot," notes sage film critic Roger Ebert). The scene only serves to underscore Alexander's sexuality as problematic, as the audience watches the couple engage in a fiercely physical knife fight that suddenly morphs into vigorous lovemaking, yet the encounter is visually bizarre and unappealing-looking: one critic reasonably described it as "borderline absurd, animalistic sex."[54] During the sex scene, Alexander predictably sees flashes of his mother's face, and hears her speak to him in a voiceover, as if to drive home the obvious parallel between the two violent women, and to imply that Alexander is just a boy with serious maternal issues. After this intense scene, the audience never sees Alexander and Roxane in bed again. Thus the film stresses that Alexander has married her not out of love, but merely for political reasons, as well as to exorcise the demons of his sensuous, controlling mother. In the absence of a tangible relationship with Hephaestion, this leaves the character of Alexander without any emotional foundation, and thus no easy way for the audience to identify with him. The film's lack of coherence about sexual and emotional issues renders the characters unnecessarily enigmatic and, above all, prevents the audience from gaining access to Farrell's portrayal.

Farrell's role in *Alexander* must finally be examined in light of the mini-renaissance of the swords-and-sandals epic after the huge critical and commercial American success of Ridley Scott's blockbuster *Gladiator* (2000), and the lesser, but still substantial, achievement of Wolfgang

Petersen's *Troy* (2004). Stone was under massive pressure from the studio (Warner Bros., which also released *Troy*) to produce an epic that
would rival the revenues and accolades earned by these two recent
films: *Gladiator* has grossed more than $188 million in the United States,
with a total of $458 million worldwide, while *Troy* has reached a very
respectable $133 million in domestic gross, and an impressive $497 million worldwide total.[55] As one preview smugly hoped for *Alexander*:
"It's gotta be better than *Troy*, right?"[56] In evaluating Stone's film, critics
justifiably placed it within the history of the epic cinematic genre, and
almost unanimously found it deficient in generic terms of grandeur,
sweep, and unity. As one critic noted: "The movie may be packed with
historical detail, but who cares when it lacks the basic coherence of
Spartacus or *Gladiator* or even *Troy*?"[57] In this context, Farrell's role can
also be set against the performances of two high-status film stars who
play the glamorous ancient heroes of these recent films—namely, Russell Crowe as Maximus in *Gladiator* and Brad Pitt as Achilles in *Troy*.
The fictional character of Maximus in *Gladiator* is granted a striking and
compelling epic trajectory, from general, to slave, to victorious gladiator, and even with his melancholy concern for the afterlife, viewers
were drawn into enthusiastic allegiance with his great heroic mission
to save Rome.[58] Homer's supreme warrior, Achilles, is given a rather
modern makeover as a romantic hero in *Troy*, but the majority of the audience was genuinely thrilled to accompany him on his dark journey
from man to myth.[59] Both of these ancient epic heroes undergo the full
range of experience in the course of their cinematic narratives, from
adversity to triumph to cathartic death, and thus both films invite the
audience to identify with the characters as heroes. In contrast, the disjointed plot of *Alexander* confuses the audience and obstructs their access to him as a character.

But the main issue that differentiates Farrell's Alexander from the
heroes of the two earlier epic films is the physical impact of the stars'
masculine sexuality on the viewing public. Crowe and Pitt are both
noteworthy products of the Hollywood star-machine, and their films
have enjoyed enormous success in furthering their extra-cinematic narratives of sexiness, masculinity, and celebrity. Crowe reached a zenith
of red-blooded maleness in the role of Maximus, with his powerful
leather-clad shoulders and chiseled face under close-cropped hair, the
epitome of every woman's gladiator fantasy. He has continued to please
audiences and critics with roles as the dashing Captain Jack Aubrey
in *Master and Commander: The Far Side of the World* (2003) and the

courageous boxer Jim Braddock in *Cinderella Man* (2005). Though he is
now a married father of a son (like Maximus), Crowe's offscreen persona has encompassed such macho incarnations as the ladies' man, the
hot-headed streetfighter, and the prickly perfectionist directors love to
hate. Pitt is currently half of the most famous celebrity couple in the
world: he and his partner, Jolie, have three adopted and three biological children as of this writing. Pitt assured his ascent as a hard-bodied
masculine screen idol by playing Tyler in *Fight Club* (1999), and added
the suave lover to his repertoire as Rusty Ryan in *Ocean's Eleven* (2001);
he later played the eponymous outlaw in *The Assassination of Jesse
James* (2007). For *Troy*, Pitt shaped his bronzed body to Olympian perfection and grew his blond hair rock-star long, as he learned to execute
Achilles' signature warrior moves with lethal precision. Pitt bares his
astonishing body in love scenes only with females (who look a little
self-conscious to be near such naked male excellence), since director
Petersen decided simply to ignore the question of Achilles' homoerotic
relationship with Patroclus, who becomes his "cousin" in *Troy*. In fact,
Stone was well aware that a forthright depiction of Alexander's sexuality in his film would isolate his character from that of the gruff family
man Maximus, as well as the newly romanticized hero Achilles. When
gay-rights groups excoriated the director's decision to cut some of the
homoerotic content from Alexander's scenes for the Director's Cut
DVD, Stone countered: "What they're saying is that we changed the
character to make him like Brad Pitt [in *Troy*]—to make him heterosexual. Which is not the case. We just don't dwell on the relationship as
much."[60] Stone's admirable artistic decision to delve into Alexander's
sexuality, rather than to avoid or revise it, resulted in an ambiguous
portrayal that audiences found difficult to apprehend or accept. Farrell's
erratic offscreen image was too unsteady for viewers to overcome the
lack of definition in the character he played.

   Why did the American audience ultimately fail to embrace Colin
Farrell in the title role of *Alexander*? Viewers were simply offered too
few insights into the qualities of character and charisma that made Alexander a legend in his own time and allowed him to emerge as arguably the most famous secular figure in all of world history. On the narrative level, Stone's film focuses on what happens to Alexander after he
has conquered the East, and so it denies the audience the salient pleasure of experiencing his rise from an eager, horse-taming boy to a visionary, globe-annexing leader. When Alexander struggles with his lonely
destiny and descends more deeply into disaster, surrounded by cagey

conspirators and resentful barbarians, the viewers are unable to feel the sympathy of identification with his tragic fall: "You know a Hollywood spectacle is in trouble when its hero yearns to go forward . . . but his soldiers just want to go home—and the audience sides with the weary mutineers."[61] A more complex and well-developed trajectory would have granted viewers the necessary perspective in order to feel allegiance to and identify with Alexander's epic journey. On the level of representation, the film makes the character of Alexander distant, elusive, indistinct, and unsympathetic. More often than not, the heroic Alexander described by the laudatory narration is at odds with the moody, drunk, and even cruel Alexander the audience actually sees onscreen. As a protagonist, Alexander has no more dangerous enemy than his own shuttered inner conflict, to which the audience is never privy. Lastly, Farrell's famous dynamism as a celebrity was stifled in his sincere attempt to flesh out the opaque Alexander written for this film. Whether Farrell's "star text" remains too unstable to inhabit the epic role of the historical Alexander is a question that has some relevance: "While film characters give us permanent and self-contained representations, stars represent unfinished narratives with unpredictable outcomes."[62] Perhaps Farrell would have turned in a better performance if he had been allowed to explore not only Alexander, but also The Great.

Notes

1. Gregory Kirschling, "Epic Proportion," *Entertainment Weekly*, May 27, 2005, 21.
2. Daniel Fierman, "Kings, Queens & Wild Things," *Entertainment Weekly*, November 19, 2004, 30.
3. Mike Clark, "*Alexander* the Great: Barely Even Mediocre," *USA Today*, November 24, 2004.
4. On the ways in which the American film audience construes the personalities of actors, see Jib Fowles, *Starstruck: Celebrity Performers and the American Public* (Washington, DC: Smithsonian Institution Press, 1992), ch. 7, "What Stars Do for the Public," 155–83.
5. Ibid., 165.
6. On the stability of star images, see ibid., 70.
7. Judith Mayne, *Cinema and Spectatorship* (London: Routledge, 1993), 123.
8. Richard Dyer, *Stars* (London: British Film Institute, 1979).
9. Christine Gledhill, "Introduction," in *Stardom: Industry of Desire*, ed. Christine Gledhill (London: Routledge, 1991), xiv.
10. Mayne, *Cinema and Spectatorship*, 124.

11. Ibid., 138.

12. Fowles, *Starstruck*, 171.

13. Donald Horton and R. Richard Wohl, "Mass Communication and Para-Social Interaction: Observations on Intimacy at a Distance," *Psychiatry* 19 (1956): 215–29.

14. Gary C. Woodward, *The Idea of Identification* (Albany: State University of New York Press, 2003), ch. 3, "Identification, Celebrity, and the Hollywood Film," 45–69, quotation on 62.

15. Ibid., 46.

16. On the role of idolization and fantasy in identification, especially among female fans of female stars, see Jackie Stacey, "Feminine Fascinations: Forms of Identification in Star-Audience Relations," in Gledhill, *Stardom*, 141–63.

17. Murray Smith, "Altered States: Character and Emotional Response in the Cinema," *Cinema Journal* 33 (Summer 1994): 35. Another system of categories for different levels of identification is developed by P. David Marshall, *Celebrity and Power: Fame in Contemporary Culture* (Minneapolis: University of Minnesota Press, 1997), 68–69.

18. Smith, "Altered States," 39–42.

19. Woodward, *The Idea of Identification*, 51.

20. Ibid., 53.

21. Ibid., 63.

22. For a no-holds-barred examination of Farrell's private life and public persona, see the unauthorized biography by Jane Kelly, *Colin Farrell: Living Dangerously* (London: John Blake Publishing, 2005).

23. Ibid., xiii.

24. Jocelyn Noveck, "Was It Good For Them, Too?" Associated Press, February 3, 2006.

25. Richard Corliss, "It's His Same Old Story," *Time*, November 29, 2004, 148.

26. Ty Burr, "Toga Party Pooper," *Entertainment Weekly*, August 5, 2005, 51.

27. Owen Gleiberman, "The Lost Crusade," *Entertainment Weekly*, December 3, 2004, 57.

28. On the DVD release of Rossen's film, see Ty Burr, "Back in the Day," *Entertainment Weekly*, October 22, 2004, 79. See also Kim Shahabudin's chapter in this volume.

29. See, for example, Burr, "Back in the Day."

30. On Farrell's box-office receipts before *Alexander*, see Dave Karger, "Irish Ayes," *Entertainment Weekly*, July 23, 2004, 10.

31. Fierman, "Kings, Queens & Wild Things," 29.

32. "November's Movie Lineup: *Alexander*," *Entertainment Weekly*, August 20, 2004, 62.

33. Quoted in Kelly, *Colin Farrell*, 200.

34. Ibid., 203.

35. Ibid., 200–201.
36. Fowles, *Starstruck*, 164.
37. Quoted in Dotson Rader, "I Found Where I Belong," *Parade*, October 17, 2004, 5.
38. Quoted in Kelly, *Colin Farrell*, 201.
39. Karger, "Irish Ayes," 10.
40. Daniel Fierman, "Great Expectations," *Entertainment Weekly*, April 23, 2004, 37.
41. Ibid., 35.
42. Karger, "Irish Ayes," 10.
43. Quoted in Jeffrey Ressner, "10 Questions for Oliver Stone," *Time*, April 19, 2004, 8.
44. Fierman, "Kings, Queens & Wild Things," 29.
45. Roger Ebert, review of *Alexander*, Chicago Sun-Times, November 26, 2004.
46. Burr, "Toga Party Pooper," 51. The reference is to the scene in Gibson's Oscar-winning film *Braveheart* (1994) where the evil King Edward tosses his son's male lover out of the castle window, a scene for which Gibson was roundly criticized by gay-rights groups.
47. Kelly, *Colin Farrell*, 202–3, 213–14. For further discussion of the casting of Olympias and Roxane, see Elizabeth Carney's chapter in this volume.
48. Fierman, "Kings, Queens & Wild Things," 31.
49. Ibid.
50. Dave Karger, "The Naked Truth," *Entertainment Weekly*, July 23, 2004, 10.
51. Gleiberman, "The Lost Crusade," 58.
52. Quoted in Kirschling, "Epic Proportion," 21.
53. Ebert, review of *Alexander*.
54. Gleiberman, "The Lost Crusade," 58.
55. For up-to-the-minute figures, see www.boxofficemojo.com.
56. "November's Movie Lineup," 62.
57. Gleiberman, "The Lost Crusade," 57.
58. On Maximus as epic hero, see Monica Silveira Cyrino, *Big Screen Rome* (Oxford: Blackwell, 2005), 229–33.
59. On the "updating" of the character of Achilles, see Daniel Mendelsohn, "A Little Iliad," *New York Review of Books*, June 24, 2004, 46–49.
60. Quoted in Kirschling, "Epic Proportion," 21.
61. Gleiberman, "The Lost Crusade," 57.
62. Woodward, *The Idea of Identification*, 69.

The Cult of Hephaestion

JEANNE REAMES

W HEN FIRST I embarked, some twenty years ago, on a critical examination of the historical figure of Hephaestion
Amyntoros and his place at the court of Alexander the
Great, I had no idea that the subject of my study would turn out to
have *fans*.

Much to my astonishment since, I have fielded literally hundreds
of enthusiastic letters from all over the globe, asking about Hephaestion. And I should add that this unexpected fascination *predated* Oliver
Stone's *Alexander*, although the film certainly elevated interest. For a few
weeks after the film was released, my educational website on Hephaestion reached over 900 visits (not mere hits) a day.[1]

But . . . fans. Hephaestion has *fans*. We all knew that Alexander had
fans—has had them since antiquity itself—yet Hephaestion would
not have been high on my list of individuals likely to inspire a cult
following.[2]

The term "fan" is, of course, derived from "fanatic" and, depending
on context, has either affectionate or negative connotations. For my
purposes, a "fan" will be neutrally defined as someone enthusiastic
about a topic as a hobby, rather than as a career, yet I think we all recognize that certain categories of fans enjoy greater social acceptability
than others.[3] Not only is it human nature to develop such interests, but
I would argue that it is healthy, too. Perhaps I should not have been so

surprised, then, to discover that Hephaestion has fans. *Who* they are tells us an indirect story about his (relative) lack of prominence in modern Alexander studies.

So—to be more precise—Hephaestion has *fangirls*.

Like "fan," the term "fangirl" (or "fanboy") can be used with either affection or ridicule, and without regard to actual age. Hephaestion's fangirls are, in fact, largely fan-*women*. I would also like to note that Hephaestion does have male fans, two-thirds of whom self-identify as gay or bisexual, but their numbers are dwarfed by his female fans, who make up 84 percent of the total.[4] By contrast, fans of Alexander break down into a variety of types with a hierarchy of social prestige ranging from military-history fans to Greek- or Macedonian-nationalist fans, gay-pride fans to fans of kings and other famous persons. One must feel a certain sympathy for Oliver Stone. Given such divergent—and often violently conflicting—attitudes toward the conqueror, it would be quite impossible to please everyone, and any perspective taken would be bound to elicit strong condemnation from some quarter.

It can be tempting for academics to regard all these fans with a jaundiced, cynical eye, especially if one has had an unpleasant experience with one strident type or another. Yet I believe most of us do, in fact, *enjoy* enthusiasm when it bubbles up independently of a course grade. What struck me most about Hephaestion's fans is that they compose subsets of society who have traditionally occupied *disempowered* social positions: women, and gay or bisexual men. If I were to say, "Hephaestion has fans," the instinctive reaction to that pronouncement is rather different than if I were to specify, "Hephaestion has female and gay fans." The clarification transforms him from Alexander's right-hand man and chiliarch into a romantic hero—a Brad Pitt of the ancient world. (Or a Jared Leto, as the case may be.)

All of which says perhaps more about *our* unconscious assumptions and automatic ordering of value than about the fans themselves. Enthusiasm for Hephaestion seems to be suspect and uncomfortably suggestive of motivations emotional and romantic. Yet is any intense interest ever devoid of emotional content? Perhaps the biggest fans of all are those of us who have devoted our careers to the study of Alexander, his court, Macedon, and related topics. Certainly no one goes into academics purely for the financial compensation.

In any case, my own dialogue with fans of Hephaestion has revealed a variety of factors that are as important as, if not more important than, fascination with any romantic relationship he may have had with the conqueror. These include Hephaestion's career and position as a behind-the-scenes power, often seen as a woman's role, as well as the intense emotional attachment between Hephaestion and Alexander (sexual or not), and—specifically for gay men—the novelty of a celebrated *military* figure who counted another man as more dear to him than his wives.

Only 15 percent of those who answered my informal survey had never read any historical or biographical work about Alexander, Macedon, or Greece—contrasting with over 70 percent who said they had read three *or more*, 46 percent who had tracked down specialist articles or monographs, and another 43 percent who had read at least one of the primary sources in its entirety (not just selections), not to mention the 26 percent who had taken more than one class in Greek history, learned the Greek language, or chosen to major in history or classics *as a direct result of their interest*.[5]

It seems that these fans are not content to stop with fiction, even if fiction was responsible for initiating their study.[6] Although referring to fictional material in the Bible rather than to historical fiction, Arnaldo Momigliano said, "Fantastic speculations about historical developments are not necessarily contrary to the interest of historical studies. They offer a scheme for the coordination of historical events. They are a constant challenge to the learned who pile up the facts without being able to organise them."[7]

It is easy to dismiss Hephaestion as Alexander's "boytoy," not to be taken seriously, just as it is easy to see his fans (women and gay men) as obsessed with a love story and nothing of real significance. Unfortunately, Oliver Stone's film did little to refute this view with Jared Leto's Hephaestion slinking about in silk robes and heavy eyeliner, giving backrubs to a frustrated Alexander. To be sure, he *is* presented as Alexander's alter ego and sounding board—the sharer of his secrets and candid advisor that Curtius paints (3.12.16). During Hephaestion's death scene, Alexander reminds him that he never let Alexander win and always told him the truth. Nonetheless, he is still presented primarily as private encourager, yes-man, and lover. The other side of Hephaestion—as military officer and chiliarch—is virtually ignored.

Nothing underscores this point more than the characters who are his foils in the film's narrative. It is not his documented conflicts with Craterus that are highlighted—conflicts that involved his public, political status—but rather historically *unattested* conflicts with Bagoas the eunuch and Roxane, Alexander's wife.[8] In fact, from the film, one would never even know that Hephaestion and Craterus were rivals at the court in the final years of Alexander's campaign.[9]

To be fair, fiction must conflate and simplify, and even the most historically faithful fictional narrative is still not history. Nor should it be; that is not the point of fiction.[10] Stone focused on Alexander's personal entanglements more than his military conquests or political choices, and thus, the main characters of his film are not Alexander's marshals, but Alexander's father (Philip), mother (Olympias), first wife (Roxane), friend-lover (Hephaestion), and father-substitute (Cleitus).[11] As a result, Stone's Hephaestion is more evident in the bedroom than the "boardroom," and as the film progresses his role increasingly involves such things as physically restraining a furious Alexander, or encouraging him in private—again, positions stereotypically associated with women. As noted above, his appointment to the second-highest place in the empire—the chiliarchy—is overlooked.

The number of scenes or camera-angle juxtapositions between Hephaestion and either Roxane or Bagoas (or both) best illustrates this—particularly in the Director's Cut DVD release of the film, titled *Alexander Revisited*. Although this longer version was not the theatrical release, it does show the original order of scenes and therefore reflects Stone's guiding vision. Thus, it is to this version that I look for an insight into Stone's Hephaestion.[12]

Three scenes are, I think, particularly key to understanding how Stone sees Hephaestion vis-à-vis Bagoas and Roxane. The first involves Alexander's visit to the harem in Babylon. In the Director's Cut, the eunuch Bagoas is much more prominent, actually introduced to Alexander, not just seen from afar. If Stone's Bagoas owes more to Renault[13] than to Curtius, nonetheless, it is immediately after this encounter and Alexander's evident fascination that we first see Hephaestion employ eyeliner—just like Bagoas. In the theatrical release, this development appears to be evidence of Orientalizing, but cutaway shots of Hephaestion watching Alexander with Bagoas in the Director's Cut make it clear that Hephaestion is startled, and perhaps feels threatened. In short, Hephaestion's first "rival" in the film is sexual, not political. Indeed, in the scene that follows (Alexander in his bedroom, reading a letter from his mother), Hephaestion functions more like a wife or mistress, to the point of wearing long, flowing robes that billow as he walks.

The second key scene is the night of Alexander's marriage to Roxane, when a teary-eyed Hephaestion lets himself into Alexander's bedroom as the king awaits his bride, in order to give Alexander a special ring.

This ring is slipped onto the ring finger of Alexander's *left* hand, and if the Greeks themselves may not have employed wedding rings, the comparison is evident to a modern audience. Hephaestion is preempting Roxane. This love triangle gets more interesting yet when Roxane walks in to find her new husband's hand on Hephaestion's cheek. She says, "You love him." Alexander disingenuously replies, "He is Hephaestion," as if that explains it all. Hephaestion leaves, and shortly after, before the marriage is consummated, Hephaestion's ring is removed and Roxane flings it across the room in a fury.[14] We might think, "So much for Hephaestion," except that as Alexander departs later, he retrieves the ring and puts it on again. If comparisons between Olympias and Roxane might seem obvious, comparisons between Hephaestion and Roxane should not be overlooked.

Third and last, we have Hephaestion's death scene.[15] Alexander speaks of the two of them growing old together, looking out from their balcony over this new empire they have built, almost as if they are an elderly couple rocking on the porch while their grandchildren cavort in the yard before them. We can almost hear echoes of an earlier exchange between Aristotle and Alexander regarding the (Platonic) notion of pure male-male love giving birth to civilization and the *polis*. If Alexander and Hephaestion do not have literal children together, they have a "brave new world" instead.[16]

In the end, and after the combined weight of parallels and juxtapositions, the primary implication in Oliver Stone's *Alexander* is not that Hephaestion is Alexander's right-hand man and a major power broker at the court because of his abilities and talents. The implication is that he is Alexander's *true* spouse, and any political power he might wield arises from his personal relationship to the king. Thus, Stone's treatment stands in a long tradition that reduces Hephaestion's significance to the personal.

I have argued elsewhere that in Macedon the personal and political overlapped, resulting in "public individuals" rather than private persons occupying public office.[17] The Macedonians merged politics with personal motivations in a way that might strike us now as suspect, and the role of Hephaestion at the court epitomizes that fusing. He was called "Philalexandros" (Friend of Alexander) by Alexander himself, in contrast to Craterus as "Philobasileus" (Friend of the king)—*not* in contrast to Roxane or Bagoas. He belonged to Alexander's marshals and displayed his stature and prominence in the public arena of court and symposium, rather than in the boudoir. He was not Alexander's "male wife," but Alexander's Friend—*Philos*[18]—and alter ego, with all that implied in Greco-Macedonian society.

Hephaestion in Modern Scholarship

When I first began to read modern Alexander histories, I was struck by the relative dearth of information about Hephaestion. Despite being the confidant, chiliarch, and *amicorum carissimus* to Alexander (Curt. 3.12.16), and despite being mentioned in the sources at least as often as those generals who outlived him to engage in their titanic clashes across the East, most modern histories had passed him over. What a curious silence.

Aside from encyclopedic entries,[19] only five summaries of Hephaestion's career went beyond a paragraph or page.[20] An article by Treves[21] dealt with his cult, not his person, and there was mention of him in three articles by Waldemar Heckel,[22] but these concerned broader topics. Most Alexander biographies tended to reserve comment about him until they reached a description of his death and its effect on Alexander: see, for example, W. W. Tarn's, which may have set a pattern. Yet the combined effect has left the impression that he was a footnote to Alexander's career, and assessments of him have ranged from dismissive to suspicious to mildly condescending.[23]

Then, in 1991, Heckel published a brief prosopographical treatment, "Hephaistion 'The Athenian,'" which for the first time asked serious questions about Hephaestion's family and their position at the court. In 1992 Heckel published *The Marshals of Alexander's Empire,* a much revised and expanded version of his doctoral thesis, in which a chapter on Hephaestion contained the most thorough and serious examination to date, but not a particularly positive assessment of his military ability. I believe it is fair to summarize Heckel's conclusions as stating that Hephaestion advanced in the army on the strength of Alexander's attachment to him, rather than on any real merit or talent of his own.[24]

This neglect or dismissal of Hephaestion might be regarded as a scholarly peculiarity, but we find a similar silence in fiction and film as well. Hephaestion is virtually absent from Robert Rossen's 1956 movie *Alexander the Great* with Richard Burton as Alexander; and in the 1964 television pilot *Alexander the Great* (aired only once in 1968 on ABC), with William Shatner as Alexander, Hephaestion does not appear at all, at least not by name. Instead, Alexander's best friend is "Cleander." Of course, both celluloid historicals were more interested in drama than accuracy, but the absence of such a significant figure is telling. We should also note that both portrayed Alexander as thoroughly *hetero-sexual*. In fact, only two novels in which Hephaestion emerges as a significant figure *also* present Alexander as primarily or exclusively heterosexual: Aubrey Menen's *A Conspiracy of Women* (1965), and Steven Pressfield's *The Virtues of War* (2004).[25] Otherwise, Hephaestion is prominent only in novels or films, including Oliver Stone's, that also address Alexander's bisexuality.[26] Yet Stone's view is, in the end, none too different from Heckel's suggestion that Hephaestion's value to the conqueror and rise in the army were based on personal affection—although Stone treated him more kindly overall.

Thus, it seems he is often linked to the issue of Alexander's sexual preferences. Those who wish to skirt the matter of Alexander's sexuality skirt Hephaestion as well, in order to avoid even raising the question. Hephaestion's ties to Alexander persist in being seen as personal and private, even sexual. In all of this, where is Hephaestion the army officer? Testimony in the ancient sources detailing his various military and political assignments dwarfs the number of attestations about his personal relationship with the king.

Hephaestion's Career

Hephaestion's friendship with Alexander has often been pointed to as the cause of his rise at the court, and Heckel went so far as to call his promotions "nepotism."[27] But nepotism implies that the one receiving the appointment is a kinsman with little or no native ability or experience. Hephaestion wasn't a kinsman—which perhaps presses the definition too far—yet it was more than nepotism. If he lacked combat command experience, a systematic listing of his assignments suggests that he did have logistical and diplomatic savvy.

Hephaestion likely began his career as one of Philip's Pages and at some point was selected to become a companion (*syntrophos*) of the prince. He was born around 356 B.C.E., as Curtius calls him a coeval of Alexander, and his father's name was Amyntor. Pella is listed as his city, but the same section names Pella as Leonnatus's city, and we know that he hailed from Lynkestis.[28] Hephaestion and Alexander likely went to school together, and he would have been one of several boys who studied under Aristotle at Mieza with the prince.[29] Later, Aristotle

wrote him letters, as did Xenocrates, the head of Plato's Academy from
339 to 314 B.C.E. (Diog. Laert. 4.14, 5.27). So perhaps he was an intellectual (or liked people to think so). He turned out to be better at logistics
and diplomacy than military combat strategy, and Curtius (3.12.16)
says that he was the king's counselor, all of which may suggest more
brains than brawn.

If he was raised and educated with the prince, his father would have
been among the king's *Hetairoi*, or Companions, so he was born into
wealth. We do not know his mother's name or the names of other relatives (although his grandfather may have been called Demetrios).[30] Of
interest, however, is his father's name: "Amyntor" and "Amyntas" are
variants much like "Stephen" and "Stefano," or "Mary" and "Maria."
Amyn*tas* was the usual version in Macedon, but Amyn*tor* was used in
Greece. Moreover, the name "Hephaestion" is uncommon in Macedon.
What all this means precisely is a matter of speculation, but it is worth
noting. The family appears to have had Greek ties of some sort (perhaps to Athens specifically).[31]

Upon graduation from the Pages' corps, Hephaestion would probably have moved into the Hypaspists or Companion Cavalry. Heckel
has made a case that the Hypaspists were the next step in the Macedonian *cursus honorum*, and indeed at Gaugamela we find Hephaestion
fighting as head of the "bodyguard" (Diod. Sic. 17.61.2), a term used
for the *agēma* of the Hypaspists in combat; Heckel has proposed that
he commanded that unit.[32] Yet on the Alexander Sarcophagus (Istanbul Museum), if the central rider in the battle scene along one side is
Hephaestion—as has been proposed—then he may have fought on
horseback at Issus. So Heckel's theory that Pages graduated into the Hypaspists may not have been absolutely correct; some may have gone
into the Companion *agēma* instead, or they may have moved back and
forth, depending. But it is clear that Hephaestion was not yet among
the special seven-man corps of *Somatophylakes*, who did not fight together as a unit, in any case.

Prior to Gaugamela, we hear nothing of Hephaestion's military rank,
and this silence led Tarn to disbelieve stories of his childhood friendship with the king.[33] Yet as Hephaestion and Alexander were coevals, it
would be *surprising* had Hephaestion received plum commands early.
Alexander could hardly risk alienating his older and more experienced
officers by granting such commissions to his *syntrophoi*.[34] Heckel has
postulated that a new king inherited the *Somatophylakes* of the prior

one, and this arrangement would have prevented Alexander from offering these posts to his own friends as soon as he took the throne. Heckel does, however, think that Alexander put Hephaestion in the *Somatophylakes* at the earliest opportunity, using him to replace Ptolemaios, who died at Halikarnassos.[35] While I agree with Heckel's basic theory about the unit, I have come to disbelieve that Hephaestion was appointed there so soon. Twice during the Bactrian campaigns, he is named separately from the *Somatophylakes,* and by both Arrian (*Anab.* 4.16.2) and Curtius (7.7.9).

So aside from possible command of the Hypaspist *agēma* at Gaugamela, Hephaestion's first important commission appears to have been joint command with Cleitus as hipparchs of the Companion Cavalry. Alexander may have had reasons beyond wanting to keep too much power out of any one man's hands, even his best friend's—the rationale that Arrian gives (*Anab.* 3.27.4). Although both Hephaestion and Cleitus had commanded the *agēmata* of Alexander's most prestigious units, to elevate Cleitus, a proven veteran, along with Hephaestion would have made the latter's appointment more palatable, even while securing for Alexander what he wanted: a man he trusted absolutely in an influential position. Prior to this, Gaugamela aside, Hephaestion had little *combat command* experience—not to be confused with having little *command* experience. In fact, it seems that he had handled several important logistical and diplomatic duties already.

The accompanying table uses a modified content analysis to organize all of the ancient citations of Hephaestion's duties and assignments, along with descriptions of their nature. Each is then assigned to one or more of five categories: diplomatic/advisory; building, founding cities; troop supply; troop movement; and combat.[36] Normally, troop movement and troop supply would be labeled simply "logistics," but I chose to separate them here because in Hephaestion's case the movement of troops was usually accomplished through hostile territory and may have included skirmishes not directly referenced by the sources. This is part of our problem: we can *in no way* assume that the table represents a comprehensive list of Hephaestion's commands. We may, at least, hope that it is representative. As for the "diplomatic/advisory" category, in addition to duties such as finding a new king for Sidon, it involves citations that suggest the informal advisory role to which Curtius refers in 3.12.16, observing that no one was as free to counsel the king as Hephaestion.

Table 1. Hephaestion's Assignments

	Assignment		Category				
Citation	Description	Diplomatic/ advisory	Building, founding cities	Troop supply	Troop movement	Combat
Curt. 4.1.16–26; Diod. Sic. 17.47.1–4	chose a king for Sidon	XX				
Curt. 4.5.10	led fleet off Palestinian coast between Haifa and Gaza			XX		
Plut. *Alex.* 41.3	Alex. wrote letter from Egypt to H., "absent on some business"	XX?		XX?		
Arr. *Anab.* 3.15.2; Curt. Diod. Sic. 17.61.3	wounded while in command of the Hypaspist *agēma*					XX
Curt. 6.2.9	in charge of Persian captives	XX				
Curt. 6.8.17, 6.11.10–20; Plut. *Alex.* 44.6	role in Philotas affair	XX				
Arr. *Anab.* 3.27.4	command of half Companions	N/A	N/A	N/A	N/A	N/A
Curt. 7.7.9	among those advising Alex. about attack on Scythians	XX				
Arr. *Anab.* 4.12.4; Plut. *Alex.* 54.3–4,	organized *proskynesis* debacle?	XX				

Continued on next page

Table 1—*continued*

Assignment		Category				
Citation	Description	Diplomatic/ advisory	Building, founding cities	Troop supply	Troop movement	Combat
Arr. *Anab.* 4.16.2; Curt. 8.1.1–10	helped subdue countryside of Sogdiana (doublet with item below?)					(X)
Arr. *Anab.* 4.16.3	peopled cities in Sogdiana		XX			
Curt. 8.2.13	while at Marakanda, sent to secure winter supplies			XX		
Arr. *Anab.* 4.22.7; Curt. 8.10.2	with Perdiccas, subdued Peukelaotis area					XX
Arr. *Anab.* 4.22.8, 4.28.5, 4.30.9, 5.3.5; Curt. 8.10.2–3	with Perdiccas, bridged Indus with boats		XX		XX	
Arr. *Anab.* 4.28.5	fortified/garrisoned Orobatis		XX			XX
Curt. 8.12.4–6	got supplies and established Omphis in father's place?	XX		XX		
Arr. *Anab.* 5.12.2; Curt. 8.14.15	Battle of Hydaspes: hipparchy under command of Alex.					XX
Arr. *Anab.* 5.21.5; Curt. 9.1.35; Diod. Sic. 17. 91.2, 17.93.1	with Demetrios, took land of "unfriendly" Porus and gave it to "friendly" Porus	XX				XX

Continued on next page

Table 1—*continued*

Assignment		Category				
Citation	Description	Diplomatic/ advisory	Building, founding cities	Troop supply	Troop movement	Combat
Arr. *Anab.* 5.29.3	built and fortified city in land of "unfriendly"Porus		XX			
Arr. *Indike* 8.18.3	trierarch for Hydaspes fleet		XX			
Arr. *Anab.* 6.2.2, 6.4.1; Arr. *Indike* 8.19.1; Diod. Sic. 17.96.1	took elephants and bulk of fighting troops down the Hydaspes left bank				XX	
Arr. *Anab.* 6.5.5–6	Mallian siege: ordered five days ahead to intercept retreat and set up base camp			XX	XX	(X)
Arr. *Anab.* 6.13.1	after siege: had command of land forces while Nearchus had fleet, awaiting Alex.			XX	XX	
Arr. *Anab.* 6.17.4	with Peithon, settled fortified cities on river near Patala		XX			XX
Arr. *Anab.* 6.18.1	fortified Patala citadel; came under attack during process		XX			(X)
Arr. *Anab.* 6.20.1	fortified harbor, docks		XX			

Continued on next page

Table 1—*continued*

Assignment		Category				
Citation	Description	Diplomatic/ advisory	Building, founding cities	Troop supply	Troop movement	Combat
Arr. *Anab.* 6.21.3	left in command of base camp				XX	
Arr. *Anab.* 6.21.5; Curt. 9.10.6–7	built Rhambakia into an Alexandria			XX		
Arr. *Anab.* 6.28.4	listed among *Somatophylakes*	N/A	N/A	N/A	N/A	N/A
Arr. *Anab.* 6.28.7	took troops and baggage by coastal route to Persia				XX	
Arr. *Anab.* 7.7.1	took troops along Persian Gulf				XX	
Arr. *Anab.* 7.14.10	role as chiliarch	N/A	N/A	N/A	N/A	N/A

Note: Assignments where Hephaestion was given independent command are represented by (X).

Of the thirty-two entries in table 1, twenty-nine are actual assignments, while the other three involve commissions: Hephaestion's appointment as joint hipparch of the Companions, his place as *Somatophylax*, and his role as chiliarch. While command of the Hypaspist *agēma* might also be considered a commission, we hear of it only in the context of an actual battle, and thus it is listed here as combat.[37] As his *Somatophylax* and chiliarch appointments are both mentioned after the fact, the time of these commissions is difficult to place. He is not certainly listed as a *Somatophylax* until the occasion of Peukestas's extraordinary appointment as the eighth member, after the army had emerged from Gedrosia; if he probably was not among their numbers before the Bactrian campaigns, he obviously was by their emergence into Carmania.

The most likely time for his formal appointment follows Alexander's reorganization of the Companion Cavalry into eight hipparchies (including the *agēma*) after reinforcements arrived in Bactria during the winter of 329/28 (Arr. *Anab.* 4.7.1; Curt. 5.2.6). By the late summer or early fall of 328, Cleitus was reassigned as satrap of Bactria, and that is likely when these reorganizations occurred.[38] Command of the Com-· panions was split seven ways (excluding Alexander's *agēma*), and while Hephaestion's hipparchy may have been chief among them, the change meant a demotion, *contra* Peter Green, who believed that he then had sole command of the Companions, or Heckel, who equated the chiliarchy with the first Companion hipparchy. N. G. L. Hammond explains, "The brevity of Arrian has contributed to some misunderstanding of Hephaestion's position."[39] His hipparchy was not the same thing as his chiliarchy, and the two should not be conflated. Rather, he held both titles, and Arrian is mistaken to speak of them as if they were one. We learn from Diodorus that "chiliarch" as used for Hephaestion's commission referred to the Persian *hazarapatish,* a civil service position.[40] His appointment to the chiliarchy did not mean that he retained sole command of the Companions. Although his hipparchy was apparently preeminent, his fellow hipparchs were theoretically his equals. In any case, and to make up for this demotion, perhaps, Alexander put him in the *Somatophylakes* at the earliest opportunity, so we might narrow his appointment to sometime between mid-328 and mid-325—but this is chiefly speculation.

As for his investiture to the chiliarchy, it must have occurred after the Mallian campaign in India, perhaps in Carmania, or at Susa at the time of his marriage to Drypetis,[41] yet we do not learn of it until after his death. If Arrian's text of the Mallian siege is confused, to say the least, one observation makes it unlikely that Hephaestion was already chiliarch. Arrian says (*Anab.* 6.12.1–2) that when the troops learned of Alexander's wounding and thought him dead, morale fell, since they could not imagine who would be their future leader, "for in the opinion of both Alexander and the Macedonians, several held an equal claim." In the Loeb edition, Brunt translates *kathestēkenai* as "equal reputation," but I believe it to have a broader meaning here. In any case, Hephaestion could not have been chiliarch *yet.* Let us turn, then, to an evaluation of his specific assignments.

Regarding the remaining twenty-nine entries, twenty were of a non-combat nature, four had logistic or diplomatic as well as combat aspects, and only five were purely combat. Of those nine (four plus five) that did involve combat, Hephaestion was *intentionally* given independent command only *twice.* On the other occasions, he was co-assigned with Perdiccas (infantry), Peithon (infantry), and Demetrios (a fellow hipparch), or he was under another's command during a set-piece battle: Nikanor or Alexander himself.

Of the two cases where he was independently assigned, one was in Sogdiana (Arr. *Anab.* 4.16.2–3, Curt. 8.1.1–10), and the other was during the Mallian siege (Arr. *Anab.* 6.5.5–6). The Sogdian assignment occurred not long after he became co-commander of the Companions, but there is doubt as to whether it was combat in nature. According to Arrian, Hephaestion was one of five commanders sent out with troops to subdue the Sogdian countryside, but no specifics are mentioned. When these five divisions rejoined, Cleitus and Artabazus were sent off again to deal with Spitamenes, Alexander mopped up the remaining rebels, and Hephaestion was left to settle people in the subdued areas. Curtius mentions *only* the assignments of Hephaestion, Cleitus, and Alexander. In his commentary on Arrian, Bosworth has suggested that Arrian mistook a single assignment in Ptolemy's account for two: first Ptolemy had listed all assignments in passing, then later returned to give details of the three most important, while Curtius's source had information only on the three.[42] This very reasonable reading would mean Hephaestion's was *not* a combat assignment at all. Therefore, we shall eliminate it from our list.

The second case, involving the Mallian siege, also looks less significant upon closer inspection. While Hephaestion was given an independent appointment that could have involved combat, he was stationed furthest from the battle, five days south, and his primary assignment was not interception of fleeing Mallians, but setting up a base camp. Heckel perhaps overestimated this command when he said that Hephaestion (not Craterus) was the one chosen to be a part of Alexander's elaborate plans at Mallia.[43] J. F. C. Fuller noted that Alexander must have known that the Mallians were not likely to break south (toward Hephaestion), nor back west (toward Ptolemy), but would turn east toward their allies, the Oxydrakai. This, they, in fact, did. Yet in an attempt to reconstruct the battle from Arrian's abbreviated account, Fuller sent Hephaestion's column south down the Ravi branch while stating that Craterus flanked Nearchus's fleet along the Chenab, after taking the elephants, Polyperchon's infantry, and several other units previously under Hephaestion. Nearchus and Craterus then made a base camp.[44] But Arrian's text (*Anab.* 6.5.5–6) simply says that Hephaestion was sent south without specifying which branch of the river he followed (if any), nor what precisely happened to Craterus with the remaining troops. Arrian speaks (*Anab.* 6.5.7) of the advance guard waiting at the confluence of the rivers until Alexander, Craterus, and Ptolemy can join them—but it is not specified who this advance guard *is*.[45] However, from the names left off the list and from what follows in 6.13.1, where we find Hephaestion and Nearchus in charge, we can guess that the advance guard consisted of Nearchus's fleet and Hephaestion's troops. It was not Craterus, then, who helped to establish the camp as Fuller implies, because Craterus joined them later—though we are not told what he did in the meantime. He drops out of Arrian's narrative, perhaps because he had dropped out of Arrian's source.[46] What makes Fuller's reconstruction particularly unlikely is that it would have required Hephaestion to enter the base camp and take command of the land forces from Craterus: improbable at best.

It must have worked the other way. Hephaestion took his column on a fast march five days south to the river's confluence, where he set up camp, met the fleet when it arrived, then kept command of the land troops as new columns came in, being no more willing to give command to Craterus than Craterus would have been to give it to him.[47] *Neither* Hephaestion nor Craterus (nor Ptolemy either) had much of a role in the Mallian campaign—nor, I believe Fuller is correct to note, did Alexander expect that they would. The king had simply needed to allow for all contingencies. He sent Hephaestion to do precisely what Hephaestion was best at—organize. It was no more a combat command than when Hephaestion had peopled cities in the pacified regions of Sogdiana. And this means that Hephaestion was *never* (to our knowledge) given an assignment in the anticipation that he would have to command alone in a battle.

One case does exist where he commanded singularly in combat, but it was a surprise attack. While fortifying Patala, his workers and engineers were ambushed by locals (Arr. *Anab.* 6.18.1). In recently pacified territory, such an attack was always possible, but his mission was not the same as going into hostile territory with orders to subdue it. In each case when he *was* sent into hostile territory, he always had another (tried) combat commander with him, and, in fact, at Patala, Peithon had initially been present.

Thus, if we count Hephaestion's assignments for *intent*, his combat duties are reduced by three. Although playing with numbers—given such a small and uncertain sample—is problematic to say the least, this produces a ratio of 22:6, or between three and four to one. In short, three-quarters of his known duties were *noncombat,* and of those that were likely to involve combat, he always shared command with someone else. The evidence suggests that he was meticulously kept away from combat command.[48]

By contrast, his first recorded assignment of *any* type was an independent diplomatic mission—choosing a new king for Sidon—where political finesse was required to balance opposing parties without angering any (Curt. 4.1.16–26; Diod. Sic. 17.47.1–2). He carried it off with aplomb, and without intervention from Alexander beyond confirmation of his choice. His next assignment was the logistical duty of skirting the Palestinian coast with the fleet, supplying water to the army while it marched (Curt. 4.5.10). Although Alexander controlled the seas, it is an error to dismiss this as "a relatively minor task."[49] Donald Engels has pointed out that no little planning would have been required to make that march during late summer.[50]

We might ask where he learned his diplomatic and logistical skills, but as our sources rarely relate the duties of junior officers, we have no idea what role Hephaestion filled in the army prior to Sidon. During battles, he would have fought among the Hypaspists or Companions, but where he served otherwise is unknown; perhaps he acted as apprentice at supply under Parmenion. Yet it seems unlikely that Alexander would have given him such important assignments without reason to think him capable, because—as we just saw—the king would later orchestrate matters to keep him *away* from combat command even while he held combat commissions. Nonetheless—and if we set aside qualitative judgments about the relative worth of combat and organization—it is Hephaestion who, of Alexander's *syntrophoi* or boyhood companions, received important independent duties at the youngest age.

We should also note the wide variety of his assignments, from troop movement to supply, from diplomacy to engineering supervision. His diplomatic assignments aside, the others share two features: all were organizational in nature, and all required some mathematical ability. From this, we might suppose that Hephaestion had a mind for detail and numbers. He also apparently had some political tact, certainly where foreigners were concerned, but also, if Curtius can be believed, among the Macedonians: "No one had greater freedom in admonishing [Alexander], but he exercised it in such a fashion that it seemed granted by the king, rather than claimed by himself" (3.12.16). The picture of Hephaestion as quarrelsome, impulsive, and tactless comes primarily from Plutarch and stands at odds with his repeated diplomatic assignments, where tact was required.

We may wonder, though, to what extent he was directly involved in logistical decision-making, and how much was the work of his advisors. Could he have been a mere political appointee? Several facts argue against this. The first and most obvious is that he continued to receive independent logistical and diplomatic assignments. Were he merely an appointee, the type of assignment would not matter, and we would not see the pattern indicated above in our breakdown of his duties. Second, the Macedonian army, while involving more specialization than most Greek armies, was still not specialized to the degree of our modern military. The king himself figured logistics on numerous occasions, and his chief combat advisor, Parmenion, also seems to have been his chief transport officer until Ekbatana.[51] Hephaestion would have been expected to participate in logistical planning, not simply to supervise those who did it. Of his twenty-eight assignments, seven—about one quarter—concerned transport and supply alone (see table).

In order to determine Hephaestion's logistical skill, we must consider the various terrains in which he was responsible for supplies—which areas were difficult, and which easy. In his work on Alexander's logistics, Engels has helpfully detailed the nature of the landscape through which the army marched, and of the seven basic regions in which Hephaestion had charge of construction or supplies, or moved troops, five were critical: Palestine, the retreat from Marakanda, bridging the Indus, building Rhambakia into an Alexandria, and the Persian Gulf. Two of these may have required supply magazines: the Persian Gulf and Palestine.[52] Of Alexander's other high-ranking officers, Erigyios and Koinos also had transport duties, as did Craterus, but the only one besides the king who had more—and more critical—supply and transport assignments than Hephaestion was Parmenion. Furthermore, Craterus was in charge of logistics only when co-assigned with Parmenion, or when Hephaestion was busy with another, more important assignment.

As Napoleon said, an army runs on its stomach, and we must not dismiss Hephaestion's significance because he was "merely" a logistics officer—and Alexander's friend. He did not rise to the chiliarchy because he was Alexander's friend. We have seen that—friend or not— Alexander avoided giving him combat commands for which, apparently, he was ill-suited. He rose to be chiliarch because after the death of Parmenion he became Alexander's chief diplomatic, logistics, and transport officer. Apparently those were his skills, and Alexander appointed him accordingly.

Hephaestion's Significance

If—as it appears—Hephaestion's assignments were of more consequence than previously thought, why have his abilities been overlooked, underrated, or outright denigrated?

One reason may be that he died before Alexander and therefore had
no part in the Successor Wars that followed—events from which modern scholars derive a more complete picture of his fellow marshals. One
scholar even speaks of him as being spared the aftermath of Alexander's death, in which he "was evidently ill qualified to compete with
the sterner and more energetic spirits that surrounded him."[53] On the
contrary—having some diplomatic-political ability, he might have
fared better than the ill-starred Craterus. If we had to evaluate the abilities of Ptolemy, Eumenes, or Antigonus based solely on their presentation in the extant histories of Alexander, we might never foresee their
later prominence, either. Bosworth notes: "Our extant sources are centrally focused on the king himself. Accordingly it is his own military
actions which receive the fullest documentation. Appointments to sa-
trapies and satrapal armies are carefully noted because he made them,
but the achievements of the appointees are passed over in silence."[54]

Yet I believe the primary reason Hephaestion has been overlooked
stems from a combination of ancient and modern biases. As I noted at
the outset of this chapter, Hephaestion's modern "fans" constitute a
fairly specific demographic—far more specific than the fans of nearly
any other figure at Alexander's court, including the conqueror himself.
Hephaestion has fangirls and gay fanboys nine times out of ten because
they are the ones most likely to recognize his significance *and* his marginalization, since it mirrors their own. Hephaestion's talents were sup-
portive, his leadership not particularly notable in combat, and his role
in Alexander's life closely mirrored that of a spouse—but he was not a
spouse, at least not formally. Had he been, he might have received more
attention. One must be able to look at him standing in Alexander's
shadow, as he so often does, and recognize his role as *éminence grise* at
the court, for good or ill.[55]

Nor do I think this an entirely modern bias. Such judgments may
partially arise from an unconscious adoption of biases found in our
primary sources. As Engels has pointed out, "Ancient Greek historians
seldom display any interest in the supply problems of armies," and, he
further observes, this has led modern scholars to overlook their importance.[56] I believe Hephaestion has suffered in our analyses for the same

reason: his career as a logistics and diplomatic officer is overshadowed by the combat talent of his chief rival, Craterus. Elizabeth Carney has argued that Olympias endured a similar fate as modern scholarship adopted the misogynistic biases of the ancients, and even (consciously or unconsciously) exacerbated them.[57]

Nevertheless, as the ancients did value combat ability over less bloody military talents, it might seem peculiar for a logistics officer— even a good one—to be raised to the second-most-important position at court: the chiliarch or *hazarapatish*.[58] This position granted "supreme control over the entire state and all the civil servants."[59] Diodorus—or really Hieronymus—described it as *deutereuonta kata tnv exousian* or "second in authority" (18.48.4), and Nepos (9.3.2) refers to "the chiliarch, who held the most elevated position after the king."[60]

This commission particularly raises debate as to how much Hephaestion owed to his personal relationship with Alexander. J. R. Hamilton says: "Hephaestion's promotion was probably the result not so much of his military and administrative abilities, considerable though these were, as of the affection that Alexander felt for his boyhood friend and of Hephaestion's complete devotion to his policies."[61] Plutarch (*Alex.* 47.5) tells us that he, like Alexander, adapted to the native Persian customs,[62] and one notes that the king assigned him frequently to interact with Persians and Indians. Certainly trust and a similar political outlook played a part—even a significant part—in his appointment. But his organizational ability has been undervalued.

In the *Cambridge History of Iran*, Ernst Badian says, "There is no support in the sources for the belief that Hephaestion held all the actual powers of a Grand Vizier."[63] While I would certainly not argue that Hephaestion's new role would have conformed precisely to that of a Persian *hazarapatish*, he did hold the title. As he came into the role so near the time of his death, there is little evidence for exactly what he did in that capacity, yet it is presumptuous to assume his new duties were not, at least partly, the usual ones that went with the title. The Macedonians had used the Persian court as a model in the past, and it is perfectly logical to assume that Hephaestion's role as chiliarch *did* include Macedonian versions of duties previously performed by his Persian counterpart.[64] They were not unique to the Persian court, but are common needs found in any large government.

In the Persian court, it was the *hazarapatish* who kept the king's appointment book and screened access to the king (Ael. *VH* 1.21); he also headed up the chancellery and was chief of the king's personal guard.[65]

Moreover, he was responsible for security and order at the court, kept an eye on world events to create digests for the king, and minded the king's comfort on campaign. He was "the highest civil servant in the state."[66] And although he did fight first among the Immortals, the *hazarapatish* was not, primarily, a military position—certainly not one of frequent combat command. It required different talents—talents that Hephaestion obviously had, given his previous record.

Hephaestion as *Hazarapatish*

Macedonian court procedure was not as intricate as Persian, but as Alexander adopted the role of Great King—with its correspondingly more complex protocol—he would have needed to create positions to fill new needs. Furthermore, and as stated previously, it has been generally accepted that the Macedonian court used the Persian as a model. For example, the institution of the Pages, the infantry Hypaspists called "bodyguards," and the royal secretary and archive may all have sprung from Achaemenid example.[67] But a chiliarch was new, and Hephaestion had the cheerless task of working out the duties of a position for which there had heretofore been no equivalent.[68] For instance, only a small number of people could approach the Persian king without going through the chiliarch first,[69] but as we know, Macedonians were accustomed to petitioning their king freely. The chief of a small kingdom had the luxury of being more readily accessible than the ruler of a large empire. Among Arrian's various explanations for the explosion between Alexander and his soldiers at Opis is the characterization of Alexander "courted as he now was in the barbarian manner."[70] The Opis affair occurred not long after the pageantry at Susa—which is also the most likely time for Hephaestion's appointment to the chiliarchy. Although there were complaints about increasing pomp and circumstance surrounding Alexander as early as 330, could some of the soldier's disgruntlement here have stemmed from recently instituted policies restricting access to the king and requiring common soldiers and lesser military and civil officers to make an appointment?[71] Carney calls the king's relationship to his soldiers "paternal," and Eleanor Roosevelt once described the presidential family: "As life grew busier at the White House, my husband had less time for family affairs, and I can remember how resentful the boys were when they found they actually had to make an appointment to see their father if they wanted to talk to him privately."[72]

Other functions of the *hazarapatish* included concern with court security, command of the king's bodyguard, and first place among the Immortals.[73] Hephaestion did not (re-)take command of the Hypaspist *agēma* (the Macedonian equivalent of the Persian Immortals), but he was a member of the seven-man *Somatophylakes*. Further, he held command over what was probably the chief hipparchy of the Companions and, as Alexander fought primarily as a cavalryman, this may have been the more prestigious position. Arrian's wording at 7.14.10, in which Alexander says that there would never be another chiliarch over the Companion Cavalry, suggests that this post was, for Alexander, linked to the role of chiliarch just as the *hazarapatish* had been linked to the Immortals—but hipparch and chiliarch are not the same role, as discussed above.[74] The *Somatophylakes* do not appear to have had a formal leader, although one of their number may have been informally recognized as senior. They oversaw court security, such as it was. When Philotas fell under suspicion, two of the six *Philoi* called to the king's tent were *Somatophylakes*.[75]

The civil servant side of the *hazarapatish*'s role included keeping the king's appointment book and, perhaps, the introduction of visitors, duties previously handled by the usher—Chares, under Alexander.[76] How or whether Chares' role altered much after Hephaestion became chiliarch is unknown. Nevertheless, once Alexander had returned to the major cities of Persia near the end of his reign, the complexity of court ceremonial would have increased over what had been known on campaign,[77] or what he had used while still posing as Persia's conqueror, not its Great King. As the demands of Alexander's new empire required more organization and formality, the demands of maintaining a royal household would have required more organization and formality, too. Perhaps Hephaestion, with Chares' assistance, had responsibility for adapting Persian protocols.

As for the king's comfort on campaign, this was traditionally the duty of the Pages. Before, they had been under the king's direct discipline, but now, perhaps, they too were expected to answer to Hephaestion. Along with the need to arrange an appointment to see the king, this must have felt like a demotion to other Companions. Were they no longer the king's *Hetairoi* if they—and their sons—had to get to the king through another *Hetairos*? The *Hetairoi* were the king's social equals, in theory, if not necessarily in practice. Making Hephaestion chiliarch would have appeared to them just another step in transforming their familiar rough-and-ready system into an Oriental, hierarchical tyranny.

It may have been organizationally necessary—but it would not have been welcome.

And, finally, the chancellery was traditionally under the purview of the *hazarapatish*. The Macedonian chancellery had heretofore been headed by Eumenes, as chief secretary. His conflict with Hephaestion— as it seems to have taken place only in the last half-year of the latter's life—perhaps stemmed from his infringing on areas that Eumenes had heretofore considered his own responsibility. In the Book of Esther, we find that (H)aman was intimately involved with the chancellery, and it was chancellery officials who were required to do him obeisance.[78] Theoretically, Hephaestion became Eumenes' superior, although Eumenes had been chief secretary from the reign of Philip onward. That change would hardly have been well received, and if Eumenes could not argue with the king's appointment, he could certainly resent the appointee.[79]

There may have been other causes for friction between the two men. The *hazarapatish* kept the king informed of world affairs, and sometimes advised him on the best course of action to take: Teribazos had advised Artaxerxes regarding Cyrus's rebellion, Prexaspes brought dispatches to Cambyses, and—however fictional—(H)aman, under the pretext of informing Xerxes of a people's "rebellious behavior," sought the destruction of the Jews. As Alexander had increasingly more things to keep track of, it would have fallen to his assistants to create digests of information for him, organize his appointment book, and read and organize his mail.[80] If, as Plutarch implies (*Alex.* 39.5), Hephaestion had read Alexander's mail in the past, then he may have been helping informally in this capacity for some while before receiving his chiliarchy, but afterward he would have had a final say on what the king actually saw—and this could have brought him into conflict with Alexander's chief secretary: a clash of prerogatives.

So Hephaestion's new role would not only have alienated the Macedonian rank and file; it probably also alienated some senior officers, including Eumenes. As the new court became increasingly complex, a position like the chiliarchy became increasingly important, but it would also have been thankless. Little wonder if, at the time of Hephaestion's death, he was less than appreciated among his colleagues. His sudden change in status and the resultant unpopularity would have affected how he was presented in the ancient histories—and he did not survive long enough either to outlive the resentment or to prove his competence. Yet that means we must be all the more careful in our acceptance of these ancient reports.

Given this detailed look at both his assignments and his appointments, it seems that Hephaestion was rather more important at the court, and more able, than has sometimes been recognized—in historical treatments *or* film. So perhaps his fans—together with his friend, the king—were right all along to take notice of the man behind the throne, Alexander's *éminence grise*.

Notes

1. Letters and e-mail have come from North and South America, Europe, Russia and the Far East, including various Pacific islands, and Australia. The majority of correspondents found my name via websites, but some letters have come by regular post to my university address. My Hephaestion website is located at http://myweb.unomaha.edu/~mreames/Hephaistion/hephaistion.html (last updated September 1, 2007).

2. In an effort to ascertain whether my own impression of Hephaestion's fans, derived from letters and e-mail, matched the demographics of those who would call *themselves* fans, I both reviewed the mail I had received over the years and ran a (very) informal online survey. Although I advertised the survey as widely as possible in a variety of places and allowed only one answer per ISP (a unique identifying number that prevents most sock-puppeting), it should be regarded as far from scientific. The results more or less matched what I had derived from the saved letters. The informal survey was taken by about 400 persons, so no individual response significantly altered the final percentages.

3. On the face of it, there seems to be little difference between the bare-chested football fan displaying body paint in his team colors in chilly weather and the Trekkie dressed in a homemade Starfleet uniform and sporting Spock ears at a science fiction convention. Yet the football fan is a jock; the Star Trek fan merely a geek.

4. In my informal survey, almost 60.0 percent identified as straight women, with another 22.5 percent as bisexual (only 2.5 percent were lesbian). Almost equal numbers of straight and bisexual men responded, but half-again as many gay men. The survey also showed a lower median age than I have encountered in postal (or even email) correspondence, a difference I believe to be an artifact of internet *fluency*, which favors a younger demographic. Even so, over half my survey respondents were twenty-four or older, and only about 20 percent were teens (eighteen or younger). If we allow for a bias toward youth, it suggests that the bulk of those interested in Hephaestion are past their undergraduate years.

5. This distinction was specified explicitly in the survey: the interest in Hephaestion had *preceded* the classes and did not follow from them.

6. About 65 percent—a little under two-thirds—of those surveyed attributed their initial interest in Hephaestion to fiction in either written or film format; 60

percent of that group specified the novels of Mary Renault (28 percent) or Oliver Stone's *Alexander* (32 percent) as their first exposure.

7. Arnaldo Momigliano, *The Classical Foundations of Modern Historiography* (Berkeley: University of California Press, 1990), 21.

8. These conflicts derive more from the novels of Mary Renault than the ancient histories and biographies. At several points in the film, Stone's indebtedness to Renault is evident. We might say that these conflicts are logical extrapolation, but such assumptions tend to reflect *our* cultural constructions—not those of the Macedonian court. See the work of Elizabeth Carney on similar assumptions about Olympias's motivations, in particular "Olympias and the Image of the Virago," *Phoenix* 47 (1993): 29-55: "Judgements of Olympias' career and motivation, her role in Macedonian political history, and her public prestige continue to reproduce the views of ancient sources uncritically" (29). The rest of the article goes on to explore why this is so, and the extent to which modern assumptions figure into the process. The same is true of Hephaestion, as we shall see.

9. If anything, from the film one would think that Hephaestion's primary rival at the court was Cleitus.

10. For a more in-depth discussion of history and historical fiction, see my "Alexander as Icon: Some Socio-Political Contexts of Alexander the Great in Twentieth-Century Fiction," in *Alexander's Empire: Formulation to Decay*, ed. Waldemar Heckel, Lawrence Tritle, and Pat Wheatley (Claremont, CA: Regina Books, 2007), 233-44.

11. It is almost a commonplace these days that Oliver Stone's films are more about Oliver Stone than about his characters, but we still might recognize a Plutarchian approach: "For it is not histories that I am writing, but lives; and in the most illustrious deeds there is not always a manifestation of virtue or vice, nay, a slight thing like a phrase or a jest often makes a greater revelation of character than battles where thousands fall, or the greatest armaments, or sieges of cities. Accordingly . . . I must be permitted to devote myself rather to the signs of the soul in men, and by means of these to portray the life of each, leaving to others the description of their great contests" (Plut. *Alex.* 1.2-3, in Plutarch, *Plutarch's Lives*, tr. Bernadotte Perrin, Loeb Classical Library, 11 vols. [1919; repr., London: Heinemann, 1994], 7:225). Even so, Plutarch did not limit his subject matter quite so much.

12. Personally, I found the Director's Cut superior in terms of logical plot development. While it remains a deeply flawed film in many ways, the choice of *thematic* advancement over chronological worked better. Such nonlinear storytelling is especially common in indigenous traditions, if also traditionally difficult for nonnative Western audiences. Kimberly Blaeser articulates the different aesthetic (and why it works) in "Like 'Reeds Through the Ribs of a Basket': Native Women Weaving Stories," *American Indian Quarterly* 21 (1997): 555-65, esp. 563-64; as does Paula Gunn Allen in the preface to her edited

collection, *Spider Woman's Granddaughters: Traditional Tales and Contemporary Writing by Native American Women* (New York: Women's Press, 1990), 8–9. These are only two examples; the difference is widely recognized in modern studies of indigenous storytelling and literature.

13. Mary Renault, *The Persian Boy* (New York: Pantheon, 1998).

14. All in a rather animalistic exchange, in which Alexander repeatedly snarls like the caged black panther seen earlier. Hephaestion represents not just a noncarnal, intellectual, male-male love, but also the "higher civilization" of Greece, while Roxane represents the barbarian wilds together with the "passions" that Aristotle warned women are "slave to." If this would fit an ancient Greek mindset, its use as symbolism in a *modern* film is rather disturbing.

15. Particularly in the theatrical release, the scene's framing was unfortunate, showing Alexander at the window, carried away articulating his vision of the future, while Hephaestion jerks in his death throes in the background. The result was comical rather than tragic; fortunately the Director's Cut has a less melodramatic demise.

16. Alexander also says that their children (by wives whom history buffs know to be sisters) will play together as he and Hephaestion once played together. Ergo, he and Hephaestion will have the ideological "child" of Alexander's empire, as well as literal children who are related by blood through their mothers.

17. Jeanne Reames-Zimmerman, "Hephaestion Amyntoros: *Éminence Grise* at the Court of Alexander the Great" (Ph. D. diss., The Pennsylvania State University, 1998), 245–55.

18. This term was probably used—at least sometimes—as a political, not just personal, title, much like the Roman emperor's *Amici*. See Reames-Zimmerman, "Hephaestion Amyntoros," 31–36, for further discussion of the slippery nature of titles at the Macedonian court, including citations of previous discussions.

19. N. G. L. Hammond and H. H. Scullard, *The Oxford Classical Dictionary* (Oxford: Oxford University Press, 1970); Pauly-Wissowa, *Real-Encyclopädie der classischen Altertumswissenschaft* (Neue Bearbeitung, 1894–1972); and Helmut Berve, *Das Alexanderreich auf prosopographischer Grundlage*, 2 vols. (Munich: C. H. Beck, 1925–1926). At the time, the 3rd edition of the *OCD* had not been published.

20. Hermann Bengtson, *Philipp und Alexander der Grosse* (Munich: Callwey, 1985), 194ff.; Elizabeth Carney, "Alexander the Great and the Macedonian Aristocracy" (Ph.D. diss., Duke University, 1975), 217–21; Ernst Kornemann, *Die Alexandergeschichte des Königs Ptolemaios I. von Aegypten* (Leipzig: Teubner, 1935), 242ff.; and two monographs by Friedrich Schachermeyr: *Alexander in Babylon und die Reichsordnung nach seinem Tode* (Vienna: Böhlau, 1970), 31–37, and *Alexander der Grosse: Das Problem seiner Persönlichkeit und seines Wirkens* (Vienna: Böhlau, 1973), 511–15.

21. Piero Treves, "Hyperides and the Cult of Hephaestion," *The Classical Review* 53 (1939): 56–57.

22. Waldemar Heckel, "The *Somatophylakes* of Alexander the Great: Some Thoughts," *Historia* 27 (1978): 224–28; "Factions and Macedonian Politics in the Reign of Alexander the Great," *Archaia Makedonia* 4 (1986): 293–305; "*Somatophylakia:* A Macedonian *Cursus Honorum*," *Phoenix* 40 (1986): 279–94.

23. W. W. Tarn, *Alexander the Great*, 2 vols. (Cambridge: Cambridge University Press, 1948), 1:177; Peter Green, *Alexander of Macedon: 356–323 BC* (1970; repr., Berkeley: University of California Press, 1991), 456 (dismissive); Ernst Badian, "The Eunuch Bagoas: A Study in Method," *Classical Quarterly* n.s. 8 (1958): 150 (suspicious); J. R. Hamilton, *Alexander the Great* (Pittsburgh: University of Pittsburgh Press, 1973), 145; and A. B. Bosworth, *Conquest and Empire: The Reign of Alexander the Great* (Cambridge: Cambridge University Press, 1988), 164–65 (mildly condescending). Some older works, such as A. R. Burn, *Alexander the Great and the Hellenistic World* (New York: Collier, 1962) and C. A. Robinson, Jr., *Alexander the Great* (New York: E. P. Dutton, 1947), scarcely mentioned him at all.

24. Waldemar Heckel, "Hephaistion 'The Athenian,'" *Zeitschrift für Papyrologie und Epigraphik* 87 (1991): 39–41, and *The Marshals of Alexander's Empire* (New York: Routledge, 1992), 65–90. If my own investigations of Hephaestion's career lead me to different conclusions than Heckel's, I nonetheless owe a great deal to his groundbreaking work.

25. Aubrey Menen, *A Conspiracy of Women* (New York: Random House, 1965); Steven Pressfield, *The Virtues of War* (New York: Doubleday, 2004). Particularly the latter goes to great lengths to avoid any hint of homoeroticism among the Greeks, not only for Alexander himself, but even with regard to less ambiguous figures or groups such as the Sacred Band of Thebes.

26. I recognize (and have elsewhere argued) that use of this term is anachronistic in discussions of ancient sexual expression, but for convenience and familiarity I have employed it here. "Sexuality" as we tend to define it today as a part of personality is largely a post-Freudian construct.

27. Heckel, *Marshals*, 71.

28. Arr. *Anab.* 6.28.4; Arr. *Indike* 18.3; Nearchus, a Cretan, is listed here as an Amphipolitan, as well. The confusion seems to stem from current town of residence versus origin, so all Arrian's passage tells us is that when Hephaestion left Macedonia, Pella was considered to be his city of residence. Also, he and Alexander are often presented as the same age, but *et sicut aetate par erat regi* (Curt. 3.12.15) does not necessarily mean born in the same year, and Hephaestion may have been a year or two older than the prince (see Jeanne Reames-Zimmerman, "An Atypical Affair? Alexander the Great, Hephaestion Amyntoros, and the Nature of Their Relationship," *Ancient History Bulletin* 13, no. 3 [1999]: 90n51, 91–93).

29. The Suda (Adler, s.v. "Marsyas") lists Marsyas as a syntrophos of Alexander; he is credited with a now lost work entitled *The Education of Alexander*, likely referencing Xenophon's *Education of Cyrus*.

30. Heckel, "Hephaistion 'The Athenian.'"

31. For a fuller discussion of what began as a query about origin and became something of an epigraphic odyssey in search of a family, see Reames-Zimmerman, "Hephaestion Amyntoros," 52–73.

32. Heckel, "*Somatophylakia*," 279–94; and on Hephaestion in particular, see 287–88.

33. Tarn, *Alexander the Great*, 2:57.

34. Berve, *Alexanderreich*, 2:170; Carney, "Alexander the Great," 217.

35. On the *Somatophylakes* in general, see Heckel, "The *Somatophylakes* of Alexander the Great," 224–28; "*Somatophylakia*," 279–94; and *Marshals*, 237–88; on Hephaestion in particular as a *Somatophylax*, see *Marshals*, 70–71, 257–79.

36. One citation of a combat nature has been excluded. Polyaenus (4.3.27) says that Hephaestion and Philotas Parmenionos led the battle at the Persian passes. This is certainly an error, as both Arrian (*Anab.* 3.18.4, 3.18.7–8) and Curtius (5.4.14–15, 5.4.29) credit Craterus with leading the main body of troops there.

37. As to why this did not fall to Nikanor as general commander of the unit (Arr. *Anab.* 3.21.8), it seems that separate men led the *agēmata*, as Cleitus did for the Companions, although Philotas was their general commander (Arr. *Anab.* 3.11.8; Curt. 4.8.26; Diod. Sic. 17.57.1), and as Admetos led the Hypaspists at Tyre (Arr. *Anab.* 2.23.2). Perhaps Hephaestion took over Admetos' position when he was killed. So also Heckel, *Marshals*, 247–49, who calls them "royal" and "regular."

38. Green, *Alexander of Macedon*, 361, for Cleitus's reassignment; Cleitus was killed at a banquet just before he set out to claim it. Burn, *Alexander the Great and the Hellenistic World*, 30, believes the cavalry redivision occurred after Cleitus's death, but it seems Cleitus had already been reassigned. G. G. Apherghis, "Alexander's Hipparchies," *Ancient World* 28 (1997): 141, places the reorganization during the winter of 329/28 when reinforcements first arrived, but that is too early. Thomas Daniel, "The Taxeis of Alexander and the Change to Chiliarch, the Companions Cavalry and the Change to Hipparchies: A Brief Assessment," *Ancient World* 32 (1991): 47, appears to place it even earlier, but obviously, the redivision must postdate the death of Philotas in late 330.

39. Green, *Alexander of Macedon*, 448; Heckel, *Marshals*, 86; N. G. L. Hammond, *Sources for Alexander the Great: An Analysis of Plutarch's* Life *and Arrian's* Anabasis Alexandrou (Cambridge: Cambridge University Press, 1993), 297. While I may not always agree with Hammond's assessments, in this case his is supported by what we know of the position of the *hazarapatish*, see note 40 below, esp. Dandamaev and Lukonin.

40. M. A. Dandamaev and V. G. Lukonin, *The Culture and Social Institutions of Ancient Iran*, tr. P. L. Kohl (Cambridge: Cambridge University Press, 1989), 111ff.; also Nepos, *Life of Konon* 9.3.2 and Hieronymus/Diodoros 18.48.4.

41. So Bosworth suggested in *Conquest and Empire*, 157.

42. A. B. Bosworth, *A Historical Commentary on Arrian's History of Alexander,* 2 vols. (Oxford: Oxford University Press,1995), 2:112–13.

43. Heckel, *Marshals,* 122–23.

44. J. F. C. Fuller, *The Generalship of Alexander the Great* (1960; repr., New York: De Capo Press, 1989), 259–63.

45. "Nearchus was sent with the fleet and ordered to proceed three days in advance of the army downstream. Alexander divided the remaining forces [those not given to Krateros] into three parts; Hephaestion was ordered to go on five days ahead, so that any who fled from [Alexander's] own force and moved rapidly ahead would fall in with Hephaestion's troops and be captured, while Ptolemy son of Lagus, to whom he also handed over part of the army, was told to follow him at an interval of three days, so that any who turned back again, fleeing from himself, might fall in with Ptolemy and his troops. The advance guard was ordered as soon as they arrived at the junction of the Acesines and Hydraotes to wait there till he [Alexander] arrived in person and till the forces of Krateros and Ptolemy joined him" (Arr. *Anab.* 6.5.5–7, in *Arrian: Selected Works: English and Greek,* rev. ed., tr. P. A. Brunt, with intro. and notes by P. A. Brunt, Loeb Classical Library, 2 vols. [Cambridge, Mass.: Harvard University Press, 1976–1983], 2:113).

46. It would not be the first time that Ptolemy glossed over the assignments of later rivals, but it seems more likely that Nearchus and Hephaestion simply moved faster than Craterus, who was burdened with elephants and other slow transport. In any case, Craterus is not flanking Nearchus all the way south.

47. Alexander may even have left instructions that Hephaestion was to be in charge, as it was the sort of assignment at which he excelled. Had Alexander actually died, Craterus would probably have lost no time in challenging Hephaestion's *imperium maius.*

48. Heckel (*Marshals,* 76) also points out that we never hear of him actually commanding the half of the Companions assigned to him.

49. So Heckel terms it (ibid., 69–70), although in the paragraph just before, with regard to appointing a king for Sidon, he does say, "Hephaestion's role suggests that Alexander had recognized early his best friend's administrative and organizational skills." Hephaestion is assigned command of the fleet directly after the siege of Tyre, for the march from Haifa to Gaza. No specific mention is made, however, of who commanded the fleet during the Gaza siege—where it supplied the army as well as transporting siege engines—or on the march from Gaza to Pelusion. It was probably still Hephaestion, but we are told only that Amyntas received ten triremes to return to Macedon for new recruits (Curt. 4.6.30).

50. D. W. Engels, *Alexander the Great and the Logistics of the Macedonian Army* (Berkeley: University of California Press, 1978), 57–60.

51. Ibid., 35, 121.

52. Again, the Palestinian march would not have been as difficult as Engels portrays—no doubt Alexander's army followed the old coastal road referred to in the Bible as "the way to the land of Philistines" (Ex. 13:17), but late summer was a harsh time for that march with a sizable army. Water needs would have been high, while wells and springs were at their lowest levels.

53. William Smith, "Hephaestion," in *A Dictionary of Greek and Roman Biography*, 3 vols. (London, 1849), 2:382–83.

54. A. B. Bosworth, "Alexander the Great and the Decline of Macedon," *Journal of Hellenic Studies* 106 (1986): 1.

55. The use of *éminence grise* here is intended to carry no particular connotation, good or bad, despite its historical usage. Yet I think we must keep in mind that one did not get ahead at the Macedonian court by being "nice," and Hephaestion would have been as aggressive and ruthless as his contemporaries.

56. Engels, *Logistics*, 59n33.

57. Carney, "Olympias and the Image of the Virago"; see also her chapter in this volume.

58. P. J. Junge, "Hazarapatis," *Klio* 33 (1940): 32, proposes that he is called chiliarch because he commands a 1,000-man bodyguard, as well as the 10,000-man Immortals. The role of *hazarapatish* or grand vizier, which the Greeks called the chiliarch, was an old one in both the ancient Near East and Egypt. Among other examples, in Num. 31:14 we find "commanders of thousands," which the *LXX* translated as *khiliarkhoi*, from the Hebrew words *sar* and *'elep*. See G. N. Knoppers, *I Chronicles*, Anchor Bible Series (New York: Doubleday, 2004), 23–24, for a discussion of *'elep/'allûp* in relation to 1 Chron. 12:37. But this early Biblical usage is strictly in a military context. In Akkadian, the term later translated as "chiliarch" is *sukkallu*, defined as "a court official" in *Chicago Assyrian Dictionary*, ed. Donald Whitcomb and Martha T. Roth (Chicago: Oriental Institute of the University of Chicago, 1921–2005); F. M. Fales and J. N. Postgate, *Imperial Administrative Records*, part 1, *Palace and Temple Administration*, State Archives of Assyria 7 (Helsinki: Helsinki University Press, 1992), use "vizier," with *sukkal dan[nu]* being the variant for "grand vizier." It also appears in the synchronistic king list (iii & iv) under the Babylonian kings. Over time, the position developed into the complex role held under the Persian Achaemenids. See also Émile Benveniste, "Chiliarque," in *Titres et noms propres en Iranien ancien*, Travaux de l'Institute d'Études Iraniennes de l'Université de Paris (Paris: C. Klincksieck, 1966), 67, 69, for more on the Persian and pre-Persian linguistic background, the most useful part of an otherwise rather confused article.

59. Dandamaev and Lukonin, *Ancient Iran*, 111. See also, and particularly, Junge's discussion in "Hazarapatis," as well as a more recent article by Andrew W. Collins, "The Office of Chiliarch under Alexander and the Successors," *Phoenix* 55 (2001): 259–83, published between my original discussion and this revision. Collins and I reach some similar and some rather different conclusions. His article, of course, is focused more generally on the office, and mine on

Hephaestion in particular, but while we both agree on the military origin and the fact that hard-and-fast "duties" should not be assumed—the office was more flexible than that—we diverge on the questions of when Hephaestion was named to the chiliarchy (he believes it was 330, and I think that too early, for reasons discussed above) and whether it was primarily a military or a civil service position (he seems to argue for the former, while I would argue more for the latter). Nonetheless, his article represents a much needed addition to the conversation about the chiliarchy.

Benveniste's "Chiliarque" confuses a military position with the Persian *hazarapatish*. While it is true that Curtius employs the term "chiliarch" in 5.2.2–3 as a military rank earned by bravery in special military games, this is *not* the civil position to which Diodorus refers in 18.48.4–5, or, apparently, the position to which Hephaestion was appointed. The military position for which Curtius employs "chiliarch" is the traditional one: a leader of 1,000 troops. For a more thorough discussion, see Collins, "The Office of Chiliarch."

60. I.e.: "primum ex more Persarum ad chiliarchum, qui secundum gradum imperii tenebat."

61. Hamilton, *Alexander the Great*, 145.

62. The phrasing gives the impression that he adapted because he agreed with Alexander, not simply to please him. This should not surprise; if they were friends, it is likely that they viewed affairs in similar ways.

63. Ernst Badian, "Alexander in Iran," in *Cambridge History of Iran*, vol. 2 (Cambridge: Cambridge University Press, 1985), 485n1.

64. Badian implies (ibid., 485) that the chief duty he acquired was command of the royal guard, presumably the Hypaspist *agēma* or the *agēma* of the Companions, but he did *not* take either of these positions. His chiliarchy was connected, militarily, to his previous position as commander of the (first?) Companion hipparch, but not the *agēma*. If he did not command the guard, that leaves us wondering just what he did, if not the other duties of a *hazarapatish*. Perhaps Badian meant to imply that he did nothing, and the appointment was honorary only, but we simply do not know enough to say, and it makes far more sense to assume that he did take on the duties of this office that Alexander had resurrected specifically for him. Junge, "Chiliarque," 38n8, says that Alexander intended to reform the position "aus der Verschmelzung persischer und makedonischer Formen," but does not enlarge on the statement; his article is intended to consider the position only under the Achaemenids.

65. Junge, "Chiliarque," 18–19, 29–34; Junge also wanted to put him in charge of the treasury, based on reliefs, but there is no support for this, nor for the contention that the *hazarapatish* personally directed all receptions: see Dandamaev and Lukonin, *Ancient Iran*, 228; J. M. Cook, "The Rise of the Achaemenids and Establishment of Their Empire," in *Cambridge History of Iran*, 2:232–31. Junge's article is a bit too inclined to ossify the role, as Collins, "The Office of Chilliarch," also notes, esp. 274 and 179. We can assume that duties varied,

depending on circumstances. For instance, Junge suggests ("Chiliarque," 19) that Aristazanes was also *hazarapatish* under Artaxerxes Ochos, even though Diodorus calls him *eisaggeleus* (16.47.3), because he seems to have led the bodyguard and is described as the most faithful of the king's friends after Bagoas, who *is* called chiliarch by Diodoros in 17.5.3. But rather than have two *hazarapati,* it may be that Aristazanes only filled a military function for which Bagoas, as a eunuch, was either not fit, or not considered to be fit. Nevertheless, Cook's description, in "Rise of the Achaemenids," 233, of Junge's claims as "overpitched" may be too dismissive. Dandamaev and Lukonin, *Ancient Iran,* are more inclined to accept them with caution.

66. Dandamaev and Lukonin, *Ancient Iran,* 22–29.

67. See discussions in E. N. Borza, *In the Shadow of Olympus: The Emergence of Macedon* (Princeton, NJ: Princeton University Press, 1990), 249–51; Heckel, *"Somatophylakia,"* 281; R. D. Milns, "The Hypaspists under Alexander III: Some Problems," *Historia* 20 (1971): 186–95; and Dietmar Kienast, *Philipp II, von Makedonien und das Reich der Achaimeniden,* Abhandlungen der Marburger Gelehrten Gesellschaft, Jahrgang 1971, no. 6 (Munich: Fink, 1973): 7–37. However, Edward M. Anson, "The Hypaspists: Macedonia's Professional Citizen-Soldiers," *Historia* 34 (1985): 246–48, would like to credit the Thebans with the precedent for the Hypaspists as professional soldiers. This does not preclude the idea that the Hypaspists may have been called the king's bodyguard in battle, as the Immortals were. As for the Pages, whether this institution was created by Philip or predates him is not a settled issue; so the imitation of the Persian court may date back at least as far as Archelaos, and perhaps even as far back as the first contact between Macedon and the East, under Alexander I.

68. Another role probably adopted by Alexander about the same time as the chiliarchy is Iolaos Antipatrou's position as cupbearer (*oinochoos,* or *masqeh* in Hebrew). This seems to have been a traditional role for a younger person of prestigious family. It was held under Artaxerxes I by Nehemiah, who was later appointed governor of Judea (Neh. 1:11b); as we noted, Prexaspes' son also held it (Herod. 3.34); see Junge, "Chiliarque," 21. The role involved tasting the king's wine to prevent poisoning, and guarding his bedchamber. These were already duties of the Pages corps, but apparently Iolaos was singled out from among them for this unique honor. See M. A. Throntveit, *Ezra-Nehemiah,* Interpretation Series (Louisville: John Knox Press, 1992), 66–67.

69. These include the representatives of the seven leading Persian clans, the queen mother, and the chief wife—as well as the *hazarapatish* himself. Dandamaev and Lukonin, *Ancient Iran,* 119. See also Nepos, *Kon.* 9.3.2–3.

70. Arr. *Anab.* 7.8.3, tr. Brunt. The full list of complaints can be found in 7.8.1–3. I hesitate to call this event a true mutiny; Carney's use of "indiscipline" is to be preferred. See Elizabeth D. Carney, "Macedonians and Mutiny: Discipline and Indiscipline in the Army of Philip and Alexander," *Classical Philology* 91 (1996): esp. 24–31.

71. Plutarch (*Demetr.* 42) tells us that Demetrios was criticized for employing too much ceremony, as well. For the *hazarapatish* keeping the appointment book, see Nepos, *Kon.* 9.3.3 and n.76 below.

72. Carney, "Macedonians and Mutiny," 28; Eleanor Roosevelt, *The Autobiography of Eleanor Roosevelt* (New York: Harper, 1961), 139.

73. See Collins, "The Office of Chiliarch," esp. 268–69, for a discussion of his military functions.

74. Bosworth, *Conquest and Empire*, 276, thinks that Alexander may have been trying to increase the prestige of the Companions over the Hypaspist *agēma*, since most of the disaffection had been among the infantry ranks, not the cavalry. As for the Companions acting as Alexander's bodyguard, certainly it was Cleitus, as commander of the *agēma*, who saved Alexander's life at Granicus (Arr. *Anab.* 1.15.8; Curt. 8.1.20; Diod. Sic. 17.20.7; Plut. *Alex.* 16.5). After Hephaestion's death, the position of chiliarch was never officially filled, though Arrian tells us that, for all intents and purposes, Perdiccas stepped into it (fr. 1a.3, 1b.5). We should recall the number of times that Perdiccas and Hephaestion were co-assigned.

75. Perdiccas and Leonnatus. Of course, since the king's life had been threatened, the Bodyguard's involvement was to be expected.

76. One certainly had to request an audience with the *hazarapatish*, but it is doubtful that he actually introduced one to the Great King. In Nepos, *Kon.* 9.3.3, Tithraustes instructs Konon on protocol, but as Konon does not, in the end, have an audience, we do not know who would have introduced him. Diod. Sic. 16.47.3 refers to Aristazanes as *eisaggeleus*, the "introducer" (herald or usher), and this is the same term used of Chares (Plut. *Alex.* 46.1), so that seems to have been a separate function. It may be, then, that Hephaestion kept Alexander's appointments, and Chares did the introducing, though the timing of Chares' appointment to that position is not entirely clear.

77. There is clear evidence that Alexander had begun employing at least some Persian court ceremonial as early as 330—to the disgust of such old-guard figures as Cleitus; see Elizabeth D. Carney, "The Death of Clitus," *Greek, Roman and Byzantine Studies* 22 (1981): 149–60. Nonetheless, what could be accomplished on campaign was quite different from what would be expected at Persepolis, Susa, or Ekbatana. Also, no doubt Alexander introduced his changes gradually. There is no evidence that he required Macedonians to treat him with the same other-worldliness with which the Achaemenid king was regarded, or even that he would have wanted them to. G. L. Cawkwell, "The Deification of Alexander the Great: A Note," in *Ventures into Greek History*, ed. Ian Worthington (Oxford: Oxford University Press, 1994), deals with Alexander's purported wish to be deified and the difference between naming himself a son of Ammon and actually claiming to *be* a god.

Although a matter of no small debate, the *proskynesis* affair seems to have been Alexander's attempt at a pragmatic regularization of court procedure.

There are always those who react to any introduction of change with vociferous complaint. The Macedonians made it clear that they were not happy to see their king adopt the procedures of the very people they had just conquered. There has been too much tendency to grant these complaints validity, unconsciously adopting the anti-Oriental biases of our sources, and forgetting that an ever-increasing empire demanded new governmental protocols. Because the complaints are always framed generally, it is impossible to know just what changes were actually instituted, aside from the extremely controversial (and ultimately unsuccessful) *proskynesis*. Much of it may have been rather innocuous—if unwelcome—bureaucracy. People naturally protest against bureaucracy, until they are the ones responsible for maintaining order. W. E. Higgins, "Aspects of Alexander's Imperial Administrations: Some Modern Methods and Views Reviewed," *Athenaeum* 58 (1980): 131, notes, "The Macedonians' sense of what conquerors traditionally had a right to expect was not the same as their king's sense of what the responsibilities of successful rule implied in a multi-national realm."

78. See C. A. Moore's discussion of arguments for and against the historical accuracy of this book in *The Anchor Bible Esther* (New York: Doubleday, 1971), xxxiv-xxxvi; and also Momigliano, *Modern Historiography*, 11. While the book is an ancient novel, perhaps of the late Persian period, and its specifics are certainly fictional, the general descriptions of court operations are apparently based on first-hand experience, and as such, instructive.

79. The conflict concerning the flute-player Euius, though not linked to the chancellery, likely resulted from Hephaestion's new position. Whatever reason Hephaestion had to assign Euius to quarters that Eumenes had requisitioned, assigning guest quarters was part of his traditional job as *hazarapatish*. Given Plutarch's description of the conflict (*Eum.* 2.1-2), it is impossible to tell whether or not Hephaestion knew that the quarters were already taken. It may have been an honest mistake, or a deliberate slight—but the assignment itself was not outside of his duties.

80. Turning again to Eleanor Roosevelt, her *Autobiography* describes several of these functions as performed for FDR and others in high office: President Wilson had his secretary Joseph Tumulty clip important editorials and news from leading newspapers (101-2); Louis Howe handled FDR's mail (116), mapped out his campaigns (158), and organized his appointments with a variety of people (176); and King George had names and occupations of people in the U.S. government as well as other information procured for him before his visit (205).

Part 4

Alexander's Dream
Macedonians and Foreigners

Oliver Stone, *Alexander*, and the Unity of Mankind

THOMAS HARRISON

NY HISTORICAL FILM treads a very fine line between the need
to ensure at least a degree of historical plausibility and the
need to generate a plot and characters capable of sustaining
the audience's attention. The viewer too is torn between appreciation of
the plot and identification of minute divergences from the historical
record—and the more informed he or she is, all the more so. I might as
well state at the outset that—despite enormous admiration for certain
aspects of the film and for the heroic efforts that went into it—in my
opinion Oliver Stone's *Alexander* does not convince. Over several view-
ings I was certainly distracted by historical details—while appreciating
the film's knowing pastiche of the Greek sources. But neither these
details—nor the Irish accents, nor the faux-heroic language—were, for
me, the heart of the problem. I suggest instead that the reasons for the
film's heroic failure are inherent in the ancient and modern historiography of Alexander—and in the interpretative choices made, against this
background, by the director.[1]

How can we identify a distinct Oliver Stone's Alexander? We should
not, of course, make the mistake of supposing that even the convenient
narrator—Anthony Hopkins's Ptolemy—speaks for the director. The
film itself warns us against this: especially in its conclusion, where

Ptolemy makes the surprising statement that "I never believed in his dream, none of us did," suggesting an opportunistic motive for his policy of "mixing the races, harmony,"[2] but also, in earlier interventions of the narrator, by blurring the boundaries of the man and the myth.[3] Robin Lane Fox has also written of a trap set for "minimalist historians": that they might "[jump] too quickly to conclusions and [write] off the film as one-sided hero-worship because they would take all Ptolemy's views as Oliver's own."[4] Just as Alexander's modern biographers smudge their portrait by acknowledging that the myth is as important as the man,[5] this strategy is in a sense an attempt to have it both ways. Despite the danger of interpreting one speaker or aspect of the film as containing the kernel of Stone's "reading" of Alexander, it is certainly possible to identify from the disparate voices of the film (together with the commentaries of the director and his advisor) a *broadly* distinct "Stone's Alexander." First, then, I will lay out some areas where these voices converge; given the danger of narratological offense, this introduction may be a little laborious.

One area of convergence is the representation of Alexander's civilizing mission. "[Stone's Alexander] is certainly a hero, and a hero with a vision," Robin Lane Fox has written. "He is consciously bringing change to an East which, in places, strikes *him* as being primitive."[6] Within the film, this theme emerges especially from Ptolemy's narration and in the dialogue between Alexander and Hephaestion on the balcony at Babylon. "Before him there were tribes," as Ptolemy puts it; "after him all was possible; there was suddenly a sense that the world could be ruled by one king and be better for all." The same point is made again by Alexander on the balcony, only with a greater emphasis on the backwardness of the peoples to be subjected:

> I have seen the future, Hephaestion, I've seen it now a thousand times, on a thousand faces: these people want, need change. Aristotle was wrong about them. . . . Look at those we've conquered. They leave their dead unburied. They smash their enemies' skulls and drink them as dust. They mate in public. What can they think, or sing, or write when none can read? But as Alexander's army they can go where they never thought possible. They can soldier, work in the cities, the Alexandrias, from Egypt to the outer Ocean. We can connect these lands, Hephaestion, and the people.

At the same time, the film presents a number of related themes. First, just as the film acknowledges the earlier backwardness of the Macedonians,[7] so, conversely, nods are made to Persia as a great civilization, and to Alexander's acknowledgment of Persia's past. (There was no room, Lane Fox has written, to establish "Persian culture in detail.")[8] "What disturbs me most," Alexander replies to Cassander's insistence on the unequal status of the barbarians,[9] "is not your lack of respect for my judgment; it's your contempt for a world far older than ours."[10] Babylonia—which arguably stands in for, or is conflated with, Persia in the absence of Persepolis or Susa—is "a great old civilization," in Lane Fox's words again, by contrast to the nomadic tribes that Alexander wants to bring into his Alexandrias.[11]

And yet this older world is apparently past its sell-by date. The film also repeats and elaborates a number of the standard tropes of Greek representations of the East.[12] Alexander's speech at Gaugamela, for example, harps on the Persian king's depriving his subjects of freedom, and his employment of assassins[13]—words reinforced by the image of Darius rigidly conducting his troops from the vantage-point of his chariot. The dialogue between Alexander and Hephaestion on the balcony at Babylon reveals that Alexander—far from wanting to draw people into the new Alexandrias to make them slaves, as the popular report passed on by Hephaestion has it—feels that by his conquest the peoples of the Persian empire have been freed:[14] "To free the people of the world, such would be beyond the glory of Achilles, beyond Heracles, a feat to rival Prometheus who was always a friend to man." This freedom appears to consist in the opportunities afforded by a newfound literacy or by service in Alexander's army; Asia had been "held down" under the Persian empire.[15]

At the same time, other definitions of freedom are in play in the course of the film. Alexander's own men, by contrast, are at Gaugamela as "Macedonian free men." In the future they will be able to boast, Alexander tells them: "I was here at Gaugamela for the freedom and glory of Greece." Freedom from what, or to do what? The only answers that the film offers elsewhere, consonant with the freedom of opportunity won by Alexander for the Persians and their subjects, are distinctly fuzzy: freedom of youth, freedom to attempt the impossible[16] and be endlessly disillusioned,[17] and freedom from fear. "How can I tell you," Ptolemy asks, "what it was like to be young, to dream big dreams, to believe when Alexander looked you in the eye you could do anything?" At the conclusion of the film, Ptolemy describes Alexander as fighting "all his life . . . to free himself from fear. . . . By this and this alone he was made free, the freest man I have ever known." If one man can be more free than all others, this arguably devalues that broader freedom. The line is curiously reminiscent indeed of Greek representations of the distribution of freedom among the Persians.[18] If one has to fight for freedom from fear, it also suggests—paradoxically?—a fear of fear. And Ptolemy's following words do indeed suggest a very different narrative, reminiscent of Ernst Badian's reading of a paranoid Alexander,[19] though he then rather clumsily turns this to a positive end: "His tragedy was one of increasing loneliness and impatience with those who could not understand,[20] and if his desire to reconcile Greek and barbarian ended in failure, what a failure. His failure towered over other men's successes."

There is clear distancing also from the rigid point of view ascribed in the film to Aristotle. (Whether this is an accurate account of the historical Aristotle's view of the barbarian world is another matter.)[21] "If we are superior to the Persians, as you say," the boy Alexander puts it, "why do we not rule them?" How can an "inferior race . . . control at least four-fifths of the known world"? "Aristotle may have called them barbarians," as Ptolemy points out, "but he never saw Babylon." And yet, as Aristotle predicts, "the East has a way of swallowing men and their dreams"; Babylon, as Ptolemy puts it (clumsily?), "was a far easier mistress to enter than it was to leave." The film conveys "Babylon, Persia" as a lush capital of somnolent excess, filled with the sounds of braying animals. That Persia is seen as merely waiting casually for the coming of the Macedonians reflects a general passivity[22]—by contrast, as Aristotle has put it earlier in the film, it is his Macedonian charges' competition with one another (an idea redolent of Athenian democratic and Persian war ideology)[23] that will draw them "from [their] frog pond," the Mediterranean, to the domination that is apparently their due.

While representing Persia and the Persian empire as a land fit to be civilized (and at the same time upholding the antiquity of its civilization[s]), the film also holds that Alexander was driven by a desire to unite Greece and Persia, and more broadly the Greeks and barbarians, or all the peoples of the earth. This is something that Oliver Stone has made explicit in comments on the film,[24] and that was central to the origins of the film project.[25] Two episodes are crucial here. The first is Alexander's marriage to Roxane (with which the Susa marriages of Alexander's companions have been elided). There the taking of Asian women as brides is a "sign of respect" that "will unify us." For dramatic effect and contrast, one presumes (though also out of an attempt at plausible reconstruction),[26] Roxane and Bactria are presented in wild, exotic form. ("I had this vision of Roxane," Lane Fox confides, "dressed in furs and hunting-robes, galloping out from a castle, shooting arrows at wild animals as she passed."[27]) The second scene crucial to this theme is that of Hephaestion's deathbed.[28] Standing on the balcony reserved for his visionary moments, Alexander expands on his plans for the future (his "last plans," as recorded by Diodorus),[29] as Hephaestion lies dying: Babylon will become the center of the world; "populations will mix and travel freely. Asia and Europe will come together. We'll grow old together." Hephaestion's immediate death seems to suggest the unrealizable nature of his other plans. (As Ptolemy concludes, "[The dreamers] must die before they kill us with their blasted dreams.")

Finally—and despite Ptolemy's curmudgeonly asides—it hardly needs to be said that in its portrayal of Alexander's pursuit of the unity of nations, or his attempt to civilize the peoples of the Persian empire, the film represents Alexander in a straightforwardly heroic light.[30] Indeed, he is almost seen as being above worldly concerns.[31] The film cannot, of course, reasonably exclude any acts of violence. These, however, are dealt with by a curious mixture of techniques. In the case of the destruction of Thebes, explicit justification is offered by Ptolemy: it was intended to stun the Greeks into surrender (the justification of the atom bomb), and, anyway, it was exceptional ("he treated most populations with magnanimity"); this and other exceptions (Gaza, Persepolis) are, according to Ptolemy, unfairly harped upon, "always remembered by those who hate Alexander and all he stood for." Other justifications lurk here. There seems to be an implication—a sinister implication?—that his actions are justified by "[what] he stood for." (And what right does he have to show "magnanimity," as if resisting him were in itself a crime?) At the same time, Thebes is dubbed that "tragic city," as if it had been no one's decision to massacre its inhabitants or sell the rest into slavery.[32]

Another explicit justification of Alexander's violence is offered by Ptolemy in the light of the Indian mutiny. "In smashing the mutiny and executing the ringleaders he did nothing in my mind that any general in wartime has not done—but clearly the army was divided and Alexander was no longer loved by all." "Of course," we might respond. But in a film that projects Alexander as the greatest hero, it is distinctly underwhelming then to be offered the view that he was unexceptional in his war crimes. The film clearly suggests a degeneration in standards as Alexander reaches the limits of his conquests ("tempers worsened; we massacred all Indians who resisted"). This might have offered the opportunity for a Bosworth-style reading of Alexander, but instead the film somehow seeks to suppress this and to keep Alexander's heroism at center stage. The bloodiness of the Indian battle scene is plastered over with an incongruously triumphant score; the music turns dark (hints of Orff's *Carmina Burana*) only as Alexander himself gets into danger.

I move now from the film's representation of Alexander's idealism to the historical status of such claims. What evidence is there for this image of Alexander—and in particular for his dream of unifying Asia and Europe, of the brotherhood of mankind? This issue is the subject of a well-known pair of (sharply contrasting) papers by two of the most prominent Alexander-historians of the twentieth century: W. W. Tarn and Ernst Badian.[33]

Tarn notoriously declared to the British Academy in 1933 that Alexander was responsible "for one of the great revolutions in human thought": the invention of the universalist idea whereby "all mankind was one and all men were brothers, or anyway ought to be." Having established that such ideas had no currency in the period before Aristotle, Tarn eliminates—or so he supposes—all alternative explanations, for example that they are a "projection backwards" of Stoic thought or from Augustus. Similar ideas, Tarn finds, are ascribed to Theophrastus, and to Alexarchus, as in the following examples: "But no one is likely to suppose that . . . that simple man thought this up for himself";[34] "it would seem that there must be some common source behind this group, and as that source has to be something later, in the sphere of thought, than Aristotle, it can only be Alexander."[35] The things that Alexander is reported as saying, Tarn then concludes, he indeed said: "[He] did say that all men were sons of God, that is brothers, . . . he did aspire to be the harmonizer and reconciler of the world—that part of the world which his arm reached; he did have the intention of uniting the peoples of his empire in fellowship and concord and making them of one mind together."[36] It emerges then that Alexander's actions are not the greatest part of his achievement: "Alexander, for the things he *did*, was called The Great; but if what I have said to-day be right, I do not think we shall doubt that this idea of his—call it a purpose, call it a dream, call it what you will—was the greatest thing about him."[37]

Twenty-five years later Badian undermined Tarn's grand thesis, pointing out both misreadings[38] and the circularity of some of Tarn's arguments. In the light of this scholarly scrap, few, if any, would now maintain Tarn's thesis wholesale. On the other hand, the recent resurgence of interest in Alexander (in the light of, and in advance of, Stone's film) has shown how such ideas have persisted. It is possible to argue, for example, that some such idealism must be predicated of Alexander in order to explain why his men followed him so far. It is this line that has been pursued by Robin Lane Fox—with his contempt for "minimalist" historians[39]—and that has found its way, mixed with the different idealism of Stone and Thomas Schühly,[40] into "Stone's Alexander."

The position argued here will be at variance with those of both Tarn and Badian: I maintain that the ideas ascribed to Alexander are plausibly contemporary, but, far from being revolutionary, they derive in large part from *Persian* royal ideology and from the Greeks' representation of Persia.

Central here is Arrian's account of the Opis banquet—a mere tailpiece to the account of the mutiny of Alexander's troops, according to Badian, recording the formal settlement of the mutiny.[41] Since this episode was elided in Stone's film with the mutiny at the river Hyphasis, it may be worth recapping the events as recounted by Arrian (*Anab.* 7.8–9). On arriving at Opis, Alexander discharged the elderly Macedonians and those who had been disabled for war, promising to give them enough to make them objects of envy. Disquiet at other aspects of his behavior—his Persian dress, the introduction of Oriental successors, and so on—spilled out, as the Macedonians called on him to release them all and proceed with the help of his "father" (i.e., Ammon). Alexander—less well-disposed to the Macedonians, Arrian says, because of barbarian flattery—ordered the arrest and execution of the ringleaders (thirteen in number) and delivered an angry speech. This set-piece took his hearers through all the achievements first of Philip and then himself (all presented as benefactions to the Macedonians). He insisted, for example, that he had taken nothing for himself (only for safekeeping) and that he took less pleasure in fine foods than they. As for their request to go home, he calls their bluff, telling them to report on arriving home that they had deserted their king ("leaving him to the care of the wild tribes you had conquered"). Alexander then withdraws into his palace, and a standoff begins. After the third day, he begins to divide up commands (7.11)—at which point the Macedonians rush to the palace as suppliants offering to give up those who had instigated the mutiny and swearing not to leave his doors by day or night until he showed them some pity.[42] There follows an emotional scene in which Alexander emerges and weeps. Then an officer of the Companions, Callines, tells the king that what grieves the Macedonians is that while he has made the Persians his kinsmen (*syngeneis*) and allows them to kiss him,[43] no Macedonian has been allowed the same privilege (7.11.6). Alexander replies that he regards all of the Macedonians as his kinsmen and will thenceforth call them so; Callines then, and anyone else who wished, approached and kissed him, and they all took up their arms and returned to the camp singing their victory song.

> But Alexander in gratitude for this sacrificed to the gods to whom he was wont to sacrifice, and gave a general feast [*thoinēn dēmotelē*], sitting himself there, and all the Macedonians sitting round him [*amph' auton*]; and then next to them Persians [*en de tōi ephexēs toutōn Persōn*], and next any of the other tribes who had precedence in reputation or any other quality, and he himself and his comrades [lit.: those around him, *hoi amph' auton*] drank from the same bowl and poured the same libations, while the Greek seers and the Magians began the ceremony. And Alexander prayed for all sorts of blessings, and especially for harmony and fellowship in the empire [*homonoian te kai koinōnian tēs archēs*] between Macedonians and Persians. They say that those who shared the feast were nine thousand, and that they all poured the same libation and thereat sang the one song of victory. (Arr. *Anab.* 7.11.8–9, tr. Brunt)

Much of the dispute between Tarn and Badian focused on details: for example, the meaning of the phrase "*homonoian te kai koinōnian tēs archēs*"—partnership in rule, partnership in the realm,[44] or (as in Brunt's translation) "fellowship in the empire." Another point of contention has been the precise nature of the seating plan. Despite the emphasis of Arrian's description on partnership, it is clear that, contrary to Tarn's reading of the passage in which "the most prominent men from every race in his Empire and from at least one people not in his Empire, Greeks, sat at his own table,"[45] the seating was arranged hierarchically, with Macedonians "around him," then Persians, and then the rest.[46] A further question is whether the same krater was used for the libation by all nationalities. For Tarn, memorably, "no witness could ever have forgotten the sight of that great krater on Alexander's table and people of every nationality drawing wine from it for their common libation."[47] Badian points out that no details are given about tables, and suggests that the "Persians and the rest poured the same libation—in an extended sense—from their own bowls." In a sense, then, the precise seating arrangements are immaterial: though Badian pours scorn on the interpretation of the banquet as an "international love feast," the occasion is clearly designed to emphasize the commonality that exists between the peoples of the empire, and in particular between the Macedonians and Persians (a point underlined also by the combination of

Magi and seers)[48]—while at the same time maintaining a hierarchy in which the Macedonians now (rather than the Persians) are top dogs.[49]

In a number of aspects of its symbolism, the event depends upon Persian precedent (and its representation in Greek sources). So, for example, as Pierre Briant has written, the concentric seating pattern reflects the way in which, in Persian royal ideology, "the king's favor was expressed by the degree of proximity one had attained with respect to his person";[50] the banquet (imitated a few years later by Peucestas) was the realization "in three dimensions" of this idea.[51] Parallel to this emphasis on proximity to the king's person is the idea of the nations of the empire arranged in concentric circles around the Persians. Herodotus ascribes to the Persians the belief that they were the best people, their neighbors the next most virtuous, and those furthest from them the worst (1.134.2–3). Arrian's reference to those tribes "who had precedence in reputation or any other quality" seems to echo this, and to be redolent not only of the caricatured representation of subject peoples in Persian art and inscriptions,[52] but also, more generally, of the finely graded etiquette of the Achaemenid court. Finally, royal banquets are a common theme in Greek representations of the Persian court.[53] Though the emphasis is usually on the luxurious nature of the occasion (or on the quantities of food required to furnish the king's table), the symbolism of such occasions emerges clearly. So, for example, Herodotus's account of the banquet given by Mardonius in Thebes includes the detail that a Theban and a Persian were seated together on each couch (9.16; cf. 5.18–20), presumably again an expression of harmony and fellowship between the peoples of the empire.

There is a similar Persian background to surrounding events. As Joseph Roisman has pointed out, Alexander's grant to his men of the right to kiss him reveals an exploitation by Alexander of the different value placed on the kiss by Greco-Macedonians and Iranians: "Among the Persians, kissing was practiced among kin or served as a sign of respect. For the Greeks, and presumably for the Macedonians, non-erotic kissing among men expressed one's strong affections to another, a joy at his presence, and his close relationship with him."[54] Alexander's defiant speech dismissing his men is also reminiscent of Persian ideology, especially in its emphasis on the listing of his conquests and his crossing of boundaries (Arr. *Anab.* 7.10.5–7, tr. Brunt):[55]

> when you reach home, tell them there that your King, Alexander, victor over Persians, Medes, Bactrians, Sacaeans, conqueror of Uxians,

Arachotians, Drangae, master of Parthyaea, Chorasmia, Hyrcania to the Caspian sea; who crossed the Caucasus beyond the Caspian gates, who crossed the rivers Oxus and Tanais, yes, and the Indus too, that none but Dionysus had crossed, the Hydaspes, Acesines, Hydraotes; and those who would further have crossed the Hyphasis, had not you shrunk back; who broke into the Indian Ocean by both mouths of the Indus; who traversed the Gadrosian desert—where none other had passed with an armed force; who in the line of march captured Carmania and the country of the Oreitans; whom, when his fleet had sailed from India to the Persian Sea, you led back again to Susa—tell them, I say, that you deserted him.

Alexander's grand gesture, then, appears now in a rather different light. If there is a contradiction in Arrian's account of Opis between the twin emphases on hierarchy and on equality between the peoples of the empire, this is an ideological theme that dates back to the Achaemenids.[56] Moreover, this is only one among a much larger number of parallels.[57] Alexander's supposed aspiration to unify Asia and Europe can be seen against the background of the Persian king's self-presentation as a global policeman sorting out the squabbles of the peoples of the empire,[58] or of (Herodotus's and others' representation of) Xerxes' desire to create an empire "bordering the aither of Zeus" (Hdt. 1.209.1, 7.8.g.203, 19.1, 54.2, 8.53.2, 109.3; Aesch. *Pers.* 189–99). Alexander's scornful dismissal of Parmenion's advice at the Granicus that they should wait to cross at dawn (Arr. *Anab.* 1.13.6–7: "All this I know, Parmenio[n], but I should feel ashamed if after crossing the Hellespont easily, this petty stream (by this epithet did he belittle the Granicus) hinders us from crossing just as we are") needs to be seen in the context of the same emphasis on rivers as boundaries in Herodotus,[59] and of the Persian king's alternating anger at and idealization of rivers;[60] more broadly, there is a "Persian" background to Alexander's domination of the landscape of Asia, his relentless determination to overcome all physical obstacles for the sake of it, whether these obstacles be city walls (Arr. *Anab.* 2.26; cf. 4.2–3), deserts (*Anab.* 3.3, 6.24–26; Plut. *Alex.* 26), or any of a series of apparently inaccessible mountain strongholds (Arr. *Anab.* 4.18.4, 21, 28–30; Arr. *Indike* 5.10; Plut. *Alex.* 58; cf. Diod. Sic. 17.82, 85).[61] Alexander's longing for geographical discovery (Arr. *Anab.* 7.16.4; cf. Arr. *Indike* 20.1), or for *grands projets*—the removal of weirs on the Tigris (Arr. *Anab.* 7.7.6–7), his redirection of the waters of the Euphrates in Assyria (Arr. *Anab.* 7.21.6–7), or the scheme (included among his so-called last plans) to forge a road west across Libya (Diod. Sic. 18.4)—again pick up from his Achaemenid predecessors' concerns:

from their attraction to vast engineering works (for example, the Athos canal, described in elaborate detail by Herodotus[62]), from their pattern of exploration prior to conquest,[63] or from the kings' intense curiosity (latched onto by Greek writers) about all affairs Greek.[64] Similarly, Alexander's kingship of "Asia"—the subject of an often sterile debate in modern scholarship[65]—is explicable against the background of Herodotus's representation of Asia as a single, distinct prize (3.88.1, 4.1, 4.4, 7.1.2), which the Persians claim for themselves (1.5, 9.116.3).[66] Even Alexander's *pothos*—the sudden desire that seizes him and drives him, for example, to capture the natural fortress of Aornos (Arr. *Anab.* 4.28.4), and that has been seen as deriving from Alexander's own speech[67]— may allude to the similar whimsical desires of his Persian predecessors.

But how are we to understand these parallels? In part, doubtless, in terms of the similar circumstances and demands of Alexander's new position as conqueror of Asia: this brought with it new concerns, similar (inevitably) to those that motivated his Achaemenid predecessors. (His removal of the weirs from the Tigris is credited to military security, for example: Arr. *Anab.* 7.7.6–7.) Certain similarities in story-patterns can also be explained in terms of the stories' transmission, their falling into predictable narrative molds.[68] The pattern whereby the natural environment bows down to Alexander's restless spirit is similarly the result of the demands of narrative, as Plutarch indeed observed in the context of Alexander's progress through Pamphylia (*Alex.* 17).[69] And yet there are clearly two other possibilities: deliberate allusion or borrowing on Alexander's part *and* on the part of his historians.

Distinguishing in any instance between these two possibilities is enormously difficult. It is also crucially important: whether an allusion is historical or historiographical makes a marked difference to the moral judgment implied by an anecdote in our sources. So, for example, Alexander's libation in the Hellespont (Arr. *Anab.* 1.11.6)—or his visit to Troy and propitiation of Athena Ilias and of Priam (Arr. *Anab.* 1.11.7–8)— recalls Xerxes' earlier libation and sacrifice in the course of the Persian Wars (Hdt. 7.43; cf. 7.54). Unlike Xerxes, however, Alexander also sacrificed to the hero Protesilaus (Arr. *Anab.* 1.11.5; cf. 6.19.5), the first man to disembark on Asian soil (and to die there) in the course of the Trojan War, and a potent symbol of the boundary between Asia and Europe at the close of Herodotus's *Histories*.[70] The intention behind Alexander's sacrifice to Protesilaus, according to Arrian, was "that his landing might be more fortunate"; Alexander learns from previous attempts to cross the Hellespont and to unite Asia and Europe—and caps the account of Herodotus. He is aligned with Xerxes, and with the Greek victors of the Persian Wars. These contrasting echoes of the Trojan War have recently been interpreted, with some ingenuity, as a deliberate exploitation on Alexander's part of the assimilation of the Trojan War with the Persian Wars.[71] This reading attempts to elide the potential awkwardness of Alexander's Trojan descent on his mother's side (Arr. *Anab.* 1.11.8).[72] An alternative reading, however, would see the conflicting traditions as the result of contrasting allusions on the part of Alexander's historians; Arrian's account, on this reading, would preserve within it anecdotes reflecting different ways of playing off the Persian/Trojan War narratives. The contrast between different ideological positions within a narrative is indeed an important clue to ascribing an allusion to Alexander or to subsequent historians. Unless we suppose that Alexander's dual (Greek and Trojan ancestry) was so well known as to demand an attempt ideologically to deal with its implications, any ideological position taken by Alexander must surely both have reflected well on him and have been relatively clear; conversely, contradiction or ambivalence might reasonably be taken as characteristic of subsequent traditions.

To return to the significance of the Opis banquet, it would be foolish to rule out the possibility that Alexander himself responded to the circumstances in which he found himself by borrowing from Achaemenid precedent. Regardless, however, of whether we are dealing with the historical Alexander and his intentions or a subsequent attempt to forge his actions into a coherent narrative, what emerges is a picture of Alexander as responsive rather than proactive, in which the contours of his campaigns are explained not by wildly fluctuating intentions (seeing himself as an avenger of the Persian Wars, or as a successor to Darius, for example) but rather by the need to respond appropriately to circumstances or to placate different constituencies. This conclusion follows from the contradictions in "Alexander's" ideological positions: seeking Persian recognition, posing as the legitimate heir by conquest to Darius III, and paying lavish homage to the founder of the Persian empire, Cyrus II,[73] yet destroying the Persian royal capital Persepolis as an act of vengeance for the destruction of the temples in Athens (Arr. *Anab.* 3.18.11; cf. Diod. Sic. 17.70–72).[74]

These contrasting positions have often been interpreted in terms of a deliberate change of tack on Alexander's part—an end to the campaign of vengeance—but as closer examination of the varying traditions of the destruction of Persepolis reveals, they can better be explained in terms of contradictions inherent in Alexander's situation. In one family of stories, his act was deliberate, in opposition to his advisor Parmenion, who operates as a kind of narrative stooge (Arr. *Anab.* 3.18.10–12; cf. Strabo 15.3.6). In another, it was all the result of high jinks that got out of control; the first act was not his at all, but that of a courtesan, Thais; and Alexander was subsequently overcome with remorse (Diod. Sic. 17.70–72; Curt. 5.7.2–11; Plut. *Alex.* 38). Many explanations have been given for this discrepancy: for example, that it was an attempt to tar Thais's lover Ptolemy.[75] But what the two versions reflect is the attempt (from the point in Alexander's campaign at which he begins to win)[76] to satisfy two incompatible constituencies and priorities. Clearly, Alexander's presentation of his campaign as a Panhellenic war of revenge was designed to be popular (regardless of whether he was genuinely convinced of it).[77] His choice of Persepolis for destruction may not have been so meaningful to a Greek audience more familiar with Susa,[78] but even if we allow that it was intended to convey a different message to the Persians and other peoples of the empire, it might still have been intended to satisfy the desire for revenge, plunder, possibly even "closure" of Alexander's Greco-Macedonian troops. If Alexander's destruction of Persepolis further undermined his attempt to accommodate the Persian elite,[79] this points to a broader problem: the way in which his rule of Asia was undermined precisely by the ideology that had propelled his conquest.[80] This need to square different constituencies, far from ceasing at this point, continued. As revealed, for example, by the *proskynesis* affair, by the continuing use of Panhellenic ideas,[81] by his hybrid royal dress, or by the presentation of his abstinence, his ability to touch pitch and not be defiled (e.g., in his speech at Opis)[82] by contrast to others such as Harpalus, the need to present himself both as a legitimate heir to the Achaemenids and as the representative of a Panhellenic ideal that set itself against the alleged luxury and decadence of the Persian empire resulted in a permanent act of ideological splits.

Can we credit *any* intentions or idealism to Alexander? If the idea of the unification of Asia and Europe, say, or of the brotherhood of men, were ideas that could be said to go against the current generally (as undoubtedly they did with his Greco-Macedonian supporters), or if they were evidently revolutionary, then it would be more attractive to ascribe such ideas to his own conviction. The fact, however, that such ideological postures were so readily available to him (packaged through Achaemenid precedent), as well as the fact that they offered one possible way to bridge the gap between Greeks and Persians, suggests to me a relatively small place for Alexander's personal conviction,[83] that his ideological agenda to some extent orchestrated itself[84]—a scenario akin to the standard picture of Alexander's or Cyrus's reception in Babylon, in which the conqueror's gestures depend on negotiations with the local ruling classes.[85] Of course, we may reasonably conjecture pragmatic motives on Alexander's part: that his desire to conquer the entire Persian empire probably snowballed over time as it became a more realistic ambition,[86] that he would have taken a care over logistics that finds little reflection in our sources,[87] and, even more broadly, that he would surely have sought—as his ideological contortions suggest—to be a ruler as well as a conqueror.[88] Alexander's personality as it comes down to us in the sources, however, is arguably little more than a patchwork of others' expectations and responses.

I return now to Stone's *Alexander*—and, as I see it, its lack of success. Many reasons could be given for this. High among them, in my view, is, in fact, an excessive concern with historical plausibility, one that obscures the storyline with detail that distracts those who can read the references, and must seem obscure and wordy to those who cannot.[89] For this viewer, more central problems were the incongruous score and the casting and directing of Colin Farrell—who seemed (perhaps appropriately, given the argument made out above) too weak an engine for the film's action,[90] veering between cliché-ridden idealism and his various sub-Freudian traumas. It would have been better, in my view, to present Alexander's psychological makeup and the possible overlapping explanations for his actions *suggestively*, through his actions and responses, rather than through clunking flashbacks, or admonitions from Philip that "it is never easy to escape our mothers."[91] Like some reviewers, I also found that the careful plotting of different regional accents obtruded. Alexander's and his companions' "Irish openheartedness and camaraderie," in the words of Lane Fox,[92] may have been intended to suggest Alexander's ultimate freedom, but they give the impression that his campaign was an act of whimsy, like a party that had gotten very, very far out of hand.

Some of the problems of the film, however, are arguably inherent in the issues discussed above. "The story is beautiful," Stone has written: "A heroic young man, a dynamic prince, then a king in his time, [he] struggled mightily with his two strong parents, succeeded them, and achieved many of his dreams on earth. I would say he was the world's greatest idealist and as a result he took the world's greatest fall."[93] Lane Fox likewise has described the story of Alexander as "the ultimate epic"[94]—ripe for film adaptation. To many or most viewers, however, Alexander must appear an awkward kind of hero. Contemporary heroes—even, or especially, in U.S. movies—are the small men fighting against the system, uncovering corruption, daring to overrule instructions to make a nuclear strike, and so forth. No matter how one emphasizes Alexander's happy-go-lucky spirit or the vast size of the Persian forces arrayed against him, it is hard—knowing the plot, and seeing the passivity of Darius at Gaugamela—not to see him as a bully without a (sufficient) cause. The fact that the film is—within limits, as we have seen—open about the violence that Alexander's campaign unleashed adds to the problem for contemporary audiences. The film asks us not to judge Alexander by contemporary standards but to use those of Alexander's contemporaries. Stone's Alexander is not one "stamped down into dust (with only his generalship exempt)," Lane Fox has written, "because nowadays we hate great men and share a moral revulsion from killing in an unprovoked war. Once people submitted, or were defeated, Alexander had no wish to go on persecuting or killing them."[95] It is perhaps too much to ask of a film audience to suspend their default moral judgment and still remain emotionally engaged.

These difficulties are only compounded by the background of contemporary events. Stone and those around him have firmly rejected the claim that the film should be read in relation to the U.S.-led war in Iraq, pointing out, for example, that it was developed many years before that war began—or was even planned.[96] In its ideological confusion and idealism, however, and in its hazy idea of a freedom without clear referent, it surely presents marked affinities—notwithstanding the director's very different political stance—with the ideological justification for U.S. intervention. More importantly, no matter what the director's expressed intentions were, the contemporary backdrop will *inevitably* inform the experience of viewers (as it did the response of reviewers). Similarly, any attempt to represent Alexander's sexuality accurately is perhaps bound to look embarrassed to a majority of modern viewers.

So how, finally, might one have cut the cake differently for contemporary audiences? A more successful Alexander for our times would perhaps have brought to the fore precisely those negative undercurrents that undermine Alexander's heroism: his increasing isolation and paranoia, the futility of his military expedition and its consequences, the inadequacy of oppositions of West and East, civilization and barbarism—in other words, bluntly put, it would have been a film informed more by Bosworth and Badian than by Lane Fox.[97] As Lane Fox himself has written, there is a "frequent theme of battle and fading idealism" in Stone's films.[98] And yet Stone's endings tend ultimately to be affirming: *Wall Street's* Bud Fox (Charlie Sheen) rediscovers his moral sense and brings down Gordon Gecko; *Born on the Fourth of July* concludes with the conversion of Ron Kovic (Tom Cruise) into a courageous leader of anti–Vietnam War protests, lauded by the Democratic convention. In the case of Alexander, the historical facts leave no room for such an optimistic turn.

Notes

My thanks to Lloyd Llewellyn-Jones and the editors for their comments on this chapter, to Michael Flower and other contributors to a discussion of Stone's *Alexander* held at Princeton University in autumn 2004, and (not least) to Robin Lane Fox: this paper is a distant descendant of an essay written for him as an undergraduate years ago.

1. Quotations are from the Director's Cut DVD unless otherwise noted.

2. "Oh, he talked of these things, but wasn't it really about Alexander and another population ready to obey him?"

3. "Did such a man as Alexander exist? Of course not, we idealize him . . ." "Son of a god. It was a myth, of course. At least it started as a myth. I know. I was there."

4. Lane Fox 2004, 41: "It was neat that we were warned to be wary of his version right at the start"; cf. "Audiences will be wary of taking Ptolemy's viewpoint entirely as Oliver's own" (167); "Ptolemy interprets his story too: he is prone to 'look on the bright side': he is analytical in ways which the real Ptolemy's history . . . was not" (158).

5. Worthington 2004, 303: "How do you like your Alexander?" (If there is no consensus on Alexander, Worthington asks again, "does it even really matter?")

6. Lane Fox 2004, 164 (italics mine). It need not be the case that Alexander's vision is shared (by Alexander's companions or *Alexander's* director).

7. In the words of Ptolemy, the Macedonians are "grandsons of goatherders, we now rule two million square miles."

8. Lane Fox 2004, 159. It might be answered that the film shows little interest in doing so, largely repeating the clichéd representation of Persia ascribed by recent historians (e.g., Briant 2002a) to an earlier generation of scholars.

9. "Alexander, be reasonable—were they ever meant to be our equals, to share our rewards?"

10. Cf. Lane Fox 2004, 164: "Unlike the older officers and Cassander,

Alexander wants respect for Persians and Iranians, by one of whom (despite them) he plans to father a son and heir."

11. Ibid.

12. See e.g., Hall 1989; Briant 2002b.

13. "Who is this Great King who pays assassins, who enslaves his own men? These men do not fight for their homes."

14. "But we freed them, Hephaestion, from the Persia where everyone lives as slaves."

15. Lane Fox 2004, 2.

16. Hephaestion: "Remember the fates of these heroes—they suffered greatly." Alexander: "Oh we all suffer. Your father, mine, they all came to the end of their time, and in the end when it's over, all that matters is what you've done."

17. "But each land, each boundary I cross, I strip away an illusion . . . yet still I push harder and harder to reach this. . . . We must go on, Ptolemy, until we find an end."

18. See esp. Momigliano 1984; for a contextualization of Greek ideas of freedom, see Raaflaub 2003.

19. Badian 1962.

20. Contrast Lane Fox 2004, 11, on Schühly's original conception: "For Thomas, Alexander's drama is a drama about beauty, not paranoia or increasing isolation." See also ibid., 55, for Colin Farrell's take on Alexander as lonely even among his companions after the death of Hephaestion.

21. Badian (1966, 302–6) posits a development in Aristotle's view.

22. A powerful theme of Hall 1989, 1993.

23. E.g., the tradition of the competition of Aristides and Themistocles for the good of Athens in Hdt. 8.79–81; see further, in the context of Aeschylus's *Persians*, Harrison 2000, 95–100.

24. In his foreword to Lane Fox 2004, Stone states: "His vision of reconciling barbarian and Greek races was too much for many Greeks, and made his last years particularly painful."

25. For Thomas Schühly's original submission, see Lane Fox 2004, 8.

26. See ibid., esp. 87–98.

27. Ibid., 39. The scene of Alexander and Roxane's wedding night unfortunately suggests the taming of a wild Bactrian by the literate European; this, together with the imbalance of the sexes in the Susa marriages (Greco-Macedonian men taking "Oriental" wives), might reasonably be taken as supporting the analogy of sexual and military conquest argued to be present in the Greek sources by Hall 1993.

28. A neat link, since Alexander's marriage seemed to mark the end of his relationship with Hephaestion.

29. See esp. Bosworth 1988a, ch. 8.

30. Cf. Lane Fox 2004, 164.

31. Ptolemy: "It was an empire not of land and gold, but of the mind . . . Hellenic civilization, open to all."

32. The divergence between the sources for the destruction of Thebes—some ascribing the decision to Alexander, others to his allies—suggests (as with the destruction of Persepolis) sensitivity. For a new interpretation of this episode, see Worthington 2003.

33. Tarn 1966; Badian 1966.

34. Tarn 1966, 262.

35. Ibid., 265.

36. Ibid., 267.

37. Ibid., 268.

38. See, e.g., Badian 1966, 288-89, on Plut. *Alex*. 27.3ff.

39. Lane Fox 1973 distances himself from the idea of the unity of mankind in favor of a civilizing (or Westernizing) mission. E.g.: "Alexander has been hailed as the founder of the brotherhood of man or criticized for betraying 'purity' of race, but it is as the first man to wish to westernize Asia that he ought to have been judged" (429).

40. For the eccentricity of which see Lane Fox 2004, 15; for Lane Fox's acknowledgment of the long roots of Schühly's interpretation of Alexander's mixture of cultures (with Johan Gustav Droysen), see ibid., 8.

41. Badian 1966, 290ff.

42. See here Heckel 2003, 225, emphasizing loyalty (relying esp. on Curt. 10.3.1-4).

43. Roisman (2003, 300) notes that Alexander is kissed rather than kissing.

44. Badian 1966, 293.

45. Tarn 1948, 2:442.

46. Badian 1966, 291.

47. Tarn 1948, 2:442; cf. Bosworth 1988a, 160-61.

48. Fredricksmeyer 2003, 260.

49. Contrast the interpretation of Cartledge 2004, 190: "This was a far cry from what some sentimentalists have interpreted as a profession of the brotherhood of man or the unity of all mankind. What about the Greeks, for example? Where did they fit into Alexander's scheme of things? For the most part, they did not."

50. Briant 2002b, 311.

51. Ibid., 310-11; cf. 766: "This concentric manifestation of royal favor was realized in three dimensions by Alexander at Opis . . . and imitated a few years later by Peucestas at Persepolis, who placed the participants in four concentric circles around the altars; the innermost circle encompassed 'the generals and hipparchs and also each of the Persians who was most highly honoured'" (Diod. Sic. 19.22.2-3; cf. Xen. *Cyr*. 8.4.3-5). For the similar arrangement of his receptions at Susa, cf. Phylarchus *FGrHist* 81 F 41, with Bosworth 1988a, 160.

52. See Briant 2002b, 734, comparing the Opis banquet with tomb reliefs of Achaemenid kings; for the representation of subject peoples in the art of Persepolis, see esp. Root 1979.

53. See e.g. Lewis 1987; Briant 1989.

54. Roisman 2003, 299 (citing Arr. *Anab.* 4.12.3-5; Plut. *Alex.* 54.4-6; Hdt. 1.134.1; Xen. *Cyr.* 1.4.27-28; Xen. *Ages.* 5.4-5).

55. See inscriptions in Kent 1953: e.g., DNa, DPe, DSm, DZc; cf. DB 1.12-17.

56. There is no need to suppose then that the suggestion of hierarchy undermines the historical expression of the idea of unity or fellowship (as supposed by Green 1991, 456).

57. Some of the following material reprises Harrison 2004.

58. See esp. Kent 1953: DSe, lines 30-34; cf. DNb (perhaps reflected at Hdt. 5.49.8, 7.9.b): "Saith Darius the King: Much which was ill-done that I made good. Provinces were in commotion (yaud); one man was smiting the other. The following I brought about by the favour of Ahuramazda, that the one does not smite the other at all, each one is in his place. My law—of that they feel fear, so that the stronger does not smite or destroy the weak."

59. Asheri 1990, 135-36; Lateiner 1989, ch. 6.

60. See esp. Hdt. 1.75, 1.188-90, 3.117 (with Griffiths 2001), 4.91, 7.34-35, 7.54, 8.109.3 (cf. Aesch. *Pers.* 790-91).

61. As Plutarch develops the theme, Alexander had a passion for surmounting obstacles, "not only his enemies, but even places and seasons of the year" (Plut. *Alex.* 26; cf. 58; Arr. *Anab.* 4.21.3). Alexander does reveal some flashes of pragmatism: e.g., when faced with the hilltop refuge of the Aspendians, he was "not prepared for a long siege" (Arr. *Anab.* 1.27.3-4; cf. 1.29.1-2, 3.24.1-3), though the Aspendians nonetheless acceded to his demands.

62. Hdt. 7.22, 37.1, 122; cf. 6.44-45, 95.2, 7.189.2.

63. Martin 1965, with, e.g., esp. Hdt. 3.1-25, 134-38, 4.43.

64. See e.g. Hdt. 3.137 (Darius's familiarity with Greek wrestling); Dinon *FGrHist* 690 F 2 (his love of Greek figs); Hdt. 8.135 (Xerxes' knowledge of Delphi); Aesch. *Pers.* 230-31, Hdt. 1.153.1, 5.73.2, 105; Ar. *Ach.* 648-51 (questioning identity of Athenians or Spartans). The king's geographical curiosity in two cases frames Herodotus's narration: Darius's wonder at the Black Sea leads to Herodotus's "eyewitness" report of his measurement of it (4.85-86); and Xerxes' amazement at the mouth of the Peneius gorge, and his thought of diverting the river, lead to Herodotus's explanation of why it has the form it does (7.128-30).

65. See, e.g., Fredricksmeyer 2000, arguing that Alexander's claim to "kingship of Asia" was a "unique creation"; contrast Nawotka 2004.

66. Herodotus's book 1 is, on one level, the story of the completion of Cyrus's conquest of Asia: 1.108, 177-78, 209. See further Harrison 2002.

67. Cf. Ehrenberg 1938.

68. Compare, e.g., Alexander's conquest of the rock of Sogdiana, spurred on by the barbarians' injunction to "look to soldiers with wings" if he wanted to

capture it (Arr. *Anab.* 4.18.6), with the Herodotean story of Zopyrus, mocked with the words "when a mule gives birth to a foal, then the city [Babylon] will be taken" (Hdt. 3.153).

69. Previous historians, Plutarch says, "imply that through some extraordinary stroke of providence the tide receded to make way for him. . . . Menander alludes to this prodigy in one of his comedies, where he says: 'Like Alexander, if I want to meet / A man, he's there before me in the street, / And if I am obliged to cross the sea, / The waves at once will make a path for me'" (Scott-Kilvert 1973, 270–71).

70. See especially Boedeker 1988.

71. Flower 2000, 107–9.

72. Ibid., 109–10: "This should not be taken to indicate that Alexander was now discarding the traditional assimilation of Trojans and Persians in Greek thought. Alexander's interconnected imitation and emulation of Achilles over-shadowed and transcended his Trojan ancestry."

73. See especially Wiesehöfer 1994, 39; cf. Bosworth 1980 and Brosius 2003, 173–79, on Alexander's "superficial" borrowings. For Alexander as *philokyros,* cf. Strabo 11.11.4; for his concern for Cyrus's tomb, see, e.g., Arr. *Anab.* 6.29.4–11; cf. 3.27.4, 5.4.5, 6.2–3.

74. The contradiction is unresolved in Brosius 2003, for whom Alexander both "pursued a carefully orchestrated ideological agenda . . . to invite comparison with Cyrus" (175) and yet "created an ideology-laden 'fantasy-world' of the Persian empire as the ultimate enemy of Greece, in which the Macedonian king led the revenge for Xerxes' invasion and took the role of the champion of the freedom of the Greeks" (174); cf. Lane Fox 2004, 73.

75. Ath. 13.37. See Nawotka 2003, 70–73, for a history of different interpretations; cf. Hammond 1992; Sancisi-Weerdenburg 1993.

76. Cf. Briant 1982, 360.

77. Flower 2000, 100–101; though contrast Nawotka 2003, 71 (emphasizing Greek unfamiliarity with Persepolis); for Persepolis see Flower 2000, 113–15.

78. It is arguable also that by this stage Alexander may have been much less mindful of public opinion on the Greek mainland.

79. Brosius 2003, 190–91.

80. The situation is almost analogous to that of any modern government that, inevitably over time, finds itself measured against its original promises and others' expectations. Cf. the powerful reading of Briant 1982, 391–92, connecting the destruction of Persepolis with Alexander's idealization of Cyrus.

81. Flower 2000, 117–18.

82. Arr. *Anab.* 7.9–10; Plut. *Alex.* 23; this idea of the monarch untouched by wealth is foreshadowed in the fourth century: Xen. *Cyr.* 1.5.1, 6.45, 2.1.30, 6.2.26–29, 8.2.19–22; cf. Xen. *Symp.* 4.31–32; Isoc. *Nicocles* 2.

83. Ironically, Alexander's convictions are taken seriously even in so negative an account as Brosius 2003, for whom, e.g., Alexander "regarded himself as the successor to the murdered Darius III" (171).

84. Cf. Brosius 2003, 175; contrast Tarn 1966, 266, arguing that the idea of the unity of mankind derives not only from the fact of Alexander's empire but from his ideas.

85. Brosius 2003, 185 (cf. Kuhrt and Sherwin White 1994, 315–16; Kuhrt 1983 on Cyrus in Babylon); contrast Brosius 2003, 185n26, on the "rose-tinted picture of the welcomed 'liberation.'"

86. Brunt 1965.

87. Engels 1978.

88. Cf. Brosius 2003, 172: "Alexander's short-term strategies, his military aggression, his violent reactions against any demonstration of resistance, the ruthless killing of local populations, and the destruction of cities and towns throughout his twelve-year campaign certainly allow that conclusion. Yet at the same time Alexander sought cooperation with the Persians, politically and militarily, which suggests that he must have realized at some point that mere conquest of territory was no guarantee for maintaining the land and the people who had been conquered."

89. E.g., the nod to Alexander's portraiture (Hephaestion says, "You still hold your head cocked, like that") or the mythological references ("my mother's god, who came to India"); cf. Lane Fox 2004, 45.

90. Edith Hall points out to me that, in her understanding of the film, the randomness and futility of Alexander's campaigns was the central point.

91. Cf. Lane Fox 2004, 53: "Colin could change to a softness in his eyes for the early scenes with his mother and imply the suffering which even Alexander, Oliver believed, had experienced in his turbulent family."

92. Ibid., 64; cf. "the combination of fierceness and emotion with an unexpected softness in the eyes. Colin was not Irish for nothing, and he also still had Alexander's youth" (49); "he had an Irish talent for the job [riding]" (50). On the rationale for the different accents, see ibid., 54.

93. Foreword to Lane Fox 2004.

94. Lane Fox 2004, 5.

95. Ibid., 167. In Schühly's original conception, according to Lane Fox (ibid., 11), "Alexander mastered the art of winning the support of people he defeated. . . . He was not in the business of . . . bringing 'Unesco' to the world. He was brought up in a Macedonia which was more like the world of the Godfather."

96. Ibid., 7.

97. Ibid., 34.

98. Ibid., 12.

References

Asheri, D. 1990. "Herodotus on Thrace and Thracian Society." In *Hérodote et les peuples non-Grecs*, ed. W. Burkert et al., 131–69. Fondation Hardt Entretiens 35. Geneva.

Badian, E. 1962. "Alexander the Great and the Loneliness of Power." *AUMLA: Journal of the Australasian Universities Language and Literature Association* 17: 80–91. (Repr. in *Studies in Greek and Roman History*, 192–205. Oxford, 1964.)

———. 1966."Alexander the Great and the Unity of Mankind." In *Alexander the Great: The Main Problems*, ed. G. T. Griffith, 287–306. Cambridge. (Orig. pub. in *Historia* 7 [1958]: 425–44.)

Boedeker, D. 1988. "Protesilaos and the End of Herodotus' *Histories*." *Classical Antiquity* 7:30–48.

Bosworth, A. B. 1980. "Alexander and the Iranians." *Journal of Hellenic Studies* 100:1–21.

———. 1988a. *Conquest and Empire: The Reign of Alexander the Great*. Cambridge.

———. 1988b. *From Arrian to Alexander: Studies in Historical Interpretation*. Oxford.

———. 1996. *Alexander and the East: The Tragedy of Triumph*. Oxford.

Briant, P. 1982. "Conquête territoriale et stratégie idéologique: Alexandre le grand et l'idéologie monarchique Achéménide." In *Rois, Tributs, Paysans*, 357–404. Paris.

———. 1989. "Table du roi: Tribut et rédistribution chez les Achéménides." In *Le Tribut dans l'Empire Perse: Actes de la table ronde de Paris*, ed. P. Briant and C. Herrenschmidt, 35–44. Paris.

———. 2002a. *From Cyrus to Alexander: A History of the Persian Empire*. Tr. P. T. Daniels. Winona Lake, IN.

———. 2002b. "History as Ideology: The Greeks and 'Persian' Decadence." In *Greeks and Barbarians*, ed. T. Harrison, 193–210. Edinburgh Readings on the Ancient World. Edinburgh. (Orig. pub. as "Histoire et idéologie: Les Grecs et la décadence Perse," in *Mélanges P. Lévêque*, vol. 2, *Anthropologie et société*, ed. M.-M. Mactoux and E. Geny, 33–47. Besançon, 1989.)

Brosius, M. 2003. "Alexander and the Persians." In *Brill's Companion to Alexander the Great*, ed. J. Roisman, 169–93. Leiden.

Brunt, P. A. 1965. "The Aims of Alexander." *Greece and Rome* 12:205–15.

———, tr. 1976–1983. *Arrian: Selected Works: English and Greek*. Rev. ed., with intro. and notes by P. A. Brunt. Loeb Classical Library. 2 vols. Cambridge, MA.

Cartledge, P. 2004. *Alexander the Great: The Hunt for a New Past*. London. Rev. ed., New York, 2005.

Ehrenberg, V. 1938. *Alexander and the Greeks*. Oxford.

Engels, D. E. 1978. *Alexander the Great and the Logistics of the Macedonian Army*. Berkeley.

Flower, M. 2000. "Alexander the Great and Panhellenism." In *Alexander the Great in Fact and Fiction*, ed. A. B. Bosworth and E. J. Baynham, 96–135. Oxford.

Fredricksmeyer, E. A. 2000. "Alexander the Great and the Kingship of Asia." In *Alexander the Great in Fact and Fiction*, ed. A. B. Bosworth and E. J. Baynham, 136–66. Oxford.

———. 2003. "Alexander's Religion and Divinity." In *Brill's Companion to Alexander the Great*, ed. J. Roisman, 253–78. Leiden.

Green, P. 1991. *Alexander of Macedon, 356–323 B.C.: A Historical Biography.* Berkeley.

Griffiths, A. 2001. "Kissing Cousins: Some Curious Cases of Adjacent Material in Herodotus." In *The Historical Craft in the Age of Herodotus*, ed. N. Luraghi, 173–77. Oxford.

Hall, E. 1989. *Inventing the Barbarian: Greek Self-Definition through Tragedy.* Oxford.

———. 1993. "Asia Unmanned: Images of Victory in Classical Athens." In *War and Society in the Greek World*, ed. J. Rich and G. Shipley, 107–33. London.

Hammond, N. G. L. 1992. "The Archaeological and Literary Evidence for the Burning of Persepolis." *Classical Quarterly* 42:358–64.

Harrison, T. 2000. *The Emptiness of Asia: Aeschylus' Persians and the History of the Fifth Century.* London.

———. 2002. "The Persian Invasions." In *Brill's Companion to Herodotus*, ed. E. Bakker, I. De Jong, and H. van Wees, 551–78. Leiden.

———. 2004. "Mastering the Landscape." In *Titulus: Essays in Memory of Stanislaw Kalita*, ed. E. Dabrowa, 27–33. Electrum 8. Krakow.

Heckel, W. 2003. "King and 'Companions': Observations on the Nature of Power in the Reign of Alexander." In *Brill's Companion to Alexander the Great*, ed. J. Roisman, 197–225. Leiden.

Kent, R. G. 1953. *Old Persian: Grammar, Texts, Lexicon.* 2nd ed. New Haven, CT.

Kuhrt, A. 1983. "The Cyrus Cylinder and Achaemenid Imperial Policy." *Journal for the Study of the Old Testament* 25:83–97.

Kuhrt, A., and S. Sherwin White. 1994. "The Transition from the Achaemenid to the Seleucid Rule in Babylonia: Revolution or Evolution?" In *Achaemenid History VIII: Continuity and Change*, ed. H. Sancisi-Weerdenburg, A. Kuhrt, and M. Cool Root, 311–27. Leiden.

Lane Fox, R. 1973. *Alexander the Great.* London: Allen Lane.

———. 2004. *The Making of Alexander.* Oxford and London.

Lateiner, D. 1989. *The Historical Method of Herodotus.* Toronto.

Lewis, D. M. 1987. "The King's Table." In *Achaemenid History II: The Greek Sources*, ed. H. Sancisi-Weerdenburg and A. Kuhrt, 79–87. Leiden. (Repr. in his *Selected Papers in Greek and Near Eastern History*, ed. P. J. Rhodes, 332–41. Cambridge, 1997.)

Martin, V. 1965. "La politique des Achéménides: l'Exploration prélude de la conquête." *Museum Helveticum* 22:38–48.

Momigliano, A. 1984. "Persian Empire and Greek Freedom." In *Settimo Contributo*, 61–75. Rome. (Orig. pub. in *The Idea of Freedom: Essays in Honour of Isaiah Berlin*, ed. A. Ryan, 139–51. Oxford, 1979.)

Nawotka, K. 2003. "Alexander the Great in Persepolis." *Acta Antiqua* 43:67–76.

———. 2004. "Alexander the Great and the Kingdom of Asia." *Eos* 91:34–43.

Raaflaub, K. 2003. *The Discovery of Freedom in Ancient Greece.* 2nd ed. Chicago.

Roisman, J. 2003. "Honor in Alexander's Campaign." In *Brill's Companion to Alexander the Great,* ed. J. Roisman, 279–99. Leiden.

Root, M. C. 1979. *The King and Kingship in Achaemenid Art.* Leiden.

Sancisi-Weerdenburg, H. 1993. "Alexander and Persepolis." In *Alexander the Great: Reality and Myth,* ed. J. Carlsen, B. Due, O. Steen Due, and B. Poulsen, 177–88. Rome.

Scott-Kilvert, I., tr. 1973. *The Age of Alexander: Nine Greek Lives,* by Plutarch. Harmondsworth.

Tarn, W. W. 1948. *Alexander the Great.* 2 vols. Cambridge.

———. 1966. "Alexander the Great and the Unity of Mankind." In *Alexander the Great: The Main Problems,* ed. G. T. Griffith, 243–86. Cambridge: Heffer. (Orig. pub. in *Proceedings of the British Academy* 19 [1933]: 123–66.)

Wiesehöfer, J. 1994. *Die 'dunklen Jahrhunderte' der Persis: Untersuchungen zu Geschichte und Kultur von Fars in frühhellenistischer Zeit (330–140 v. Chr.).* Zetemata 90. Munich.

Worthington, I. 2003. "Alexander's Destruction of Thebes." In *Crossroads of History: The Age of Alexander,* ed. W. Heckel and L. Tritle, 65–86. Claremont, CA.

———. 2004. *Alexander the Great: Man and God.* London.

"Help me, Aphrodite!"
Depicting the Royal Women of Persia
in Alexander

LLOYD LLEWELLYN-JONES

I'M GONNA GO where the desert sun is; where the fun is; where the harem girls dance," sang Elvis Presley in his 1965 musical *Harum Scarum* (also known as *Harem Holiday*). Presley plays the role of Johnny Tyronne, an action-movie star and ladies' man, traveling through the Middle East on a goodwill tour to publicize his latest film, *The Sands of the Desert*. In the process of his Arabian Promotion Tour, he fights off wicked sheiks and bandits and encounters all the mysteries of the East embodied in a bevy of sexy lovelies named Emerald, Amethyst, and Sapphire, the sultry concubines of a sultan's harem, before falling head-over-heels in love with the Princess Shalimar, whom he marries and takes home to the West—to liberation—to America: "Go East—and drink and feast—go East, young man!" In effect, the film's plot fulfills the theme song's promise that going East will reward a young man with all his desired fantasies, or with "*1001 Swingin' Nights*," as the film's publicity campaign promised.

Of course, the Presley film is a piece of trivial hokum (even Presley fans are agreed as to the abysmal quality of the production), but in many ways Johnny Tyronne's fantasy of the East bears a close relationship

243

with that of Alexander the Great, at least as Oliver Stone envisages things. "Go East, young man; you'll feel like a Sheik, so rich and grand, with dancing girls at your command"—the lyrics seem to voice Alexander's sole motivation for his conquest of Persia. Take for example scene 36 of *Alexander*, as it appears in the fourth edition of the shooting script (dated August 21, 2003). The scene is set in the royal apartments of Darius III's palace in Babylon:

> (*Music of pipes and flutes can be heard coming from a garden below them [Alexander and his companions].* . . . *Intrigued by the music, Alexander moves down a staircase into* . . . *a cool garden paradise. As Alexander descends, Darius' lovers appear, in ones or twos, then threes, accumulating quickly like flowers in their curiosity to set eyes on the young conqueror.* . . . *To Alexander's enchanted eyes, it's a vision of Paradise more than a harem. The Persians have constructed a world from water pools, to food, fragrance, music, clothes, and love, all designed to seduce the senses.*)

> PERDICCAS (agog): By the gods! What is this?!
> CRATERUS: I venture one for each night of the year! No wonder Darius ran—when he had this to come back to!
> CASSANDER (aside): Time for a woman, Alexander?
> ALEXANDER: I think you'll manage well without me, Cassander.

> (*The fat, older eunuchs prostrate themselves, their world aflutter at this invasion of throbbing Greek masculinity. Women keep appearing from small apartments— partially concealed by foliage and rock—and several play flutes and various shapes of lyres, luring the men.*)

> LEONNATUS: Help me, Aphrodite! How will I ever go back to Lysidea after this?
> NEARCHUS: I advise you not to touch, Leonnatus. I'll take care of it for you.

> (*The men ravish the women with their eyes, their tastes different, their lust similar . . .*)

The script is peppered with unashamed Orientalist clichés: "from water pools, to food, fragrance, music, clothes, and love, all designed to seduce the senses," it reads. In the theatrical release of the film shown in cinemas worldwide, the sledgehammer stereotypes are even more painfully obvious, as will be demonstrated below. Numerous questions arise out of this set up: why did Stone indulge himself with these outmoded and, essentially, historically inaccurate visions of the East, and how do these cinematic perceptions of the Orient fit in with a bigger Hollywood convention of picturing the East? In this chapter I explore how *Alexander* utilizes the image of the royal women of Persia and question the functions they serve in the film's visual and narrative dialogues. I also examine Stone's stereotyping of the effeminized East and his relationship to the historical reality of Achaemenid women and, in particular, the royal harem.

That *Alexander*'s narrative essentially follows the military occupation of an apparently weakened—if ancient—Eastern civilization by a young and energetic Western superpower ("Operation Persian Freedom," as the *New Yorker* put it)[1] forces us to consider the movie within the larger colonialist/imperialist framework so often employed in Hollywood's rendition of East-West encounters, wherein the East is portrayed in a negative light. As Max Alvarez has noted, "the culture for which Hollywood has shown its greatest contempt has been the Middle East[ern] culture."[2]

It was in 1978 that Edward Said famously broached a theory that film critics, among others, could use to explain the negative, exotic, and often erotic settings that Hollywood's vision of the East routinely promotes. *Orientalism* describes how Western colonialist discourse has represented the "colonies" and cultures of the Middle Eastern world in a way that justifies and supports the West's imperialist enterprise. Put more succinctly, Orientalism is an idiosyncratic means of representing Otherness. "The Orient," wrote Said, "was almost a European invention, and has been since antiquity a place of romance, exotic beings, haunting memories and landscapes, remarkable experiences."[3] While his focus was on European literature—academic writing, travel reports, and novels—his theory has been applied readily to the visual arts and even to popular culture.

The craze for Orientalist painting in Europe and the United States in the late nineteenth century, for example, had an enormous influence on the burgeoning American film industry, and in Hollywood the representation of the East—typically titillating viewers with the thrills of passion, adventure, and exotic settings—was already becoming conventionalized by the 1910s. Even the most cursory glance reveals Hollywood's wide range of narrative formulas for Orientalism: Biblical epics and historical biopics with Middle Eastern settings vied for audience attention with Foreign Legion adventures and Arabian Nights fantasies.

The relationship between Orientalism and cinema is a prime example of what Said has called "a marvellous instance of the interrelations between society, history, and textuality."[4] But while Orientalism offers insights into movies made throughout the twentieth century, a closer look suggests that the oppositions illuminated by Said are in fact blurred, complicated, and undone by the films themselves. As Matthew Bernstein has noted, there may well be contradictions between the visual style of a film and the logic of a film's narrative, so that, "like all representational texts, Orientalist films sustain a measure of ideological contradiction and incoherence."[5]

Bernstein's discerning comment certainly works for Stone's *Alexander*, for there is a dichotomy in the way the narrative and characters of the film are structured and utilized and the way in which the film is visualized in terms of set design, costume design, and mise-en-scène.

Any engagement with Alexander the Great's life, including cinematic portrayals, cannot just accept a prima facie imperialist/Orientalist reading; there is more to Alexander than the sum of his parts. One is forced to recognize, say, the mythic and legendary aspects of Alexander's career interwoven with the historical facts. Indeed, the legendary elements of his life are as closely fixed in the popular imagination as his gargantuan military exploits. And just as history enjoys an interesting interaction with myth, so too it can be argued that the polarization between East and West so vehemently argued for by Said in *Orientalism* is overstated.

While the "imagining" of the East that Said articulates is central to this chapter, it is important to qualify both the embedded duality and the hostile relationship outlined in *Orientalism* and to emphasize that the "Other" is part of the totality as a defining aspect of the "Self." In other words, Orientalism is compulsory, for while the East gives the West its identity, in return the West defines itself by projecting an identity onto the East. It follows therefore that the Orient, and for us the Persians especially, have to be seen as part of the totality of the Western narrative and must be moved from an essential "Other" to an integral part of the "Self." This is a concept Alexander the Great seems to have struggled with after his conquest of Persia and his defeat of Darius III. His adoption of Achaemenid court dress and protocol, his adoption of Persian youths into the Macedonian military, and the mass marriages at Susa are just some of his attempts at a greater acceptance of the dialogic nature of the East-West relationship.

In filmic terms, the scenes in *Alexander* that are set in the East (Babylon, Bactria, India) serve to define the Western scenes (exclusively Macedon). Or, if one prefers, the Alexander of the early scenes, Alexander of Macedon, is only one-half of the more complex Alexander of the later scenes: Alexander the Great King. The Eastern narrative is an essential part of the film, since it qualifies Alexander's achievements, the man he becomes, and the future he aspires to.

Nonetheless, while recognizing the complex discourse between East and West in Alexander's character and in aspects of the film narrative, the way in which Oliver Stone, together with his design team, chose to articulate that dialogue in visual terms is at loggerheads with a more sophisticated understanding of and response to Orientalism. The look of the film's Eastern scenes is acutely disappointing, not so much in the painstaking details of sets and costumes, but in the general and overall visualization of the East, which relies too heavily on hackneyed Orientalist clichés. Essentially this film falls into a category of particularly low, passé, and even offensive visualization of the East, which we might term the "jewel in the navel" school of Orientalism. If we consider, as we will below, how Stone steeps his audience in an onscreen vision of a fantasy East, then his reading of the East-West dialogue is no more sophisticated in its depiction of the Orient than that of *Harum Scarum*.

Designs on the Past

Before turning to the movie's representation of the royal women of Persia, it is important to expand our understanding of how set and costume design functions in an epic movie and to ask why such a clichéd vision of the East was formulated in *Alexander*'s production design.

When it comes to film design, it should be noted that the Hollywood epic generally presents a stereotypical view of the ancient world; Hollywood does not take risks. The sense of the past contained in the epic movie genre is largely based on visual conventions inherited from Victorian historical paintings, early twentieth-century stage designs, and film designs from Hollywood's formative era, so that the presentation of ancient life varies little in Hollywood filmmaking, relying instead on visual clichés developed through repetition and based on audience familiarity.[6] Experienced moviegoers know what their ancient world is *supposed* to look like, and any film that seriously challenges this is unlikely to gain popular acceptance or box-office success.[7]

When making *Gladiator* (2000), Ridley Scott used the paintings of the Victorian artist Lawrence Alma-Tadema to re-create the "look" of imperial Rome, much as Cecil B. DeMille used the same artist to inspire his set designs for *Cleopatra* (1934).[8] Oliver Stone too fell back on Hollywood's tried and tested vision of antiquity. During the initial design stage, costume designer Jenny Beavan warned Stone that the look

of the film was in danger of turning into "some bad 1950s Hollywood
big movie." Stone retorted, "But I like bad Hollywood movies of the
1950s!"[9] His affection for Hollywood's epic tradition manifested itself
when he invited the heads of the various design departments to a special screening of D. W. Griffith's 1916 silent masterpiece *Intolerance*,
with its famous scenes set in Babylon on the eve of its conquest by
Cyrus the Great. This film had a fundamental impact on the way the
final cut of *Alexander* was produced, especially in relation to the representation of Eastern women.
    This is not to say that Stone and his design team were not meticulous
about historical detail. As the historical consultant for the costume design department, I was involved with the project for almost two years
(and what follows is to a large extent based on first-hand knowledge of
how the film was crafted, and my own response to the process)—I was
often overwhelmed by the design team's concern for and attention to
the minutiae of the historical reality of Alexander's world. As far as I
am concerned, Oliver Stone is a historian's film director, with an enormous respect and passion for the past, a facet of his character I found
enormously appealing each time we communicated. And his quest to
render Alexander's world accurately was infectious: all members of the
design team, from designers to prop- and costume-makers, strove for
historical authenticity.
    The production designer, Jan Roelfs, created a feasible and tangible
past world for *Alexander*. Of the many sets he and the set decorator,
Jim Erickson, created, the exterior and interior sets for Babylon were
by far the most impressive: "Babylon is definitely the richest set I've
ever done," Roelfs was quoted as saying. "Alexander's entry into Babylon is the pinnacle of his career. He's never seen such splendour in
his life, never before encountered a culture which in many ways is
superior to his own."[10] The lush Hanging Gardens of Babylon, one of
the Seven Wonders of the ancient world, were incorporated into the
design as Erickson called upon his gardening skills and horticultural
knowledge to acquire plants appropriate to the historical time and
place. Scenic artist Steve Mitchell painted a 150-foot-long, 45-foot-tall,
wraparound cyclorama depicting a photo-realistic, microscopically detailed panoramic view of Babylon as seen from the apex of the palace
terrace. Perhaps the most dazzling part of the set is Darius III's bedroom, which Alexander takes as his own. The intricate wooden screens
were all hand-carved in Morocco, as was the huge overhead fan featuring the woven image of the Persian supreme deity, Ahuramazda. This

meticulous and painstaking attention to detail is emblematic of the care taken by everyone involved with the production to ensure that Alexander the Great's world was faithfully recreated for modern audiences.[11]

Likewise, Jenny Beavan strove for accuracy in all the costumes. Beavan is an outstanding designer with a string of credits to her name and is completely *au fait* with the specific demands of period movies, having designed films such as *Anna and the King* (1999), *Gosford Park* (2001), and *A Room with a View* (1985), for which she won an Oscar. Her approach to costume, like mine, is organic, involving draping costume-stands with lengths of cloth in order to achieve the correct drape of weight for Greek and Persian robes, rather than designing them on paper first. I had a personal involvement with the costumes for the Persian and Bactrian royal women, having been given the task of locating headdress prototypes while on a trip to Istanbul, and working closely on the cut, drape, and belting of Persian court robes with cutter Jane Law.[12]

Yet despite this striving for authenticity, films are products of their time; even in the earliest silent pictures, elements of contemporary living were frequently incorporated into the look of the film, to make the remote ancient world more accessible to the audience. One of the most interesting dilemmas in designing ancient spectacles is reconciling a modern perspective with the historical horizon of the period described: conflating the look of the past with the look of the present, without committing serious anachronisms.

The notion of historicism contends that we should try to understand the past from its own perspective, eliminating our modern conceptions of the past during the process of research. A historicist would therefore argue that the design of a historical film should be as authentic as possible, and in many respects Stone can be classed as a historicist director. However, current issues of taste, perception, and reception are always and unavoidably present whenever history is narrated, whether in academic scholarship or imaginative fiction. This is very much the case with Hollywood epics, where a variety of voices (director, designers, stars) converge, merge, or clash. The result is not so much "realist history" as "designer history," a term coined by the influential film historian Charles Tashiro to describe a situation in which "historical references become secondary to design, although they are never totally absent. . . . Designer history . . . combines the apolitical focus of costume melodrama with the impersonal affect of the traditional History Film. The past becomes a movement of empty forms and exquisite objects."[13] Tashiro goes on to suggest that makeup, hairstyles, and costumes in the typical epic are often adjusted to conform to a contemporary look. If this is the case, then designer history is a facet of the look of *Alexander* too, an aspect of the film's production I found hard to understand during my time working on the movie. So while Beavan's team was able and willing to create a meticulous reconstruction of the gold and purple cloak found in a royal Macedonian grave at Vergina for Alexander to wear for his triumphal entry into Babylon,[14] Beavan was also responsible for creating a set of fantastical "harem outfits" for the concubines of Darius's Babylonian harem and, more alarmingly, some bizarre "Greek" costumes for Angelina Jolie's Olympias that had nothing to do with authentic Macedonian dress of the late fourth century B.C.E., but spoke volumes about contemporary designer fashion and Jolie's own taste in clothes.

In a similar vein, Oliver Stone's own voice could dictate design decisions. Beavan took pains to ensure that Roxane's wedding robes, for example, followed the ancient Near Eastern precedent in which the bride wore red; her head was crowned with a high cap, covered with a rich red veil, and her face was obscured beneath a metallic *burqa'a*, all of which were feasible garments for a Bactrian princess, carefully based on finds of fourth-century Scythian female dress.[15] As Beavan recalls, "When I researched [Roxane's wedding robe], I found that Afghanistani [*sic*] techniques haven't changed much in two thousand years. . . . They sewed gold into clothes, which we did both for Roxane and Alexander's wedding costumes."[16] But at Stone's insistence Roxane's headdress was further augmented with an anachronistic crown of flowering lotus buds replicated from the headdress of Queen Pu-abi of Sumer, which he had seen during an early research trip to the British Museum.[17] That the headdress predated Alexander's marriage to Roxane by almost two and a half millennia was not an issue for Stone; such is the clout of the auteur.

Yet despite the director's peccadilloes (or an actress's irritability), it must be conceded that the overall attention to detail and the quest for historical accuracy in *Alexander*'s design are admirable and stand head and shoulders above the cluttered design concept of *Troy* (2003), which clearly took as its inspiration *Intolerance* and its bafflingly intricate design (even D. W. Griffith thought of it as "a pastiche of more or less authentic details").[18] Upon its cinematic release, *Alexander*, while not receiving worldwide critical acclaim, was nonetheless noted for the excellence of its design. Typical is the review in *Variety*:

Startling visions of antiquity, the likes of which have never before been put on the screen, will surely stay in the mind long after the dramatic vicissitudes have been forgotten: Alexander outwitting a much larger Persian army at Gaugamela, the legendary Hanging Gardens of Babylon . . . , Alexander's triumphant entry through the giant portals of Babylon, the throbbing heart of the ancient world that is extravagantly evoked by production designer Jan Roelfs and a vast artistic team. . . . Enormous effort has gone into imagining the look of Alexander's ever-expanding empire, from the décor of the buildings to weapons and jewellery design, for which Roelfs and costumer Jenny Beavan and their teams deserve high marks. Careful CGI work usefully amplifies the grandeur of the Gaugamela battle, Babylon and Alexandria, augmenting shooting done in Morocco, northern Thailand and London studios.[19]

And, for the *Hollywood Reporter*: "Babylon with its legendary Hanging Gardens lives up to its reputation as one of the wonders of the ancient world. . . . Technically, this production has exciting battles, eye-catching sets and brilliant colorful costumes."[20] So it is not the production design per se that is at fault, and neither set design nor costume design is wholly responsible for the clichéd "look" of the East. The problem must lie in the mise-en-scène and the way in which the women of Persia are utilized in the onscreen vision of the East.

Open Sesame: *Alexander*'s Fantasy Harem

That the word "harem" is problematic is undeniable. Influenced by vague notions of the Turkish *seraglio*, today we have a tendency to imagine Eastern women as shut away inside palaces, out of the sight of men (but not necessarily out of harm's way), having as their only link to the world beyond the palace walls the eunuchs, the half-men who served them and occasionally "serviced" them. The image of an Ottoman-style harem, a secluded and closely guarded pleasure palace filled with scantily clad, nubile concubines idling away their days in languid preparation for nights of sexual adventure in a sultan's bed, has become an integral part of the West's fascination with the mysterious East. Interest in stories of the "lustful Turk" and his concubines was fueled in the mid-eighteenth century by the publication of free translations of the Arabic *Alf Leila wa Leila* under the title *Tales of a Thousand and One Nights*. These racy—and highly inaccurate—versions of the Arabic stories immediately satisfied the European taste for representations of a passionate and violent Orient.[21] Thus in his introduction to *The Arabian Nights Entertainments*, B. R. Redman commented that the setting of the stories

> is a world in which all the senses feast riotously upon sights and sounds and perfumes; upon fruit and flowers and jewels, upon wines and sweets, and upon yielding flesh, both male and female, whose beauty is incomparable. It is a world of heroic, amorous encounters. . . . Romance lurks behind every shuttered window; every veiled glance begets an intrigue; and in every servant's hand nestles a scented note granting a speedy rendezvous. . . . It's a world in which palaces are made from diamonds, and thrones cut from single rubies. . . . In short, it is the world of eternal fairy tale—and there is no resisting its enchantment.[22]

Yet the allure of the erotic East finds its most vivid expression not in literature but in nineteenth-century Orientalist paintings, typified by the harem and hamam scenes of Jean Auguste Dominique Ingres, and because of this, argues Kristian Davies, "even mentioning one's interest in Orientalism brings a rolling of the eyes, implying that one has an interest in lurid things. The result of the criticism is that there are two types of Orientalist painting: depictions of women, and then everything else."[23]

By the early twentieth century, harem fantasies inspired by the canvases of the Orientalist painters were being played out on the stages of the West in performances as "highbrow" as Diaghilev's 1910 Ballets Russes Paris premiere of *Schéhérazade*[24] or as popular as the hoochy-cooch "belly dance" of Little Egypt at the 1893 Chicago World's Fair. Here the audience was promised scenes of "Life in the Harem. Dreamy Scenes in the Orient. Eastern Dances. The Sultan's Diversions."[25]

Western cinema quickly appropriated the harem fantasy, and from the mid-1910s Hollywood created a harem stereotype adjacent to, and dependent on, the canvases of the Orientalist artists of the earlier century. Since then, Hollywood's view of the East has not simply been symptomatic of the colonialist imagination, but also a product of the (Western) male gaze. Hollywood rescue fantasy films, like *Harum Scarum* or *The Sheik* (1921), metaphorically render the East as a female who is saved from her own destructiveness, while also advancing the narrative of the rescue of women (Eastern or Western) from "Arab" men.

Gender is therefore an essential component of Orientalism, and the veiled and "secluded" harem girls in Orientalist films and paintings ironically expose more flesh than they conceal. The process of exposing the female Other serves to allegorize the Western male's ability to dominate and possess her, and, as a symbol or metaphor of the East, the harem girl is ripe for Western domination through, it is to be assumed, penetration.

This desire to project the Orient as feminine is formulated as early as Griffith's *Intolerance*, where Babylon signifies sexual excess by drawing on the New Testament vision of "Babylon the Great, the Mother of Harlots and the Abominations of the Earth."[26] Griffith himself was deeply inspired by Eugène Delacroix's epic 1827 canvas *The Death of Sardanapalus*, depicting the demise of the Assyrian king amid the brutality and sensuality of his court.[27] Griffith used the painting to recreate "Babylon's last bacchanal."[28]

In *Alexander*, Babylon also represents feminine excess. The Macedonian army enters through the lavish Ishtar Gate to a thundering anthem of gongs, cymbals, drums, and brass composed by Vangelis and called "The Dream of Babylon." The theatrical release of the film adequately captures the vision of what Stone's script (scene 34) demanded:

> Subtitle: *Babylon, Persia. 331 BC*
>
> Resplendent with finery, Alexander, hair crowned with gold laurel, royal purple cloak clasped with jewels, surrounded by his closest companions [enters] through the blue-tiled Ishtar Gate. Crowds on the parapets cheer and shower flowers upon him as the cavalry and infantry saunter in to the lilting sound of flutes, drums, and horns. Thousands of people are jammed together in the vast square, all shouting, hypnotically— "Sikander!" Never has he been so adored! Alexander's amazed, overwhelmed. Inside the gate—the streets are filled with crowds of mixed races, many performing the Persian *proskynesis*, sending a kiss to the king from their lips, some, of lower rank, prostrating themselves to their knees. Gifts have been brought from all over the kingdom—caged lions, leopards and livestock. . . . Alexander feels himself sucked into the eyes of the populace, feeling its beastly love.

As Alexander progresses through the streets, Stone opts to focus on Colin Farrell's face. In slow motion, and at an unusual skewed angle, the camera captures Alexander's obvious bliss—with closed eyes and smiling lips—while he is bathed in a shower of pink and red rose petals; this is Alexander in an ecstasy bordering on sexual delight. And with this shot, Vangelis's theme changes: a harp glissando introduces a musical dream-state with a bewitching use of percussion, female choir (no male voices at all), and harp; it reflects Alexander's erotic reverie.[29] A voiceover from the narrator, Ptolemy, accompanies the scene: "So it came to pass, in a dream as mythical to all Greeks as Achilles defeating the Trojans, Alexander entered Babylon. . . . But in the end I believe Babylon was a far easier mistress to enter than she was to leave." Here the city is alluded to as a "mistress," with all the sexual connotations of the word, so that Alexander's conquest of her (his entry into her) has to be regarded as an act of sexual penetration. But Babylon is a willing mistress, and the girls of the royal harem, as we will see, are envisaged as an extension of the city's sexual compliance.

   Alexander's visual infatuation with Babylon's material abundance, emphasized through the mise-en-scène of monumental architecture, exotic costumes, flora, and fauna, as well as details of strange social customs, cannot be divorced from Orientalist colonial travel reports obsessed with the details of perceived Eastern sensual overindulgence. Thus *Alexander* visually reproduces what Said refers to as the "imaginative geography" of Orientalism and the feminization of the East, symbolized by "the sensual woman, the harem, and the despotic—but curiously attractive—ruler,"[30] in this case Raz Degan's good-looking King Darius.

   In *Alexander* we accompany, quite literally, the perspective of the "discoverer"—and it is precisely this point of view that defines his historical position. In *Alexander* the camera relays the hero's dynamic movement across a passive space, in this case the public spaces of Babylon and then Darius's private palace, stripping those spaces of any mystical enigma as the spectator gains access to the treasures of the East through the eyes of the discoverer-protagonist. Alexander's progression through city and palace becomes increasingly more intimate as the conqueror and his companions penetrate into the heart of the palace: scene 34 (as we have seen) is set at the Gates of Babylon; scene 35 takes us to the King's Apartments inside the Babylon Palace; and scene 36 takes us to the Interior Babylon Garden of the King's Palace, the harem.

   In *Alexander* the image of the harem offers an "open sesame" to an unknown, alluring world. As a director Oliver Stone is not alone in this regard: other historical epics like Robert Rossen's *Alexander the Great* (1956) and King Vidor's *Solomon and Sheba* (1959), as well as musicals such as Vincente Minnelli's *Kismet* (1955) and Walter Lang's *The King and I* (1956), use the motif of the ruler or conqueror within his harem to transmit the idea of the autocracy and sexual authority of the male protagonist. The harem sequence in *Alexander* propels the audience, like Alexander himself, into the unknown world of the East, although it should be noted that the scene as it appears in the film does not necessarily replicate the original script.

The first hint the film's audience gets of the Oriental pleasures to come occurs in scene 35 (as enumerated in the script):

(*Darius's bedchamber. Discussing the necessity of capturing the defeated Persian king in order to legitimize Alexander's rule over his empire, Alexander and his companions pause to marvel at the material manifestations of an age-old civilization.*)

ALEXANDER (in wonder): Imagine the minds that conceived this! With architects and engineers like these we could build cities such as we've only dreamed!
PTOLEMY: Aristotle might have called them barbarians, but he never saw Babylon.[31]

But all thoughts of the reality of conquering and controlling "a world far older than ours," as Alexander puts it, are soon pushed aside. Distracted by the music of pipes, flutes, harps, and light female laughter coming from a garden below them, Alexander and his men move down a staircase and into a garden-harem. The antiquity and nobility of the East are suddenly subordinated by a vision of hedonistic, enchanted decadence. On the soundtrack Vangelis's "Gardens of Delight" begins with a dreamy female solo voice accompanied by harp, strings, and delicate finger-cymbals, setting the mood for a scene of sensual pleasures.

As Alexander and the companions enter the harem they are greeted with an exquisite sight. The camera privileges the Macedonian position as we see the harem from above, from Alexander's viewpoint, and we gaze down into the lushly planted hothouse, where the women display themselves like rare orchids.

PERDICCAS (agog): By the gods! What is this?!
CRATERUS: No wonder Darius ran—when he had this to come back to! I venture one for each night of the year!
LEONNATUS: Help me, Aphrodite! How will I ever go back to Lysimache after this?[32]
NEARCHUS: I advise you not to touch, Leonnatus. Here, I'll take care of it for you.

Nearchus prepares to move on the girls, but he is held back by Alexander, who silently asserts his authority and forbids his men to handle them roughly. This is a marked change from the original script, where Alexander is more complacent in enjoying the sexual availability of the harem's occupants:

ALEXANDER (to Hephaestion): . . . Aristotle was perhaps too prescient! Do these images fool us—with their beauty—and degrade our souls?
CASSANDER (overhearing, amused): Come now, Alexander, what's temptation for, but to be enjoyed? Either way, it is pleasant torture, is it not?

Originally the script allowed Alexander to enter into the hedonism enjoyed by his men and indulge in "his own vision of temptation in the form of a lustrous black-ringleted, gelded boy of 17—Bagoas—dark, soft eyes, piercing in their tenderness and pain." In the theatrical release, Alexander's sexual arousal is curtailed; he exchanges a brief glance with Bagoas, but Stone does not allow Alexander to have any sexual stirrings in this palace of pleasure, and Alexander remains strangely detached from his exotic surroundings. In the script the Macedonians are so excited by the sight of the concubines that, like wound-up teenagers with overactive libidos, they burst into a mock fight: "The 'Great King' is bowled onto the cushions by the rushing tackle of Perdiccas, Craterus, and Cleitus. . . . They wrestle the good-natured Alexander across chairs and carpets, yelling and laughing, knocking over valuable objects and a bowl of fruit. Cassander and the others watch, but . . . Bagoas can[not] believe the freedom this madcap king displays."

The theatrical release, however, omits this scene of the rough and tumble of male-to-male bonding and takes Alexander and his men out of the frame, opting instead to concentrate on the softer, sultry, and sensuous delights of the harem: the bodies of the concubines. The camera privileges the male point of view as it spotlights individual women. Through a series of fluid edits we, like Alexander's men, focus first on a dark-eyed girl lightly strumming a lyre, then a fair-haired girl coyly lifting her peacock-feather fan to her cheek, and next a loose-limbed beauty stroking the soft white fur of her fat Persian kitten. The rapid cutting means that the women of Darius's harem change from the active observers as visualized in the script ("Darius' lovers appear . . . quickly . . . in their curiosity to set eyes on the young conqueror") to the passive observed of the camera's lens/Alexander's gaze. Stone's use of the camera and of editing to capture the exotic beauty of individuals within the harem pays homage to Griffith's *Intolerance*, wherein the girls of Babylon are put on display for public auction, a scene in turn inspired by Edwin Long's epic 1875 painting The Babylonian Marriage Market.[33] Griffith's setting is more crowded than the painting, but the director compensates for this through the skillful use of the moving camera and slick editing. No fewer than sixty shots are used in this sequence, fifty-seven of which are rapid cuts allowing the audience to move "through the looking-glass of nineteenth-century painting into the reality of the magic world of the movies."[34] Griffith uses his camera to pan along a line of girls stretched out on the floor in front of the auction podium, and one by one he lets his audience see them toying with their mirrors, waving their fans, or merely gazing at the ground; like Stone's harem girls, Griffith's seraglio of beauties are busy doing nothing, simply basking in their gorgeousness and languidly waiting for their sexual adventures to begin. Commenting on the portrayal of the Babylonian women in Intolerance, Henrietta McCall has noted: "The women suffer the same fate as Long's maidens: they had been prettified to conform with modern tastes and wore flimsy robes that clung or were shaped to the body with jewelled girdles. The women had to be recognizably 'Babylonian' to western eyes, that is, exotic, mysterious, and beautiful, and prone to lounge on tiger-skins."[35]

In terms of costume, the girls of 1916 and 2004 have much in common: they wear the same standard Hollywood fantasy-harem ensembles of low-slung skirts that show midriffs and hips, wrap-around brassiere-tops, a variety of gossamer veils, and an abundance of tinkling jewelry. As in the Orientalist harem paintings of the nineteenth century, the exposure of flesh is paramount.

After allowing the camera to linger on the harem inmates, Vangelis's "Gardens of Delight" theme picks up with a laid-back and rhythmical Eastern-sounding percussion. It is at this juncture that the film's clichéd image of the harem descends to its nadir as each harem girl begins to sway her hips, rotate her abdomen, and twist her arms in a slow and sensual belly-dance. The girls of Darius's harem are very willing performers, it seems; they bloom before the rugged Macedonian invaders and dart liquid glances into the eyes of the welcome intruders, inviting them to share in the sensual delights of this secret world of women. The image created by Stone puts one in mind of Sir William "Oriental" Jones's eighteenth-century conception of the harem as a grand brothel, with the inmates performing in an erotic costume drama:

> A thousand nymphs with many a sprightly glance
> Form'd round the radiant wheels an airy dance
> Celestial shapes! In fluid light array'd
> Like twinkling stars their beamy sandals play'd;
> Their lucid mantles glitter'd in the sun
> (Webs half so bright the silkworm never spun)—
> Transparent robes, that bore the rainbow's hue,

And finer than the nets of pearly dew
That morning spreads o'er every flower.[36]

The confusion between harem and brothel is a common one: Emmett
Murphy, for instance, includes a chapter on the harem in his book *Great
Bordellos of the World*, arguing that "although not every harem is a bor-
dello, . . . not every . . . house of women is a harem. . . . The Turkish word
for inn, *serai*, will be accepted in the Islamic world for hostelry and
whorehouse, this [later] became known in the West as the *seraglio*."[37]
Similarly, in the popular imagination of the West there is little difference between concubine and courtesan. Alexander's men undoubtedly
regard the women as sexually available—not surprising, given the obvious come-ons the girls exude. "I venture one for each night of the
year!" is Craterus's wide-eyed observation, and here the script draws
on the popular ancient Greek perception that the Great King was surrounded by 360 enthusiastic concubines—one, *almost*, for every night of
the year.[38] "Help me, Aphrodite!" is an appropriate plea. The Western
male dream of the wanton and available odalisque is promulgated
by Stone in a fashion worthy of Delacroix and Ingres or—by direct
descent—Edwin Long.

Orientalist art, and by extension Orientalist cinema, prioritizes male
visual pleasure, a form of gratification bound up in imperial identity.
Adding the gloss of antiquity to the Orientalist image, especially the
decadence of Babylon and the ubiquitous image of the harem, supports
the ideology and gives Western prejudice a rich pedigree, seemingly
steeped in historicity. In this regard, Stone's *Alexander* has to be seen as
the latest in a long line of beautiful, if deeply misunderstood and dangerous, Orientalist clichés.

The Inner Court: *Alexander* and the Historical Harem

So, what is the reality? To explore the truth about the royal harem in the
Persian empire, we must dispel the images created in *Alexander*. We
also need to expand our understanding of what a harem really is; we
must realize that although a harem can be a physical space, an identifiable area of a palace or house used by women—and by children, eunuchs, and privileged men, for that matter—"harem" can also simply
refer to women grouped together, without a defining space. But we can
take the word much further: as Hugh Kennedy has recently stressed, in
Arabic usage a caliph or sultan would use the word to refer to his

women and, more generally, to all those under his immediate protection: children, siblings, courtiers, and slaves[39]—a group of people rather than a particular building or a specific location. It is difficult to know how the ancient Persians actually referred to a harem, in either its physical or ideological form, but the Old Persian term *viθ* seems to carry with it the double sense of "house" (in the sense of "palace") as both a building and a household. The word also seems to suggest the concept of an "inner court," again in the double sense of a space and a people, parallel to the Arabic *harem*, or, for that matter, the modern Farsi *andarūnī*.[40] I use "harem," then, to refer to a flexible space and a distinct group of people—male and female—who inhabit that permeable, but hierarchically bound, space.

It makes sense to believe that there was a conception of "harem" in ancient Persia; the ideology of harem is, after all, a hallmark of almost all absolute monarchies throughout the ages, so why should it be absent from the Achaemenid empire—the largest world empire to that date? Yet in the most recent work on the ancient Persian court, some scholars have totally denied its presence. Most puzzling is Maria Brosius's methodical ostracism of it from her important study *Women in Ancient Persia*.[41] While she notes the wide array of royal females found at the Achaemenid court, and observes that there was a distinct hierarchy of women ranging in importance from the king's mother and the king's wife and wives (of Persian stock) to the non-Persian concubines and, ultimately, slaves, she does not attempt to qualify these women as a specific unit within the court.

This does not make sense. In any developed court system, the presence of women of definite social status would have called for a hierarchical structure reflected in such issues as court protocol (audiences, dining, etc.) and even designated (if not permanent) social and living spaces. Whether she realizes it or not, Brosius is in fact dealing with the women of the royal harem, although her limited understanding of what the term actually implies is problematic. She writes: "It is clear . . . that there is no truth in suggestions that women lived in seclusion and were confined to the palace."[42] She is also misguided in her suggestion of a "Greek notion that women lived in the seclusion of the palace, hidden away from the outside world."[43] I am aware of no Greek text of the Classical period that specifically says this.[44] Misunderstandings arise from the cavalier translation of the Greek term *gynaikeion* or *gynaikonitis* as "women's quarters." Recent research has revealed that this is widely off the mark.[45] "The place where the women are" is a better translation of the Greek word, suggesting any temporary space utilized by women and by family. In the ancient Greek understanding, *gynaikeion* is never a fixed, let alone secluded, female-only space. To read Persian court structures through an imperfect understanding of the.Greek terminology is futile. For Brosius to think of "harem" only in terms of secluded female-only space or as a form of purdah is a grave misunderstanding.

Pierre Briant goes further in his resistance to the concept of a Persian royal harem and dismisses any notion of it as a Greek fantasy coined in the overheated imaginations of Herodotus, Plutarch, and Ctesias.[46] This opinion is in sharp contrast to Richard Frye's earlier estimation that "the harems of the Achaemenid rulers were large, for they contained not only the wives and concubines of the king but all the women of the family, such as sisters, mothers and others."[47] Frye limits his interpretation of "harem" to females of a spatially defined inner court, which is strictly speaking inaccurate (although his use of the word "others" could imply men); nonetheless, Frye, like Ernst Herzfeld, Albert Olmstead, Erich Schmidt, and David Lewis, has argued in favor of a royal harem institution lying at the heart of imperial dynastic policy.[48]

It is only since the 1980s, and with work emanating from the influential Achaemenid History Workshop, that scholars have concentrated on an allegedly skewed Greek vision of the Persian court and thereby come to regard the harem as a byproduct of Greek fantasy literature.[49] Briant's reaction to the notion of harem is emblematic of his approach to much of Achaemenid culture in general, whereby he systematically attempts to alienate Persia from the cultural *koine* of the ancient Near East and see it as a society freed from the more alien mores of the Neo-Babylonian and Assyrian past on the one hand, while being equally free from the Orientalist gloss provided by Greek authors on the other. Briant, has, for instance, rejected the notion that all individuals identified as "eunuchs" in the context of the Achaemenid empire were castrated males; he suggests that "eunuch" was how "Greek authors transmitted a term that the court of the Great King considered a court title."[50] But as Shaun Tougher has warned in his major study of eunuchism in antiquity, Greeks knew what eunuchs were and therefore "being too skeptical [about the sources] can be as dangerous as being gullible." He goes further to suggest, "One is left with the impression that Briant simply prefers not to consider some eunuchs to be castrated men as he finds it hard to accept that they could be powerful elite officials. A wider knowledge of eunuch history undermines this stance."[51]

I suggest that Briant is susceptible to the same fault in regard to the harem, and that a wider understanding of the harem system in other court cultures suggests that the sources we have for an Achaemenid harem find ready parallels elsewhere. For Briant the word "harem" conjures up so effectively the misguided stereotypes promulgated by Stone's *Alexander* that he seems unable to move beyond the Orientalist fantasy to consider the reality of the political resonances and power plays of the women of the royal harem, found in monarchic systems worldwide over many successive centuries. Scholarship has to rise above the harem cliché, reexamine the root and meaning of the word, and recognize that, in the absence of any other purposeful term, "harem" is the most appropriate one to use to describe the domestic makeup of the Persian royal household.[52]

I do not believe that the royal women of Achaemenid Persia lived in purdah, nor did they inhabit a world of sultry sensuality, but I do believe that they formed part of a strict hierarchical court structure that moved in close proximity to the king. As a component of his harem (in the true sense of the word), they participated in the peripatetic lifestyle of the court. It is logical to recognize the harem as a vital component of Persian court culture and to recognize its political importance in the maintenance of dynastic power. The Achaemenid dynasty was essentially a centrally run family business, and at the heart of the operation lay the harem, the king's inner court. For the women, men, and servants of the royal family, prestige (and access to power) lay in their proximity to the king.[53]

Moreover, the high status of royal females was reflected in their inaccessibility, their removal from general public view. This does not negate any financial power or autonomy they might have held; nor does it suggest that they lived in secluded segregation. While women could be holders and maintainers of their own lands and estates, while they could manage their own finances and travel independently of the king, these capabilities do not necessarily indicate a desire on their part to be public figures. Common conceptions of "harem" popularly incorporate a lack of freedom for women. But "freedom" in the modern sense of the word does not equate with ancient concepts of public visibility. True power and prestige lay in a woman's removal from an overt public life. The Greek reports of royal and noble women progressing through the empire within their curtained carriages is not fantasy;[54] it is an observation of Persian custom in which women of status augmented their

privileged social position by separating themselves from the common
gaze. There was no honor in being exposed. To intrude upon a woman's
privacy was therefore tantamount to an insult.

Alexander would have known this; after all, he was a product of a
harem himself, the son of a polygamous union.[55] Philip II's many wives
must have been housed in fairly close proximity within the palace at
Pella, and so as a concept, harem—an inner court—would have been familiar to Alexander (and let us not forget that there was a long history
of Persian influence at the Macedonian court).[56] But the concept of Macedonian polygamy is entirely underplayed in *Alexander*: when Philip
takes a new bride, Eurydice, the suggestion is that Olympias will be divorced or at least exiled, and that any sons born to Philip's new queen
will supersede Alexander and his sister. At worst, Philip is a serial
monogamist. During script consultations over the staging of Philip's
assassination in the theater, it was suggested that his other wives be
represented seated together too, but this was quickly dismissed as
overcomplicating the narrative. In Stone's film polygamy and concubinage are products of "Oriental despotism" alone, and Alexander, the
child of a monogamous union, is as thrilled and flabbergasted by the
display of sexual hedonism he finds in the Persian court as any of his
Macedonian soldiers.

Two specific points arise from Stone's portrayal of the harem that
seriously undermine the historical reality of the institution as well as
Alexander's calculated use of it. Firstly, Stone opts for the glossy Hollywood fantasy harem and thereby writes out of history the type of people
who actually constituted the inner court. This cinematic harem is filled
with young and, presumably, fertile concubines, while the older women
of the inner court, the mature females, the mothers and their children
(boys and girls), are invisible. In careful consultation with the assistant
director, I had strongly suggested that the harem comprise women
and children of diverse ages and divergent social strata (king's wives,
sisters, daughters, concubines, children, eunuchs, and slaves), and indeed the script does call for "young and old women, eunuchs, slaves . . .
and . . . females of the extended royal branch." The vision I had in mind
resembled the type of extended family I had been privileged to encounter among a nomadic tribe in modern Iran, in which the *andarūnī* consisted of all the males of the family (fathers, sons, and brothers) and
their respective wives (who were also mothers), of grandmothers, and a
whole array of male and female offspring ranging from infants to adolescents. But when the time came to film the Babylon harem sequence at

Pinewood Studios, the older women and the children disappeared from the scene.

Second, Stone does not understand that being seen by unrelated males would bring great shame upon the women of the royal household. Alexander and his men violate their domestic space and thereby affront the personal honor of the inhabitants of the inner court; we should expect the women to react accordingly.[57] But not here: these harem girls are brazen; they dance and coquettishly interact with the conquerors. Why do they not flee in terror? Why do they not veil themselves? Why do they not resist? Instead they capitulate; more than that, the concubines willingly open up and blossom.

Interestingly, the Turkish director Ferzan Özpetek deals differently with a very similar scenario. His 1999 film *Harem Suare* ("The Last Harem") traces the daily life of the imperial harem in Istanbul at the twilight of the Ottoman empire. The story follows Safiye, the sultan's favorite concubine, as she gains power and authority within the inner court by overcoming plots and intrigues until she secures her position by bearing the sultan a son and becoming an official wife. When the empire falls, the sultan escapes to Europe, leaving all his wives and concubines behind in Istanbul, and it is left to Safiye to fight for their rights under the new and indecisive Republic.

The most remarkable scene in the film occurs immediately after the sultan has fled the Dolmabahçe Palace, as the Republican guards enter the private heart of the complex to issue orders that the harem is to be disbanded and the women are to leave the security of the palace and return to their natal homes. As the guardsmen enter into the sanctity of the domestic space, the concubines huddle together for protection, terrified at the fate that may befall them. Humiliated at this breach of propriety, they reach for their veils or any makeshift covering that will protect them from the violation of the unwanted male gaze until Safiye orders the guards to show respect and withdraw, which they eventually do.

Özpetek has stressed that his main concern was to "unravel one of the most crucial knots of my original culture: the end of the Ottoman Empire, portrayed in one of the places dearest to the imagination—the harem."[58] But he does not choose a belittling course; the disbanding of the last harem represents for Özpetek the breakdown of the old order because he recognizes that the inner court represents the heart of the Ottoman empire, and with the destruction of the harem the political relevance of the sultanship ceases.

Oliver Stone fails to realize the political value of the inner court of Achaemenid Persia, let alone the dynastic consequences of Alexander's acquisition of Darius III's harem. The possession of a predecessor's harem, and in particular the females of the household, ensured the successor's hold on the throne, and the control of the harem gave a new ruler the potential to legitimize his reign through the physical posses-sion of a former monarch's household—and the sexual command over the women of any former ruler must not be overlooked here. Darius the Great had capitalized on this when in his bid for power he had married all the available royal women of the line of Cyrus II—the former wives and/or sisters of Cambyses and Bardiya—whereupon he incorporated them into his harem and established them as the highest-ranking of all his existing wives. He quickly fathered children by his new acquisitions and promoted his sons born in the purple above those born before his accession.[59] In this Darius I was following a common Near Eastern practice: Ramses II of Egypt, for instance, routinely inherited the women belonging to the harem of his father, Seti I, as a demonstration of dynastic longevity;[60] upon his military victory and subsequent acces-sion to the throne of Israel, David claimed the female harem of Saul;[61] and Solomon peacefully inherited his father's harem of women and servants.[62] A challenge to both David and Solomon came in the form of rebellions within the royal house when two of David's sons, Absalom and Adonijah, rebelled against the Israelite kings and attempted to win the royal concubines and incorporate them into rival royal harems.[63]

Historically, at least in the Greek and Hebrew sources, Persian con-cubines were generally considered to be attractive girls;[64] they were bought in slave markets,[65] or were received as gifts or as tribute and were collected from different parts of the empire.[66] Concubines were also captured from rebellious subjects.[67] The Greeks referred to these women as pallakai, a term denoting low-class females, perhaps of the demimonde, but the appellation cannot be justified for what we know about the status of Persian concubinage, and the concubines of Persian kings should not be classed as even reputable disreputable women.[68] Artaxerxes I is known to have fathered at least eighteen sons from his concubines, and Artaxerxes II had 150 sons by his concubines.[69] While the official take was that children born to concubines were regarded as inferior to children born to a royal wife (and the Greeks routinely called them nothoi, "illegitimate"), "the history of the succession of Achae-menid kings tells another story."[70] As a result of wars, epidemics, the high infant mortality rate, or succession struggles within the royal household, an opportunity sometimes arose for the son of a concubine to ascend (or claw his way) to the throne. Darius II Ochus was crowned Great King despite being the son of a Babylonian concubine named Cosmartidene, suggesting that concubinage was not necessarily a dormant institution and that concubines could gain access to high status and even become queen mothers.[71] The reality of the harem was that circumstance or ambition could change the course of dynastic politics.

With this in mind, Oliver Stone's version of Alexander's appropriation of the royal harem makes little sense. It is highly unlikely that upon entering Babylon in January 330 B.C.E. Alexander encountered any of Darius's concubines and eunuchs (let alone royal blood kin) left behind in an empty palace. This was simply not the Persian practice. We know that Alexander took hold of Darius III's harem not at Babylon, but much earlier, at Issus, soon after his November 333 victory, for the peripatetic Persian court had, as always, accompanied the Great King on campaign.[72] We learn that the human booty acquired after Issus included 29 pot-tenders, 13 milk-dish makers, 17 drink-mixers, 70 wine-bearers, 46 chaplet-weavers, 40 perfumers, 227 bakers, and no fewer than 329 concubines.[73] As Margaret Miller explains, "Alexander had captured what was certainly rather than possibly a royal household."[74] But Alexander was merely keeping up the Greek practice of acquiring Persian concubines as war booty: after the battle of Plataea, for instance, we hear that the concubines of Persian officers and satraps were included in the human loot together with specialized servants and eunuchs.[75]

Having captured the harem of Darius, Alexander continued in the Persian tradition and had the personnel of the inner court accompany him on campaign until 330, when we hear that the core of the royal women were housed in the royal palace at Susa with the instruction that they be taught Greek.[76] It is highly likely that Alexander had decided to marry at least one of the daughters of Darius around this time, but it was not until his return to Susa nine years later that he finally married into the royal clan. While Alexander's Achaemenid brides, Stateira, the daughter of Darius III, and Parysatis, daughter of Artaxerxes III, were of fundamental importance to his claim to the Persian throne (and they far overshadowed Roxane's significance in his Eastern policy), it is important not to overlook the symbolic value of Alexander's acquisition of Darius III's harem en masse in 333 and certainly the blow that the appropriation of the royal concubines meant to Darius. In the Old Testament, Yahweh threatens David with the promise that "I will take your women before your eyes"[77]—and that threat resonated within all the kings of the ancient Near East. In her excellent study *The Imperial Harem: Women and Sovereignty in the Ottoman Empire*, Leslie Peirce makes a vital observation on the nature of absolute monarchy, such as was the Achaemenid dynasty, and its intimate relationship with the women of an inner court:

> Sex for the Ottoman sultan, as for any monarch in a hereditary dynasty, could never be purely pleasure, for it had significant political meaning. Its consequences—the production of offspring—affected the succession to the throne, indeed the very survival of the dynasty. It was not a random activity. Sexual relations between the sultan and chosen women of the harem were embedded in a complex politics of dynastic reproduction.[78]

Daniel Ogden, in his discussion of Alexander's marriage into the Achaemenid clan, goes further and makes an important observation on the nature of marriage in ancient absolute monarchies. According to Ogden, Alexander's Persian marriages highlight

> a certain paradox, in Greek terms, of marriages made by an absolute monarch. In Greek culture marriage (*gamos*) was a contract between two men who were, if not equal, at any rate equally free. In some sense an absolute monarch's women could only ever be concubines, since he could never enjoy the symmetrical relationship with their fathers that is normally integral to *gamos*. Here then is another reason why the distinction between wives and concubines could have become engulfed in a royal context.[79]

For Darius III, the Macedonian king's seizure of the Persian royal harem heralded the end of Achaemenid rule, for Alexander's appropriation of the reproductive capabilities of the women of the inner court immediately jeopardized the legitimacy of Darius's reign. In this respect, Oliver Stone's trivialization of the royal harem as a brothel-like pleasure palace fails to do justice to a decisive moment in Alexander's political career.

Princess of a Thousand Roses: Stateira

All of the ancient sources recall Alexander's courtly treatment of the royal women of Persia, but it is possible that his relationship with Queen Stateira, wife of Darius III, was especially close.[80] She is said to have died in childbirth before the battle of Gaugamela in 331, although the exact time of her death is problematic. Arrian tries to convince his

readers that Alexander never touched Darius's queen, although if Stateira died later than the spring of 332, there is every possibility that she
carried Alexander's child, not Darius's.[81]

Alexander never married Darius's queen, but in 324 he took her
daughter, Princess Stateira, as his wife. He had captured her at Issus, together with her mother, her grandmother Sisygambis, her sister Drypetis, and her five-year-old brother Ochus, the only known son of Darius
III. Nevertheless, Alexander waited another nine years to solemnize
their union, despite the fact that Darius offered Alexander his daughter's hand in the immediate aftermath of Issus. Argead kings often asserted their claim to the throne by marrying the widow of a predecessor,
but since Queen Stateira had died in 332, Alexander's only alternative
in 324 was to marry her daughter, who, it has been suggested, stood in
for, and in a sense "became," the mother.[82]

As Briant has recently discussed, a myth has emerged in the Western
tradition about Alexander's relationship with "the most beautiful
woman in Asia"—and here he too speaks of an amalgamated Stateira, a
legendary beauty who is, in fact, a mixture of mother and daughter.[83]
Given that the two historical Stateiras seem to have had somewhat
tragic fates—the elder Stateira surviving her royal husband and dying,
perhaps, giving birth to his enemy's heir; the younger meeting her
death at the hands of Roxane, Alexander's Bactrian bride—a whole variety of artistic treatments of a suffering Stateira and a vengeful Roxane
emerged in the arts of the West in the post-Renaissance period. In Vero-
nese's great canvas of 1565–70, *The Family of Darius before Alexander*, Stateira, dressed in blue and pink brocade, kneels before the Macedonian
king, the image of modest Italian beauty.

In contrast, Defoe's willful and lusty heroine of 1724 dresses in Persian garb and delights her London audience with such wildly exotic
"Eastern" dances that the lusty male drinkers in a tavern nickname
her "Roxana" in homage to Alexander's barbaric queen.[84] Costes de la
Calprenède's novel *Cassandre* (1642–45) narrates the story of Alexander
the Great as a "secret history" in which the cousins Roxane and Stateira
compete for Alexander's favor. The romance proved hugely influential
for the English playwright Nathaniel Lee, who, in *The Rival Queens* of
1677, presented on stage the stereotypes of the two Eastern queens—
the fierce Roxane and the gentle Stateira—who between then unman
the noble Alexander and promulgate the moral bankruptcy of his court,
in much the same way that the rival mistresses of Charles II, Barbara
Palmer, Lady Castlemaine (Roxane), and Frances Stuart, Duchess of

Richmond (Stateira), jockeyed for position in the morally corrupt Restoration court.[85]

It is unlikely that Oliver Stone conscientiously drew upon this long tradition of placid Stateiras or on the mother-daughter syncretism, but his film presents us with a curiously familiar vision of the Persian princess. She makes her first appearance in silence, observing the shenanigans in the harem from the lofty retreat of a balcony, surrounded and safeguarded by her imperious ladies-in-waiting and eunuchs. She looks splendid: dressed in a rich red court robe and a bejeweled turban with a light silk veil and clutching a feather fan, she is every inch a princess. As the music swells, the girls gyrate their hips, and the Macedonians overheat, Stateira makes her entrance into the harem garden. All the action stops as the women, eunuchs, guards, and slaves of the Persian court prostrate themselves in deference to Darius's daughter. The onscreen dialogue runs like this:

OLD EUNUCH (making an announcement): Great King, Alexander!
PHARNAKES (taking over): The Princess of a Thousand Roses, the eldest daughter of the formerly Great King Darius, Stateira.
STATEIRA (mistaking Hephaestion for Alexander): Noble Alexander, I come to beg for the lives of my sisters, my mother, my grandmother.

(There is laughter from Alexander's men at the princess's mistake in appealing to Hephaestion and not to Alexander. She turns to Pharnakes in embarrassment and distress.)

ALEXANDER (gently): You are not wrong, Princess Stateira (motioning towards Hephaestion); he too is Alexander.
STATEIRA (in broken Greek spoken with an Iranian accent): Please, I plead for my family's lives. Sell me as a slave, Great King but do not . . .
ALEXANDER: Look now, into my eyes, princess, and tell me how would you like to be treated?
STATEIRA: As I am: a princess.
ALEXANDER: Then so be it. You and your family shall be treated as my family. (There are murmurs from the crowd.) You shall live in this palace for as long as you choose. Have you any other requests for me, my noble princess?
STATEIRA: No, everything I wish I have . . . (she falters)
PHARNAKES (aiding her): "Requested."
STATEIRA (repeating): Requested.
ALEXANDER (full of tender admiration): You truly are a queen.

The image of Stateira Oliver Stone chooses to advance is that of a gentle and passive princess who is a victim of dire circumstance, yet a woman whose nobility stands out despite her desperate situation. It is a deeply romantic portrayal and draws on another popular Orientalist stereotype: the beautiful captive princess rescued by the liberator-hero. In *Harum Scarum* Elvis Presley had encountered Princess Shalimar in much the same misty-eyed way that Alexander meets Stateira, in the heart of the exotic and erotic harem, and the audience anticipates that, like Shalimar, Stateira will find her future in the arms of the Western hero. Stateira smiles nervously and modestly lowers her fluttering eyes away from Alexander's liquid gaze; for his part, Alexander too seems besotted by this vision of reticent yet regal perfection.

Stateira's royal title elaborates upon the Orientalist cliché; she is not merely "Princess" but "Princess of a Thousand Roses."[86] The title has no legitimate Achaemenid pedigree,[87] although it must be said that we know next to nothing about the court titles used by royal women in Persia. All that can be said with some certainty is that women of the royal house were honored with the title *dukšiš* (pl. *dukšišbe*), which can be generically translated as "princess."[88] Here, however, Stateira's elaborate title has a decidedly exotic tone, and its link to roses is consistent with Western fantasies of the blossoming sensuality of the Eastern woman. Take, for example, Guy de Maupassant's description of a fantasy sultan's concubines: "These flower-women, women flowers, he [the sultan] prefers . . . to any others, and spends his nights in the hothouses where he hides them . . . in a harem."[89] In *Alexander* it is interesting to observe too the hothouse atmosphere of Darius's garden harem, where all the concubines are exotic and colorful blooms (remember the script's description of the girls: "like flowers in their curiosity to set eyes on the young conqueror"), but where Stateira, with her regal bearing and her rich red silk robes, is the single rose among all Persian women.

Added to this is the sound of Stateira's voice: it falters over the formation of unfamiliar words and is encased within a charmingly pleasant Persian accent (Annelise Hesme, who played Stateira, although French, based her accent on an Iranian learning English). What effect does this have on the audience? It certainly weakens Stateira's power within the scene, since she becomes dependent on Pharnakes for help in speaking, but simultaneously the linguistic fallibility of this elegant noblewoman heightens her erotic charms too; there is something delightfully submissive in Stateira's hesitant speech and something decidedly erotic in her mysterious accent. In a wider context, Stateira's style of speech is consistent with the way in which the Persians were

imagined to speak in antiquity and the way they are represented en
masse throughout the film.⁹⁰ In early script discussions Stone was keen
for the Persian characters to speak in modern Farsi with English subtitles superimposed onto the screen for clarity, but this was vetoed by
the production company, who were concerned about audience reactions. Instead, the Persian characters were given the onscreen accent of
modern Iranians speaking English. Not that there is much "Persian" dialogue in the film as a whole, because the Persian characters are given
surprisingly little to say; Darius has no dialogue whatsoever, and his
lines are limited to a short series of staccato commands: "Envelop him,
Bessus" and "Go!" That Stateira's broken "Greek" becomes, to a large
extent (and with the exception of Pharnakes), the most eloquent words
spoken by these otherwise silent Persians should be a matter of concern.

Despite the pretty mise-en-scène of the Stateira/Alexander sequence, essentially this is an anticlimactic moment in the film, and the
scene goes nowhere. The character of Stateira disappears from the film
narrative at this point, only to emerge briefly once again as Ptolemy
narrates the events of Alexander's return to Babylon from India and his
eventual marriage to Stateira and Parysatis, both of whom are shown in
long-shot witnessing his second triumphal entry into the city from the
roof of the palace.⁹¹ At best Stateira serves as a foil to the fiery character
of Roxane; her usefulness in the narrative of the film is overlooked and
underplayed.

The Stateira/Alexander sequence is ahistorical in many ways and is
not even an accurate retelling of one of the more famous events of
Alexander's Persian campaign, his capture of the royal women at Issus.
In the ancient sources it is, notoriously, Stateira's grandmother Sisygambis who mistakes Hephaestion for Alexander and who then appeals to Alexander's mercy, and it was to Sisygambis that Alexander directed his attention, as befitted her role as the matriarch and guardian
of the Achaemenid line.⁹² As Bosworth puts it, "Alexander scrupu-
lously cultivated the Queen Mother."⁹³

So why did Stone overlook the importance of Sisygambis in *Alexander*, given her prominence in the classical sources and later traditions?
In fact, he didn't. The fourth draft of the Alexander script contains a
long scene devoted to the famous meeting; I record it here in full:

[FEMALE] VOICE (off set): Where is this Alexander?

(*Emerging from the largest apartment, pushing through the retinue, a dominant
older woman emerges. Arthritic, close to 75, richly dressed and made-up, the*

dignified Sisygambis, mother of Darius, immediately quietens the rowdy Mace-
donians, as the eunuchs prostrate with great respect.)

OLD EUNUCH (in a sobering voice): Great King!—Sisygambis! Queen
    Mother of the (pause) formerly Great King, Darius—and his eldest
    daughter, the Princess of a Thousand Flowers, Stateira!

(With Sisygambis is Darius' daughter, Stateira (21), beautiful, statuesque.
Eunuchs help, but the Queen Mother, who can't see very well, mistakes Hephaes-
tion for Alexander—and bows.)

SISYGAMBIS (translated by the Old Eunuch): Noble Alexander, I speak
    simply—I beg of you the lives of my grandchildren!

(Sisygambis, irritated, realizes her mistake and notices Alexander. Prince Phar-
nakes, now a Persian ally of Alexander's, steps forward to aid the translation.)

SISYGAMBIS (translated): Great King, I beg you forgive me—do not
    punish my family for my insult—

(Alexander is charmed by her manner—clearly, in her time, a woman of
power.)

ALEXANDER: No, you are not wrong Queen Mother (indicating
    Hephaestion)—he too is Alexander. And looks far more so than I.

(Laughter from the Greeks, but Sisygambis is cold and severe, her voice meant to
carry as she bows again.)

SISYGAMBIS (translated): Please do not mock my plea for my
    grandchildren's lives! Bring me death, Great King, but . . .
ALEXANDER (translated): Look now in my eyes, Queen Mother! (pause)
    Tell me—how would you like to be treated?
SISYGAMBIS (pause, a trap?): Why, as I am Great King—a Queen.
ALEXANDER: Then you and your family shall be treated as my own
    family . . . (murmurs all around). Is there anything else you desire,
    Queen Mother?
SISYGAMBIS: No. Everything I desire is contained in my first wish,
    Great King.

(Though Sisygambis has lived far too long to believe in the magnanimity of any-
one, she mutters a realization to the equally-suspicious Stateira, who translates
for her now in an impeccable Greek accent—)

STATEIRA: My grandmother, O Great King, is not used to such
    treatment from barbarians. But now she understands why her son,
    my father, fled from you in battle, like a coward. (Gathering herself)
    My grandmother would like me to tell you—she no longer considers
    herself to have a son.

(The murmurs of an astonished Persian court, as Alexander steps close to Sisy-gambis and places his hand warmly on her shoulder. From the outside we now hear a roar of an assembling crowd.)

ALEXANDER: Princess Stateira, tell her if she so desires, she now has a son.

(Sisygambis is deeply flattered and amazed, and puts her time-worn hand over his, and kisses him on the lips, in the royal style. This provokes strong reaction from the Macedonians, amazed by Alexander's inclusiveness. To some, like Par-menion, it smacks of Alexander joining the Persian royal family rather than the other way around. The Persians are equally puzzled—such an idealist this young beardless king seems!)

This powerful scene not only captures the intensity of the celebrated meeting, but also catapults the character of Alexander into another sphere, in which he is shown as a gentle and caring individual craving a mother's warmth. This, allegedly, is what the historical Sisygambis offered him, and Alexander accorded all the honors of the role of Queen Mother to the aging woman and thought of her as a true mother.

So why did this important scene not make it from page to screen? Oliver Stone had cast the legendary French actress Jeanne Moreau in the role of Sisygambis—a coup in itself—and the scene was almost ready to be filmed when contractual disagreements led to Moreau's withdrawal from the production. The actress's departure meant that the scene had to be quickly rewritten with the roles of Sisygambis and Stateira amal-gamated into the single part subsequently (and hurriedly) learned and performed by Annelise Hesme. Such are the day-to-day pressures and bombshells of the film industry. But the impact on the film of Jeanne Moreau's departure is striking.

As it stands in the script, the Sisygambis scene immediately dispels many of the Orientalist clichés inherent in the Stateira/Alexander se-quence, most notably the somewhat sickly romanticism surrounding the princess. Incorporating the figure of a wise old matriarch would have put the political importance of the women of the royal harem back into the film and forced the audience to view the females of the inner court as a collection of women of different ages and differing social strata. Moreover, Sisygambis's rejection of Darius as her son and her fostering and support of Alexander emphasize the political importance of the women of the Achaemenid family as guarantors of the right to rule. In the unfilmed scene even Stateira allies herself with the con-queror and helps legitimize his rule. She becomes more than a passive foil to Roxane, while Queen Sisygambis, for her part, becomes a well-drawn counterpart for Alexander's mother, Olympias, who is of course denied the title Queen of Babylon and, kept at a distance in Macedon, has little public recognition as Queen Mother.

More frustratingly, the withdrawal of Jeanne Moreau necessitated a heavy rewriting of the end of the film. The third draft of the script included a series of montage shots showing the fates of key characters in Alexander's life. By the time the fourth draft was written, the montages had disappeared, but Ptolemy still narrated what happened to the principal characters in the fateful weeks following Alexander's death. He takes particular stock of the Persians:

> PTOLEMY (with bitter irony): Roxane too, like Olympias, played by stern rules. Supported by several generals, days after Alexander's death, she had Stateira poisoned. It was reason enough for many to believe that she was the one behind Hephaestion's sudden demise—but this is unproven in my mind. Bagoas disappeared from the histories entirely, a wise move perhaps—but I will say only his love and devotion for Alexander was unquestionable—As was Sisygambis', the Queen Mother, who when she heard the news of her adopted son's death, dismissed her slaves, turned to a wall in her chambers, and fasted to death within six days.

The planned montage sequence would have enhanced Ptolemy's narration, but unfortunately the sequence was never filmed. The audience is left in darkness about the fates of many of the characters whose lives they have been following onscreen for three hours.

Conclusion

In the version of the film shown in cinemas, we never learn the fate of Stateira; she simply disappears from the narrative, having played no part in the essential storyline. This is symbolic perhaps of the use of all Persian women in the film, or indeed, of Persian history and culture in *Alexander* generally. Persia—here representing "the Orient"—is marginalized as an exotic treat for the eye and an unusual experience for the ear. Oliver Stone does not allow Achaemenid Persia to be taken seriously as a political force, a military entity, or a cultural power. The women of the Persian court are used only as visual stimuli, and the true nature of the harem in the Achaemenid period—the role royal women played within the power structure of the inner court and, by extension, the empire—is entirely overlooked in favor of hackneyed "Oriental"

images. In terms of film narrative, the movie has nothing to offer the
Persian women. Stateira's role contributes little to the film, and her political usefulness to Alexander the Great King is utterly disregarded.

Alexander displays all the familiar Orientalist notions about the infe-
riority and picturesqueness of Eastern societies. The lure of the East as
set out in *Alexander* has two dimensions: one of space—the call of far-
distant lands and alien peoples; and one of time—the pursuit of the *historical* "Other." The unifying factor of both dimensions is the portrayal
of the Eastern woman, and in particular the "harem woman," who embodies most rigidly the mythic elements of the Western perception of
the Orient: domestic submissiveness, erotic willingness, and exotic sensuality. "Help me, Aphrodite!" is thus the exhilarated cry of a Western
man caught up in an Oriental fantasy of his own making. In terms of its
portrayal of East-West relationships, *Alexander* is a stale cultural statement and a worn-out reflection of the continuing Western preoccupation with an imaginary exotic Orient. "Help me, Aphrodite!" has the
hollow ring of Elvis Presley's encouragement to "go East, young man!"

Notes

1. Lane 2004, 125.
2. Alvarez 1998, 27. For a detailed examination of Hollywood's use of
Middle Eastern culture, see Shaheen 2003.
3. Said 1978, 1.
4. Said 1978, 24.
5. Bernstein 1997, 11.
6. For the Academic Painters and their recreations of antiquity, see Liversidge and Edwards 1996; Ash 1999; Wood 1983. Hollywood's debt to these artists is still felt today: see Landau 2000, 64–67. For the influence of Victorian theater design on cinema art direction, see Finkel 1996; Mayer 1994.
7. The 1954 film *The Silver Chalice*, set in late first-century C.E. Syria and Ju-
daea, radically altered this design formula: the set and costume designs blend
the semiabstract and the impressionistic, which, coupled with a poor script,
made the film a box-office flop. See further Hirsch 1978, 34–36; Elley 1984,
117–18.
8. Landau 2000, 64.
9. Lane Fox 2004, 124.
10. *Alexander* pressbook.
11. On the design process, see Lane Fox 2004, 73–98.
12. For details see ibid., 121–30; Llewellyn-Jones 2004, 1–2.
13. Tashiro 1998, 95–96.

14. Andronikos 1980, 36 fig. 9. Compare Lane Fox 2004, 109, 152.

15. Reeder 1999, 118–20, 122, 150–52.

16. *Alexander* pressbook.

17. Dated ca. 2600 B.C.E. See Reade 1991, 45 fig. 55. Compare Lane Fox 2004, 162. Lane (2004, 125) described the headdress as a "deluxe birdcage."

18. Drew 2001, 57.

19. McCarthy 2004, 45–47.

20. Honeycutt 2004, 28.

21. For examples of Orientalist ideology within the European translations of the *Alf Leila wa Leila,* see Kabbani 1986; see also Mernissi 1997, 2001.

22. Redman 1932, ix.

23. Davies 2005, 247. For Ingres's Eastern women, see Lemaire 2000, 198–203; Ribeiro 1999, 197–236. On women in Orientalist art more generally, see Del-Plato 2002; Thornton 1993.

24. Mernissi 2001, 68–69.

25. Çelik 2000, 81.

26. Rev. 17:5.

27. For a discussion of the painting and a background to the nineteenth-century mania for the ancient Near East, see Bohrer 2003, 54–59.

28. Drew 2001, 68–69.

29. Some critics were less than kind about Vangelis's score. Kurt Loder wrote: "The soundtrack score of this movie, by the Greek synth virtuoso Vangelis, is an abomination in itself, an ugly mush of oozing string washes, pounding tympanis, swooning chorales and tiny tinkling chimes. There's no one up on the screen at any point suffering as much abuse as the audience that's forced to endure this aural assault." See http://www.mtv.com/movies/news/articles/1494174/11242004/story.jhtml.

30. Said 1985, 90, 103.

31. In the script (fourth draft) the scene reads:

PTOLEMY: Aristotle might have called them barbarians, but he never saw Babylon.

ALEXANDER (in wonder): Imagine the minds that conceived this, Ptolemy! With architects and engineers like these we could build cities such as we've only dreamed!

32. In the fourth draft of the script, Leonnatus calls his wife Lysidea.

33. See Bills 1998, 105–8; Bills et al. 2004.

34. Hanson 1972, 506.

35. McCall 1998, 210; see further Bahrani 2001.

36. Jones 1772, cited in Lytle Croutier 1989, 71.

37. Murphy 1983, 109.

38. Deinon *FGrH* 690 F 27; Plut. *Artax.* 27.2; Heracleides (*FGrH* 689 F 1) notes 300 concubines. Olmstead (1948, 424) argues that the presence of 360 concubines

can be linked with the number of days in a calendar year, but the figure is too convenient to be taken seriously and is probably a Greek fantasy of the number of women available for the Great King's pleasure. The number of concubines in the royal household probably fluctuated, and it is possible that at times they actually exceeded 360 in number.

39. Kennedy 2004, 160–99.

40. Lit. "the inside"—the private quarters of well-to-do houses, in contrast to the *bīrūnī*, the public rooms, usually reserved for men. Like "harem," *andarūnī* also refers to the people who make up the inner household. For aspects of gendered space, see Laffon and Laffon 2004, 122–33.

41. Brosius 1996.

42. Ibid., 188.

43. Ibid., 43.

44. Plut. *Them.* 26 alone suggests the complete seclusion and policing of wives and concubines, but this is an unreliable source and Plutarch has a definite agenda here. His adventure story of Themistocles' flight and exile in a curtained palanquin, like a woman, necessitates Plutarch's digression on the *extreme* control Persians have over their wives, concubines, and slaves. In his *Life of Artaxerxes*, which revolves around the workings of the inner court in some detail, nothing of this strict seclusion is suggested. For the unreliability of Plutarch on this matter see Nashat 2003, 21, 23.

45. See Morgan 2005.

46. He refers to the "myth of the harem." See Briant 2002, 283–86.

47. Frye 1962, 97.

48. Herzfeld 1941, 234–36; Olmstead 1948, 86–87, 214–15, 411–12; Schmidt 1953, 245–64; Lewis 1977, 22.

49. See in particular Sancisi-Weerdenburg 1987, 1993.

50. Briant 2002, 276–77.

51. Tougher 2008, 22–23. I am grateful to Dr. Tougher for sharing his thoughts on this subject.

52. Fighting against the tide, Balcer (1993, 273–317) writes with common sense on the concept of the early Achaemenid harem. See also Llewellyn-Jones 2002.

53. Carney (2000, 15) is wrong to believe that Persian royal women had no political role; they were denied any public office, but this does not mean that they were deprived of any indirect route to political power. For a discussion of this notion see Garlick, Dixon, and Allen 1992.

54. Xen. *Cyr.* 6.4.11; Diod. Sic. 11.56.7–8; Plut. *Them.* 26.

55. Ogden 1999; Carney 2000.

56. On the housing of the Macedonian royal women, see Carney 2000, 27–28; Ogden 1999, 273–77. On Persian influence at the Macedonian court, see Carney 2000, 15–16.

57. For a full discussion of female shame and its connection to domestic space, see Llewellyn-Jones 2003, 155–214.

58. See http://www.filmfestivals.com/cannes99/html/regard20.htm.

59. Brosius 1996, 47–64; Ogden 1999, 45.

60. Leblanc 1999.

61. See 2 Sam. 12:8.

62. De Vaux 1961, 115. See now also important studies of women and the ancient Near Eastern harem by Solvang 2003 and Marsman 2003.

63. See 2 Sam. 15:16, 16:21–22, 20:3; 1 Kings 2:13–25.

64. Plut. *Artax.* 27; Diod. Sic. 17.77.6; Esther 2:3.

65. Hdt. 8.105; Plut. *Them.* 26.4.

66. Gifts: Xen. *Cyr.* 4.6.11, 5.1.1, 5.2.9, 39; tribute: Hdt. 3.97; collected from around the empire: Esther 2:2–3.

67. Hdt. 4.19.

68. See Hdt. 3.1–2; Brosius 1996, 31–34.

69. Plut. *Artax.* 26; Just. *Epit.* 9.1. See further Lewis 1977, 75.

70. Brosius 1996, 33.

71. Ctesias 47. Ctesias also notes that Darius II's wife and half-sister, Parysatis, was also the daughter of a Babylonian concubine named Andia. Egyptian history follows the same pattern found at the Persian court: Aset, the mother of the great warrior king Thutmose III, was a woman of unexceptional rank within the harem of Thutmose II until an accident of history propelled her son to the throne and advanced her to the exalted role of King's Mother. See Redford 2002, 63.

72. Diod. Sic. 17.36.2; Curt. 3.11.24.

73. Ath. 13.608a.

74. Miller 1997, 37.

75. Hdt. 7.83.2, 9.76.1–3, 9.81.2. Likewise, Parmenion captured a number of Persian women of high status at Damascus in 333. These included the wife of Artaxerxes III and three of his daughters, including Parysatis, whom Alexander later married. See Heckel 2006, 274.

76. Diod. Sic. 17.67.1.

77. See 2 Sam. 12:1–12.

78. Peirce 1993, 3.

79. Ogden 1999, 44.

80. Curt. 3.11.20–12.17, 3.12.21–26; Just. *Epit.* 11.9.11–16; Val. Max. 4.7 *ext* 2.

81. For a discussion of this point, see Carney 2003, 247–48.

82. Odgen (1999, 45) speculates: "This may explain the difficulty surrounding the bride's name in the sources. In Arrian's official Susan wedding list she is called Barsine, but the vulgate sources refer to her as Stateira. . . . It was quite common for the wives of Macedonian princes to change their names. . . . Philip's first wife Audata may have changed her name to Eurydice

on marriage in order to evoke the most 'legitimate' (in Philip [II]'s judgement at any rate) of Amyntas III's wives, Philip's mother, Eurydice." For a discussion of the Stateira-Barsine confusion, see also Hamilton 1969, 55; Heckel 2006, 255–57.

83. Briant 2003, 395–426.
84. Defoe 1724 (1998). I am grateful to Jed Wentz for this reference.
85. See Marsden 2001; Ballaster 2005.
86. In an earlier version of the script she is called "Princess of a Thousand Flowers."
87. Although one of Artaxerxes I's concubines bore the Iranian name Alogune, meaning "rose-colored." See Ctesias 47.
88. See Brosius 1996, 27–28; 2006, 41. It is not certain whether concubines shared this title too; I would find it unlikely.
89. De Maupassant 1886, 45 (my translation).
90. See Munson 2005.
91. This scene and narration do not appear in the Director's Cut DVD.
92. Curt. 3.11.20–12.17, 3.12.21–26. See also Carney 2000, 108.
93. Bosworth 2003, 216.

References

Allen, Lindsay. 2006. *The Persian Empire: A History.* London.
Alvarez, Max. 1998. "Heroes & Villains." *Extra!* September–October.
Andronikos, Manolis. 1980. "The Royal Tombs at Vergina: A Brief Account of the Excavations." In *The Search for Alexander,* ed. J. Carter Brown et al., 26–38. Boston.
Ash, Russell. 1999. *Victorian Masters and Their Art.* London.
Bahrani, Zainab. 2001. *Women of Babylon: Gender and Representation in Mesopotamia.* London.
Balcer, Jack Martin. 1993. *A Prosopographical Study of the Ancient Persians Royal and Noble, c. 550–450 B.C.* Lampeter.
Ballaster, Rosalind. 2005. *Fabulous Orients: Fictions of the East in England 1662–1785.* Oxford.
Bernstein, Matthew. 1997. "Introduction." In *Visions of the East: Orientalism in Film,* ed. Matthew Bernstein and Gaylyn Studlar, 1–18. London.
Bills, Mark. 1998. *Edwin Longsden Long RA.* London.
Bills, Mark, et al. 2004. *The Price of Beauty: Edwin Long's 'Babylonian Marriage Market' (1875).* London.
Bohrer, Frederick Nathaniel. 2003. *Orientalism and Visual Culture: Imagining Mesopotamia in Nineteenth-Century Europe.* Cambridge.
Bosworth, A. B. 2003. "Alexander and the Iranians." In *Alexander the Great: A Reader,* ed. Ian Worthington, 208–35. London.

Briant, Pierre. 2002. *From Cyrus to Alexander: A History of the Persian Empire.* Tr. Peter T. Daniels. Winona Lake, IN.

———. 2003. *Darius dans l'ombre d'Alexandre.* Paris.

Brosius, Maria. 1996. *Women in Ancient Persia (559–331 BC).* Oxford.

———. 2006. *The Persians. An Introduction.* London.

Carney, Elizabeth D. 2000. *Women and Monarchy in Macedonia.* Norman, OK.

———. 2003. "Women in Alexander's Court." In *Brill's Companion to Alexander the Great,* ed. Joseph Roisman, 227–52. Leiden.

Çelik, Zelma. 2000. "Speaking Back to Orientalist Discourse at the World's Columbian Exposition." In *Noble Dreams—Wicked Pleasures: Orientalism in America, 1870–1930,* ed. Holly Edwards, 76–97. Princeton, NJ.

Cook, John M. 1983. *The Persian Empire.* London.

Davies, Kristian. 2005. *The Orientalists: Western Artists in Arabia, the Sahara, Persia and India.* New York.

Defoe, Daniel. 1998. *Roxana, the Fortunate Mistress; or, A history of the life and vast variety of fortunes of Mademoiselle de Beleau: afterwards called the Countess de Wintselsheim in Germany: being the person known by the name of the Lady Roxana in the time of Charles II.* Oxford. (Orig. pub. 1724.)

DelPlato, Joan. 2002. *Multiple Wives, Multiple Pleasures: Representing the Harem, 1800–1875.* London.

de Maupassant, Guy. 1886. *Un cas de divorce.* Paris.

de Vaux, Roland. 1961. *Ancient Israel: Its Life and Institutions.* London.

Drew, William M. 2001. *D. W. Griffith's* Intolerance: *Its Genesis and Its Vision.* Jefferson, NC.

Elley, Derek. 1984. *The Epic Film: Myth and History.* London.

Finkel, Alicia. 1996. *Romantic Stages: Set and Costume Design in Victorian England.* Jefferson, NC.

Frye, Richard Nelson. 1962. *The Heritage of Persia.* London.

Garlick, Barbara, Suzanne Dixon, and Pauline Allen, eds. 1992. *Stereotypes of Women in Power: Historical Perspectives and Revisionist* Views. New York.

Grosrichard, Alain. 1998. *The Sultan's Court: European Fantasies of the East.* London.

Hamilton, James R. 1969. *Plutarch: Alexander: A Commentary.* Oxford.

Hanson, Bernard. 1972. "D. W. Griffith: Some Sources." *Art Bulletin* 54:505–8.

Heckel, Waldemar. 2006. *Who's Who in the Age of Alexander the Great.* Oxford.

Herzfeld, Ernst. 1941. *Iran in the Ancient East.* Oxford.

Hirsch, Foster. 1978. *The Hollywood Epic.* London.

Honeycutt, Kirk. 2004. "Alexander." *Hollywood Reporter,* November 19.

Irwin, Robert. 2006. *The Lust of Knowing: The Orientalists and Their Enemies.* London.

Jones, William. 1772. *The Seven Fountains.* London.

Kabbani, Rana. 1986. *Europe's Myths of Orient.* Bloomington, IN.

Kennedy, Hugh. 2004. *The Court of the Caliphs: The Rise of Islam's Greatest Dynasty*. London.

Laffon, Martine, and Caroline Laffon. 2004. *A Home in the World: Houses and Cultures*. Paris.

Lal, Ruby. 2005. *Domesticity and Power in the Early Mughal World*. Cambridge.

Landau, Diana. 2000. *Gladiator: The Making of the Ridley Scott Epic*. New York.

Lane, Anthony. 2004. "War-Torn." *New Yorker*, December 6.

Lane Fox, Robin. 2004. *The Making of Alexander*. Oxford: R & L.

Leblanc, Christian. 1999. *Nefertari "l'aimée-de-Mout."* Paris.

Lemaire, Gerard-Georges. 2000. *The Orient in Western Art*. Paris.

Lewis, Donald W. 1977. *Sparta and Persia: Lectures Delivered at the University of Cincinnati, Autumn 1976, in Memory of David B. Bradeen*. Leiden.

Lewis, Reiner. 2004. *Rethinking Orientalism: Women, Travel and the Ottoman Harem*. London.

Liversidge, Michael, and Catharine Edwards, eds. 1996. *Imagining Rome: British Artists and Rome in the Nineteenth Century*. London.

Llewellyn-Jones, Lloyd. 2002. "Eunuchs and the Harem in Achaemenid Persia (559–331 BC)." In *Eunuchs in Antiquity and Beyond*, ed. S. Tougher, 19–49. London and Swansea.

———. 2003. *Aphrodite's Tortoise: The Veiled Woman of Ancient Greece*. Swansea.

———. 2004. "The King and I: Costumes and the Making of *Alexander*." *CA News* 31 (December): 1–2.

Lytle Croutier, A. 1989. *Harem: The World Behind the Veil*. New York.

Macfie, Alexander L. 2002. *Orientalism*. London.

MacKenzie, John M. 1995. *Orientalism: History, Theory and the Arts*. Manchester.

Marsden, Jean I. 2001. "Tragedy and Varieties of Serious Drama." In *A Companion to Restoration Drama*, ed. S. J. Owen, 228–42. Oxford.

Marsman, Hennie J. 2003. *Women in Ugarit and Israel: Their Social Position in the Context of the Ancient Near East*. Leiden.

Mayer, David. 1994. *Playing Out the Empire: Ben-Hur and Other Toga Plays and Films: An Anthology*. Oxford.

McCall, Henrietta. 1998. "Rediscovery and Aftermath." In *The Legacy of Mesopotamia*, ed. S. Dalley, 183–213. Oxford.

McCarthy, Todd. 2004. "An Enervating Epic." *Variety*, November 22.

Mernissi, Fatima. 1997. *Êtes-vous vaccine contre le harem?* Casablanca.

———. 2001. *Scheherazade Goes West: Different Cultures, Different Harems*. New York.

———. 2003. *Fantasies de l'harem i noves Xahrazads*. Barcelona.

Miller, Margaret C. 1997. *Athens and Persia in the Fifth Century BC: A Study in Cultural Receptivity*. Cambridge.

Morgan, Janett. 2005. "Cultic Activity in the Classical Greek Household." Ph.D. diss., Cardiff University.

Munson, R. V. 2005. *Black Doves Speak: Herodotus and the Languages of Barbarians.* Washington, DC.

Murphy, Emmett. 1983. *Great Bordellos of the World.* London.

Nashat, G. 2003. "Women in Pre-Islamic and Early Islamic Iran." In *Women in Iran from the Rise of Islam to 1800,* ed. G. Nashat and L. Beck, 11–47. Urbana.

Ogden, Daniel. 1999. *Polygamy, Prostitutes and Death: The Hellenistic Dynasties.* London.

Olmstead, A. T. 1948. *History of the Persian Empire.* London.

Peirce, Leslie P. 1993. *The Imperial Harem: Women and Sovereignty in the Ottoman Empire.* Oxford.

Reade, Julian. 1991. *Mesopotamia.* London.

Redford, Susan. 2002. *The Harem Conspiracy: The Murder of Ramesses III.* DeKalb, IL.

Redman, Ben R. 1932. *The Arabian Nights Entertainments.* London.

Reeder, Ellen D. 1999. *Scythian Gold.* New York.

Ribeiro, Aileen. 1999. *Ingres in Fashion.* London.

Said, Edward W. 1978. *Orientalism: Western Conceptions of the Orient.* London.

———. 1985. "Orientalism Reconsidered." *Cultural Critique* 1:89–107.

Sancisi-Weerdenburg, Heleen. 1987. "Decadence in the Empire or Decadence in the Sources? From Source to Synthesis: Ctesias." In *Achaemenid History,* vol. 1, *Sources, Structures and Synthesis,* ed. Heleen Sancisi-Weerdenburg, 33–45. Leiden.

———. 1993. "Exit Atossa: Images of Women in Greek Historiography on Persia." In *Images of Women in Antiquity,* ed. Averil Cameron and Amélie Kuhrt, 20–33. London.

Schmidt, Erich F. 1953. *Persepolis I: Structures, Reliefs, Inscriptions.* Chicago.

Shaheen, Jack G. 2003. *Reel Bad Arabs: How Hollywood Vilifies a People.* Moreton-in-Marsh.

Solvang, Elna K. 2003. *A Woman's Place Is in the House: Royal Women of Judah and Their Involvement in the House of David.* Sheffield.

Tashiro, Charles S. 1998. *Pretty Pictures: Production Design and the History Film.* Austin.

Thornton, Lynne. 1993. *La femme dans la peinture Orientaliste.* Paris.

Tougher, Shaun. 2008. *The Eunuch in Byzantine History and Society.* New York.

Wood, Charles. 1983. *Olympian Dreamers: Victorian Classical Painters 1860–1914.* London.

Yeazell, Ruth. B. 2000. *Harems of the Mind: Passages of Western Art and Literature.* New Haven, CT.

Part 5

Ways of Viewing Alexander

Viewing the Past

Cinematic Exegesis in the Caverns of Macedon

VERITY PLATT

I N   T H E   I N T R O D U C T I O N to his *Life of Alexander,* Plutarch compares his work as a biographer to that of a painter:

> Just as painters get the likenesses in their portraits from the face and
> the expression of the eyes, wherein the character shows itself, but make
> very little account of the other parts of the body, so I must be permitted to
> devote myself rather to the signs of the soul in men, and by means of
> these to portray the life of each, leaving to others the description of their
> great contests. (1.3, tr. B. Perrin)

As Plutarch firmly states, "It is not Histories that I am writing, but Lives"
(*Alex.* 1.2); the genre calls not for a detailed narrative of great deeds, but
for a focus on those details of deportment and conduct—"a slight thing
like a phrase or a jest" (1.2)—that reveal something of the subject's inner
life.[1] Like a painted portrait, the biography attempts to capture the essence of its subject by alighting on the particular, the idiosyncratic. In ancient portrait traditions, the iconographical details of body and dress
were designed to signify the social, public role of the subject. The portrait's "verism," however—its communication of individuality—lay in
the rendering of facial features. For Plutarch, the themes suggested by

bodily iconography can easily be left for the historians; the biographer's task, like the painter's, is to focus on the "signs of the soul."

Such a visual analogy is particularly appropriate for a life of Alexander, a leader famed for his active interest in artistic production, educated engagement with sculptors and painters, and careful control of his image. By the time Plutarch was writing in the second century C.E., Alexander's facial features had been disseminated all over the Greco-Roman world in the form of coins, sculptures, paintings, and mosaics, his "melting eyes," half-turned head, and wild hair easily recognizable by any educated ancient viewer.[2] While Alexander was famed for commissioning works by masters such as Lysippus, Apelles, and Pyrgoteles, he was also himself an image, repeatedly viewed, replicated, and appropriated by patrons and viewers keen to possess some element of his glamorous legacy.[3]

This dual presentation of the Macedonian king as both a viewing subject and consumed object is an important element of Oliver Stone's *Alexander*. Like Plutarch, Stone treats Alexander's historical achievements with a pointed (and arguably necessary) selectivity, presenting his military campaigns through a series of highly stylized, impressionistic episodes. Rather than following a traditional historical narrative, the film's primary focus is on "the signs of the soul," as Stone attempts a coherent exploration of Alexander's inner journey, structured not only by his martial achievements, but also by episodes exploring his familial and romantic relationships. In terms of contemporary cinematic genres, *Alexander* is not a historical epic, but a *biopic*, signaled by the conspicuous absence of the customary epithet "the Great" in the film's title.[4] While Stone certainly addresses Alexander's heroic legacy—the glamorous youth whose image has been so readily exploited by history—the film's most innovative episodes are those that explore Alexander's psychological motivations. In these scenes, he is not simply presented as the object of the cinematic gaze, but as a viewer himself, through whom the film focalizes its investigation of the cultural and emotional pressures exerted upon the hero by mythical and familial paradigms (often conflated, for better or worse, through the Oedipal structures of Freudian psychology). Thus, while artistic representations of Alexander himself appear frequently throughout the film, we also see a series of sculptures, paintings, and mosaics that, in their presentation of familiar mythical archetypes, comment upon Alexander's role within Greek tradition—his struggle to bear the weight of the past and yet to surpass these cultural models, providing a new heroic paradigm for the future as "a visionary whose dreams, deeds and destiny echo through eternity."[5]

If Alexander as cultural commodity illustrates the forces of image creation and consumption, then historical cinema functions as the apogee of such a reciprocal relationship, feeding upon the images of the past in order to reanimate the iconic with sound and motion. Within Hollywood tradition, Stone stands as a director both celebrated and reviled for his readiness to manipulate and reframe visual history (as demonstrated by his use of genuine archival footage in *JFK*), blurring the boundaries between fiction and "authentic" evidence in service of his (often unorthodox) master narrative.[6] In this sense, *Alexander* is no exception. A self-conscious use of visual history is apparent from the film's opening credits, and echoed in its closing ones. In both, a series of ancient representations of Alexander, including a marble portrait bust and the Alexander Mosaic, frame the film with a claim for both historical authenticity and artistic status, hinting at complicity in the mythmaking that surrounds—and constitutes—Alexander's legacy.[7] Do such portraits reveal "signs of the soul," constituting a chain of authoritative visual testimonies of which Stone's film—with "Oxford historian Robin Lane Fox" as advisor—is the culmination? Or do they paradoxically demonstrate the impossibility of accessing and reanimating the "real" Alexander, a figure whose passions and motivations can only ever be imagined, who, as the Egyptian cartouche and Assyrian reliefs also depicted in the credits suggest, is given a multiplicity of forms by the many different cultures that lay claim to him? Throughout, the film plays with the contestability of historical narrative, switching between Ptolemy's partisan reminiscences (dictated in Alexandria, that repository of ancient learning) and vividly rendered flashbacks that often focalize through Alexander himself.[8] Shifting cinematic effects achieved through the use of colored filters and differently grained film stock—a typical Stone strategy—also contribute to the self-consciously "constructed" nature of each episode.[9] We should not forget that this is the director of *Natural Born Killers*, a master of editing and manipulation whose aim is seldom cinematic illusionism; rather, visual representations are part of a wider body of contested and problematized material that Stone openly appropriates and maneuvers in order to make his cinematic "case."[10] While his films are often fueled by a strong, even aggressive ideological focus, they tend to provoke debate rather than lay claim to the final word; in Stone's cinematic corpus we are continually reminded of both the power and the *subjectivity* of the visual.[11]

While the opening portraits of *Alexander* establish the film's concerns with authenticity, artistry, and multiculturalism, works of Greek art are given visual emphasis in several episodes, and appear throughout the cinematic narrative almost as a "guide to viewing." Recognizably Late Classical or Hellenistic sculptures, wall paintings, and mosaics feature prominently in the Alexandrian scenes: the library contains a monumental wall painting reminiscent of the Alexander Mosaic (a pastiche depicting the Macedonian troops fighting Indian elephants rather than Persians), as well as a wall-mounted version of the Mosaic itself (complete with Colin Farrell's features) and the Gnosis stag-hunt mosaic from Pella, which is often assumed (probably erroneously) to depict Alexander and Hephaestion.[12] These references to Alexander's military victories and the activities of the Macedonian court serve as visual counterparts to Ptolemy's narration; they are records of "eyewitness" experience that call upon details of warfare and hunting in order to support their allusions to Alexander's most important political and sexual relationships. While foreshadowing and reflecting events that reverberate through the film and testifying to Ptolemy's membership in Alexander's close circle of Macedonian nobles, these images also function as markers of authenticity within the set itself. In this sense they situate the film within a cinematic tradition of lavish reconstructions of the ancient world—dating back to the extravagant sets of Cecil B. DeMille—while simultaneously making a claim for the hard-won academic status of Stone's film, which was marketed as a carefully researched attempt to understand the "real" Alexander.[13]

However, like the portraits that frame the film as a whole, this use of images supposedly contemporary with the historical figure of Alexander raises an awkward conundrum, for issues of authenticity and artistry are particularly fraught with regard to the Alexander Mosaic.[14] Its relationship to a lost fourth-century "original," its dubious value as historical evidence for the battles of Issus or Gaugamela, and its find context within a Pompeian atrium house all problematize the image's reception, testifying, like Ptolemy's shaky narrative, to the precarious foundations of Alexander's place in history, and the desire of subsequent generations to replicate and consume his image. Works of art within the film, then, function as both cinematic signifiers (visual tropes that comment upon *Alexander*'s place within the "swords-and-sandals" tradition) and metahistorical ones (which claim authenticity while illustrating the difficulties inherent in accessing the "real" figure of Alexander).

Within the flashback scenes that show us Alexander in action, works of art act as clues to the themes and motivations underlying the cinematic narrative. While on one level they simply form part of the historically reconstructed backdrop and are seldom commented upon by actors within the film, on another they function as a form of visual commentary and interpretive aid for the knowledgeable viewer. Take, for example, the mural that decorates one wall of Olympias's bedroom in the Macedonian palace, the location for many scenes from Alexander's fraught family drama. Inspired, perhaps, by the fourth-century B.C.E. chariot-based compositions of Hades abducting Persephone in one of the royal tombs at Vergina, and the Pella mosaic of Theseus abducting Helen, the wall painting depicts Olympias's ancestor Achilles dragging the body of Hector behind his chariot at Troy.[15] Though the mural is never explicitly acknowledged by Olympias, pointed editing nevertheless uses the image to reinforce the epic fantasies with which she inspires her son, "my little Achilles." As an image of vengeance and heroism—and a proleptic image of doom—the Achilles fresco gives visual form to the queen's ambitions and explains what Stone calls Alexander's "bargain" with his mother, "the notion that, like Achilles, it was better to die young but achieve everlasting fame than to live a long life but win no glory."[16] In this sense, the image functions as a visual counterpart to the fact that Alexander sleeps with a copy of the *Iliad* beneath his pillow. This detail, picked up from Plutarch's *Life of Alexander,* is used as a taunt by Cassander before the battle of Gaugamela, and is revealed on the night of Alexander's wedding to Roxane, thus providing a leitmotif that reinforces the themes of heroic achievement and untimely death that drive Stone's mythically conceived narrative.[17]

While these artworks provide a form of silent commentary upon the cinematic action, one key scene from Alexander's childhood subjects a series of paintings to a detailed form of exegesis in which the relationship between their visual content and Alexander's enacting of mythical paradigms is privileged through detailed camerawork and explicit dialogue. This is the episode in the caves beneath the Macedonian royal palace, where Philip guides his son through a series of torch-lit chambers adorned with Archaic-style wall paintings depicting characters from Greek mythology—Achilles, Prometheus, Oedipus, Medea, and Heracles. Each represents a heroic or tragic archetype with a powerful bearing on both Alexander's place in history and his psychological motivations. This pedagogic scene, in which the father warns his son of future dangers, plays an important part in portraying the uneasy relationship between Philip and Alexander. On the one hand, it stresses their intimacy and shared ambition. On the other hand, it adumbrates the emotional upheaval of Alexander's attempts to escape his father's shadow. The images themselves provide an opportunity for the director to explain the mythic archetypes that structure the events of the film to an audience unfamiliar with Greek tragedy or epic poetry, and in this sense they have a double function as a pedagogic device. We view *with* Alexander, and are thus drawn into the web of legend and fantasy that shapes his engagement with the world. They also allow for a reflexive comment upon Alexander's own eventual transformation into a viewed and consumed object: excited by the glamour of Philip's tales, the youth cries, "One day I'll be on walls like these!" a comment that both resounds with dramatic irony (he will be more like these tragic figures than he might wish) and reminds us of his future iconic—and cinematic—status.

How relevant is each myth? As Plutarch tells us, Alexander claimed descent from both Heracles (on his father's side) and Achilles (on his mother's), a divine lineage to which Philip and Olympias each allude in the rape scene.[18] Like Heracles, Alexander has a noble purpose, will perform mighty deeds across the known world, and can look forward to apotheosis. Yet as Stone was keen to point out in a 2005 interview in *Cineaste,* Heracles was also a tragic figure, the frenzied murderer of his wife and children. The full relevance of the archetype will become clear only toward the end of the film, when Alexander violently rejects the pregnant Roxane.[19] In this sense, the images are anticipatory, encouraging the viewer to engage dynamically with the cinematic narrative, participating in the sequence of foreshadowings, echoes, and flashbacks with which Stone attempts to give the picture coherence.

The figure of Achilles, on the other hand, is integrated into the film at a far more fundamental level. He is a powerful factor in Olympias's attempts to shape her son's fortunes, omnipresent in the texts and images whose influence Alexander feels so keenly, and also, through Achilles' love for Patroclus, a heroic model for Alexander's relationship with Hephaestion. Stone has emphasized Achilles' significance for Alexander's early death, specifically referring to the speed with which both heroes follow their lovers to the grave—a motif that is echoed and foreshadowed on the eve of the battle of Gaugamela, when Alexander promises Hephaestion, "I will follow you down to the house of death."[20] In the cave scene, the young Alexander specifically states that Achilles is his "favorite" mythical figure because "he loved Patroclus and avenged his death."

While these two myths anticipate Alexander's exploits as warrior and lover, others develop the film's tragic and psychological themes through specific allusions to figures familiar from Attic tragedy— Medea, who murdered her children to spite her unfaithful husband, and Oedipus, who unwittingly killed his father and married his mother. The figure of an exotic, infanticidal mother echoes Olympias's mythologizing treatment of Alexander, for in encouraging him to enact the fate of Achilles, she is ultimately responsible for his early death ("My mother would never hurt me!" he protests to Philip, in a further ironic twist). It also gives force to the theory, espoused by Hephaestion toward the end of the film, that in forging ever further east, Alexander is trying to escape Olympias's far-reaching influence.[21] Yet, as the figure of Oedipus suggests, Alexander's relationship with his mother also has erotic undertones (brought to the surface by Angelina Jolie's eroticized performance). Philip states to Alexander that Oedipus's tragedy arose from "knowledge that came too late," anticipating, perhaps, his son's marriage to a foreign princess presented as a "pale reflection" of Olympias ("The myth becomes real!" Alexander claims, before seducing Roxane), and his symbolic murder of his father in the form of Cleitus.

Stone has insisted that the influence of Freud on his presentation of the Philip-Olympias-Alexander triangle is negligible and unproblematic: "I was amazed to find various detractors writing seriously about Freudian impulses when Freud clearly acknowledged that many of his theories were based on Greek myth."[22] Yet such protestations seem rather disingenuous and potentially anachronistic, given that most contemporary viewers (and certainly a multitude of critics) have interpreted the relationships the film explores through the lens of Freudian psychology, rather than Sophoclean and Euripidean tragedy.[23] However one chooses to interpret the layering of myth and psychoanalysis at work in these elements of the film, it is clear that the "family tragedy" represents the psychological heart of *Alexander*, and that the representation of a powerful, ambiguous maternal figure and a patricidal son in the Macedonian caves has a compelling influence on the viewer's understanding of the plot. While the Freudianisms may seem rather heavy-handed when spelt out literally, Stone's strategy of displacing them onto mythical archetypes presented in image form adds a certain subtlety to the narrative, and at least leaves the act of metaphorical interpretation (or pop psychology) to the viewer.

The most nuanced archetype that Alexander encounters in the cave is the image of Prometheus, eternally tormented by Zeus's eagle as punishment for bestowing on men the life-giving force of fire. The condemned Titan functions as a provocative analogy for Alexander himself, whose legacy can be interpreted as either a form of enlightened imperialism, the gift of "the dreamer who gave a new meaning to the world" (if we are to follow Stone's use of William Tarn and Ulrich Wilcken), or an aggressive, self-aggrandizing form of *Realpolitik*.[24] The representation of Prometheus's punishment provides a powerful leit-motif for Stone in the form of Zeus's eagle. This reappears throughout the film as both a real bird, soaring through the opening credits and appearing before the battle of Gaugamela as a favorable omen, and in various artistic representations. These take the form of visual echoes of the cave painting itself (presented as Alexander's hallucinations during moments of high emotional stress), and a stylized, embroidered hanging in the court of Babylon, which sways ominously above Alexander's deathbed in the opening and closing scenes. As the bird of Zeus, the eagle both symbolizes the god's favor toward his descendant and defines the limits of Alexander's achievements. It is a symbol of power: the divine power to which he lays claim through his heroic deeds; the earthly power he wrests from potentates such as Darius; and the patriarchal power that he struggles to emulate and surpass throughout his life. When viewed in relation to the fate of Prometheus, the eagle also represents punishment, alluding to the tragic paradigms that influenced Stone's structuring of the film, and Alexander's hubristic attempts to transcend the limitations of human achievement "as a new sort of man who would seek to match and challenge the ancient gods."[25] More than any other image within the cave scene, the eagle draws attention to the themes of epic heroism and tragic melodrama that shape the film's otherwise fragmented, episodic narrative, functioning as an important connecting device amid the collage-effect of competing visual forms.

    While the mythical figures depicted in the caves provide models for Alexander's psychological state and clues for the interpretation of his subsequent actions, they also function as an extra layer of visual representation within the film—static images within the moving spectacle of cinema that demand both the protagonists' and the viewers' attention. As an alternative (and yet closely related) medium to that of film, the painted image is loaded with a special semiotic urgency when it appears on screen, particularly when shot in closeup and presented as the focus of interpretative dialogue.[26] Stone's self-conscious use of different forms of media such as archival and neo-documentary footage and

black-and-white video sequences in earlier films (most notably *JFK*) is a
key element of his directorial strategy, and it is significant that the
pointedly symbolic use of images within the Macedonian caves is one
of the few places in *Alexander* where Stone completely departs from his
historical sources and plays freely with the materials available to him.
Whereas the other Greek or Macedonian works of art that appear in the
film are adaptations of known originals (such as the Alexander Mosaic)
or careful pastiches based on contemporary sources (such as the Achilles fresco in Olympias's bedchamber), the cave paintings are a work of
complete cinematic fiction. While they are depicted in a schematic linear
style familiar from early Archaic vase paintings, employing red and
black pigments and incised lines within silhouetted forms, the only image that has close stylistic and compositional parallels in the extant archaeological record is that of Prometheus and the eagle. A number of
Tyrrhenian amphorae dated to the second quarter of the sixth century
B.C.E. depict the liberation of Prometheus by Heracles, as Zeus's eagle
approaches his prey with a beady eye, sharp beak, and a powerful wing-
span.[27] Oedipus, however, is never depicted blinding himself prior to
the Hellenistic period, but is more commonly shown in Archaic and
Classical vase painting approaching the sphinx, while Medea is more
often depicted contemplating the murder of her sons than actually committing the fatal act (which was considered *beyond* the limits of representation in antiquity).[28]

To point out these anachronisms and inventions is not to criticize the
director and his team—as Robin Lane Fox happily declares in the commentary on the theatrical release DVD of *Alexander*, "This is a scene of
pure imagination from Oliver; there's absolutely no evidence at all that
there were cave paintings." The shift from "authentic" images to imaginary ones is a significant marker of the film's attempts to move beyond
the constraints of historical evidence and give a unique shape to the Alexander story. As potent symbols of heroism, violence, and loss, the images do a lot of interpretive "work," giving visual form to the mythico-
tragic themes already present in the Alexander corpus, and providing
simple, identifiable narratives for the viewer to follow through the film.
But the paintings also complicate the sense of "history" that *Alexander*
espouses. Even for an audience unschooled in classical art, their style is
recognizably different, more "primitive" than the paintings, sculptures,
and mosaics hitherto shown. Whereas naturalistic, classicizing forms
dominate Ptolemy's garden, the Alexandrian library, and the palace
at Pella, the style of the cave paintings beneath the Macedonian court

represents something far more ancient, expressed through linear, schematic forms full of motion and violence. While contemporary art-historical scholarship has long distanced itself from the language of primitivism in its analysis of Archaic styles, the association between non-naturalistic, abstracted forms and the "childlike" or "primitive" is still readily drawn in general culture, and it is not surprising that a Hollywood film should exploit this notion. Here the concept of primitivism is associated with the primeval, the mysterious and disturbing, with the central tragedy of human fate. It is telling that the only stylistically parallel image presented in the film is the rough-hewn wooden image of Phobos ("Fear"), to whom Alexander prays before the battle of Gaugamela, an abstracted face with large eyes that recalls the Medea image within the caves.[29] The frontality and disturbing gaze of both images are inspired by the apotropaic form of the Gorgon, suggesting an attempt to master primordial forces of fear and violence by controlling them in image form.[30]

The Archaic, then, functions as a stylistic signifier that draws attention to a deep sense of historical inevitability in Greek culture, a tragic sensibility embodied in the film by the figure of Philip, whose gnomic comments about the inexorable authority of mythic archetypes dominate his exegesis of the cave paintings. The images thus make the audience aware of the cultural paradigms shaping Alexander's destiny, while drawing attention to a certain intergenerational tension, expressed by the contrast between the drunken, disillusioned king and his ambitious, wide-eyed son.[31] In the events that follow, Alexander will transcend the limitations imposed on mortal achievement by the divine status quo, surpassing the success of his father. Yet he will be forced to suffer the consequences, repeatedly coming up against limiting factors in which the figure of Philip is ever present—as a ghost who takes the place of Cleitus in the murder scene, and in the form of the vengeful eagle, a symbol of patriarchal authority that marks the boundary between success and failure, life and death. The Archaic style of the paintings adumbrating this tension plays an important part in constructing the forces of history that inspire and constrain Alexander, and it is highly significant that the exegetical process in the caves is led predominantly by Philip, representative of what Stone calls the "Classical Greek pessimism" of an older era.[32]

In giving form to the concept of the "primitive," however, the paintings also suggest the power of the subconscious, particularly when linked to the later figure of Phobos. In this sense, they give visible form to the Freudian narrative that shapes Alexander's relationship with his parents and lovers. While the classicizing images adorning the court of Ptolemy signify reason, intellect, and culture, the Archaic forms beneath the palace of Macedon suggest the dark forces of anger and desire, the id that drives the family drama. In this sense, the leitmotif of the eagle not only symbolizes the authority of Zeus, but it also comes to function as a sign of the father, the "No" against which Alexander, like Prometheus, must struggle in order to define himself, and to which he must ultimately submit. There is, of course, cinematic precedent for the use of winged predators as oppressive signs demanding interpretation in relation to such psychological struggles. Hitchcock's film *The Birds* famously uses montages of flying birds as symbols of violence and rupture, interpreted by Slavoj Žižek as signs of the maternal superego, the irruption of repressed desires in the lives of the protagonists.[33] While Stone's directorial strategy is worlds apart from Hitchcock's, the web of association that *Alexander* weaves around the Archaic, the psychological, and the mythical through the use of these motifs seems to cry out for such modes of interpretation, especially given the divinatory power attributed to birds in antiquity and the ominous way in which the eagle is used to foreshadow or reflect Alexander's fate throughout the film.

Alexander makes a number of cinematic allusions, from the nod to *Citizen Kane* in the opening deathbed scene to the spectacular DeMille-style sets in Alexandria and Babylon. Besides these references to classic Hollywood cinema, the use of ancient art as a means of commenting upon the plot and structure of the film is also suggestive of various European productions of the 1960s—notably Jean-Luc Godard's *Le Mépris* (1963) and Federico Fellini's *Fellini-Satyricon* (1969). In a 2005 interview with *In Camera* magazine, Stone's director of photography, Rodrigo Prieto, discussed his use of differently colored filters in *Alexander,* commenting that Stone wanted the early scenes in the film to have "an 'innocent' look with primary colors when Alexander is a child in Macedon, similar to Jean-Luc Godard's *Le Mépris*. It meant I had to work without a filter, but the very fine grain of Eastman EXR 50D 5245 gave me a clean, transparent feel."[34] The pellucid, Mediterranean quality of the Macedonian scenes certainly shares a similar light and color palette with Godard's film, which explores the relationship between a scriptwriter and his wife on the set of a Cinecittà film of the *Odyssey,* directed by Fritz Lang (playing himself).[35] The film-within-a-film includes interpolated shots of various Greek sculptures (a bust of Athena, the Artemision "Poseidon," the Knidian Aphrodite). These images act as signs of "antiquity," seeming to offer some kind of visual commentary on Lang's project and the relationships within the broader narrative, in which the protagonists rapidly start to conform to the characters of the *Odyssey* itself. The "Contempt" of the title refers both to the tasteless commercialism of Hollywood (represented by the producer Prokosch, who wants a crowd-pleaser in which Lang's Penelope is unfaithful to Odysseus) and to the troubled relationship between the screenwriter and his wife. The "debasement of classical antiquity"[36] (represented by iconic sculptures of the Greek gods) by the American film industry is presented as parallel to the writer's debasement of his wife (played by the equally iconic Brigitte Bardot).[37]

It is ironic, then, that in alluding to *Le Mépris*, Stone is echoing a film that deliberately sets out to reject the very Hollywood blockbuster approach to the classical world of which *Alexander*, with its $150 million budget, is a prime example. Is the "innocent" look Stone requested of his cinematographer really to be taken as such, given Godard's notorious antipathy to Hollywood spectacle? Is it just one of many cinematic tropes that Stone appropriates and discards according to the shifting requirements of his project? Or is it, like his rhetorical rejection of Freud, a means of disarming potential critics? It is perhaps significant that in explaining his film-within-a-film to the Hollywood producer in *Le Mépris*, Lang claims that it represents "the fight of the individual against the circumstances, the eternal problem of the old Greeks. . . . It's a fight against the gods, the fight of Prometheus and Ulysses." The allusions to Lang's concept of the Greek mentality in *Alexander*, complete with the cave painting's representation of Prometheus, suggest that Stone is seeking to reconcile Hollywood spectacle with art-house production values. By including an homage to *Le Mépris*'s portrayal of the ancient Mediterranean, expressed through lighting effects and the gnomic use of Greek art, *Alexander* claims to be a different kind of epic film, distanced from the "sword-and-sandals" aesthetic of its rival blockbusters *Gladiator* (2000) and *Troy* (2004) by its nonlinear, episodic narrative (not unlike the *Odyssey*, in fact, although Alexander never gets home . . .) and its self-conscious academicism. Stone's response to his blockbuster's potential "debasement" of the Greek past is to incorporate nouvelle vague effects, such as an ostentatious use of colored filters (also used in the opening scene of *Le Mépris*), which express cinema's attempts to acknowledge the very *impossibility* of accessing antiquity. That he does so with such confidence expresses the chutzpah and highhandedness that has so often infuriated Stone's critics.

While *Le Mépris* explores the aesthetic and moral distance of the ancient world as embodied by its sculptural representations of the gods,
Fellini-Satyricon explores the rupture between antiquity and modernity
through extensive use of Roman painting.[38] Indeed, the most obvious
cinematic parallel to the cave painting scene in *Alexander* is the episode
in *Satyricon* that takes place between Encolpio and Eumolpo in the picture gallery. In each, an older man discusses a series of painted images
from "the past" with a younger one, offering a form of *paideia* (or "education") that problematizes the relationship between history (represented by the painted fragments) and the cinematic present. "I show
you masterpieces which could not be painted today," Eumolpo claims.
"The whole of civilization, shagged out."[39] Whereas the *Alexander* scene
presents the viewer with pastiche signs of the "Archaic," Fellini creates
his *pinacotheca* from an assorted jumble of reproduced painted fragments, including a still life from the House of the Stags in Herculaneum, the painted glass tondo of Septimius Severus and his family, and
mummy portraits from the Fayum. The power to educate through visual *exempla* is a key aspect of the original *pinacotheca* scene in Petronius's *Satyricon* (on which Fellini's film is based), which performs a
complex negotiation of the relationship between learning, erotic desire,
and myth. In this sense, the passage provides a perfect model for Stone's
Alexander, where visual mythical *exempla* are employed to explore the
sexual, familial, and cultural paradigms that shape and constrain the
film's protagonist.[40]

Important differences in the viewing of ancient art in each film, however, typify the awkward reconciliation that *Alexander* effects between
conventional Hollywood epic, nouvelle vague cinematic artistry, and an
academically informed use of history. In *Fellini-Satyricon*, images replicated from Roman paintings are juxtaposed at random, fragmented and
surreally presented with no obvious connection to the filmic narrative.
In this way they reflect the film's own eclectic, often tangential relationship to ancient culture, as well as the episodic, fragmented structure of
both the film and Petronius's text. As Fellini claimed, they represent
"the potsherds, crumbs and dust of a vanished world."[41] Maria Wyke
has commented that the film addresses "cinema's relation to classics
and cinema's value as a means of reconstructing and consuming ancient
Rome in the present," a conundrum that is given striking visual form in
the final frame of *Satyricon*, when the dialogue breaks off (like Petronius's text) in mid-sentence, and Encolpio's face fades into that of a
Roman fresco.[42] The film's ending thus problematizes the ambiguous

status of the cinematic image, suggesting that it is just another form of defamiliarized, fragmented "representation," distanced from both the lost reality of antiquity *and* the world of the contemporary viewer.[43]

As suggested above, Stone's *Alexander* also addresses the irrevocability of the past and the subjectivity of the visual. The presentation of Archaic paintings within the cave scene employs flickering light, shifting camera angles, and choppy editing, so that we are never given a lingering view of the images displayed, but are dependent for our understanding on Philip's highly personal exegesis. One might also view the paintings according to Plato's allegory of mimesis, in which man's failure to perceive the forms of "truth" is compared to the viewing of illusory, projected images on a cave wall—a powerful metaphor for the cinema itself. In this sense, the mythical archetypes depicted function as metaphors through which we might try to understand the historical figure of Alexander, but ultimately illustrate our distance from him, so acting as a reflexive comment on the status of the film.

However, the thematic use of mythical leitmotifs throughout *Alexander* and the pointed interpretation of these metaphors by Philip (and, to a lesser extent, Olympias, Ptolemy, and Hephaestion) give the film a psychological and narrative coherence that *Fellini-Satyricon* disavows. While acknowledging the influence of mythic narratives and the subjectivizing force of history upon our understanding of Alexander, the images are also designed to *explain,* rather than problematize, the function of such devices within the film, in a far less elusive manner than Godard's and Fellini's surreal juxtapositions. This paradox goes some way toward accounting for the peculiar nature of *Alexander,* and, perhaps, its negative critical response. For Stone's nod to European art-house explorations of the relationship between modernity and antiquity stands cheek by jowl with the big-budget drama of Hollywood spectacle. On the one hand, a film intended for a mass audience calls for narrative comprehensibility, an attempt to give shape to the necessarily episodic nature of the biopic, to the mess of "history." Yet, on the other hand, Stone's awareness of the contestability of historical truth and the subjective nature of his sources means he must acknowledge the necessary distance that prevails between the film and its subject. *Alexander* purports to break down generic boundaries, demonstrating how, in the twenty-first century, the old barriers between Hollywood and Europe (or between studio and independent films) have been broken down— or, perhaps, how Hollywood has voraciously absorbed any cinematic styles and gestures originally conceived in opposition to it.

Such a bold claim is, perhaps, particularly appropriate for a film about an individual who surpassed the achievements of his predecessors and attempted to break down cultural barriers and incorporate the forces of the Other into his grandiose worldview. Certainly, critics were not slow to find parallels between the director and his subject. But Stone's attempt to unify different cinematic forms creates a veneer of unity that, like Alexander's empire, collapses all too easily under the strain of artistic and historical contradictions. And just as debate continues to rage over the nature of Alexander's own achievements (enlightened imperialist or savage tyrant?), so it will continue to surround the works of Stone himself. Roger Ebert was representative of the critical response to *Alexander* (though more sympathetic than some) in his description of it as "an ambitious and sincere film that fails to find a focus for its elusive subject."[44] The question remains: is that *Alexander's* predicament, or its raison d'être?

Notes

1. On Plutarch's *Life of Alexander* see Wardman 1955; Hamilton 1969, esp. xxxvii–xliii; Hammond 1993, esp. 5–6, 163–67; and Prandi 2000. Translation from *Life of Alexander*, in Plutarch, *Plutarch's Lives*, tr. Bernadotte Perrin, Loeb Classical Library, 11 vols. (1919, repr., London, 1994), 7:225.

2. On the material culture of Alexander's Macedon, see Yalouris, Andronikos, Rhomiopoulou et al. 1980; on the dissemination of Alexander's image in the Hellenistic and Roman world, see Stewart 1993; Cohen 1997.

3. Plutarch's *Life of Alexander* and Pliny's *Natural History*, for instance, include several scenes in which Alexander views paintings, sculptures, and engraved gems (Plut. *Alex.* 37.3, 39.5), commissions works of art, engages with artists, and comments upon their creative enterprise (Plut. *Alex.* 4.1–2; Plin. *HN* 35.85–87). Significantly, we know the names of his court artists, the sculptor Lysippus (Plut. *De Alex. fort.* 2.2.3 = *Mor.* 335A–B; *Alex.* 4.1), the painter Apelles (Plin. *HN* 35.85–87), and the gem-carver Pyrgoteles (Plin. *HN* 37.8).

4. See Crowdus 2005, where the film critic claims that *Alexander is* "more of a character portrait than a historical chronicle" (13), functioning as a form of "psychohistory" (17). As Stone himself has claimed, his films are intended "first and foremost to be dramas about individuals in personal struggles" (12). On the Hollywood biopic, see Custen 1992.

5. Warner Bros. promotional material, Director's Cut DVD. See http://alexanderthemovie.warnerbros.com. My discussion is based on the Director's Cut DVD unless otherwise noted.

6. See the essays collected in Kunz 1997, addressing Stone's "rhetorical" use of history. On the controversy over *JFK*, see the annotated screenplay (Stone and

Sklar 1992), and discussions by Romanowski 1993; Mackey-Kallis 1996, 33–57; Riordan 1996; and, for a summary, Lavington 2004, 153–74.

7. Fiona Greenland kindly informs me that the bust is adapted from a cast in the Ashmolean Museum Cast Gallery, based on a marble sculpture in the British Museum originally from Alexandria.

8. On the role played by the Ptolemies in constructing the history of Alexander, see Mossé 2004, 168–70.

9. On the effects created by different film stocks and colored filters in *Alexander*, see Prieto 2005.

10. See Kunz 1997, xix, on Stone's use of grainy stock, flashback and fantasy sequences, and hyperkinetic editing; he is "a director who is ready to try any cinematic resource available to convey his vision with authority."

11. See Green 1997 on *Natural Born Killers*, where he argues that Stone's body of work challenges any notion of history as authoritative. Lavington (2004, 268) comments, "The story of Alexander seems tailor-made for Stone—a corpus of agreed facts with many grey areas, leaving themselves open to subjective interpretation."

12. On the Alexander Mosaic, see Cohen 1997; Moreno 2001. On the Pella mosaics, see Robertson 1982; Salzmann 1982; Cohen 1997, 62–63.

13. On DeMille's cinematic reconstructions of antiquity, see Wyke 1997, esp. 132–37.

14. On the original painting's possible attribution to the artist "Helen of Egypt," see Cohen 1997, 59.

15. See Andronikos 1994; Cohen 1997, pl. VIIIb.

16. Crowdus 2005, 13. How appropriate for Jolie that Achilles was played in *Troy* (also released in 2004) by her future partner, Brad Pitt.

17. Plut. *Alex.* 8.2. On the mythologizing of Alexander both in his lifetime and by later historians, see Carlsen et al. 1993; Bosworth and Baynham 2000; Mossé 2004, 167–209.

18. Plut. *Alex.* 2.1.

19. Crowdus 2005, 20, quoting Stone: "Alexander, by turning his back on his son through Roxane, is metaphorically doing the same thing."

20. Ibid., 19: Stone claimed that "in following Hephaestion so closely to his death, Alexander kept the vow Achilles made in *The Iliad*."

21. As Philip states prophetically in the cave scene, "It is never easy to escape our mothers, Alexander."

22. Crowdus 2005, 16. As many reviewers have acknowledged, the Freudianisms are hard to ignore, especially given the narrative prominence of the "primal scene" in which the boy Alexander watches Philip try to rape his mother, an event he echoes in his treatment of Roxane on his own wedding night. As Breskin states in an interview with Stone (1997, 37–42), the director has been frequently criticized for his treatment of women as stereotypes and

plot devices rather than sympathetic or fully rounded characters. For archived press reviews of *Alexander*, see http://www.imdb.com/title/tt0346491/external reviews.

23. Of the many mentions of Freud in reviews of *Alexander*'s theatrical release, see for example McCarthy 2004; Thomson 2004; and Ansen 2004.

24. See Crowdus 2005, 14-15, quoting Stone and mentioning his admiration for Tarn (1948) and Wilcken (1932).

25. Crowdus 2005, 19 (quoting Stone).

26. On painting in film, see Bazin 2003 (orig. 1967); Walker 1993.

27. See *LIMC* 7.1:541-42, s.v. Prometheus, nos. 67-69 (=*ABV* 97.28-30).

28. See *LIMC* 7.1:3-8, s.v. Oidipous: nos. 10-72 depict Oedipus and the Sphinx; only a small number of extant representations, dating from the late fourth century B.C.E. to the third century C.E., depict him as blinded (nos. 82-88). On Medea contemplating the murder of her sons in the fourth-century B.C.E. painter Timanthes' famous version, see, e.g., *Greek Anthology* 16.135-43, with Bergmann 1996.

29. While there are very few surviving representations of Phobos in Greek culture (see *LIMC* 7.1:393-94, s.v. Phobos), allusions to the personification in literary contexts often refer to its use as a shield device, suggesting a visual parallel with *gorgoneia* (see Hes. *Theog.* 933-34, Paus. 5.9.14, on the chest of Kypselos).

30. On the Gorgon, see Mack 2002.

31. As Philip says to the young Alexander in this scene, "No man, no woman can be too powerful or too beautiful without disaster befalling them. . . . The glory they give, in the end they take away."

32. Crowdus 2005, 19 (quoting Stone).

33. Žižek 1991. See also Samuels 1997; Morris 2000.

34. Prieto 2005. Prieto also claimed to have used the whole range of Kodak film: "I was trying for something different for each scene to enhance the sense of travel and passage of time and, thanks to these different negatives, I was able to modify the texture, grain and contrast continuously."

35. On *Le Mépris*, see Goldmann 1976, 74-78; Marie 1986; Aumont 1990; Rakovsky, Zimmer, and Lefèvre 1991; Wyke 1997, 183-84. All quotations are from the 2003 Momentum Pictures World Cinema Collection DVD release.

36. Wyke 1997, 184.

37. Significantly, at several points in the film Bardot's character studies an Italian collection of erotic paintings from Pompeii, given to the couple by the American producer Prokosch: just as the frescoes themselves have been stripped from their context and commodified in book form as a form of pornography, so Bardot's image had become an object of ocular possession and exchange (a process that Godard ridicules in the extended opening scene, which reduces Bardot's body to a series of "part objects" in a parody of Hollywood's cinematic scopophilia). See Coates 1998; Salama 2005.

38. On *Fellini-Satyricon,* see Fellini 1978; Moravia 1978; Wyke 1997, 188–92.
39. Eumolpo continues: "You are not to wonder that the art of painting is dead, young man. We all of us see more beauty in a bag of gold—I do—than all the work of Apelles or Phidias." Translated subtitles from the 2004 MGM DVD release.
40. On the *pinacotheca* scene in Petronius's text, see Elsner 1993.
41. Fellini 1978, 17. In his preface to *Satyricon,* 18–19, Fellini claimed that his cinematic procedure evoked antiquity "not through the fruit of a bookish, scholastic documentation, a literal fidelity to the text, but rather in the way an archaeologist reconstructs something alluding to the form of an amphora or a statue from a few potsherds. Our film, through the fragmentary recurrence of its episodes, should restore the image of a vanished world without completing it, as if those characters, those habits, those milieux were summoned for us in a trance, recalled from their silence by the mystic ritual of a séance."
42. Wyke 1997, 188.
43. As claimed by Moravia, 1978, 164, who, incidentally, also wrote the novel on which Godard's *Le Mépris* is based.
44. Ebert 2004.

References

Andronikos, M. 1994. *Vergina II: The Tomb of Persephone.* Athens.
Ansen, David. 2004. "Not So Great: Oliver Stone's 'Alexander' Will Conscript You for a Long Forced March." *Newsweek,* November 29, 60.
Aumont, J. 1990. "The Fall of the Gods: Jean-Luc Godard's *Le Mépris* (1963)." In *French Film: Texts and Contexts,* ed. S. Hayward and G. Vincendeau, 217–29. London.
Bazin, A. 2003. "Painting and Cinema." In *The Visual Turn: Classical Film Theory and Art History,* ed. A. Dalle Vacche, 221–25. New Brunswick, NJ.
Bergmann, B. 1996. "The Pregnant Moment: Tragic Wives in the Roman Interior." In *Sexuality in Ancient Art: Near East, Egypt, Greece, and Italy,* ed. N. B. Kampen, 199–218. New York.
Bondanella, P., ed. 1978. *Federico Fellini: Essays in Criticism.* New York.
Bosworth, A. B., and E. Baynham, eds. 2000. *Alexander the Great in Fact and Fiction.* Oxford.
Breskin, D. 1997. "Oliver Stone: An Interview with the Director." In *The Films of Oliver Stone,* ed. D. Kunz, 3–64. Lanham, MD.
Carlsen, J., et al. 1993. *Alexander the Great: Reality and Myth.* Rome.
Coates, P. 1998. "*Le Mépris*: Women, Statues, Gods." *Film Criticism* 22: 38–49.
Cohen, A. 1997. *The Alexander Mosaic: Stories of Victory and Defeat.* Cambridge.
Crowdus, G. 2005. "Dramatizing Issues That Historians Don't Address: An Interview with Oliver Stone." *Cineaste* 30 (Spring): 12–23.

Custen, G. F. 1992. *Bio/Pics: How Hollywood Constructed Public History.* New Brunswick, NJ.

Ebert, Roger. 2004. Review of *Alexander. Chicago Sun-Times,* November 24.

Elsner, J. 1993. "The Seductions of Art: Encolpius and Eumolpus in a Neronian Picture Gallery." *Proceedings of the Cambridge Philological Society* 39: 30–47.

Fellini, F. 1978. "Preface to *Satyricon.*" In *Federico Fellini: Essays in Criticism,* ed. P. Bondanella, 16–19. (Orig. pub. in *Fellini's Satyricon by Federico Fellini,* ed. D. Zanelli, tr. E. Walter, 43–46. New York, 1970.)

Goldmann, A. 1976. "Deserts of Belief: Bunuel—Pasolini—Godard." *Australian Journal of Screen Theory* 1:67–78.

Green, D. 1997. "*Natural Born Killers* and American Decline." In *The Films of Oliver Stone,* ed. D. Kunz, 259–71. Lanham, MD.

Hamilton, J. R. 1969. *Plutarch: Alexander: A Commentary.* Oxford.

Hammond, N. G. L. 1993. *Sources for Alexander the Great: An Analysis of Plutarch's Life and Arrian's Anabasis Alexandrou.* Cambridge.

Kunz, D., ed. 1997. *The Films of Oliver Stone.* Lanham, MD.

Lavington, S. 2004. *Oliver Stone.* London.

Mack, R. 2002. "Facing Down Medusa (An Aetiology of the Gaze)." *Art History* 25:571–604.

Mackey-Kallis, S. 1996. *Oliver Stone's America: "Dreaming the Myth Outward."* Boulder, CO.

Marie, M. 1986. "Un monde qui s'accorde à nos désirs." *Revue Belge du Cinéma* 15:25–36.

McCarthy, Todd. 2004. "An Enervating Epic." *Variety,* November 22, 45–47.

Moravia, A. 1978. "Dreaming up Petronius." Tr. Raymond Rosenthal. In *Federico Fellini: Essays in Criticism,* ed. P. Bondanella, 161–68. (Orig. pub. in *New York Review of Books,* March 26, 1970, 40–42.)

Moreno, P. 2001. *Apelles: The Alexander Mosaic.* Tr. David Stanton. Milan.

Morris, C. D. 2000. "Reading the Birds and *The Birds.*" *Literature Film Quarterly* 28:250–58.

Mossé, C. 2004. *Alexander: Destiny and Myth.* Tr. J. Lloyd. Edinburgh.

Perrin, Bernadotte, tr. 1919. *Life of Alexander.* In Plutarch, *Plutarch's Lives,* vol. 7. 11 vols. Loeb Classical Library. (Repr., London, 1994.)

Prandi, L. 2000. "l'Alessandro di Plutarco." In *Rhetorical Theory and Praxis in Plutarch,* ed. L. Van der Stockt. Louvain and Namur.

Prieto, Rodrigo. 2005. "A Life of Epic Proportions: Alexander the Great." *In Camera,* January, 10–11.

Rakovsky, A., J. Zimmer, and R. Lefèvre. 1991. "Sur *Le Mépris* de Jean-Luc Godard." *La Revue du Cinéma* 469:54–66.

Riordan, J. 1996. *Stone: The Controversies, Excesses and Exploits of a Radical Filmmaker.* London.

Robertson, M. 1982. "Early Greek Mosaic." In *Macedonia and Greece in Late Classical and Early Hellenistic Times*, ed. B. Barr-Sharrar and E. N. Borza, 241–49. Studies in the History of Art 10. Washington, DC.

Romanowski, W. D. 1993. "Oliver Stone's *JFK*: Commercial Film-making, Cultural History, and Conflict." *Journal of Popular Film and Television* 21, no. 2 (Summer): 63–71.

Salama, M. 2005. "Is the Visual Essentially Pornographic? The Politics of the Body in Godard's *Le Mépris* and *Weekend*." *Critical Sense* 13, no. 1: 41–66.

Salzmann, D. 1982. *Untersuchungen zu den antiken Kieselmosaiken von den Anfängen bis zum Beginn der Tesseratechnik. Archäologische Forsuchungen* 10. Berlin.

Samuels, R. 1997. *Hitchcock's Bi-Textuality: Lacan, Feminisms, and Queer Theory*. Albany, NY.

Stewart, A. F. 1993. *Faces of Power: Alexander's Image and Hellenistic Politics*. Berkeley.

Stone, O., and Z. Sklar. 1992. *JFK: The Book of the Film*. New York.

Tarn, W. 1948. *Alexander the Great*. 2 vols. Cambridge.

Thomson, Desson. 2004. "*Alexander*, The Not-So-Great." *Washington Post*, November 26.

Walker, J. A. 1993. *Art and Artists on Screen*. Manchester.

Wardman, A. E. 1955. "Plutarch and Alexander." *Classical Quarterly* n.s. 5:96–107.

Wilcken, U. 1932. *Alexander the Great*. Tr. G. C. Richards. London.

Wyke, M. 1997. *Projecting the Past: Ancient Rome, Cinema and History*. London.

Yalouris, N., M. Andronikos, K. Rhomiopoulou et al. 1980. *The Search for Alexander*. New York.

Žižek, S. 1991. *Looking Awry: An Introduction to Jacques Lacan through Popular Culture*. Cambridge, MA.

Blockbuster!

Museum Responses to Alexander the Great

JOHN F. CHERRY

Alexander as Blockbuster

"*Blockbuster*: a term derived from the popular name of the huge German bombs used in World War II to blast large sections of a city; in the museum sense, it refers to a revolutionary, powerful exhibition" (Dean 1996, 159). Judged by all the usual measures, Oliver Stone's film *Alexander* falls into the "blockbuster" category. As described in considerable detail by Robin Lane Fox in *The Making of Alexander* (2004), it entailed fifteen years of development and planning, a production budget of $160 million, and a Warner Bros. publicity campaign that spent $35 million in the United States alone. The construction of numerous lavish soundstages; outdoor, on-location filming in exotic locales (Morocco and Thailand); extended battle scenes on a vast scale involving thousands of extras and animals; a panoply of big-name Hollywood actors and actresses; a three-time Academy Award–winning director in overall charge—these things all add up to a blockbuster. The usual cycle of hype and anticipation led up to the U.S. opening on November 24, 2004, followed by the red-carpet celebrity premiere, the keen scrutiny of ticket sales during the opening weeks, and the gleeful tabulation of critical responses (some positive, but mostly fairly negative).[1] And after the general release, the predictable marketing followups: posters, T-shirts, the official guide to the movie, the release on DVD, the Director's Cut DVD, and the like.

Blockbusters aim for maximum publicity in order to attract the maximum attendance, which is necessary to recoup the staggering costs of production. The very size of the anticipated viewing audience— augmented by those who, while not themselves paying to watch the movie, are nonetheless aware of a major cinematic event—affords enhanced commercial opportunities, and this can generate some significant and intriguing responses. One example must suffice here: the apparent impact of Stone's *Alexander* on book publishing in related fields.

Table 1 presents summary information, for the period from 2002 to 2006 (bracketing the movie's release in 2004), about the numbers of published books of direct relevance to Alexander the Great. The data come from searches of the listings provided by Amazon.com and similar sources, and while hardly a scientific sample or even an exhaustive one, they provide a reasonably representative overview of changes during the period in question. The most obvious feature is the three- or fourfold increase in the total of books published in 2004, as compared with those in 2002 and 2003, with further growth by 50 percent in 2005. Since *Alexander* opened in the United States late in 2004 (on Thanksgiving weekend), it can be assumed that the majority of the books appearing in 2004 were planned specifically to take advantage of an anticipated spike of interest in all things to do with Alexander.

Many of these books are reprints that reflect the publishers' desire to squeeze additional revenue from existing titles in their lists: the impetus is most transparent in the case of Robin Lane Fox's standard study *Alexander the Great* (1973), re-released in the month prior to *Alexander*'s opening and advertised as an "unofficial movie tie-in," with an image from the movie and an endorsement by its director on the cover. A few newly written scholarly studies and biographies certainly make fresh contributions to the literature (e.g., Cartledge 2004; Rogers 2004), but the majority of publications are hackneyed retellings of Alexander's expedition that offer little that is new. Most of the dozen new books written for children or the educational market appear to be strategically timed additions to ongoing series ("Dead Famous," "Signature Lives," "Heroes and Villains," "Kids Who Ruled," etc.), as do some of those aimed at adult readers ("Weekend Biographies," "Great Empires of the Past," "Ancient Lives," "Rulers of the Ancient World," etc.). Some books intended for a general readership, not surprisingly, play up

Table 1. Published Books Relating to Alexander the Great, 2002–2006

Type of Book	2002	2003	2004	2005	2006
Scholarly studies	4	44	99	7	11
Biographies, historical accounts, and other writings for the general reader	0	1	9	11	5
Fiction (including historical novels, mysteries, fantasy)	3	1	5	6	2
Children's books	1	0	1	7	4
Reprints (facsimiles, paperback and revised editions)	1	1	7	15	4
Totals	**9**	**7**	**31**	**46**	**26**

Primary source of data: Amazon.com.

Note: Figures for 2006 include titles of books advertised as forthcoming in 2006, but not yet published at the time of writing (May 2006).

themes of likely wide appeal: sex (Chugg 2006), the "mystery" of Alexander's death (Doherty 2004; Phillips 2005), the puzzle of his lost tomb (Chugg 2004; Saunders 2006), military history (Heckel 2003; Fuller 2004; Lonsdale 2004; Warry 2005; Lonsdale 2006; Heckel and Hook 2006), or—most bizarre of all—Alexander as a model for modern business strategists (Figueira et al. 2001; Bose 2003; Kurke 2004).

Overall, one sees from this brief review of recent publishing history an almost unseemly rush into print of more than one hundred Alexander books since 2004, a good many of them tired-looking retreads, and the majority probably conceived in response to the chance for good sales generated by interest in a cinematic epic set in the ancient world. It serves no purpose to kick against the pricks of market forces—and, if we are to be fair, the last such chance to cash in on Alexander at the movies (Robert Rossen's *Alexander the Great*, 1956 was half a century ago, in an age entirely innocent of the internet or DVDs). My point is not to pass judgment but rather to emphasize that blockbusters evidently do have consequences.[2]

In this chapter my intention is to contribute to our understanding of the varied responses to Alexander by examining how he has been presented in museum settings—specifically, in the surprising number of large-scale, international loan exhibitions on this subject that have been mounted in the course of the past quarter-century. These too can be characterized as blockbusters. Tracing the emergence of this form of display in recent decades will provide some context for subsequent discussion of the Alexander exhibitions themselves.

The Museum Blockbuster: A Little History

The term "blockbuster" has a hazy etymology, at least as applied to entertainment. It may, as noted above, refer to the high-explosive aerial bombs capable of destroying whole city blocks (thus, the movie "hit" and the box-office "bomb"); equally, it may derive from theater slang for a play successful enough to drive competing theaters on the same block out of business, or to generate crowds that wind around several city blocks. The word has come to be applied more loosely to any form of production (whether a play, film, novel, computer game, or even a drug) that is costly to create, very popular, and financially successful. In the world of Hollywood, a movie that exceeds the threshold of $100 million in sales is considered a blockbuster[3]—although one that includes famous stars and captures the public attention is (oddly) accorded the same status, even if it is actually a financial failure.

At the heart of the notion of a blockbuster lies the deliberate creation of an "event," funded on an unusual scale, much anticipated in the media and by the public, and explicitly designed to draw massive crowds and generate revenue. (Albert Elsen [1986, 24] playfully puts it this way: "The blockbuster can be defined as a large-scale loan exhibition which people who normally don't go to museums will stand in line for hours to see.") It was in the 1970s that museums in North America first embraced the possibilities of this form of cultural production, although it was to some extent prefigured by earlier centennial exhibits and world's fairs, as well as by certain individually very popular shows.[4] Many (e.g., Conforti 1986; Spear 1986, 358) would trace the motivation for, and the history of, museum blockbusters to the decade (1966–77) of Thomas Hoving's directorship at the Metropolitan Museum of Art (see Hoving 1993). It was then, certainly, that sophisticated marketing techniques were introduced to draw upon broad-based public interest in large-scale temporary art exhibitions with mass appeal—most notably "Treasures of Tutankhamun" (or, more popularly, "King Tut"), on display in North America from 1976 to 1979. This exhibition, which more than a million people visited during its run at the Metropolitan Museum in 1978–79, resulted in unprecedented revenues for the various art museums of a six-museum consortium that hosted the show. Of the Metropolitan Museum's $4.5 million income from admissions in 1979, $2.8 million resulted from the Tutankhamun exhibition alone, and 40 percent of its total income came from merchandising; no less than $17.4 million was realized by sales at these six museums of "official" King Tut reproductions. As the National Gallery of Art's website notes:

> This exhibition established the term "blockbuster." A combination of the age-old fascination with ancient Egypt, the legendary allure of gold and precious stones, and the funeral trappings of the boy-king created an immense popular response. Visitors waited up to 8 hours before the building opened to view the exhibition. At times the line completely encircled the West Building.[5]

Other museums, inevitably, were quick to jump onto the bandwagon, especially at a time of growing constraints on museum operating budgets but also increased enthusiasm for corporate, foundation, and governmental sponsorship of popular exhibitions. It was the start of what Tom Csaszar (1996–97) has dubbed "the spectacular, record-breaking, sold-out, smash-hit, blockbuster supershow!" After King Tut, the Met presented exhibitions on "The Vatican Collections" (1983), "Van Gogh" (1986), "Mexico: Splendors of Thirty Centuries" (1990), "Seurat" (1991), and "The Origins of Impressionism" (1994). All attracted more than half a million visitors, as did shows on Ansel Adams (1985–86) and Andrew Wyeth (1987) at the National Gallery, which exceeded even these figures with audiences of 1,053,223 for its Auguste Rodin show (1981–82) and 990,474 for "Treasure Houses of Britain" (1985–86). Attendance records were set and then broken by successive blockbuster-style exhibitions in North America and Europe. Boston's Museum of Fine Arts drew 432,000 visitors to its 1978 Pompeii exhibit, and exceeded that mark with shows of works by Renoir (1985–86) and Monet (1990). Exceptional crowds flocked to the Art Institute of Chicago to view Monet displays not once, but three times (in 1975, 1990, and 1995), as well as shows on the Vatican treasures, Alexander the Great, Gauguin, Renoir, and Georgia O'Keefe. The Philadelphia Museum of Art joined the game with its 1970 Van Gogh exhibit (410,000 visitors), followed by shows on Chagall, Pissarro, Picasso, the Annenberg Collection, the Barnes Collection, and Cézanne (777,800 visitors, in

1995). Underpinning these shows and the audiences they attracted was, of course, the commercial sponsorship that made them possible. As Brian Wallis (1986, 28) pointed out, the growth of corporate support for blockbusters closely coincided with the expansion of multinational corporations, just a handful of which (notably IBM, Exxon, Philip Morris, and Mobil) actually account for a large proportion of all such sponsorships. Growth in this sector was spectacular during this period, with American corporate sponsorship of the arts growing from just $22 million in 1967 to almost $1 billion two decades later.

There has been considerable discussion, and not a little gnashing of teeth, among museum professionals about the desirability of the museum blockbuster event, even while they recognize it as a cultural and commercial development that is probably irreversible (see, e.g., Elsen 1986; Spear 1986; Freedberg et al. 1987; Csaszar 1996–97). Museum directors generally embrace the publicity their institutions receive, the enhanced attendance figures, the influx of sponsorship monies they would not otherwise be able to attract, and the revenues generated by auxiliary activities (sales of lavish catalogues and tie-in merchandise, tickets to lectures and other social activities, restaurant services, parking, etc.) that help keep their accounts in the black. On the other hand, the huge crowds at sold-out shows and the "mechanization" of exhibition attendance—admission by timed tickets only, heavy reliance on rented audio guides, strictly enforced pedestrian traffic flow through the exhibit (leading inexorably to the museum shop)—are hardly conducive to ideal viewing conditions and a fully satisfactory museum experience for visitors.[6] Curatorial staff tend to lament the constant pressures they face in putting together blockbuster installations, with consequent neglect of long-term needs for the conservation, study, display, and publication of the permanent collections in their museums.

These are all important pragmatic considerations, but less important than the degree to which any blockbuster exhibition is driven by marketing considerations, rather than intellectual coherence and historical value. Corporate or private donors provide substantial funding in order to have their name linked prominently with a prestigious museum on brochures, posters, catalogues, even on the sides of buses. To become known as a cultural sponsor through underwriting of this sort can generate valuable positive publicity that is worth the cost to the donor, and much appreciated by the museum and by local businesses.

Yet, as with aristocratic patrons of the arts in bygone centuries, generosity usually comes with strings attached. One may wonder (although it is often difficult to ascertain) whether the advertising and corporate subventions that make the production of these large exhibitions possible have had any direct influence on what is exhibited and what is written about it. Are viewpoints or subjects offensive to powerful groups censored, either through deliberate suppression or through failure to attract the necessary sponsorships (Haacke 1984)? Elsen (1986: 27) notes:

> The type of blockbuster that genuinely worries me, and which I have reservations about supporting, is the one that is motivated by politics. In my opinion shows like "Tutankhamun" and "Irish Treasures" were attempts to create favorable American public opinion towards specific countries or ethnic groups. The "Irish Treasures" show temporarily diverted public attention from the civil strife in Northern Ireland; Tut did more for Egypt after he was dead than while alive, and in my judgment his exhibition did much to change American public opinion about Sadat and Egypt. I believe, despite denials, that certain major museums are encouraged, if not used, by the State Department to host exhibitions that in its judgment are in line with current U.S. foreign policy.

As we will see below, such concerns become particularly delicate when large and prestigious international loans require the consent of foreign governments, as well as funding through their ministries of culture or government-owned banks. There is the opportunity not only for nations to advertise and promote their cultural heritage, but also for them to "sell" a particular perspective on themselves—Alexander the Great, for example, as a quintessential and exclusive part of the cultural heritage that defines Greek nationhood. Blockbusters, in short, become bound up in a peculiar form of cultural diplomacy intended to promote international goodwill—and, of course, commerce (Haacke 1984; Wallis 1986, 1994).

The Search for Alexander Exhibition(s)

We may now return to Alexander. The ancients liked to debate whether his stupendous achievements should be ascribed to ability and personality or merely to dumb luck (as in Plutarch's early rhetorical work *De virtute aut fortuna Alexandri*). No matter which argument is most persuasive, luck has certainly played a big role in Alexander's modern museum career. As noted above, the blockbuster emerged as a new phenomenon in the museums of North America and western Europe in the late 1970s, heralded—so far as the ancient world is concerned—by the

"Treasures of Tutankhamun" (1976–79) and "Pompeii" (1976–78) exhibitions in New York, Boston, and London. And it was during this very
period—to be precise, at 3 p.m. "on Tuesday, November 8, 1977, the day
on which the Greek Orthodox Church celebrates the feast-day of the
archangels Michael and Gabriel," as the excavator, Manolis Andronikos, melodramatically put it (1980, 32)—that Tomb II, the so-called
Royal Tomb, allegedly that of Alexander's father, Philip II, was opened
in the Great Tumulus of Vergina in Greek Macedonia. Astonishingly,
within less than three years, the fruits of these excavations formed the
highlight of a blockbuster loan exhibition, "The Search for Alexander"
(SFA), which traveled between a consortium of seven museums in the
United States and Canada on a three-year tour from November 1980
until July 1983 (see table 2).

As we now know from many subsequent examples, the central focus
of nearly all archaeological blockbusters has been the exhibition of
treasure from distant epochs and faraway places. Some of that is captured in the title of the first of two shows quickly assembled in Thessaloniki in the summers of 1978 and 1980 in order to capitalize on the new
discoveries at Vergina: "The Treasures of Ancient Macedonia: History
and Legend in Art." Although they included a good many of the same
pieces included in SFA, the name of Alexander himself was not in-
voked. Doing so was evidently an entrepreneurial decision taken to
maximize the breadth and popularity of the exhibition created for the
North American tour. A prosaic description of that show's content
might have been "Art and Architecture in the Late Fourth Century and
Hellenistic Period in Macedonia and the Rest of Greece"—the title, in
fact, of a November 1980 symposium held in the National Gallery of
Art in Washington, DC, in conjunction with SFA (Barr-Sharrar and
Borza 1982)—but such a title would hardly attract blockbuster crowds.
Similarly, highlighting the true impetus for the show (namely, the recent excavation of Macedonian royal tumulus burials) would have little
impact, given how few among the general public at the time would
have been able to identify Philip II. So it was almost by sleight of hand
that the center of gravity of the show was shifted onto Alexander himself, and various other populist "hooks" were also exploited to the full:
goldwork of exquisite manufacture in stunning quantities; the thrill of
opening royal tombs; a murder mystery (who *really* plotted the assassination of Philip II?); the opportunity to view objects never before on
display in North America; the notion that archaeology is an unending
search (a quest "for data about the ethos of Alexander and the material

Table 2. Exhibitions Discussed in This Chapter

"The Treasures of Ancient Macedonia: History and Legend in Art"
Thessaloniki, Greece, summer 1978

"Alexander the Great: History and Legend in Art"
Thessaloniki, Greece, summer 1980

"The Search for Alexander"
Washington, DC, November 16, 1980–April 5, 1981
Chicago, IL, May 16–September 7, 1981
Boston, MA, October 27, 1981–January 10, 1982
San Francisco, CA, February 20–May 16, 1982
New Orleans, LA, June 27–September 19, 1982
New York, NY, October 27, 1982–January 3, 1983
Toronto, Canada, March 5–July 10, 1983

"Ancient Macedonia"
Melbourne, Australia, November 25, 1988–19 February, 1989
Brisbane, Australia, March 11–April 20, 1989
Sydney, Australia, May 20–July 23, 1989

"Alessandro Magno: Storia e Mito"
Rome, Italy, December 21, 1995–May 21, 1996

"Alexander the Great—The Exhibition"
St. Petersburg, FL, October 1, 1996–March 31, 1997

"Alexander the Great in European Art"
Thessaloniki, Greece, September 22, 1997–January 11, 1998

"Alexander the Great: East-West Cultural Contacts from Greece to Japan"
Tokyo, Japan, August 5–October 5, 2003
Kobe, Japan, October 18–December 21, 2003

"Alexander the Great: Treasures from an Epic Era of Hellenism"
New York, NY, December 10, 2004–April 16, 2005

"The Myth of Alexander the Great"
Tashkent, Uzbekistan, June 2006

"Alexander the Great: The Road to the East"
St. Petersburg, Russia, February 13–May 1, 2007

culture of his own time and place," as J. Carter Brown rather blandly stated in his foreword to the SFA catalogue).[7]

The composition of the SFA exhibition is revealing in these respects.[8] No less than 55 percent of the 173 items on display were objects of gold or silver, a veritable treasure show. Objects from the recent excavations at Vergina actually constituted only 10 percent of the exhibition (Yalouris et al. 1980, catalogue nos. 156–73), but they were given added glamour by being described as "the climax of the search," emphasized in the catalogue by the use of color plates and a breathless account of the discovery by the excavator, Manolis Andronikos, himself. Almost 100 objects in the exhibition (57 percent) were on loan from Greece: principally drinking vessels in precious metals (37), pieces of jewelry or other cosmetic accoutrements (51), and arms and armor (8). This makes it clear that nearly all of the 36 pieces of statuary and 24 coins or jetons, half of them depicting Alexander, were contributions from the American rather than the Greek side; in fact, of the 30 items in the show that represent Alexander directly or indirectly, only five were actually loans from Greece (nos. 4, 7, 153, 155, 171). In short, a Greek show centered on fourth- and third-century B.C.E. Macedonian art and archaeology (including a small selection of new items from the Vergina excavations) was refocused for its American audience by putting the incomparably famous Alexander front and center, even though his relevance to the bulk of the objects on display is quite generalized (that is, they merely illustrate artistic production at and for the mid-fourth-century Macedonian royal court in which Alexander was raised).

Public interest in the SFA exhibition was stimulated not only by unprecedented levels of publicity, but also, for example, by the July 1978 cover story on the Vergina excavations in *National Geographic* (whose circulation exceeds ten million) and by television specials. Effective media communication was doubtless greatly assisted by the fact that one of the two major commercial sponsors of the show was the publishing giant Time, Inc. (Mobil also provided financial support for the audiovisual section of the exhibition). The other chief financial underwriter was the government-controlled National Bank of Greece. Indeed, in SFA we see a perfect alignment for the creation of a blockbuster: the endorsement and active collaboration of several agencies of the Greek government, especially the Ministry of Culture and Sciences and some of its leading archaeologists; investment in the exhibition by corporations with deep pockets and a hunger for positive publicity; and the enthusiastic cooperation of the directors of seven of the largest and most powerful museums in North America.

Csaszar (1996–97, 25–27) has rightly noted that blockbusters should be evaluated not only in terms of their success with the public, as measured by attendances and revenues, but also by whether all the effort and expense (and the risks associated with transporting unique objects) are justified by having any effect on the ways in which we see art history. As Csazar (1996–97, 25) asked, do large exhibitions "in the end confirm and reinscribe our view of a figure or era, or . . . elevate their subjects into a new level of discourse?" In the case of SFA, this is not easy to judge. It certainly intensified an interest in Alexander and ancient Macedon, both academic and popular, that continues unabated to the present day. No fewer than nine symposia and other scholarly meetings took place in conjunction with the SFA exhibition over a period of fifteen months between late 1980 and early 1982, and many of the papers delivered there were subsequently published (e.g., Adams and Borza 1982; Barr-Sharrar and Borza 1982).[9] Works of reference on the coinages of Alexander were prepared or reprinted to accompany the SFA symposia (Gardiakos 1981; Oikonomides 1981). Little, Brown and Company—the publisher responsible for the SFA catalogue (Yalouris et al. 1980)—also in 1980 published *The Search for Alexander,* a heavily illustrated, readable biography by Robin Lane Fox explicitly timed to coincide with the exhibition and television special (and for the most part reproducing the romantically heroic view of Alexander espoused in his much longer study of 1973).

Most of this activity, of course, took place when it did because of the various SFA installations, but some of it would likely have happened even without them, as scholarly responses to the breathtaking discoveries in the royal tombs at Vergina. Overall, its chief impact was to illustrate Alexander's Macedonian heritage, while offering little revision to standard views of the man himself. The text of the SFA catalogue, far from seeing a need to revisit the complex issues around Alexander's ethnicity and cultural background in light of the new finds, unapologetically presented him as a quintessentially Hellenic icon, a Greek-speaker embarked on a Hellenic *mission civilisatrice* to the East (Yalouris et al. 1980, 10–38). Since it was written by Greek archaeologists, for a Greek-organized exhibition with significant Greek governmental backing, this comes as no surprise; but it is a clear example of how the whole tenor of a blockbuster show can closely reflect its sponsors' views.

Alexander in the Antipodes

In 1988, six years after SFA's North American tour ended, there opened in three Australian venues an exhibition more than twice as large entitled "Ancient Macedonia" (AM). As its catalogue states, this exhibition was "a gesture of goodwill to Australia for its bicentenary by the government of Greece" (Greek Ministry of Culture 1988, ix). It was organized in Greece by the Ministry of Culture and the Hellenic National Committee of the International Council of Museums and in Australia by the Museum of Victoria, managed by the International Cultural

Corporation of Australia, indemnified by the Australian government, funded by the telecommunications company OTC and the Australian Bicentennial Authority (and, in a minor way, by the Macedonia Thrace Bank), with transportation provided by Olympic Airways and Australian Airlines. This, in short, was a very serious international collaboration. The staging of AM in Australia makes sense when it is remembered that this country has one of the world's largest populations of people with Greek ancestry outside Greece and Cyprus; Melbourne is the third-largest Greek-speaking city in the world, and since 1984 has enjoyed a special sister-city relationship with Thessaloniki in northern Greece. The fact that the exhibition opened in 1988, the year of the Australian bicentennial, was of course not accidental and doubtless helped boost attendance figures.

Although it shared a number of objects in common with SFA, this show did not highlight Alexander as the central attraction (although he is, of course, present, represented in a few sculptures and coins). It sought, instead, to showcase the remarkable recent advances in understanding of Macedonian archaeology, including the discoveries at Derveni (1962) and Vergina (1977), and finds from many other rescue and research excavations of recent decades. This itself was a radical move, given that Macedon has long been treated as less than, and outside, the mainstream archaeology of the southern Greek mainland and the Aegean—the "Other," as it were, of Greek archaeology (Andreou et al. 2001; Margomenou et al. 2005). Now the finds at Vergina, and political realignments within Greece itself that favored the north, combined to produce a new level of interest in this part of the Greek world.

The show's catalogue is a model of scholarship: bilingual throughout, it provides 402 detailed catalogue entries, each illustrated in full color, of objects from more than 50 sites, drawn entirely from northern Greek museums.[10] It differs from SFA by providing comprehensive coverage of the art and culture of Macedon from Early Neolithic times until the Roman conquest in 146 B.C.E. The range of materials on display was thus far broader, both chronologically and in terms of artifact types; having less emphasis on stone statuary and precious metals, the exhibition is dominated by vases, terracottas, and bronze- and ironwork of many periods. The dominant period, however, is the fourth century and the age of Philip II and Alexander, clearly signaled by the inclusion of some of its most spectacular gold and silver objects. This broad temporal sweep, indeed, provided the backdrop for a narrative, developed in the various introductory essays that occupy the first hundred pages of the AM catalogue, in which a steady march toward civilization is seen as culminating in the "Macedonian Hellenism" that was to be borne by Alexander to the depths of Asia, projecting Greek Macedon onto the world stage. In this respect, the aim of AM was little different from that of SFA.

What *was* different was the political and cultural setting. It was in 1980, the year SFA opened, that General Tito's death signaled the beginning of the constitutional crisis and ethnic conflicts in the Republic of Yugoslavia that were to lead to its breakup a decade later. The Republic of Macedonia did not declare independence from Yugoslavia until September 1991, when it became known as FYROM (the Former Yugoslav Republic of Macedonia), but ethnic tensions between Greeks and Macedonians were on the rise throughout the 1980s. They were fueled on one side by Greek fears of the rise of a non-Greek Greater Macedonia encompassing parts of Greece, Bulgaria, Albania, and the former Yugoslavia. On the other side were FYROM's claims for a Macedonian identity incorporating history and symbols that Greece regards as exclusively its own (for example, the Macedonian star, seen most famously on the lid of the gold larnax from Tomb II at Vergina, was co-opted by FYROM after independence as the device on its new state flag; the previous year, Greece had placed it on the reverse of a 100-drachma coin, bearing the head of Alexander on the obverse).[11] Confrontations over the Macedonian problem played out most vigorously not in the Macedonian region itself, but among diaspora communities in large cities such as Toronto or Melbourne where opportunities exist for substantial numbers of Greek and Yugoslav Macedonians to meet face-to-face; and, as vividly documented by Loring Danforth (1995), marches and protest meetings by one side or the other not infrequently resulted in violent conflict.

This was the backdrop to the AM exhibition. To bring such an ambitious blockbuster show to Australia at this time was hardly a neutral act of cultural diplomacy. Consisting exclusively of objects from Greece itself and endorsed in the catalogue by welcoming messages from the president of the Hellenic Republic and its minister of culture, the exhibition hammered home the message that Alexander, Philip II, and their entire cultural heritage reaching back into the mists of prehistory were unequivocally *Greek*. Not surprisingly, it was not well received by the local (Yugoslav) Macedonian population. At the opening and during the early days of the show's run at the Australian Museum in Sydney, for instance, the museum's entrance was guarded by a police line, with additional security and canine units required to manage protests by the local Macedonian community.[12]

Alexander's Afterlife in Rome and Thessaloniki

The original Thessaloniki exhibitions of 1978 and 1980, while obviously mounted to showcase the 1977 discoveries at Vergina, also exhibited a strong degree of interest in artistic responses to Alexander long after his death—as the subtitle "History and Legend in Art" indicates. In fact, of the 62 items illustrated in the exhibition's catalogue, no less than 30 percent are of Byzantine or later date (Ninou 1980, 75–94): Coptic textiles; Byzantine manuscripts; sixteenth- to nineteenth-century engravings, paintings, and etchings; examples of traditional Greek folk art; and twentieth-century paintings and sculpture, all relating in one way or another to Alexander.

The recognition that any "search for Alexander" is inevitably framed by the context of his *Nachleben*—the rich, 2,000-year-long traditions first of mythmaking (greatly stimulated by the widespread dissemination of the *Alexander Romance*) and later of artistic and literary responses to the ancient authors rediscovered in the Renaissance—seems to have been either overlooked or willfully ignored in the SFA exhibition. Its principal catalogue, published for the Washington, DC, opening, included as an afterthought just four items entitled "related works of later periods lent from Greece" (Yalouris et al. 1980, 190–91, cat. nos. A–D). Interestingly, subsequent installations of this show paid considerably more attention to materials postdating antiquity.[13] *Supplement* II to the SFA catalogue, prepared for the Boston show (Herrmann 1981), presented eighteen additional works from the ancient world, but also a further twenty-eight engravings, etchings, drawings, oil paintings, watercolors, marble reliefs, and tapestries dating from the thirteenth to eighteenth centuries, drawn from American collections; these included important works by (or after) artists such as Andrea del Verrocchio, Salvator Rosa, and Charles Le Brun, as well as pages from illustrated Iranian and Mughal manuscripts of the *Shahnameh* (the Persian *Book of Kings*, in which Alexander figures prominently). SFA's last North American stop, in Toronto, was also accompanied by a supplemental catalogue (Royal Ontario Museum 1983), whose first dozen entries relate to the afterlife of Alexander, as represented in Gandharan art, seventeenth-century French etchings, eighteenth-century Italian paintings, nineteenth-century reproductions of ancient Alexander representations, and a twentieth-century Rajput miniature painting of Alexander.

Two major subsequent exhibitions, held in Rome and Thessaloniki in 1996–97, greatly expanded on these modest beginnings. In many ways, they represent the most ambitious, open-minded, and interesting of all the shows reviewed here.

"Alessandro Magno Storia e Mito" (AMSM), organized by the Fondazione Memmo, was on display at the Palazzo Ruspoli in Rome from December 21, 1995, until May 21, 1996. To judge from its massive 400-page catalogue (Di Vita 1995), this was a brilliantly conceived show, with loan items from forty-three museums in eleven countries. The first 200 pages of the catalogue are given over to a series of sixteen essays on everything from "Alexander and Rome" to "The Demonization of Alexander in Sassanian Iran" and "Alexander-Iskandar 'dhu'l-Qarnayn' in the Art of Islam." Written by leading scholars in their fields (e.g., Giovanni Pugliese Carratelli on Alexander's political campaigns in the East, and Paul Bernard on his city-foundations in Central Asia), these contributions are themselves liberally illustrated with images of landscapes, sites, and monuments, as well as many artifacts and works of art that did not form part of the exhibition itself. Even before reaching the "Catalogue of Works" that makes up its second half, a reader will find in this volume a rich overview of Alexander studies and some serious scholarly contributions to the field.

Organized in eleven sections of very unequal size, the exhibition began in a predictable manner with small groups of objects illustrating "Royal Origins" (items from tombs at Pydna and Vergina, portraits of Philip II and Olympias), "Image of a Sovereign" (Alexander portraits in various media, including a newly discovered statue from Perge in Turkey), "Models, Masters, Friends, Adversaries" (Homer, Aristotle, Hephaestion, Diogenes, Demosthenes), and "The Conquest" (mainly arms and armor, and depictions of Alexander's battles). But it is with section 5, "The Persians: The Great Enemy," that the exhibition spreads its wings, putting on display a range of stone reliefs, metalwork, seals, and even an Elamite administrative tablet: astonishingly, AMSM is the only exhibition among all those under discussion that devoted space to the material culture of the Achaemenid empire, whose defeat was, after all, the very raison d'être for Alexander's expedition. It goes on to showcase aspects of his Eastern encounters and impact in imaginative ways. For instance, in section 8 curators set groups of pottery and small objects from sites in Swat (Pakistan), dating to the two or three centuries before his arrival there, alongside examples of the Gandharan styles of sculpture and architecture that developed in the same region in the centuries following his death. In what must have been for the visitor a most colorful climax to the entire show, the final sections (representing well over one-third of the items on display) explore the apotheosis of Alexander, and his development as a mythical figure in the Christian middle ages and in Islam, as seen especially in dozens of sheets from Byzantine, early medieval, Persian, and Mughal illustrated manuscripts.

AMSM was certainly an exhibition of blockbuster proportions, a museological venture requiring international collaboration on an unusual scale. A team of sixty scholars contributed essays and entries to the impressive catalogue, the first four pages of which are taken up with lists of individuals, committees, museums, institutions, patrons, and sponsors. The show succeeded, or so it seems to me, partly because—notwithstanding its sprawling scope—it managed to achieve a balance lacking in most of the other Alexander exhibitions. A visit to this show would have offered the general public a richly varied and satisfying visual experience (and one not dependent merely on the glitter of gold), yet the research underlying its installation and the writing of the catalogue also created a significant contribution to Alexander scholarship. Similarly, AMSM manages to convey a picture of Alexander as a Macedonian of his own unique time and place, while giving equal attention to the peoples and cultures of the East with whom he came in contact. Finally, it is, so far, the only show that pays more than lip service to the fact that it is not the historical Alexander, but rather an ever-changing mythical figure, that has dominated the popular imagination throughout much of the Old World for the past two millennia.

If we return to Csaszar's question (1996–97, 25), noted above, about the capacity of blockbusters to "elevate their subjects into a new level of discourse," the exhibition "Alexander the Great in European Art" (AGEA), on display in Thessaloniki in autumn 1997, provides a decisively affirmative answer. The city that year bore the title of Cultural Capital of Europe, and it can hardly have been a difficult decision to choose Macedonia's most famous son as the subject of a major art exposition to celebrate and promote the region. But resisting the easy option of an updated reinstallation of "Treasures of Ancient Macedonia" or some version of SFA, the organizers made the inspired decision to focus on responses to Alexander in European art, bringing together 138 works (including a number of books, maps, and manuscripts), which—with

the single exception of a Roman copy of a Lysippan head of Alexander—
date from the early Renaissance to the early twentieth century. Three
dozen art historians from museums and galleries across Europe contributed essays and very detailed entries for the catalogue.

The arrangement of AGEA was inventive and engaging. Like the
catalogue's massive and useful bibliography, organized by year rather
than alphabetically, it could have been laid out chronologically to show
a progression of shifting responses to the deeds and character of Alexander; equally, it might have been organized according to medium,
bringing together all the oil paintings, or engravings, or tapestries in
the show. Instead, the guiding principle was a series of twenty-three
topics, most of them key incidents in the life of Alexander to which
Renaissance, Baroque, and later artists were especially drawn, not infrequently as exempla of behavior for European rulers to emulate or
avoid, and sometimes with the intention of creating an ekphrastic rendition of a specific passage from an ancient author.[14] Each chapter of the
catalogue is thus prefaced by a relevant extract from Plutarch, Curtius,
Arrian, or one of the other written sources from which these artists drew
inspiration and which inflected their attitudes to Alexander. Chapter II
is given over entirely to early printed editions and translations of such
works, as well as influential historical studies from the eighteenth and
nineteenth centuries.

As can be readily seen from the lists of Baroque artworks on Alexander themes compiled by Andor Pigler in his most useful book *Barokthe-
men* (1974, 1:340–48), certain subjects were treated much more often
than others. Indeed, they sometimes came to take on a life of their own,
with complex interplay between the ancient sources, previous representations of the theme, and its allegorical or political significance, along
with the insertion into the painting of likenesses of the commissioning
patron and his family, and even of the artist himself. A case in point
is the story of Alexander's gift of his mistress Campaspe to his court
painter Apelles, represented by ten works of art in AGEA and a long
essay for chapter IX of the catalogue by Sylvia Ferino-Pagden (1997).
Beginning as a minor anecdote about art in Pliny and Aelian (and not
even mentioned by the major Alexander historians), from the Renaissance onward it regularly occurs in artistic cycles celebrating the life of
Alexander. Yet Alexander himself is somewhat incidental to the main
significance of this episode, which became an allegory of painting itself,
with interlocking notions of the king as an understanding patron of the

arts, the painter as a connoisseur of absolute beauty and thus desirous of it, and the beautiful model representing a challenge set by nature to art. By juxtaposing works of art on this single subject from very different eras and traditions, AGEA succeeded brilliantly in teasing out and illuminating such complexities, and certainly more vividly than previous purely literary studies of it had done (e.g., Cast 1981). The same holds true of other well-represented subjects accorded special attention in the exhibition: the marriage of Alexander and "Roxana," Alexander's visit to Diogenes, and the family of Darius before Alexander.

In short, AGEA offered a remarkable array of visual responses to Alexander the Great in European art. It too was certainly a blockbuster:[15] nothing on this scale or on this theme had been exhibited in one place before, and the quality of the artworks was remarkable (for example, the section on the family of Darius before Alexander included a Parmigianino, a Primaticcio, and two works apiece by Raphael and Rubens). The show itself may have been very enjoyable, but it has also left a lasting legacy in the depth of fresh scholarship reflected in its catalogue. Indeed, it is likely to remain the standard work of reference on this subject for some time to come.[16]

Alexander in the "Blockbuster Mill"

Perhaps the oddest of all the Alexander-themed exhibitions in recent years is the one put on display in 1996–97 at the Florida International Museum in St. Petersburg, a museum that had itself opened only the year before. It is one of a new breed of venues—other examples are "Wonders: The Memphis International Cultural Series" (in Tennessee) and the "Mississippi Arts Pavilion" (in Jackson)—that are closer to entertainment theme parks than traditional art museums. Although organized as nonprofits, they have the unashamedly commercial objectives of promoting tourism and economic development, particularly in mid-sized cities without major art museums of their own. Generally housed in convention centers or large buildings converted from other uses (a department store, for example), they need no art experts on their permanent staff, since they themselves do not own any art, and they make no pretensions to scholarship. "With no collections of their own, they borrow high-quality or historically important art and artifacts from foreign institutions. Then they surround the objects with mystery, drama and romance through atmospheric installations and lively audio-tour narrations" (Rosenbaum 1997, 45).

Exhibitions in these "blockbuster mills," as they have been dubbed, tend to share an approach based on the transformation and theatrical enhancement of large interior spaces to evoke the appropriate time and place—pharaonic Egypt, czarist Russia, Napoleonic France, and so on. Elaborate settings are constructed to provide visitors with a "you-are-there" feeling and to showcase the star objects in the show: for example, a huge circular stone tomb to house the jade burial suit of a Han dynasty emperor (in the Wonders Series "Imperial Tombs of China" exhibition of 1995), or piles of sand and a massive mirrored hall with faux columns (for the "Splendors of Ancient Egypt" installation at the Florida International Museum in 1996). Unlike traditional museums, which can negotiate international art loans by making their own collections open to loan requests, the blockbuster-mill museums must pay substantial amounts of cash to foreign lenders to secure loans of objects. That, in turn, makes their shows financially risky ventures and frequently necessitates not only high ticket prices, but also local government assistance in the form of loan guarantees or direct grants.

How did this new concept of the museum play out in response to Alexander? Details of the show "Alexander the Great—The Exhibition" at the Florida International Museum (FIM) are scarce, since it seems to have generated neither a catalogue nor a permanent website.[17] In the FIM website's own words:

> Over 500 masterpieces from more than 45 museums and collections around the world were assembled to tell the fascinating story of one of the world's most extraordinary men—Alexander the Great. Artifacts in the exhibition included a pebble mosaic nearly 10 feet (3 meters) long showing Alexander hunting a lion, jewelry, original weapons used by the Macedonian army and classic marble statues as well as delicate miniature representations in bone.

The show was curated by Robert Bianchi (formerly curator of Egyptian, Classical, and Middle Eastern Art at the Brooklyn Museum), who freely admitted that he had set out to create a great tourist attraction. The advertising brochure claimed: "You'll follow in Alexander's footsteps as the entire museum is transformed into ancient Greece and the exotic lands he conquered. You'll not only see what Alexander saw, you'll feel what he felt."

Just as in the original SFA exhibition fifteen years earlier, the hook to pull in the crowds was the name of Alexander, even though the actual centerpiece of the installation was a gallery dedicated to the gold objects from the tomb of Philip II at Vergina. Nevertheless, with the exception of a group of small gold discs, this gallery actually contained nothing but replicas. Furthermore, despite FIM's reference to "classic marble statues" among the "500 masterpieces," a number of cases in the exhibition displayed merely modern casts of ancient sculpture. As if to make up for aspects of the show that visitors might find rather disappointing, an artist from a department-store design firm was brought in to re-create the façade of the tomb of Philip II with its hunting fresco—not so much as a replica of the façade in its current state as a re-creation of what it might have looked like when new. It is readily apparent from the detailed photographs of this fresco published by Andronikos (1993, 101–13) that it is badly faded and poorly preserved; but the artist, undaunted, applied an approach drawn from "visual merchandising" to produce a garish version with an excess of color, reportedly more reminiscent of Poussin than ancient Macedon (Rosenbaum 1997, 47).[18]

The St. Petersburg show seems simply to have followed the organizing concepts of the SFA exhibition, but without the benefit of access to a comparably wide array of important original material or to much scholarly input. It was not adjudged a success, in any event, being seen by only 173,000 visitors (FIM had planned on 525,000)—possibly because tickets were very expensive, or because the exhibition's timing unfortunately coincided with local race riots, or because FIM was still quite new and not yet well known; or perhaps word got around that the show was not very good. Whatever the case, the museum's more recent offerings indicate that it has moved away from expensive international loan exhibitions involving antiquities in favor of crowd-pleasing shows on such themes as the *Titanic*, baseball, Barbie dolls, and Princess Diana.[19]

Into the Twenty-first Century: Alexander in Japan and Uzbekistan

In the large-scale Alexander exhibitions discussed so far, we can detect two main foci of interest. One puts the spotlight on Alexander in his own time and place (mid-fourth-century B.C.E. Macedon), on the treasures of the Macedonian royal court, and on Alexander as a great and emphatically Greek king. The other sees him as a ruler whose travels to the ends of the known world were of revolutionary significance to subsequent political and cultural developments throughout the eastern Mediterranean, the Middle East, and beyond; but also as someone who became a largely mythical figure, a legend difficult to nail down securely, a backdrop against which all manner of responses have been projected, from Roman times until the present. In the most recent museum blockbusters devoted to Alexander, one sees these same two impulses on display.

An intriguing example of the latter is a 2003 exhibition mounted at the Tokyo National Museum and the Hyogo Prefectural Museum of Art in Kobe under the title "Alexander the Great: East-West Cultural Contacts from Greece to Japan" (EWCC), and accompanied by a Japanese-English catalogue (Nishioka 2003).[20] Endorsed by the Greek minister of culture, co-organized by the Hellenic Cultural Organization, and containing objects from more than a dozen Greek museums, the show was staged as part of the outreach activities of the "Cultural Olympiad 2001–2004" program, preparatory to the Olympic Games in Athens. It was not, however, a Greek loan of a prepackaged group of art objects celebrating the glories of Hellenic culture in the Age of Alexander and their enduring power. Indeed, only about 40 of the 184 items on display actually came from Greece; and, notwithstanding the huge reproduction on the catalogue's cover of the well-known sculpted head of Alexander from Yannitsa now in the Pella Museum, the introductory essay by Katsumi Tanabe begins: "In opening, let us be clear that this is not an exhibition of the [sic] Alexander the Great, nor one of Greek art. Although we have employed the name of this king, we have done so only as a symbol of Hellenistic culture" (Nishioka 2003, 19). In other words, co-opting the king's name, as always, helps pull in the crowds.

EWCC's real purpose was to illustrate a thesis—a somewhat tenuous and certainly controversial one—concerning the process of transmission and assimilation of artistic styles and cultural conceptualizations between the Greek world and, eventually, the Far East. In the words of the organizers (Nishioka 2003, 16):

> The vibrant traditions of Greek art, born in the Mediterranean, were transmitted by Alexander's expansion to fuse with the glorious courtly art of the conquered Achaemenian Persia. The Gandharan Buddhist art witnessed a merging of Greek, Iranian, and Indian gods into the Buddhist pantheon. At the end of this long eastward journey, these elements of various origins also crystallized in Japanese art.

Thus, to cite a single example, the show sets side by side and draws connections of influence between representations of Boreas, god of the north wind, on fourth-century B.C.E. Attic red-figure vases; a Kushan-period Buddhist relief from Gandhara in Pakistan, showing the wind god Oado with his mantle full of wind (perhaps with Boreas as the model); and his transformation into the thirteenth-century Japanese god of wind as depicted at the Myouhouin Temple in Kyoto. The show makes the claim that a very wide range of Greek gods and sea creatures were transmitted to western and central Asia and the Indian subcontinent by Alexander's invasion, and there gave palpable shape to the hitherto invisible gods of the East. It is thus an exhibition about Alexander only in the secondary sense that his actions served as the catalyst for the artistic transformations on a continent-wide scale that the selection of objects for EWCC sought to illustrate.

EWCC was also very much an exhibition of its own time. Only in the post–Cold War era of globalization has it become either practical or even desirable to draw together, as this show does, artworks found in no fewer than twenty different countries, including several of the former Soviet Central Asian republics, Afghanistan, Pakistan, Russia, China, and Japan. The growing interest, both scholarly and popular, in cultural transmissions along the Silk Road is another symptom of these changes in global geopolitics. Above all, new research possibilities have opened up recently in Uzbekistan, Tajikistan, Kazakhstan, and Afghanistan, sparking interest in the material consequences of Alexander's activities in these regions—ancient Bactria and Sogdia, in particular (e.g., Romey 2004; Holt 2005). In fact, the most recent Alexander exhibition illustrates these developments well. "The Myth of Alexander the Great" opened in June 2006 at the Gallery of Fine Art at the National Bank of Uzbekistan in Tashkent. An Italian-Uzbek collaboration, it included over 200 works (architecture, murals, sculpture, terracottas, and coins) drawn from museum collections in Italy and from excavations in southern Uzbekistan.[21]

Back to New York

The shows in Japan and Uzbekistan are very different in content and purpose than "Alexander the Great: Treasures from an Epic Era of Hellenism" (TEEH), on display at the Onassis Cultural Center in New York from December 10, 2004, to April 16, 2005. This not only represented the first of the two foci of interest noted above (324), but was essentially a reversion to the dominant themes of the SFA exhibition a quarter-century earlier; in fact, many pieces from the previous show returned to New York for TEEH. Underwritten and organized by a single sponsor, the Alexander S. Onassis Public Benefit Foundation (USA), at whose prestigious address on Fifth Avenue in Manhattan the exhibition made its sole appearance, TEEH was accompanied by a lavishly produced, large-format color catalogue, distributed free of charge at the entrance (Pandermalis 2004). Seventy percent of the roughly two hundred items on display were on loan from Greece, almost entirely from museums in Macedonia.[22] Roughly the same size as the earlier SFA show, this exhibition was, if anything, narrower in the range of objects on display, although also more coherently organized in terms of its main themes, and the various essays introducing them in the catalogue. These included portraits, coins, arms and warfare techniques of the Macedonians, the symposium, women in Macedonia, and jewelry; there were additional concluding sections devoted to some very recent finds in Macedonia—the "Lady of Aigai," a rich, royal, female burial of ca. 500 B.C.E. excavated at Vergina in 1998, and the remarkable paintings from the late fourth-century Macedonian tomb at Aghios Athanasios, near Thessaloniki, discovered in 1994.

TEEH was, to be sure, an opulent blockbuster, staged in a location where it would receive maximum publicity. It also did not hurt that Greece was still very much on the public's mind in the immediate aftermath of the 2004 Olympic Games in Athens, nor that Oliver Stone's *Alexander* was released less than two weeks before TEEH opened its own doors.[23] Mounting a show at such an auspicious time and in so central a location, its curator, Dimitrios Pandermalis, could reflect upon a quarter-century of previous Alexander exhibitions; he also had at his disposal a myriad of new finds resulting from the great expansion of archaeological research in northern Greece since the late 1970s, as well as the fruits of intensive scholarly study and publication in the field of Classical and Hellenistic Macedonian archaeology during this same period. To be sure, TEEH capitalized on recent discoveries, and publicity for the show emphasized that it included splendid objects never before displayed to the public (or at least not in the United States).

Yet neither new finds nor new scholarship seems to have had much impact on the overall conceptualization of this exhibition, which replicates that of SFA to an extraordinary degree in its myopic focus on treasure and burial, on arms and armor, jewelry, and symposiastic vessels. In a show organized by a Greek Foundation dedicated to "the dissemination of Hellenic civilization" in North America, one would naturally not expect to see much reference to provocative and politically sensitive questions such as the ways in which differing Macedonian and Greek ethnic identities found expression in material culture.[24] Alexander is described, uncompromisingly, as a "great Greek king" and his age as "an epic era in the history of Hellenic civilization."[25] The audience reaction TEEH seems mainly designed to elicit is simple gape-jawed admiration of the art on display, with no questions asked. Alexander himself, as in SFA, makes very few appearances; in fact, his name is attached to the exhibition's title mainly as a crowd-pleasing hook (in the manner of several of the blockbusters discussed here), alongside the emotive words "treasures," "epic," and "Hellenism." New York deserved to see a much more thoughtful, inventive, and nuanced exhibition than this one.

Conclusion

Although my reaction to TEEH is one of disappointment, because it attempted so little that was different or even challenging for its audience, it is not my intention to rate this or indeed any of the other blockbuster Alexander shows as either good or bad, after the manner of rottentomatoes.com. Nonetheless, exhibitions can be popular, enjoyable to visit, and a success in financial terms, yet also fall far short of the possibilities offered by the material itself. Several of the shows discussed here seem to me to be open to this criticism. To use the term coined by the historian John Staudenmaier (1993), they were "clean" exhibitions—that is, full of interesting artifacts and works of art, but almost completely devoid of any of the "messy" cultural or social stories that might have been told about them.

Underlying such reluctance to tell engaging yet sometimes complicated stories is the need for blockbusters to "play it safe," in view of their expense, the risk factors, and the large audiences they require. Moreover, the criteria for choosing subjects deemed suitable for blockbuster treatment are limited, being governed mainly by the requirement that they have the high profile that will more readily attract sponsorship. Since the 1970s, the range of subject-matter for exhibition blockbusters has been narrow. Planners of art shows seem inexorably drawn to hagiographic retrospectives of a small group of canonical, "great" male artists. In the same way, the (at least) ten large-scale exhibitions devoted to Alexander the Great over the past three decades may well reflect the nature of the blockbuster phenomenon itself as much as his inherent interest and suitability as a subject for presentation in a museum setting.

Every museum director would doubtless proclaim a desire to inspire and present ideas by engaging the audience. Learning something about (art) history is one reason for visiting a museum, but not the only one; and since visitors come to museums for many reasons and with very varied expectations, it is desirable to meet them halfway. Whether lavish and expensive blockbusters succeed in this regard is a moot point. Shearer West (1995, 75), in a devastating critique of the art blockbuster, characterizes it as follows: "Its purpose is money, its excuse education and entertainment, and it engenders a vast machinery of public relations, media hype and consumerism." This may be too cynical. Obviously, behind the scenes of any blockbuster there are political agendas and market forces at work, which we need to recognize and react to as the case demands: in the Alexander shows considered here, there are some rather obvious examples of the good, the bad, and the ugly in this respect.

What West's analysis brings out clearly is that the objects on display in a blockbuster are presented as "cyphers which can only be interpreted by the initiated," and thus it actually "alienates the majority of the population through its academic presentation of works of art, and assimilates its educated constituency by forcing it to collaborate with the commercialization of art" (1995, 75). In the final analysis, this pinpoints something of the unease one feels about the responses to Alexander in the exhibitions discussed in this chapter. The search for a populist profile has in several instances resulted in the co-optation of Alexander's name to provide an ostensible focus for a show that is in reality not wholly, or even mainly, about the man himself. Equally, the material on display has all too often been treated as a sort of icon to be worshiped and admired—with Alexander's "greatness" relentlessly asserted in emotive purple prose—yet not fully understood. It is just as difficult, it would seem, to present Alexander satisfactorily in a museum blockbuster as in a cinematic epic.

Postscript

Since this chapter was written in May 2006, yet another large-scale Alexander blockbuster show has been staged: "Alexander the Great: The Road to the East," at the State Hermitage Museum in St. Petersburg, Russia (February 13–May 1, 2007).[26] This was evidently an ambitious and comprehensive exhibition, with more than five hundred artifacts on display, covering the period from the fifth century B.C.E. until the end of the nineteenth century. The museum's website reports that the exhibition's main theme was the transformations ushered in by the Age of Alexander and their consequences for both the West and the East: "[His] influence affected a huge territory extending from Greece to India and right up to Mongolia and other states beyond the frontiers of the Oecumene. . . . At the focus of attention is the historic role played by Alexander in the destiny of Western Europe, Russia and the East, and Hellenism as a global process of interaction between civilizations and cultures." To a considerable extent, the St. Petersburg exhibition appears to mirror the general aims of the 1995–96 Rome exhibition ("Alessandro Magno: Storia e Mito"), but in its clear interest in displaying materials from areas well to the north and east of anywhere Alexander himself ever went, it also shares a certain sympathy with the ambitions of the 2003 Japanese show "Alexander the Great: East-West Cultural Contacts from Greece to Japan."

Notes

1. For my own critical response to the movie *Alexander,* see Cherry 2005. For other reviews, see the website http://www.rottentomatoes.com.

2. Revision of this chapter two years after it was written allowed the opportunity to see what has happened to the volume of Alexander-related books since 2006 (as recorded in Table 1). Amazon.com lists only nine books published or scheduled to appear in 2008—in other words, a reversion to "normal," pre-2004 rates of publication. The spike occasioned by the release of *Alexander* is thus abundantly clear.

3. A movie can, of course, be a huge financial success overall, even if actual attendance in movie theaters proves to be disappointing, since subsequent sales of the DVD and other tie-in merchandise can be substantial.

4. Conforti (1986, 18), for example, presents photographs of what he terms "the art mob" waiting to see the "Berlin Treasures" exhibition of 1948 at the National Gallery in Washington, DC, and the huge lines that formed outside the Metropolitan Museum of Art in 1962 to view the *Mona Lisa.*

5. See http://www.nga.gov/past/data/exh410.shtm. The year 2005 saw the launch of a new American and British tour of Tutankhamun's treasures ("Tutankhamun and the Golden Age of the Pharaohs"), obviously intended to repeat the experience of the 1970s. Sponsored by Egypt's Supreme Council of Antiquities, in partnership with Arts and Exhibitions International, AEG Exhibitions, and the National Geographic Society, the exhibition was on display from 2005 until 2010 in Los Angeles, Fort Lauderdale, Chicago, Philadelphia, London, Dallas, Atlanta, Indianapolis, San Francisco, and Toronto. Some three million people were initially expected to view the show, but this figure was substantially exceeded, with nearly four million visitors at the first four stops on the tour (see http://www.kingtut.org/). According to the promoter, the show

drew 937,613 to the Los Angeles County Museum of Art between June 16 and November 20, 2005; 707,534 to the Museum of Art in Fort Lauderdale, FL, between December 15, 2005, and April 23, 2006; 1.04 million to the Field Museum of Natural History in Chicago between May 26, 2006, and January 1, 2007; and 1.37 million to the Franklin Institute in Philadelphia between February 3 and September 30, 2007.

6. The time-ticketed exhibit (i.e., one requiring the purchase of a special ticket, in addition to any general admission charge to the museum, valid only for a specified time and date) seems to have been first introduced by the Art Institute of Chicago in 1983 and was adopted by most other major museums shortly thereafter (Csaszar 1996–97, 23). In a sort of ripple effect, many much smaller museums sell timed tickets to special exhibitions (even though far from blockbuster in scale and thus not requiring crowd control), perhaps precisely to create a buzz by suggesting that the show may be mobbed and sold out.

7. The brutally cynical view of the archaeological blockbuster is nicely encapsulated in the words of Jon Thompson, executive director of "Wonders: The Memphis International Cultural Series," in Memphis, TN: "We use blood, guts, gold and sex to get people in the door and then we show them the world's greatest works of art" (quoted in Rosenbaum 1997, 45).

8. It is more accurate to speak of "SFA exhibitions" in the plural, since the precise composition of the SFA show at each of its seven stops along the North American tour varied considerably; this is why there were no fewer than six supplements to the original SFA catalogue prepared for the initial Washington, DC, exposition (Yalouris et al. 1980). The details of what was (and what was not) exhibited in each of the seven cities, together with lists of the supplements and the various symposia and scholarly meetings held in conjunction with the exhibitions, have been usefully documented in Oikonomides and Bolchazy 1987.

9. For titles, abstracts, and other information about these papers, see Oikonomides and Bolchazy 1981 and 1982.

10. The museums lending to this exhibition were: Aiani, Amphipolis, Dion, Florina, Kavala, Kozani, Pella, Philippoi, Polygyros, Serres, Thasos, Thessaloniki, and Veroia. Except for replicas of the two gold larnakes and the gilded gorytus (bow-and-arrow case) from Tomb II at Vergina (cat. nos. 223–25), all objects were originals.

11. Visitors to Greece during this period were greeted by slogans, stamped on tourist brochures and maps, such as "Macedonia Is Greek: Read History!" and "Macedonia has been Greek for 5,000 years" (downgraded in later versions to "4,000 years"!). For other examples of this propaganda war fought with historical and archaeological symbols, see Brown 1994; Karakasidou 1997. Eighteen years after Macedonia became independent, this dispute continues undiminished; Greece, a NATO and European Union member country, is blocking efforts by Macedonia to join both alliances unless it changes its name to FYROM in all

international dealings (even though most countries now recognize Macedonia as the Republic of Macedonia).

12. For this information I thank Glenn Ferguson, manager of exhibitions at the Australian Museum, who also noted that the museum's records indicate an attendance of about 70,000 for the Sydney installation of AM.

13. See note 8 above.

14. These topics included: Images of Alexander [A.]; the artists' sources and the diverging assessments of A.; A. and Bucephalus; A. and Diogenes; the sacrifice at the tomb of Achilles; the battle of Granicus; A. cutting the Gordian knot; A. in the studio of Apelles; A., Apelles, and Campaspe; A. and his doctor, Philip; the family of Darius before A.; A. safeguarding the works of Homer; A. at the temple in Jerusalem; A. ordering the founding of Alexandria; the battle of Gaugamela; the triumphant entry into Babylon; A. and Thalestris; the marriage of A. and "Roxana"; A. and Porus; Mount Athos carved in the form of A.; A. and Julius Caesar; another A.: Alessandro Farnese; and a modern Greek A.

15. I have been unable to locate information on attendance figures or revenues for either AMSM or AGEA.

16. The AGEA catalogue was issued in two versions: one in modern Greek with full illustrations, the other in English without them. Unfortunately, both are now extremely difficult to locate, either for purchase or in academic libraries. This appears to be a problem generic to the catalogues of blockbuster shows of this sort, since their catalogues are usually underwritten and distributed by museums, banks, or governmental agencies, rather than commercial publishers.

17. The information presented here is culled mainly from the excellent short article "Blockbusters, Inc." by Lee Rosenbaum (1997), and from the brief entry on the Florida International Museum's former website at http://www.florida museum.org/index.html.

18. A photograph of FIM's Philip II tomb façade replica can be seen online at http://www.creativeartsinc.com/gm_alex.html.

19. Even these moves did not suffice to save this museum and its concept. See "Florida International Museum's Next Project? Its Future," *St. Petersburg Times,* April 29, 2008 (http://www.tampabay.com/news/religion/article 469738.ece). In 2006 the museum moved to a smaller space in St. Petersburg College's Downtown Center; in 2008 the museum officially became part of St. Petersburg College and was retitled the Florida International Museum at St. Petersburg College.

20. That this show was regarded by its organizers as a blockbuster is clear from the description of it in the catalogue as "a mammoth exhibition." Oddly, the executive vice director of the Tokyo National Museum, Yasuhiro Nishioka, in his preface to the catalogue makes the obviously false claims that "no major exhibition has ever been dedicated to him [Alexander]" and "we have been the first to present to the world [an exhibition] on Alexander the Great." What he actually appears to mean is made clearer a few sentences later: "Though a number

of exhibitions have already been devoted to him, they were either too small in scale or too narrow to my liking, and they were conceived only from the Western point of view" (Nishioka 2003, 17).

21. Details of this latest Alexander exhibition are sketchy, and my information is drawn solely from http://culture.uzreport.com/news. A conference organized by the Italian Embassy in Uzbekistan and the Arts Academy of Uzbekistan took place, in association with this exhibition's opening, on June 20, 2006.

22. The remaining artifacts, with a very few exceptions, were drawn from American collections, especially the American Numismatic Society in New York, the Metropolitan Museum of Art in New York, and the Museum of Fine Arts in Boston. U.S. museums contributed to only three sections of the exhibition (on portraits, numismatics, and jewelry).

23. To the best of my knowledge, no exhibitions about Alexander were organized in Greece to coincide with the 2004 Olympic Games. However, the sumptuously illustrated volume written for the general public, *Alexander the Great: Tracing His Path, 2300 Years Later* (Zafiropoulou 2004), reveals an Olympic tie-in, since it was published by International Sports Publications for the Athens 2004 Organising Committee for the Olympic Games, which holds the copyright.

24. For an up-to-date historical discussion of these issues with reference to Alexander, see Cartledge 2004, 91–133.

25. What is intended by the use of the word "epic" in the exhibition's title is never made clear. The Onassis Public Benefit Foundation's then president, Stelio Papadimitriou, refers in his preface (in Pandermalis 2004, 7) to the way in which Alexander lived out his life "according to the legend of the Homeric hero Achilles," but this is not a theme pursued in the exhibition. Pandermalis himself (ibid., 9) writes of the famous Macedonian symposia as "almost epic in style," but carries the idea no further.

26. See the museum's website: http://www.hermitagemuseum.org/html _En/04/2007/hm4_1_154.html. I have been unable to locate a copy of the catalogue accompanying the show, published by the State Hermitage Publishing House and edited by A. A. Trofimova (director of the Department of the Ancient World at the museum).

References

Adams, W. L., and E. N. Borza, eds. 1982. *Philip II, Alexander the Great and the Macedonian Heritage.* Washington, DC: University Press of America.

Andreou, St., M. Fotiadis, and K. Kotsakis. 2001. "The Neolithic and Bronze Age of Northern Greece." In *Aegean Prehistory: A Review,* ed. T. Cullen, 259–327. *American Journal of Archeology,* Supplement 1. Boston: Archaeological Institute of America.

Andronikos, M. 1980. "The Royal Tombs at Vergina: A Brief Account of the Excavations." In *The Search for Alexander: An Exhibition,* ed. N. Yalouris, M. Andronikos, and K. Rhomiopoulou, 26–38. Boston: Little, Brown.

———. 1993. *Vergina: The Royal Tombs and the Ancient City*. Athens: Ekdotike Athenon.

Barr-Sharrar, B., and E. N. Borza, eds. 1982. *Macedonia and Greece in Late Classical and Early Hellenistic Times*. Studies in the History of Art 10. Washington, DC: National Gallery of Art.

Bose, P. 2003. *Alexander the Great's Art of Strategy: Lessons from the Great Empire Builder*. New York: Gotham Books.

Brown, K. S. 1994. "Seeing Stars: Character and Identity in the Landscapes of Modern Macedonia." *Antiquity* 68:784–96.

Cartledge, P. A. 2004. *Alexander the Great: The Hunt for a New Past*. Woodstock, NY: Overlook Press.

Cast, D. 1981. *The Calumny of Apelles: A Study in the Humanist Tradition*. New Haven, CT: Yale University Press.

Cherry. J. F. 2005. "*Alexander*, the Ill-timed?" Review of Alexander Stone's *Alexander*. http://www.lsa.umich.edu/UMICH/modgreek/Home/_TOPNAV_WTGC/Media%20and%20Culture/Review%20of%20oliver%20Stone.pdf

Chugg, A. 2004. *The Lost Tomb of Alexander the Great*. London: Periplus.

———. 2006. *Alexander's Lovers*. Morrisville, NC: Lulu Press.

Conforti, M. 1986. "Museum Blockbusters: Hoving's Legacy Reconsidered." *Art in America* 74, no. 6: 18–23.

Csaszar, T. 1996–97. "The Spectacular, Record-breaking, Sold-out, Smash-hit Blockbuster Supershow! A Phenomenon of Museum Culture." *New Art Examiner* 24 (December 1996–January 1997): 22–27.

Danforth, L. M. 1995. *The Macedonian Conflict: Ethnic Nationalism in a Transnational World*. Princeton, NJ: Princeton University Press.

Dean, D. 1996. *Museum Exhibition: Theory and Practice*. London: Routledge.

Di Vita, A., ed. 1995. *Alessandro Magno: Storia e mito*. Exhibition catalogue. Rome: Leonardo Arte.

Doherty, P. C. 2004. *The Death of Alexander the Great: What—or Who—Really Killed the Young Conqueror of the Known World?* New York: Carroll & Graf.

Elsen, A. 1986. "Museum Blockbusters: Assessing the Pros and Cons." *Art in America* 74, no. 6: 24–27.

Ferino-Pagden, S. 1997. "Alexander, Apelles and Campaspe." In *Alexander the Great in European Art, 22 September 1997–11 January 1998*, ed. N. Hadjinicolaou, 135–49. Thessaloniki: Organisation for the Cultural Capital of Europe.

Figueira, T. J., T. C. Brennan, and R. H. Sternberg. 2001. *Wisdom from the Ancients: Enduring Business Lessons from Alexander the Great, Julius Caesar, and the Illustrious Leaders of Ancient Greece and Rome*. New York: Perseus Books Group.

Freedberg, S. J., G. Jackson-Stops, and R. E. Spear. 1987. "On 'Art History and the "Blockbuster" Exhibition.'" *The Art Bulletin* 69:295–98.

Fuller, J. F. C. 2004. *The Generalship of Alexander the Great*. Repr. ed. Cambridge, MA: Da Capo Press.

Gardiakos, S., ed. 1981. *The Coinages of Alexander the Great.* 3 vols. Chicago: Argonaut.

Greek Ministry of Culture. 1988. *Ancient Macedonia.* Athens: Greek Ministry of Culture; National Hellenic Committee-ICOM; International Cultural Corporation of Australia.

Haacke, H. 1984. "Museums, Managers of Consciousness." *Art in America* 72, no. 2: 9–17.

Hadjinicolaou, N., ed. 1997. *Alexander the Great in European Art, 22 September 1997–11 January 1998.* Exhibition catalogue. Thessaloniki: Organisation for the Cultural Capital of Europe.

Heckel, W. 2003. *The Wars of Alexander the Great* (*Essential Histories*). London: Routledge.

Heckel, W., and C. Hook. 2006. *Macedonian Warrior: Alexander's Elite Infantryman.* Botley, Oxford: Osprey.

Herrmann, J., ed. 1981. *Supplement II to the Catalogue "The Search for Alexander."* Boston: Museum of Fine Arts.

Holt, F. L. 2005. *Into the Land of Bones: Alexander the Great in Afghanistan.* Hellenistic Culture and Society. Berkeley: University of California Press.

Hoving, T. 1993. *Making the Mummies Dance: Inside the Metropolitan Museum of Art.* New York: Simon & Schuster.

Karakasidou, A. N. 1997. *Fields of Wheat, Hills of Blood: Passages to Nationhood in Greek Macedonia, 1870–1990.* Chicago: University of Chicago Press.

Kurke, L. B. 2004. *The Wisdom of Alexander the Great: Enduring Leadership Lessons from the Man Who Created an Empire.* New York: AMACOM.

Lane Fox, Robin. 1973. *Alexander the Great.* Harmondsworth: Allen Lane.

———. 1980. *The Search for Alexander.* Boston: Little, Brown.

———. 2004. *The Making of Alexander.* Oxford: R & L.

Lonsdale, D. J. 2004. *Alexander, Killer of Men: Alexander and the Macedonian Way of War.* London: Constable & Robinson.

———. 2006. *Alexander the Great: Lessons in Strategy.* Strategy and History 22. London: Routledge.

Margomenou, D., J. F. Cherry, and L. E. Talalay. 2005. "Reflections on the 'Aegean' and Its Prehistory: Present Routes and Future Destinations." In *Prehistorians Round the Pond: Reflections on Aegean Prehistory as a Discipline,* ed. J. F. Cherry, D. Margomenou, and L. E. Talalay, 1–21. Kelsey Museum Publication 3. Ann Arbor: Kelsey Museum of Archaeology.

Ninou, K., ed. 1980. *Alexander the Great: History and Legend in Art.* Thessaloniki: Archaeological Museum of Thessaloniki.

Nishioka, Y., ed. 2003. *Alexander the Great: East-West Cultural Contacts from Greece to Japan.* Exhibition catalogue. Tokyo: NHK Puromoshon.

Oikonomides, A. N., ed. 1981. *The Coins of Alexander the Great: An Introductory Guide for the Historian, the Numismatist and the Collector of Ancient Coins.* Chicago: Argonaut.

Oikonomides, A. N., and L. J. Bolchazy. 1981. "Scholarship, Research and *The Search for Alexander." Ancient World* 4:67–89.

———. 1982. "Scholarship, Research and *The Search for Alexander." Ancient World* 5:3–9.

———. 1987. "Tables and Indices for the Catalogue and Supplements of *The Search for Alexander* Exhibition (1980–1983)." *Ancient World* 16:115–18.

Pandermalis, D. (curator). 2004. *Alexander the Great: Treasures from an Epic Era of Hellenism.* Exhibition catalogue. New York: Alexander S. Onassis Public Benefit Foundation.

Phillips, G. 2005. *Alexander the Great: Murder in Babylon.* London: Virgin Books.

Pigler, A. 1974. *Barockthemen: Eine Auswahl von Verzeichnissen zur Ikonographie des 17. und 18. Jahrhunderts.* 3 vols. Budapest: Akadémiai Kiadó.

Rogers, G. M. 2004. *Alexander: The Ambiguity of Greatness.* New York: Random House.

Romey, K. M. 2004. "The Forgotten Realm of Alexander." *Archaeology* 57, no. 6: 18–25.

Rosenbaum, L. 1997. "Blockbusters, Inc." *Art in America* 85, no. 6: 45–53.

Royal Ontario Museum. 1983. *The Search for Alexander: Supplement to the Catalogue.* Toronto: Royal Ontario Museum.

Saunders, N. 2006. *Alexander's Tomb: The Two-thousand Year Obsession to Find the Lost Conquerer.* New York: Perseus Books Group.

Spear, R. E. 1986. "Art History and the 'Blockbuster' Exhibition." *The Art Bulletin* 68:358–59.

Staudenmaier, J. M. 1993. "Clean Exhibits, Messy Exhibits: Henry Ford's Technological Aesthetic." In *Industrial Society and Its Museums, 1890–1990: Social Aspirations and Cultural Politics,* ed. B. Schroeder-Gudehus, 171–89. Chur, Switzerland: Harwood Academic Publishers.

Wallis, B. 1986. "Museum Blockbusters: The Art of Big Business." *Art in America* 74, no. 6: 28–33.

———. 1994. "Selling Nations: International Exhibitions and Cultural Diplomacy." In *Museum Culture: Histories, Discourses, Spectacles,* ed. D. J. Shearman and I. Rogoff, 265–81. Media and Society 6. Minneapolis: University of Minnesota Press.

Warry, J. 2005. *Alexander 334–323 BC: Conquest of the Persian Empire.* Praeger Illustrated Military History. Westport, CT: Praeger.

West, S. 1995. "The Devaluation of 'Cultural Capital': Post-Modern Democracy and the Art Blockbuster." In *Art in Museums,* ed. S. Pearce, 74–93. New Research in Museum Studies 5. London: Athlone.

Yalouris, N., M. Andronikos, and K. Rhomiopoulou. 1980. *The Search for Alexander: An Exhibition.* Boston: Little, Brown.

Zafiropoulou, S. 2004. *Alexander the Great: Tracing His Path, 2300 Years Later.* Athens: International Sports Publications.

Afterword

OLIVER STONE

I'VE LEARNED MUCH from the foregoing essays by this distinguished panel of historians, and it's certainly exciting to feel Alexander once again breathe among us, analyzed and redigested in ways peculiar to our present era. When the film was released in 2004–5, I found that very few film reviewers around the world were able to identify with Alexander's concepts of war and conquest, largely because of the experiences we suffered in the last century; insofar as both men invaded the Middle East and specifically targeted Babylon/Baghdad, many took the facile way out of condemning the film by negatively associating Alexander with President George W. Bush.

On the other hand, there appeared a large and fresh body of Internet users who seemed to be discovering Alexander for the first time and communicated their newfound enthusiasm for the classical world in chat groups, some even taking summer holidays together in Macedonia. Perhaps the movie failed in the English-language countries, but it was a success in the Spanish-, German-, French-, Russian-, Korean-, Japanese-, Italian-, Swedish-, and Arabic-speaking countries; in many of them it was the top-grossing film of that season. The film ended up in the top twenty films of the year in the foreign markets outside of the United States, and ranked higher worldwide than four of the five Academy Award–nominated films, which tells us something about the balance of power the English language holds when it comes to depicting global reality.

But I'd be at fault to claim success when the film continued to haunt me for two years after its release. I needed that extra time, as I found out and will explain later, to sort out some of the unanswered questions I still had about this highly complicated man, questions that I failed to answer dramatically enough.

I take humbly the criticisms of Professor Llewellyn-Jones, who was one of our consultants on Persian matters. I believe I did err fundamentally in my understanding of the Persian harem, allowing a cloud of Hollywood fantasy to obscure my realistic judgment as to what it was really like; I do wish Jeanne Moreau had done the movie and I had stuck by my original dialogue between Alexander and Sisygambis, as it showed an overlooked aspect of Alexander. I also take to heart Elizabeth Carney's "Olympias and Oliver" about my tendency toward sexual stereotyping. Hers is a tough piece, and yet I wonder if Professor Carney's feminist point of view has itself created a rather heartless abstraction that sees life through the single prism of sexuality. Important as gender may be, is it the determinant motive of history? Are there not other factors?

Is Olympias a stereotype? Is Angelina Jolie's performance over the top? Some would say "yes!" but others might say, "This person was so exaggerated, so outrageous, I can't really relate to this person—but I certainly have known someone *like this*." Perhaps an eccentric aunt, a friend, an enemy, or someone you've only read about but allowed to enter your imagination. What I'm suggesting is that a stereotype can work because it is memorable, and also because it is sometimes necessary—as in a satire like *Natural Born Killers* or a melodrama like *Scarface*—to bring the stereotype into an extreme closeup to force the eye once again to awaken and see. Angelina Jolie magnifies a fierce Medea-like apprehension of reality; she comes *out of the screen* with the guts of a Joan Crawford, Faye Dunaway, or Bette Davis, all of whom at times were considered stereotypical, over-the top women in their films, but with time have grown more credible in our consciousness because they *do*, in fact, *reflect a certain truth* in life. Tucked away in our ancient memories are stereotypes of authoritative figures—dinosaurs, all manner of predatory animals, headmasters and teachers, cannibals, nuns, business partners, mother and father, etc.—all of whom, in some way, have become giant and determining closeups in our lives. Is this a stereotype? No. I think this is a unique phenomenon, because I think the person who is larger than life, who is "in your face," is achieving something very *fresh* to the eye in making sure you *remember* him or her. This is drama. And somehow we are mislabeling the uncomfortable, the alien, the Other, as the stereotype because we are keeping it away from ourselves, outside our emotional comfort zone.

I still wonder that historians have not raised the question of why Alexander, after leaving Macedonia, would not see his mother for the eleven further years that he lived. There certainly seems to have been some sort of emotional conflict at the root of this situation. In the film, we show Alexander shocking the Greeks with his egalitarian treatment of Asian women (and men)—in his marriage to Roxane and his treatment of Stateira. In the harem at Babylon, he pronounces all women and eunuchs free to go home forthwith, which provokes the first of the protests from his Greek companions. I wonder if Professor Carney, in referencing "domineering dowagers and scheming concubines," smears rather than elucidates. Her negativity would bar the director or the writer from pursuing a subject where a woman *is actually* a devourer or a dominatrix. This is not to say that all women are, but certainly these are fascinating characters, and it's the right of a dramatist to bring out that character. To protest, in the name of feminism, against the existence of these women is to distort history; as we know, there have been, through time, many strong, original, independent women who have acted for benefit and destruction. Let us not sacrifice character to avoid stereotyping. Perhaps Professor Carney could fault me for not having concentrated enough on the positive image, but then again she perceives the Vietnamese heroine, Le Ly Hayslip, from my film *Heaven and Earth* (1993), as a sexual victim, which I think is partly true, but fails to comprehend the greater significance of Le Ly's overcoming her adversities and forgiving her persecutors. Perhaps the professor would deem this a stereotype as well, but if so, it was the prime conflict of Le Ly's life. I also think the portrayal of strong, if conventional, married housewives in my *World Trade Center* (2006) is positive and inspiring. I wonder finally at the balance of Professor Carney's argument— if she gives Alexander his due for the enormous respect he generally displayed for women, *including* his mother. This policy, atypically, extended to his own men when they committed sexual crimes against Asian women.

Professor Thomas Harrison takes up the William Tarn versus Ernst Badian debate, but I'm less interested in this heavily trod aspect of the story, since I don't think it can be answered—nor need it be. The

response is in *what* Alexander *did,* and not his motives, which I suspect
were something like most of ours: highly ambivalent, at times glorious,
at times wretched. I sometimes feel professional historians, generally
apart from the human give and take of the marketplace, expect too
much from their leaders—requiring them to act from abstract principles
in a harsh world full of chaos. We can certainly say in Alexander's de-
fense that he kept the expedition marching eastward for seven more
years after Babylon, with a greatness of vision that could motivate a
120,000-man army. By leading from the front and sharing the burdens
of his men, he showed himself above the comfort lines of materialism,
and as a known foe of official corruption, he set high standards by punishing those found guilty of stealing, raping, and plundering (including
his school friend Eumenes). From all accounts written of Alexander, we
see, time and again, his great passion, pain, and self-torture in incidents
such as the murder of Cleitus, the burning of Persepolis, the mutiny in
India, the kissing of Bagoas in front of his men, and the bestowing of official acceptance on Asian men and womenfolk. There is no ancient
ruler, outside of legend, that I have ever heard commit such potentially
self-incriminating actions. This is, of course, one of the reasons his name
continues to endure—who was ever remotely like him? "In the doing,
always in the doing" is the dialogue I took the liberty of attributing to
Alexander.

Conquest is also a form of evolution. If Alexander had a smaller vision, he would have retreated long before to Babylon and consolidated
his empire. He would have brought his mother, his sister, and his en-
tourage to the Persian court. He would have made a stronger, more pa-
tient effort to combine Macedonian and Persian custom. This unification
of cultures would have been a lifetime challenge for any emperor, and
would certainly have changed the course of history. Why did he not?

I see Alexander more as an explorer, like many others of such a nature, not quite knowing what's going to come up on the horizon, yet
boldly reaching for the new electrical charge of change. He stayed in
motion until the end, and never returned to his Rome, London, Paris,
Berlin, or Mongolia, as other conquerors have. He comes across in many
ways as a man who was making it up as he went along—from Babylon
through Afghanistan, Pakistan, and India, and back to Babylon—where
in the end, he remained unsatisfied, dreaming of his expedition to the
West. I would call him not an imperialist, as present fashion would have
it, but rather a "proto-man," an enlightened monarch naturally in
search of one land, one world—the unity, so to speak, of the womb. If

Alexander had had a longer life, his empire might have yielded perhaps six or seven capitals—such as Babylon, Alexandria, Athens, Car-
thage, Rome, South Spain, a world with nerve centers that would have
foreshadowed, to a surprising degree, the global world centers we have
today—but with *one world government*, centered on enlightened monarchy, or, barring that, some form of governing body.

In unconsciously pursuing this "one world" concept, under the
guise of a personal quest, the Alexander of the drama we created would
have to be a man who believed he was the right force to bring the world
into a greater sense of unification and prosperity, that he was a step in
the evolutionary process. And given the cataclysms possible, I do think
Alexander ruled extraordinarily well for *twelve years* over men, both
noble and bestial, in a social fabric that not only maintained itself, but
greatly expanded in terms of culture, scientific discovery, and economic
progress. It's so easy—I think too easy—to dismiss this great effort, to
declare it broken after twelve years of rule. But can we say it really
broke apart? Even if dissolved into four parts, the basic communal en-
ergies remained in place, and his creation culminated shortly, within
150 years, in the burgeoning Roman empire.

These and other points in the essays are fascinating to debate, but I
cannot address them here in greater detail, nor can I re-shoot. Yet I was
unable to let the film go from my consciousness, and as a result a third
version of *Alexander,* called "Alexander Revisited," comprising two acts
and one intermission, was finally released worldwide on digital video
in 2007, two and a half years after the initial theatrical release. This version was not made for theatrical projection: at best two shows a day
could be seated, which means less turnover and less ancillary income to
theater exhibitors, which makes this running time economically unfea-
sible for the present system. This represents my final version, as it contains all the essential footage we shot. I don't know how many filmmakers have been given the opportunity to make *three* versions of the
same film—partly, no doubt, because of the success of video and DVD
sales in the world. But I felt that if I didn't do it now, with the energy
and memory I still have for the subject, it would never quite be the
same again. For me, this is the complete *Alexander,* and even if I am two
years late in delivering it, it's not really a question of right or wrong,
but—as in any experiment with the unknown—one of trial and error.
Flaws and all, I've arrived at the clearest interpretation I can offer.

In the third and newest version, we begin the film with a radical
change in structure, adhering to an earlier draft of the script, with

Alexander's death leading to Ptolemy's memories, leading directly to the battle of Gaugamela, kicking off the film within the first ten minutes. This was dramatically Alexander at his clearest peak, and this battle between East and West was one that determined the course of history.

The earlier version, showing the young boy's growth, sowing the seeds of the man before we'd ever seen him, I found too conventional in hindsight. These same scenes take on a heightened meaning when seen on the back side of his victory at Gaugamela—with moments such as Olympias teaching her child the ways of the snake and the overcoming of fear. These boyhood themes play out in the cave at Pella when Alexander tells his father, Philip, that one day he too will exist alongside the mythic heroes on cave walls like these.

At this point, we return to the present-time narrative with Alexander, at twenty-five—emperor of the greatest empire yet seen—entering the Gates of Babylon. From there, we plunge into the darker abysses of human nature, culminating in a transcendent triumph in India—hardly the defeat some have called it.

Dr. Verity Platt, abetted by Dr. Joanna Paul, describes the film's psychological heart as a family tragedy, which adheres to the classical Greek drama of Aeschylus and Sophocles. Dr. Platt points to the "id" of Alexander in the scene with the young boy and his one-eyed father in the cave. As Robin Lane Fox pointed out, there is no evidence whatsoever for the existence of these caves—they are a dramatist's imagination—although they're not inconceivable. The scene was cut several different ways, painfully, to conform to a theatrical length of three hours, but in so doing a certain rhythm and background to the film was lost. I think this was a crucial misdirection on my part, as these ancient myths are little known to most modern folk—so in *Alexander Revisited*, the images in the caves unfold in the order in which they were originally written in the script; in allowing the scene to run its natural length, I believe a greater realization comes to us of how Alexander was built from equal parts of Achilles, Oedipus, Heracles, Jason, Prometheus— and that chilling mother for all time, Medea, an unfair caricature to some, but nonetheless an enduring one.

In expressing to his father his desire to be remembered on cave walls like these, Alexander continues the quest of the royal Macedonian boy carrying in his genes the glory and torture of the heroes he cannot yet understand, to which end he becomes one of the greatest Greek tragic heroes of all. To this day, few scholars have truly given Alexander the full credit for his imaginative achievement—the fact that he outperformed

his favored hero, Achilles, and in eerie similarity, by following Hephaestion to an early grave, as Achilles did Patroclus, gave up long life
for great glory. Yet we somehow accept Achilles more readily, as he
comes from an older time and through the mythical voice of Homer.
One of the realities in front of us that we so often fail to see, blinded as
we are by our limitations of time and place, and quick in our pride to
condemn the overachiever who challenges preconceptions of mind,
body, and time, is that Alexander acted out the similar effects of all of
these myths in his own life! And in doing so, in a realistic and nonmythic
narrative, Alexander stands alone; no other man of historical action—
Napoleon, Julius Caesar, Genghis Khan—comes close to Alexander in
either glory or failure. With his bloody murders and tragedies, not only
does Alexander give us great history, he gives us great drama, as well as
everlasting mystery.

Why in these two and a half thousand years have so few even tried
to make this dramatic tale workable in a three- to five-act structure?
Certainly many of the scholars included in this volume have acknowledged the complexity of dramatizing this life. Dr. Paul perhaps goes to
the nut of it in my mind by reminding us of Aristotle's *Poetics*, which
calls not for the single hero, but the single action to unite the drama of
disparate themes (murder, revenge, victory, love, loss, etc.). I hope the
third version of the film finds that focus. In any case, allow me on paper
to follow the lead given by Dr. Paul.

In that cave in Pella, Philip brings the full weight of his Greek classical pessimism to bear on his son's idealism ("No man or woman can
grow too powerful or beautiful without disaster befalling"). This one-
eyed Cyclops brings us back to the archaic age of Titans and Olympians
when fathers ate their sons, and sons murdered their fathers, *and* committed incest with their mothers. In the new version, Philip has the time
to tell the full story in which Zeus, in some kind of cosmic black humor,
mixes the Titans' ashes with human dust. He implies that the human
race, as in tales of the Garden of Eden, is cursed from its inception. The
father, in Dr. Platt's analogy, becomes the great "No" who slams the
door on Alexander's fate. This becomes increasingly manifest when
Olympias later warns Alexander, at nineteen, of the risks presented by
Philip's newborn son from another wife—and that it is Alexander's fate
to become another Parmenion to his emperor father. Thus in the cave,
the primal conflict of Alexander's life is set in motion—*the war* with his
father, which, as Dr. Platt points out, plays out in Alexander's patricidal
conscience when he sees the ghost of his murdered father before he
murders Cleitus.

Befitting the power of his father, young Alexander is introduced in the cave to the eagle of Zeus, who signifies divine favor and also, in the case of Prometheus, divine punishment—both of which Alexander will duly suffer. As we see that eagle come and go through the film, it will become, like his father, a motif of Alexander's destiny working itself out. Fear will be the enemy in Alexander's life. The wooden image of Phobus is what he prays to on the eve of Gaugamela—"Conquer your fear and you will conquer death," he tells his assembled troops before the battle. To the end of his life, Alexander strove to overcome these fears, including that great hornet's nest Greek tragedy is generally based on—the terrors brought on by mothers and fathers.

In the cave, then, we discover what is subconscious for Philip and unconscious for Alexander. In this ancient mixing of the dust of Titan and man lies the madness at the heart of the human DNA—something left over from our reptile brain, frozen in such fear that it is no wonder Philip drank a strong Greek wine to drive the Furies from his mind. How condescending of modern critics to refer to Philip as a drunkard! Who wouldn't drink if surrounded by such fears? What are modern tranquilizers but similar bulwarks against the modern Furies? Alexander is the one who will ride out these fears to find the "new man" Philip hints at.

In sharp contrast to this world, there is an enlightened Greek classical look to Ptolemy's Alexandria sixty years later, with its clean architectural lines, numerous scrolls, and well-proportioned statues of Olympian gods; this entire "modern" interlude, following upon the cave scene, signals reason, intellect, and culture. Ptolemy takes us in another direction, into the future, to ponder a subtheme—the meaning and sanctity of history. This confused many people who wanted a clean narrative line, but in the end this subtheme ties very much into the single action proposed by Aristotle: that is, *was* Alexander corrupted by his action or not? Ptolemy raises for me the issue of what is history—oral, mythological? Because Ptolemy dictates his vision to his scribes, are we to believe that it is more real because it is written? The question grows on us as Ptolemy himself, in the last scene, undermines his own version of Alexander's history. Professor Solomon points to this in his examination of the importance of Ptolemy and his role as a potential co-conspirator in Alexander's death. To complete the idea, we now acknowledge at the end of the film something from which I retreated in the original editing: the disappearance of Ptolemy's memoirs in the great fires that destroyed the Library.

This third version expands rather than reduces the much-criticized prologue and epilogue of the older Ptolemy. Sometimes more is better, as there is a rhythm in the clean narrative line of a story that, when truncated, loses coherence. Allowing Anthony Hopkins's sonorous voice to work its way into our mind is a key to understanding this story. And he is a mellifluous actor, sublime in his older man's relaxation in the role; in this expanded form, he frames and unites the new structure.

It is old Ptolemy who understands the true significance of Alexander's ring, which, as a younger man, he sees in the opening scene of the film falling from the king's dying hand. Now aged, Ptolemy stares at the same cracked ring on his finger and muses on the fact that it belongs to "the true heir to the empire," Alexander and Roxane's thirteen-year-old son, who was murdered by Cassander, and thus robbed by history. And it is with a similar but hardened regret that Ptolemy now wears this ring, perhaps troubled by the feeling that he has betrayed Alexander's legitimacy and contributed to the fracturing of his empire—for which he is now making amends in writing his forgiving history. Among possible crimes of self-interest, Ptolemy could be accused of seizing Egypt, the empire's richest province, for himself, of hijacking the body of Alexander to Alexandria, in order to legitimize his own rule as pharaoh, and, as chief of Alexander's bodyguard, even of complicity in the king's murder—at least as much as Alexander was complicit in Philip's murder. If I had pushed this parallel more dramatically (by showing Ptolemy actually plotting the murder with others), it would have resonated more strongly with the audience, but at the same time it would have been the more speculative history.

An important shift in Alexander's trajectory and development comes in Babylon, where he is, indeed, lost. His dream is now clouded by Darius's escape to the northeast, as well as his army's growing rapaciousness and impatience to plunder and loot the East and return to Macedon. Which is precisely what Alexander will not do—in contradiction to his father's plans for revenge on the Persians. Revenge was never motive enough for Alexander. With his fiercely original mindset, the enemy was there to learn from and grow with, to build upon, and win over; and in so doing he would change—or let's say, for those who prefer Persian to Greek rule, "improve upon"—an empire built on a corruption, loss of freedom, and cruelty repellent to most Greeks.

Yet now, on this balcony in Babylon, the new "emperor of Asia," sharing his vision with Hephaestion, has presumably achieved all the glory he dreamt of while studying those cave walls in Pella. Yet Alexander remains deeply unsatisfied ("I see the future, Hephaestion. . . . These people need, want, to be freed"). It is a Promethean fate to realize one's dream so young, and then again to find that the dream is never static, but ephemeral and ongoing. Cannot even Alexander's worst detractors give the man credit for this astounding energy and purpose? The man did not loot the East, but sought to create something, and in the nature of his improvised actions, seemed to be building toward a goal of binding East and West together; the man himself was in the end married to three Eastern princesses, and in promoting such marriages among his own generals and soldiers, seemed to understand that through generosity, more breeds more, and less, less. He didn't need to state that there could be a unified world—as Professor Harrison might have wanted for the record—because the action lay in the doing, not the saying. It was always in this realm that Alexander functioned best. True, there were Phoenician sailors, traders, and hardy travelers of all kinds who wandered the world before Alexander, but they were hardly Microsofts or General Electrics or Toyotas, who could lead the way. Alexander became, by accretion, the first multinationalist. His was an idea so vast and unknown in its time that—given the enormous diversity of the present world—it could only have existed at the beginning of recorded time.

This idealism naturally requires an heir: someone must succeed Alexander in order for empire to become dynasty. It is fatally ironic that Roxane, mistaking the ring's significance and reducing it to an item of Hephaestion's lust, throws it violently out of their wedding bed. Hephaestion is far more accepting of Roxane than she of Hephaestion, whom she sees in an illogical, archaic way as a biological threat to her and her son's supremacy. There is an additional adversarial scene between Roxane and Hephaestion in the new version, but it is the ring scene in the wedding chamber at Bactria that seals Hephaestion's fate at the hands of Roxane. Of course, this is my conjecture as a dramatist, perhaps as irrelevant as my harem fantasies, but let us not forget that Hephaestion died young, as suddenly and mysteriously as Alexander; nor should we underrate him as one of Alexander's best and most trusted generals, sent on numerous missions of importance. It would be only human nature to expect that in a closed society of ambitious Macedonian generals, combining large amounts of testosterone and wealth, Hephaestion's insider status would be envied and hated by those who would want either to take his power or dissuade him from further expeditions so that they could actually *enjoy* their wealth. If there was a conspiracy behind Hephaestion's death—and subsequently Alexander's—logic points to these generals, among them Cassander, Perdiccas, Ptolemy, Craterus, Antigonus, and the absent Antipater. Certainly Roxane had supporters among these factions, and from the ruthless manner in which she disposed of Stateira and her unborn heir after Alexander's death, we can only surmise that Roxane had become a strong and willful woman, like Olympias. She cannot be dismissed as a suspect without motive in the death of Hephaestion.

When Hephaestion dies, he reminds Alexander unselfishly, given his own dire state—"You won men's hearts. . . . But how beautiful a myth it was, Alexander. . . . They all did [reach and fall]—Achilles, Prometheus—in whose company you now stand and shine, Alexander." This is, in truth, what Alexander wanted as a youth. How true to life that now Alexander can no longer recognize himself or set a limit to his inexorable ambitions—to explore Arabia, North Africa, Italy, the Gates of Gibraltar. He cannot, tragically, garner satisfaction from his feats because he must go on. And thus, sadly, he can only feel the brokenness of his dream, his sense that he's closer to the end than the beginning. As with Patroclus and Achilles, when Hephaestion dies, the wheels are clearly set in motion for Alexander's own death, which arrived within eight months.

In the third version of Alexander's death, I included a scene between Bagoas and Alexander, alone at night, where we hear their simple, final expressions of devotion to each other. Bagoas appeals to Alexander in another light, that of a third gender, the transsexual, which Alexander, ever curious, explored and came to love. There was also an introductory scene with Bagoas at the harem, which I cut from the film for fear of alienating masculine audiences. I was clearly pushing the mass audience's tolerance for Hephaestion as it was, but with Bagoas we risked turning the entire film into a debacle. A large part of this has to do with the tremendous amount of hostility the eunuch received at the early screenings we held for Warner Bros. personnel. Having been attacked, not necessarily justly, for so many excesses in the past, I faltered in my path; I think I lost heart. But as I don't see this issue as either victory or loss, but more as a function of time and fate, I was happy to have the chance to restore it in this third pass. With Bagoas allowed to play himself out, even in the most awkward moments, some may understand that he truly loved Alexander; their last scene together chills me when Bagoas cries, as it shows how deeply Alexander was loved—as much as

any woman could have loved him. It shows Alexander as he was—
"loved by all." At the same time, I believe Hephaestion was Alexander's true soulmate, as evidenced by his monumental funeral games,
which I very much wanted to shoot, but which we could not afford.

In his last moments on earth, Alexander reaches up to embrace the
eagle of Zeus flying out of the Persian fan above his bed; in truth, the
tiny fly-like image on the fan is the *faravahar* that represented the divinity of the Zoroastrian god of light, Ahuramazda.

In Alexander's fevered imagination, the *faravahar* blends with Zeus's
eagle—divine symbols of Eastern and Western religions that merge into
the Alexandrine One—and as he dies, the ring he is offering up to his
divine ideal crashes to the floor, broken, like his empire, into pieces. As
Prometheus did, Alexander has ascended to the lofty heights between
man and the gods, and with his tortured (poisoned?) Promethean
death, he passes on the gift of "fire" (civilization) to the next generation.
Thus, to repeat, the ring is representative of more than this "heir" Ptolemy speaks of, and more than the love between Alexander and Hephaestion (no "Rosebud" here). The ring for me is the eternal symbol of
that beautiful Greek ideal—the "love of man"—that unity of man, that
dream of one world, which is and has repeatedly been shattered.
Alexander's dream, like Prometheus's, will live on in other forms, including our movie in the early twenty-first century, and beyond—but
for now, as with all men, it seems that Alexander has reached the end.
As Ptolemy concludes, "All men reach and fall . . . reach and fall."

Yet viewing Alexander's life through a more optimistic prism, I feel
that he died a tired but content man. Dr. Paul, in pointing to Aristotle's
"single action," has opened my eyes to what I missed at the time. It was
there certainly in my subconscious from the beginning, struggling to be
heard, but its implications frightened me. The theme, the main action of
this piece, was always murder—the murder of Philip—and whether Alexander was involved or not. But, in hindsight, I think I subconsciously
avoided going to the bottom of this murky pond because I was scarred
from the numerous personal attacks on me as a conspiracy theorist
after *JFK* and *Nixon*. If I had admitted that this was a movie about
Alexander's possible conspiratorial involvement in that murder, it
would have represented a great risk to the fortunes of an expensive
movie. I truly feared that the movie would have been murdered in its
cradle, as had a previous project of mine on Martin Luther King Jr.,
where I was trying to illustrate a man's character under pressure rather
than the possibility of a conspiracy behind the murder.

If Alexander did knowingly murder his father—which I doubt—he is despicable, and I have far less respect for this character, and have done history a disservice in misinterpreting him. But there still remains the strong possibility that Alexander did know of the murder through his mother. And even if he did not know of it, he was, as I tried to show in their final scene together, sorely compromised by blood. After this meeting with Olympias, he never saw her again. Was this because she was in some way involved? Certainly her public behavior was re- marked upon by many when she flaunted her joy at her husband's death—an argument, to my mind, *against* her involvement. Bearing in mind that the crime of patricide is one of the most heinous and strongly condemned in Greek tragedies, Alexander assumed the throne, not un- like most Macedonian kings, under suspicious circumstances.

It is certainly possible that Pausanias did murder Philip, who had many enemies in the clan-based society of Macedon. He also had fierce foes in Greece, and it is quite logical that Darius and Persian gold con- tributed to his death in some way in order to abort Philip's planned in- vasion. Furthermore, it is possible Olympias was involved with Greek or Persian factions, or both. For her, much was at stake—a new son and heir had just been born of pure Macedonian blood; she was still an out- sider to the local power base of nobles, and Alexander was only half- Macedonian. Indeed, if he was the son of Zeus as she claimed, then he was not Macedonian at all! Nor did Olympias waste time disposing of Eurydice and the newborn heir after the assassination. Her ruthlessness is evident, but did she actually involve herself in Philip's murder? The behavior of Alexander in their bedroom scenes makes it clear that he is riddled with doubt. At the least he must wonder how she can gloat so openly over his father's death. The essence of it is that Alexander is as- cending to an ambivalent throne—but one that he wants badly, as his mother makes him see.

We have here the potential for a startlingly original Greek tragedy— mother kills father; son, loving both, assumes throne in bad conscience, which haunts him till he redeems his honor late in life. The protagonist in the end may be ambushed by the past, but, unlike Oedipus, he over- comes it. I don't know offhand of any parallel Greek play with this storyline, and this is what infused me with the passion to try for these parameters. Thus all of Alexander's actions, as played out by Colin Far- rell, are based on this profound insecurity over his throne. In the cam- paign tent scene before Gaugamela, during a discussion among the generals, Parmenion questions whether Persian gold actually paid for

Philip's death. Watch Alexander's reaction closely, and you'll see that insecurity. I have read accounts to the effect that at Issus, in his first great battle with the Persians, Alexander blundered in his tactics (somewhat like George W. Bush trying to show up his father in modern Iraq) by overestimating the power of his cavalry to turn the tide of battle, and it was Parmenion's sturdiness that saved the day.

We see this insecurity again in Alexander's reaction to his mother's letter on the balcony at Babylon with Hephaestion ("My father thought me weak, my mother divine—which am I, Hephaestion? Weak or divine?"). This is a key question. Certainly the Greek concept of fatherhood was opaque, allowing Alexander, who had so little physical resemblance to his father, to wonder. This all comes to a culmination when Alexander faces the elephants in India. Movie audiences take heroism for granted far too easily in film—and thus in history. They expect it, which is a shame, as we repeatedly undercut its true meaning. In this climactic scene, we have Alexander, practically alone in the heart of the battle, taking on the Indian king astride an elephant twice the size of his great horse, Bucephalus. Alexander's action is a classic heroic sacrifice, meant to motivate his lagging men into action—as was historically true at the battle of Multan, when this suicidal heroism in fact turned the tide of battle in favor of the Greeks, but led to Alexander's most grievous wound. We should remember that Alexander prided himself on never having been defeated in battle, and to preserve this record of invincibility, he seemed to be willing to die. Yet to me there seems even more at stake.

It is an amazing moment in the film as he transcends the normal limits of life. With an arrow piercing his lung, what is the last thing, the very last thing, that crosses his dying mind? In dramatic terms, we suggest that it is his last moments in Pella, years before, with his mother arguing for the assassination of his father. Is he complicit because of his mother's hate? Can he bring her to justice, as Orestes did his mother? What a horrible twist of fate to have to choose between matricide and patricide. The answer is never made clear. And yet when she says, "Great power, wealth, conquest—all your desires—the world is yours! Take it!" he does. And because of this dishonorable desire in himself for power at any price, we are suggesting that Alexander will always *feel* complicit.

Recovering with great willpower from his near-fatal wound in India, he gives in to his army's wishes and returns to Babylon. Yet as the ashen Alexander is put on a horse for all his men to behold, he sees the pale, fleshy shade of his father, Philip, staring down at him from a cliff of cheering soldiers. The ghost nods to him, as if with final approval of his kingship. It is as Philip promised long ago in the cave in Pella—"a king is not born, Alexander, he's made—by steel and suffering!" Alexander has truly ascended to his father's station and become the true king.

It is then, after long absence, that the eagle of Zeus returns to the sky above. Alexander, who has nearly died in this battle, shines again— though briefly. I'd like to believe that the violation (murder?) of Philip is expiated from Alexander's soul. And as a man now wholly free of the fear of father and mother that has governed his long journey from home, Alexander returns to his death (foretold) in Babylon.

I began my own journey on this long ago when I first read Mary Renault's account of Alexander, and it brings me to a very special place in my life. It is going to be very hard to repeat that feeling each one of us on the film shared of being in the presence of such a great person for such a long time. He made us better than ourselves. I hope this film can, in some way, be a memorial to the memory and greatness of his achievement. I don't think this film will ever fit any single category of film made in Hollywood. It ends with so many ambiguities, and it was so long ago. It still leaves my mind excited with that sensation of a past lived by people like *us,* who passed on a fire of memory of a time when young men could dream of taking and holding power, and truly changing the course of the world! "In the doing, always in the doing" will ring for me as Alexander's theme, his *cri de coeur.* And if he leaves us in the end with more questions than answers, his are grand questions well worth asking—and his achievements glorious ideals to live by.

Contributors

ELIZABETH D. CARNEY teaches in the history department at Clemson University in South Carolina. Most of her work deals with the political history of ancient Macedon, especially the role of women. She has published two monographs, *Women and Monarchy in Macedonia* and *Olympias, Mother of Alexander*, as well as articles on symposia, discipline in the Macedonian army, the royal burials in Vergina, and Ptolemaic monarchy, particularly the career of Arsinoe Philadelphus.

PAUL CARTLEDGE is A. G. Leventis Professor of Greek Culture at the University of Cambridge and a professorial fellow of Clare College. He has written, cowritten, edited, or coedited over twenty books, most recently *Ancient Greek Political Thought in Practice* and *Ancient Greece: A History in Eleven Cities*. He has been the historical consultant to five major television series.

JOHN F. CHERRY is the Joukowsky Family Professor of Archaeology and professor of classics and anthropology in the Joukowsky Institute for Archaeology and the Ancient World at Brown University. He has led several archaeological survey projects in Greece and has also done fieldwork in the United Kingdom, the United States, Italy, and southern Armenia. He has coauthored or coedited twelve books, including most recently *Explaining Social Change: Studies in Honour of Colin Renfrew* (coedited with Chris Scarre and Stephen Shennan) and *Prehistorians Round the Pond: Reflections on Aegean Prehistory as a Discipline* (coedited with Despina Margomenou and Lauren E. Talalay).

MONICA SILVEIRA CYRINO is professor of classics at the University of New Mexico. She is the author of *Big Screen Rome, In Pandora's Jar: Lovesickness in Early Greek Poetry, A Journey through Greek Mythology,* and *Aphrodite* and the editor of *Rome, Season One: History Makes Television*. She has appeared as an academic consultant on the television show *History vs. Hollywood* on the History

Channel and is the recipient of the American Philological Association's national teaching award in classics (1998–99).

FIONA ROSE GREENLAND completed her doctorate in classical archaeology at Oxford University, where she focused her research on visual culture and architecture in the interior of Roman Tarraconensis (Spain). She lectured at New College, Oxford, for four years and has published numerous articles and reviews on the material culture of ancient Roman Spain. Greenland served as a historical consultant to Oliver Stone's *Alexander.* She is now pursuing a doctorate in sociology at the University of Michigan in Ann Arbor, Michigan.

THOMAS HARRISON is Rathbone Professor of Ancient History and Classical Archaeology at the University of Liverpool. A specialist in Greek history and historiography, his publications include *Divinity and History: The Religion of Herodotus, The Emptiness of Asia: Aeschylus' Persians and the History of the Fifth Century,* and (as editor) *Greeks and Barbarians.*

ROBIN LANE FOX is a Fellow of New College, Oxford, and University Reader in ancient history. His books include *Alexander the Great, Pagans and Christians,* and *A History of the Classical World,* all of which are in print and have been widely translated. *Travelling Heroes: Greeks and Their Myths in the Age of Homer* is his most recent book. He was the historical consultant on Oliver Stone's *Alexander* and served as a cavalry commander in the film's major battles.

LLOYD LLEWELLYN-JONES lectures in Ancient History in the School of History, Classics and Archaeology at the University of Edinburgh, Scotland. He is the author of *Aphrodite's Tortoise: The Veiled Woman of Ancient Greece,* as well as *Ctesias' History of Persia: Tales of the Orient* (with James Robson) and *Greek and Roman Dress from A to Z* (with Liza Cleland and Glenys Davies). He was a historical consultant for the costume department on Oliver Stone's *Alexander* and has contributed to documentaries for American and British television.

JOANNA PAUL is a lecturer in classical studies at the University of Liverpool, where she specializes in modern receptions of classical antiquity, particularly in the cinema. Her study of the relationship between film and the classical epic tradition is forthcoming from Oxford University Press. She has also published articles on Fellini's films set in the ancient world and is working on a project that explores modern receptions of Pompeii and Herculaneum.

VERITY PLATT is an art historian with special interests in the relationship between art and religion, theories of representation, Roman wall painting, and funerary art. Her book *Facing the Gods: Epiphany and Representation in*

Graeco-Roman Art, Literature and Religion is forthcoming from Cambridge University Press. She is assistant professor of art history at the University of Chicago.

JEANNE REAMES studied Macedonian history under Eugene N. Borza at Pennsylvania State University. She is currently the Martin Professor of History (2009/10) at the University of Nebraska, Omaha. Her interests include the ways in which Alexander's image has been appropriated, reinterpreted, and fictionalized throughout history. She coedited *Macedonian Legacies: Studies on Ancient Macedonian History and Culture in Honor of Eugene N. Borza* and is doing research for a monograph about Hephaestion, Craterus, and power politics at the court of Alexander.

KIM SHAHABUDIN has studied the reception of the ancient world in the cinema since 1999. She has presented papers and published articles on the 2004 film *Troy*, the cinematic casting of bodybuilders as Hercules, and the mythological Cyclops in the cinema. She is editing a collection of essays on classical reception in mass media and coauthoring a monograph on Greece and Rome in the cinema. She is currently conducting research at the University of Reading into teaching and learning and continues to lecture on classical reception.

MARILYN B. SKINNER is professor of classics at the University of Arizona in Tucson. Her research areas include Roman literature of the Republican and Augustan eras and sexuality and gender in antiquity. Her books include *Catullus' Passer: The Arrangement of the Book of Polymetric Poems*; *Catullus in Verona*; *Sexuality in Greek and Roman Culture*; and, as coeditor, *Roman Sexualities*.

JON SOLOMON is the Robert D. Novak Professor of Western Civilization and Culture at the University of Illinois at Urbana-Champaign, where he is also professor of classics and of cinema studies. His research ranges from classical philology to medieval, Renaissance, and Baroque adaptations of the classics to contemporary cinema. In addition to *The Ancient World in the Cinema*, which helped create a new subfield of classical studies and pedagogy, Solomon has published essays on *Gladiator* and *Troy*. Current projects include a study of *Ben-Hur* as a prototype for commercial success and synergy, an edition and translation of Boccaccio's *Genealogy of the Pagan Gods*, and an analysis of classical allusions in contemporary cinema.

OLIVER STONE has written and directed numerous films, including *World Trade Center, Salvador, The Doors, Wall Street, Nixon, Heaven and Earth, Born on the Fourth of July*, and *W*. He won "Best Director" Academy Awards for *Platoon* (1986) and *Born on the Fourth of July* (1989) and "Best Adapted Screenplay" for

Midnight Express (1979). After serving in the U.S. Army in the Vietnam War, Stone attended film school at NYU. He first wrote a script for a film about Alexander the Great in 1986 and revised it periodically until he started the film project in earnest in 2003. His *Alexander* was released theatrically in the United States in 2004 and later released in three versions on DVD: *Alexander* (2005), *Alexander*: Director's Cut (2005), and *Alexander Revisited*: The Final Cut (2007).

Index

box office (*continued*)
16–17, 36–37, 43–44, 178; for foreign markets, 88, 337; Hollywood epics as box office hits, 3–4, 19, 108; as measure of success, 8, 36–37, 60, 94–95, 168; for Rossen's *Alexander the Great*, 94–95; for Stone's other films, 44–45
Briant, Pierre, 227, 260, 261
Brosius, Maria, 259–60
budget for Stone's *Alexander*, 36, 60, 296, 305
Burton, Richard: as Alexander in Rossen's *Alexander the Great*, 92, 106, 109, 173; in Rattigan's *Adventure Story*, 59, 63; in *The Robe*, 95, 104
Bush, George W., 21–22

Carney, Elizabeth D., 9, 128, 132n15, 135–67, 202, 203, 207n8, 214n70, 276n53, 338–39; article by, 135–67; contributor's note, 353
Cartledge, Paul: contributor's note, 353; introduction by, 3–12
casting, 4, 25; age difference and, 9, 148–49, 152–53, 161n51, 161n52; of Alexander for films and television, 113n1, 116n39; audience expectations and reactions to, 169–71; of characters (*see specific characters*); conventions and selection of actors for epic roles, 25–26, 104–5; critical reception of, 169, 172–73; ethnicity and, 18–19; negative reactions to, 37, 168–69; for Rossen's *Alexander the Great*, 104–5
cave paintings, 10, 148, 150–51; Archaic style and the primitive, 292–95; as exposition or foreshadowing, 26, 289–93, 295, 298; and Oedipal intergenerational struggle, 290, 294–95, 342–44, 350–51; as original invention for the film, 292–94, 342; and Plato's allegory of the Cave, 26, 298; Prometheus myth and, 291–92, 344; as proto-cinema, 26, 297–98
censorship, 311
Channon, Chips, 58
Cherry, John F., 11; article by, 305–36; contributor's note, 353

A Child's Night Dream (Stone), 87
cinematic technology, 20; film stocks, 20, 287, 295, 300n9; filters, 287, 295, 296; as reminder of subjectivity, 287
cinematography, 9, 20, 55, 295
civilizing mission, as motive, 187, 220–21, 223, 236n39, 315, 348; and "empire of the mind," 67
Cleitus: in classical tradition, 191, 196, 197, 210n38, 215n74; in literary tradition, 57; as paternal figure, 57, 72, 78, 79, 83, 85, 186, 291, 294, 343; Rattigan's characterization of, 72–73, 78, 79, 83–84, 85; Rossen's characterization of, 93, 98, 102, 159n24; Stone's characterization of, 48, 57–58, 72–73, 83, 159n24, 186, 291, 294, 343
Cleopatra (DeMille), 247
Cleopatra (Mankiewicz), 3
coins: as evidence of Alexander's visit to Delphi, 64–65; as images in film, 100, 106, 110; as material artifacts, 286, 314, 315, 327; as talismans, 8
color coding, 55–56
computer-generated imagery (CGI), 20; in *Troy*, 29
conspiracy, 39, 80, 83, 346–47, 348
costumes, 4, 10, 247–48, 249; "designer history" and creation of effective, 249–50; for female characters, 4, 150, 154, 161n52, 163n76, 163n77, 250; historical accuracy of, 150, 154, 248–50; Stone's directorial vision as influence on, 247–48, 250
Cowan, Elliot, 41
Craterus, 63, 186, 197–98, 200–202, 210n36, 211n46, 211n47, 347; as depicted in Stone's *Alexander*, 244, 255–56, 258; as political rival of Hephaestion, 185–87
credits, 38–39, 106–7
critical reception: audience reception influenced by reviews, 36–37, 58; casting and, 169, 172–73; combative rhetoric deployed during, 16–17; design production and, 250–51; historical accuracy and, 40; preproduction interest and, 16; of Rattigan's *Adventure Story*,

370

Index

Tarn, William W. (*continued*)
of Alexander, 64–65; Rattigan and, 63,
66, 70, 72, 79–80; Tarn/Badian debate,
10, 38, 114n15, 224–26, 339–40; universal brotherhood theme and, 38, 66, 70,
102, 224, 239n84, 292
Tashiro, Charles, 249–50
television series, proposed, 92, 113n1
Thais, 231
Thebes, 6, 88, 223, 236n32
300 (Snyder), 29–30
tie-ins, 306–7
Titans, 47–48, 73, 77, 292, 343–44
title, Stone on significance of, 50n10
Toplin, Robert Brent, 40
Tougher, Shaun, 260
Troy (Petersen), 3–4, 19, 22–23, 177–78; *Alexander* compared and contrasted with,
21–23, 37; sexuality in, 32n29
Tynan, Kenneth, 59, 60

unity of mankind, 66, 69, 101–2, 105, 111,
112, 223, 236n39, 236n49, 239n84, 324–
26, 348
U Turn (Stone), 46–47

Vangelis, 25, 253, 275n29
Venizelos, Evangelos, 18
versions of Stone's *Alexander*, 12n8,
207n12. *See also specific film titles*

Voight, Jon, 46–47
"vulgate tradition," 64, 71, 76, 105, 140.
See also specific authors

Wakhevitch, George, 58
Wallis, Brian, 310
Wall Street (Stone), 44–45, 234
war, 20–22, 32n33, 86, 233, 337; Alexander
as symbol of militarism, 21
White, Hayden, 111
Wilcken, Ulrich, 66, 80, 292
Winkler, Martin, 20
women: as absent in Stone's films, 142–43,
160n29; Amazon figures, 155; criticisms
of Stone's stereotypical treatment of,
300n22; dancing girls in Hollywood
epic, 96; Greek sexual paradigm and
passivity of, 121; political agency of Persian royalty, 155, 261, 272–73, 276n53;
violence against, 64–65. *See also* harem;
and specific characters
World Trade Center (Stone), 45, 339
Worsley, T. C., 88
Worthington, Ian, 38
Wright, F. A., 66

Xenophon, 126, 131n9

Žižek, Slavoj, 295

WISCONSIN STUDIES IN CLASSICS

General Editors

William Aylward, Nicholas D. Cahill, and
Patricia A. Rosenmeyer

E. A. Thompson
Romans and Barbarians: The Decline of the Western Empire

Jennifer Tolbert Roberts
Accountability in Athenian Government

H. I. Marrou
A History of Education in Antiquity
Histoire de l'Education dans l'Antiquité, translated by George Lamb

Erika Simon
Festivals of Attica: An Archaeological Commentary

G. Michael Woloch
Roman Cities: Les villes romaines by Pierre Grimal, translated and
  edited by G. Michael Woloch, together with A Descriptive
  Catalogue of Roman Cities by G. Michael Woloch

Warren G. Moon, editor
Ancient Greek Art and Iconography

Katherine Dohan Morrow
Greek Footwear and the Dating of Sculpture

John Kevin Newman
The Classical Epic Tradition

Jeanny Vorys Canby, Edith Porada, Brunilde Sismondo Ridgway,
  and Tamara Stech, editors
Ancient Anatolia: Aspects of Change and Cultural Development

Ann Norris Michelini
Euripides and the Tragic Tradition

Wendy J. Raschke, editor
The Archaeology of the Olympics: The Olympics and Other Festivals in Antiquity

Paul Plass
Wit and the Writing of History: The Rhetoric of Historiography in Imperial Rome

Barbara Hughes Fowler
The Hellenistic Aesthetic

F. M. Clover and R. S. Humphreys, editors
Tradition and Innovation in Late Antiquity

Brunilde Sismondo Ridgway
Hellenistic Sculpture I: The Styles of ca. 331–200 B.C.

Barbara Hughes Fowler, editor and translator
Hellenistic Poetry: An Anthology

Kathryn J. Gutzwiller
Theocritus' Pastoral Analogies: The Formation of a Genre

Vimala Begley and Richard Daniel De Puma, editors
Rome and India: The Ancient Sea Trade

Rudolf Blum
Hans H. Wellisch, translator
Kallimachos: The Alexandrian Library and the Origins of Bibliography

David Castriota
Myth, Ethos, and Actuality: Official Art in Fifth Century B.C. Athens

Barbara Hughes Fowler, editor and translator
Archaic Greek Poetry: An Anthology

John H. Oakley and Rebecca H. Sinos
The Wedding in Ancient Athens

Richard Daniel De Puma and Jocelyn Penny Small, editors
Murlo and the Etruscans: Art and Society in Ancient Etruria

Judith Lynn Sebesta and Larissa Bonfante, editors
The World of Roman Costume

Jennifer Larson
Greek Heroine Cults

Warren G. Moon, editor
Polykleitos, the Doryphoros, and Tradition

Paul Plass
*The Game of Death in Ancient Rome: Arena Sport and Political
   Suicide*

Margaret S. Drower
Flinders Petrie: A Life in Archaeology

Susan B. Matheson
Polygnotos and Vase Painting in Classical Athens

Jenifer Neils, editor
Worshipping Athena: Panathenaia and Parthenon

Pamela A. Webb
*Hellenistic Architectural Sculpture: Figural Motifs in
   Western Anatolia and the Aegean Islands*

Brunilde Sismondo Ridgway
Fourth-Century Styles in Greek Sculpture

Lucy Goodison and Christine Morris, editors
Ancient Goddesses: The Myths and the Evidence

Jo-Marie Claassen
Displaced Persons: The Literature of Exile from Cicero to Boethius

Brunilde Sismondo Ridgway
Hellenistic Sculpture II: The Styles of ca. 200–100 B.C.

Pat Getz-Gentle
Personal Styles in Early Cycladic Sculpture

Catullus
David Mulroy, translator and commentator
The Complete Poetry of Catullus

Brunilde Sismondo Ridgway
Hellenistic Sculpture III: The Styles of ca. 100–31 B.C.

Angeliki Kosmopoulou
*The Iconography of Sculptured Statue Bases in the Archaic and
Classical Periods*

Sara H. Lindheim
*Mail and Female: Epistolary Narrative and Desire in
Ovid's Heroides*

Graham Zanker
Modes of Viewing in Hellenistic Poetry and Art

Alexandra Ann Carpino
Discs of Splendor: The Relief Mirrors of the Etruscans

Timothy S. Johnson
A Symposion of Praise: Horace Returns to Lyric in Odes IV

Jean-René Jannot
*Religion in Ancient Etruria
Devins, Dieux et Démons: Regards sur la religion de l'Etrurie antique,*
translated by Jane K. Whitehead

Catherine Schlegel
Satire and the Threat of Speech: Horace's Satires, Book 1

Christopher A. Faraone and Laura K. McClure, editors
Prostitutes and Courtesans in the Ancient World

Plautus
John Henderson, translator and commentator
Asinaria: The One about the Asses

Patrice D. Rankine
*Ulysses in Black: Ralph Ellison, Classicism, and
African American Literature*

Paul Rehak
John G. Younger, editor
Imperium and Cosmos: Augustus and the Northern Campus Martius

Patricia J. Johnson
Ovid before Exile: Art and Punishment in the Metamorphoses

Vered Lev Kenaan
Pandora's Senses: The Feminine Character of the Ancient Text

Erik Gunderson
Nox Philologiae: Aulus Gellius and the Fantasy of the Roman Library

Sinclair Bell and Helen Nagy, editors
New Perspectives on Etruria and Early Rome

Barbara Pavlock
The Image of the Poet in Ovid's Metamorphoses

Paul Cartledge and Fiona Rose Greenland, editors
Responses to Oliver Stone's Alexander : *Film, History, and Cultural Studies*